War Poets of English Literature

War Poets of English Literature

Attied Khawar Balwan
and
Ranbir Kaur

RANDOM PUBLICATIONS
NEW DELHI (INDIA)

War Poets of English Literature

ISBN 978-93-5111-583-0

Published in 2015 in India by

RANDOM PUBLICATIONS

4376-A/4B, Gali Murari Lal, Ansari Road
New Delhi-110 002
Phone : +9111-43580356, 011-23289044, 011-43142548
e-mail: sales@randompublications.com,
info@randompublications.com, randomexports@gmail.com

Reprinted 2023

Type Setting by : Friends Media, Delhi-110089
Digitally Printed at : Replika Press Pvt. Ltd.

Preface

A war poet is a poet in time of and on the subject of war. The term, which is applied especially to those in military service during World War I.

For the first time, a substantial number of important English poets were soldiers, writing about their experiences of war. A number of them died on the battlefield, most famously Edward Thomas, Isaac Rosenberg, Wilfred Owen, and Charles Sorley. Others including Robert Graves, Ivor Gurney and Siegfried Sassoon survived but were scarred by their experiences, and this was reflected in their poetry. Robert H. Ross characterised the English "war poets" as a subgroup of the Georgian Poetry writers.

Many poems by British war poets were published in newspapers and then collected into anthologies. Several of these early anthologies were published during the war and were very popular, though the tone of the poetry changed as the war progressed. One of the wartime anthologies was The Muse in Arms, published in 1917. Several anthologies were also published in the years after the war had ended.

Modern poetry grew out of the First World War. English verse altered under the impact of mass murder in the trenches 1914-1918 and ceased to be cosy. The war spread to Russia and Italy and Turkey and into the Middle East, but the Western Front in France was the focus of attention at home. The opening bombardment on the Somme was heard in London.

Poetry came closer to news. Poets became war correspondents of feeling and suffering rather than celebrants of glory, honour, patria and remembrance. They ceased to be crudely national.

By World War II the role of "war poet" was so well-established in the public mind that "Where are the war poets?" became a topic of discussion.[citation needed]. Robert Graves gave a radio talk 'Why has this War produced no War Poets?' in October 1941 and Stephen Spender also addressed the question at about the same time (as did T. S. Eliot a year later). Alun Lewis and Keith Douglas are the standard critical choices amongst British war poets of this time.

This book will prove useful not only to the students of English literature but also to the teachers and readers of English literature.

I would like to thank my team for standing beside me throughout my career and writing this book. My special thanks go to "Random Publications" who have published the book.

– Attied Khawar Balwan and Ranbir Kaur

Contents

1

Introduction to War Poets

THE FIRST WORLD WAR AND THE POETS

One of the greatest tragedies the world has ever experienced was the First World War. With absolute determination, nations dedicated every ounce of human talent, energy and resources to the destruction of human life. Millions were killed; millions were disabled by hideous wounds, mental breakdown, bereavement. Life was worsened throughout Europe and the effects were long-lasting.

In the history of mankind war has been a rare and quite abnormal state of affairs, and when wars broke out in earlier centuries most were confined to quite small numbers of participants fighting for a few hours or days with simple weapons in small areas of land.

The First World War announced the century of war. It was to be a century in which whole nations would suffer and support war and the destructive power developed by scientists would create death, misery and brutalisation, on a new and quite astonishing scale. The human race had moved into the era of scientific savagery.

The poets played their part in this war as promoters of it, onlookers, soldiers and victims. What sets them apart is that the poets were those most gifted to express the experience of those shocking years. And their work includes some of the greatest poems in the English language.

WWI POETRY

This seminar is intended as an introduction to First World War poetry. First time users are strongly advised to read the Seminar Introduction, which gives a brief overview of the genre as well an explanation for the poetry selected for this seminar. A seminar map is also available, listing all the pages in this seminar.

THEME

In order to provide a focus for this seminar, all of the 'featured' poems have been selected for their appropriateness to a given theme. The theme selected is that of injury and the physical, mental and other consequences of this.

THE POEMS

WILFRED OWEN (1893–1918)

Biography

Owen was born on 18th March 1893 in Oswestry, Shropshire, son of Tom and Susan Owen. After the death of his grandfather in 1897 the family moved to Birkenhead (Merseyside).

His education began at the Birkenhead Institute, and then continued at the Technical School in Shrewsbury when the family were forced to move there in 1906-7 when his father was appointed Assistant Superintendent for the Western Region of the railways. Already displaying a keen interest in the arts, Owen's earliest experiments in poetry began at the age of 17. After failing to attain entrance to the University of London, he spent a year as a lay assistant to the Revd. Herbert Wigan at Dunsden before leaving for Bordeaux, France, to teach at the Berlitz School of English.

During the latter part of 1914 and early 1915 Owen became increasingly aware of the magnitude of the War and he returned to England in September 1915 to enlist in the Artists' Rifles a month later. He received his commission to the Manchester Regiment (5th Battalion) in June 1916, and spent the rest of the year training in England.

1917 in many ways was the pivotal year in his life, although it was to prove to be his penultimate. In January he was posted to France and saw his first action in which he and his men were forced to hold a flooded dug-out in no-man's land for fifty hours whilst under heavy bombardment. In March he was injured with concussion but returned to the front-line in April. In May he was caught in a shell-explosion and when his battalion was eventually relieved he was diagnosed as having shell-shock ('neurasthenia'). He was evacuated to England and on June 26th he arrived at Craiglockhart War Hospital near Edinburgh.

Had Owen not arrived at the hospital at that time one wonders what might have happened to his literary career, for it was here that he met Siegfried Sassoonwho was also a patient. Sassoon already had a reputation as a poet and after an awkward introduction he agreed to look over Owen's poems. As well as encouraging Owen to continue, he introduced him to such literary figures as Robert Graves (a friend of Sassoon's) which in turn, after his release from hospital, allowed Owen to mix with such luminaries as Arnold Bennett and H. G. Wells.

The period in Craiglockhart, and the early part of 1918, was in many ways his most creative, and he wrote many of the poems for which he is remembered today. In June 1918 he rejoined his regiment at Scarborough and then in August he returned to France. He was awarded the Military Cross for bravery at Amiens, but was killed on the 4th November whilst attempting to lead his men across the Sambre canal at Ors. The news of his death reached his parents on November 11th 1918, the day of the armistice.

SIEGFRIED SASSOON (1886–1967)

With war on the horizon, a young Englishman whose life had heretofore been consumed with the protocol of fox-hunting, said goodbye to his idyllic life and rode off on his bicycle to join the Army. Siegfried Sassoon was perhaps the most innocent of the war poets. John Hildebidle has called Sassoon the "accidental hero." Born into a wealthy Jewish family in 1886, Sassoon lived the pastoral life of a young squire: fox-hunting, playing cricket, golfing and writing romantic verses.

Being an innocent, Sassoon's reaction to the realities of the war were all the more bitter and violent — both his reaction through his poetry and his reaction on the battlefield (where, after the death of fellow officer David Thomas and his brother Hamo at Gallipoli, Sassoon earned the nickname "Mad Jack" for his near-suicidal exploits against the German lines — in the early manifestation of his grief, when he still believed that the Germans were entirely to blame).

As Paul Fussell said: "now he unleashed a talent for irony and satire and contumely that had been sleeping all during his pastoral youth." Sassoon also showed his innocence by going public with hisprotest against the war (as he grew to see that insensitive political leadership was the greater enemy than the Germans). Luckily, his friend and fellow poet Robert Graves convinced the review board that Sassoon was suffering from shell-shock and he was sent instead to the military hospital at Craiglockhart where he met and influenced Wilfred Owen.

Sassoon is a key figure in the study of the poetry of the Great War: he brought with him to the war the idyllic pastoral background; he began by writing war poetry reminiscent of Rupert Brooke; he mingled with such war poets as Robert Graves and Edmund Blunden; he spoke out publicly against the war (and yet returned to it); he influenced and mentored the then unknown Wilfred Owen; he spent thirty years reflecting on the war through his memoirs; and at last he found peace in his religious faith. Some critics found his later poetry lacking in comparison to his war poems. Sassoon, identifying with Herbert and Vaughan, recognized and understood this: "my development has been entirely consistent and in character" he answered, "almost all of them have ignored the fact that I am a religious poet."

RUPERT BROOKE (1887–1915)

For one whom Yeats proclaimed "the handsomest young man in England," Rupert Brooke has not aged well. The neo-Romanticism of Brooke and the Georgian Poets was one of the casualties of The Great War. Paul Fussell (in *The Great War and Modern Memory*) sees irony as one of the by-products of the First World War, and one of the many ironies of the war is that Rupert Brooke is remembered as a war poet at all, because he is actually not a war poet — not in the same sense that Siegfried Sassoon, Robert Graves and Wilfred Owen are war poets. Rupert Brooke is rather a pre-war poet. To borrow Blake's contrast, Brooke wrote *Songs of Innocence* (if not naïveté), while Sassoon and Owen (and others) wrote *Songs of Experience*.

Brooke's entire reputation as a war poet rests on only 5 "war sonnets" (6 if you count "Treasure" — unnumbered in his short sonnet cycle). Brooke's war experience consisted of one day of limited military action with the Hood Battalion during the evacuation of Antwerp. Consequently, his "war sonnets" swell with sentiments of the most general kind on the themes of maturity, purpose and romantic death — the kind of sentiments held by many (but not all) young Englishmen at the outbreak of the war. Brooke's "war sonnets" are really more a declaration occasioned by the ups and downs of his tumultuous personal life than a call to war for his generation.

Brooke was already a promising young poet when Britain entered the war the day after his 27th birthday. Unfortunately, the publication of his (pre-) "war sonnets" coincided with his almost mythological (pre-war) death: on Easter Sunday, 1915, Dean Inge read his sonnet "The Soldier" from the pulpit of Saint Paul's; on April 23rd (St. George's Day, the traditional observance of Shakespeare's birth) Brooke died in the Aegean Sea (from blood poisoning) on his way to battle at Gallipoli and was buried on the Island of Skyros. Winston Churchill wrote his obituary for *The Times*, Lascelles Abercrombie for the *Morning Post*. As D.H. Lawrence exclaimed: "he was slain by bright Pheobus' shaft... it was a real climax of his pose... bright Pheobus smote him down. It is all in the saga. O God, O God; it is all too much of a piece: it is like madness."

Brooke was born in 1887 at Rugby where his father was a housemaster. His dominating mother exerted a tremendous influence on him. Brooke traveled in Europe where he prepared a thesis, *John Webster and the Elizabethan Drama*, which won for him a fellowship at King's College, Cambridge. He roamed across North America and the South Seas for the *Westminster Gazette* sending back narratives and poems. Brooke was an energetic aesthete skilled at playful, irreverent satire ("Heaven") and not afraid to shock his audience with graphic descriptions ("Channel Crossing").

EDWARD THOMAS (1878–1917)

Edward (Philip) Thomas was born in Lambeth, London, of Welsh descent and he was educated at St Paul's college and then Lincoln College at Oxford University (where he studied history). A prolific writer of prose (including biographies of Richard Jefferies, Swinburne, and Keats), and a moderately successful journalist, he began writing poetry in 1912 under the pseudonym Edward Eastaway) but did not devote himself fully to the medium until 1913 after a meeting with Robert Frost, the American poet, who by then was living in England.

Thomas enlisted in 1915 with the Artists' Rifles as a private but was killed two years later at Arras having achieved the rank of 2nd Lieutenant. His poems include some of the most noted pieces from the genre, capturing the love of the English countryside unlike any other.

ISAAC ROSENBERG (1890–1918)

Returning, We Hear The Larks

Sombre the night is.
And though we have our lives, we know
What sinister threat lurks there.
Dragging these anguished limbs, we only know
This poison- blasted track opens on our camp -
On a little safe sleep.
But hark! joy - joy - strange joy.
Lo! heights of night ringing with unseen larks.
Music showering our upturned list'ning faces.
Death could drop from the dark
As easily as song -
But song only dropped,
Like a blind man's dreams on the sand
By dangerous tides,
Like a girl's dark hair for she dreams no ruin lies there,
Or her kisses where a serpent hides.

Dead Man's Dump

The plunging limbers over the shattered track
Racketed with their rusty freight,
Stuck out like many crowns of thorns,
And the rusty stakes like sceptres old
To stay the flood of brutish men
Upon our brothers dear.
The wheels lurched over sprawled dead
But pained them not, though their bones crunched;
Their shut mouths made no moan,

They lie there huddled, friend and foeman,
Man born of man, and born of woman;
And shells go crying over them
From night till night and now.
Earth has waited for them,
All the time of their growth
Fretting for their decay:
Now she has them at last!
In the strength of her strength
Suspended - stopped and held.
What fierce imaginings their dark souls lit?
Earth! Have they gone into you?
Somewhere they must have gone,
And flung on your hard back
Is their souls' sack,
Emptied of God-ancestralled essences.
Who hurled them out? Who hurled?
None saw their spirits' shadow shake the grass,
Or stood aside for the half-used life to pass
Out of those doomed nostrils and the doomed mouth,
When the swift iron burning bee
Drained the wild honey of their youth.
What of us who, flung on the shrieking pyre,
Walk, our usual thoughts untouched,
Our lucky limbs as on ichor fed,
Immortal seeming ever?
Perhaps when the flames beat loud on us,
A fear may choke in our veins
And the startled blood may stop.
The air is loud with death,
The dark air spurts with fire,
The explosions ceaseless are.
Timelessly now, some minutes past,
These dead strode time with vigorous life,
Till the shrapnel called 'An end!'
But not to all. In bleeding pangs
Some borne on stretchers dreamed of home,
Dear things, war-blotted from their hearts.
A man's brains splattered on
A stretcher-bearer's face;
His shook shoulders slipped their load,
But when they bent to look again

The drowning soul was sunk too deep
For human tenderness.
They left this dead with the older dead,
Stretched at the cross roads.
Burnt black by strange decay
Their sinister faces lie,
The lid over each eye;
The grass and coloured clay
More motion have than they,
Joined to the great sunk silences.
Here is one not long dead.
His dark hearing caught our far wheels,
And the choked soul stretched weak hands
To reach the living word the far wheels said;
The blood-dazed intelligence beating for light,
Crying through the suspense of the far torturing wheels
Swift for the end to break
Or the wheels to break,
Cried as the tide of the world broke over his sight,
'Will they come? Will they ever come?'
Even as the mixed hoofs of the mules,
The quivering-bellied mules,
And the rushing wheels all mixed
With his tortured upturned sight.
So we crashed round the bend,
We heard his weak scream,
We heard his very last sound,
And our wheels grazed his dead face.

WOMEN'S POETRY AND VERSE

There is a strong but neglected tradition of women's poetry written in response to the events of the First World War. Many of these poems are the products of direct experience of the processes of war — making weapons, nursing the wounded, the loss of brothers, sons, or lovers in the trenches — by women on active service in the battle areas as well as by women involved in the war effort at home. The range of this poetry is wide. It is often experimental and in advance of the male poetic response. Some of the women poets are well known in other contexts — like Rose Macauley, Edith Nesbit, and Edith Sitwell — others are largely unknown. It was an American woman poet, Harriet Monroe, who founded and edited *Poetry*, the first American periodical devoted exclusively to verse, and who published some of Rosenberg's work. Below are some examples of such works by a number of women poets of the period.

Munition Wages

Earning high wages?
Yus, Five quid a week.
A woman, too, mind you,
I calls it dim sweet.
Ye'are asking some questions -
But bless yer, here goes:
I spends the whole racket
On good times and clothes.
Me saving? Elijah!
Yer do think I'm mad.
I'm acting the lady,
But - I ain't living bad.
I'm having life's good times.
See 'ere, it's like this:
The 'oof come o' danger,
A touch-and-go bizz.
We're all here today, mate,
Tomorrow - perhaps dead,
If Fate tumbles on us
And blows up our shed.
Afraid! Are yer kidding?
With money to spend!
Years back I wore tatters,
Now - silk stockings, mi friend!
I've bracelets and jewellery,
Rings envied by friends;
A sergeant to swank with,
And something to lend.
I drive out in taxis,
Do theatres in style.
And this is mi verdict -
It is jolly worth while.
Worth while, for tomorrow
If I'm blown to the sky,
I'll have repaid mi wages
In death - and pass by.

Pluck

Crippled for life at seventeen,
His great eyes seem to question why:
With both legs smashed it might have been

Better in that grim trench to die
Than drag maimed years out helplessly.
A child - so wasted and so white,
He told a lie to get his way,
To march, a man with men, and fight
While other boys are still at play.
A gallant lie your heart will say.
So broke with pain, he shrinks in dread
To see the 'dresser' drawing near;
And winds the clothes about his head
That none may see his heart-sick fear.
His shaking, strangled sobs you hear.
But when the dreaded moment's there
He'll face us all, a soldier yet,
Watch his bared wounds with unmoved air,
(Though tell-tale lashes still are wet),
And smoke his woodbine cigarette.

The Wind on the Downs

I like to think of you as brown and tall,
As strong and living as you used to be,
In khaki tunic, Sam Brown belt and all,
And standing there and laughing down at me.
Because they tell me, dear, that you are dead,
Because I can no longer see your face,
You have not died, it is not true, instead
You seek adventure in some other place.
That you are round about me, I believe;
I hear you laughing as you used to do,
Yet loving all the things I think of you;
And knowing you are happy, should I grieve?
You follow and are watchful where I go;
How should you leave me, having loved me so?
We walked along the tow-path, you and I,
Beside the sluggish-moving, still canal;
It seemed impossible that you should die;
I think of you the same and always shall.
We thought of many things and spoke of few,
And life lay all uncertainly before,
And now I walk alone and think of you,
And wonder what new kingdoms you explore.
Over the railway line, across the grass,

While up above the golden wings are spread,
Flying, ever flying overhead,
Here still I see your khaki figure pass,
And when I leave the meadow, almost wait
That you should open first the wooden gate.

The Call

Who's for the trench -
Are you, my laddie?
Who'll follow French -
Will you, my laddie?
Who's fretting to begin,
Who's going out to win?
And who wants to save his skin -
Do you, my laddie?
Who's for the khaki suit -
Are you, my laddie?
Who longs to charge and shoot -
Do you, my laddie?
Who's keen on getting fit,
Who means to show his grit,
And who'd rather wait a bit -
Would you, my laddie?
Who'll earn the Empire's thanks -
Will you, my laddie?
Who'll swell the victor's ranks -
Will you, my laddie?
When that procession comes,
Banners and rolling drums -
Who'll stand and bite his thumbs -
Will you, my laddie?

Over the Top

Ten more minutes! - Say yer prayers,
Read yer Bibles, pass the rum!
Ten more minutes! Strike me dumb,
'Ow they creeps on unawares,
Those blooming minutes. Nine. It's queer,
I'm sorter stunned. It ain't with fear!
Eight. It's like as if a frog
Waddled round in your inside,
Cold as ice-blocks, straddle wide,

Tired o' waiting. Where's the grog?
Seven. I'll play yer pitch and toss -
Six. - I wins, and tails yer loss.
'Nother minute sprinted by
'Fore I knowed it; only Four
(Break 'em into seconds) more
'Twixt us and Eternity.
Every word I've ever said
Seems a-shouting in my head.
Three. Larst night a little star
Fairly shook up in the sky,
Didn't like the lullaby
Rattled by the dogs of War.
Funny thing - that star all white
Saw old Blighty, too, larst night.
Two. I ain't ashamed o' prayers,
They're only wishes sent ter God
Bits o' plants from bloody sod
Trailing up His golden stairs.
Ninety seconds - Well, who cares!
One -
No fife, no blare, no drum -
Over the Top - to Kingdom Come!

In most cases each poet or topic includes the following:

- An introduction to the poet/topic
- A featured poem, appropriate to the seminar's theme
- Some literary criticism of the featured poem
- Other relevant information or texts
- A selection of other poems appropriate to the poet/topic
- Access to the WWI Poetry Discussion Board

2

British Poets and the War between Britain and France

INTRODUCTION

From the fall of the Bastille on July 14, 1789 throughout the revolutionary and Napoleonic wars, which continued almost without cessation until Napoleon's final defeat at Waterloo on June 18, 1815, British poets responded to war activities to an extent unprecedented in British history. Blake's *The French Revolution*, passages of Wordsworth's *The Prelude* as well as a number of his sonnets, Coleridge's *France: An Ode* and *Fears in Solitude*, Byron's *Napoleon's Farewell* and parts of *Childe Harold*, and Shelley's *Henry and Louisa* are among the best known representatives of this poetic response. But many of these poems were unpublished during the war period. Furthermore, these poems have generally been examined within the context of the total body of work of the principal Romantic poets, an approach which has served to obscure the fact that the war was a primary poetic preoccupation of the age. However important, the war poems by the major poets constitute a small segment of a vast body of contemporary verse both in favour of and opposed to the war. To understand more fully the larger, generalized tradition of Romanticism, one must consider the more specific, topical tradition of war verse which influenced and was influenced by both the greater and lesser Romantic poets.

The quality of the war verses varies greatly, ranging from plainly nationalistic songs, which embody rhetorical effect rather than intrinsic poetic merit, to the most seriously intended works of art with their metaphoric use of the war experience. As many varieties of poetic mode as possible are included within this collection to present the poetically as well as the politically revolutionary aspects of the period. The doggerel and the simple call-to-arms in song, for example, are not only historical facts of the time; they are the outgrowth of the will to write for an ever-expanding, more democratic audience, one that for the first time included the workingman. Nationalistic verse had been written before, but with the growth of the popular periodical press and with both readers and writers of poetry drawn from the middle and the working classes, the simple stanza-plus-refrain form acquired a poetic respectability which it had not previously had. The virtue of this form was its accessibility to readers accustomed to the simple rhythms and repetitive patterns of the familiar jingle or nursery rhyme as well as to the popular ballads customarily found in chap books and broadsides.

The French Revolution provided a ready focus for British poets. Even before the Revolution took place, the thinking which inspired it—the writings of Voltaire, Rousseau, and others—had excited many minds in Britain, and there was wide-spread sympathy for victims of Bourbon oppression. This attitude may be attributed to the more republican nature of British political philosophy which was buttressed by the recent revolt against Britain itself by the American colonies. The American Revolution seemed to have had many of the same republican objectives as the French, and the favourable considerations it provoked in some British minds were readily applied to French revolutionary action.

The overthrow of the Bastille was regarded as the overthrow of the feudal, tyrannic rule of the Bourbons, and poets celebrated it in these terms immediately and for some years to follow. The famous "Swan of Litchfield," Anna Seward wrote *Sonnet to France on Her Present Exertions* which appeared in at least six publications from August through October 1789; Cowper's section in *The Task* which prophetically anticipated the destruction of the Bastille was reprinted in at least two periodicals; Coleridge wrote the *Destruction of the Bastille*(first published in 1834); and there appeared a spate of unsigned works in newspapers and periodicals expressing the same sentiments. The approbation accorded the fall of the Bastille was also expressed in Britain through annual festivities held on the fourteenth of July, a day celebrated by many Whigs and radicals alike during the early years of the French Republic. The tenacity with which some Britons held to the significance of the event is further demonstrated by the fact that some Britons marked the date with poetic celebration even after Britain and France were at war and the ideals of the Revolution had become tarnished.

The initial positive response in Britain to the French Revolution altered as the excesses of the revolutionary tribunals were reported. In terms of the poetry, the approval of earlier events in France perceptibly changed in 1792 with the imprisonment of the King and Queen of France, and particularly in 1793 with the execution of the royal couple and Britain's official entry into the war against the Republic of France. Much of the anti-revolutionary poetry centered upon the plight of the deposed monarchs. Edmund Burke's personal and highly sentimental view of the Queen, "glittering like the morning-star, full of life, and splendor, and joy," fixed an image which could be used to full effect by the anti-revolutionary poets. Burke's representation of Marie

Antoinette as the principal figure in a tragedy about the death of chivalry in which the "glory of Europe is extinguished forever," was rebutted by Thomas Paine's more factual account in *The Rights of Man*, but Burke's tragic queen, the wife and mother, proved more appealing, and the majority of British poets dealt with the Queen sympathetically. *Stanzas supposed to be Written Whilst the Late Queen of France was Sleeping, by Her Attendant in the Temple* is typical of the poetry which echoed Burke's image of the Queen. A rare instance of an attack on the French Queen was Blake's notebook ballad, *Let the Brothels of Paris be opened,* in which the Queen is personally held responsible for the suffering of the French people:

The Queen of France just touchd this Globe
And the Pestilence darted from her robe.

Blake's poem was not published at that time but, as David V. Erdman suggests, although Blake's works "did not reach the awakening citizens who were reading Paine and rushing together in republican societies, they did nevertheless reflect the stir and tumult of that awakening."

Wordsworth and Coleridge reflect that awakening as well. The young "revolutionary and radical" Wordsworth's personal and political involvement in the French Revolution is well documented, but it is too often overshadowed by the portrait of "the level-headed elderly man, shrewdly practical, settling down to an uneventful domestic life, a confirmed Tory in politics." The fact is that Wordsworth's response to the Revolution was sympathetic and supportive:

... I gradually withdrew
Into a noisier world, and thus ere long
Became a patriot; and my heart was all
Given to the people, and my love was theirs.

Although Wordsworth reacted against the excesses of the Revolutionary Tribunals, there is little evidence that he ever reacted against his faith in man. His belief in Utopian institutions may have been destroyed by his experience with France, but his somewhat mystical belief in the elemental passions and sentiments of common people remained intact and it was this belief rather than a political philosophy, which led him into sympathy with the French Revolution in the first place.

Coleridge treated the Revolution and the subsequent war with France in prose and verse. Philosophically wary of the ideals of Rousseau and his concept of "natural religion," Coleridge was concerned with analyzing the philosophical foundations of the Revolution. *France: An Ode*, 1798 is a poetical version of Coleridge's political philosophy, and in the fifth stanza of that poem he expresses his notion that the ideal of freedom belongs to the individual and cannot be found in a society or in the institutions of human government. In *Fears in Solitude*, 1798, Coleridge presented the dilemma of war: the poem is forceful in describing the horrors of warfare but admits the necessity for Britons to "repel an impious foe." Coleridge believed that Britain's war against Napoleon was a struggle of those who possessed a higher conception of liberty and justice against a materialist foe.

Southey, like Wordsworth and Coleridge, began as an anti-war poet who gradually reversed his position to become a staunch supporter of the war. His early anti-tyrannic *Joan of Arc* drew fire from Anna Seward in *The European Magazine*, 1797 and his *The Soldier's Wife* was parodied in *The Anti-Jacobin*.The 1799 *Annual Anthology*, which was edited by Southey, printed his *The Soldier's Funeral* and *The Battle of Blenheim*. But this and the 1800 *Annual Anthology*, which published war verse by Coleridge as well, contained poems written during the pre-Napoleonic stage of the protracted war, though Southey had already come to favour the war against France. The biting irony of *The Battle of Blenheim* directed—as was so much of Southey's war poetry—against the inhumanity of war stands in striking contrast to his vindictive *Ode Written During the Negotiations with Bonaparte, in January 1814* in which he argues against the peace negotiations and in favour of the complete destruction of Napoleon:

When innocent blood
From the four corners of the world cries out
For justice upon one accursed head.

Although the change in Southey's view of the war occurred long before he became poet-laureate in 1813, he was attacked by Leigh Hunt, among others, for his political reversal. His shift from radical politics to a "Philanthropic brand of Toryism" can be seen as a response to the change in 1796 in the character of the war itself. What had begun as a revolution against French tyranny in 1796 was seen as a war which seemed to have as its goal total European domination by France. The concept of one tyranny being substituted for another became the subject matter of Southey's war poetry, as well as that of Coleridge, Wordsworth, and others. Nevertheless, the selections of Southey included here, particularly the earlier works, proved not only popular but influential.

While Thomas Campbell was not so prolific a war poet as Southey, his work was often reprinted and his war verses provided a model which was imitated by others. Although Campbell consistently supported Britain, he maintained a poetic objectivity which enabled him to deal artistically and compassionately with the scourges of war, as in *The Soldier's Dream*.

The role of Robert Burns as a war poet must be considered in terms of his influence on the poetry of the period in general, and part four of this introduction will deal with his contribution in some detail. Burns died in 1796, and the few war poems he wrote were of mixed quality, from the touching *The Soldier's Return* to the nationalistic *The Dumfries Volunteers*, but all his poetry was well received and well circulated during this period.

The war was so popular a subject that a commentator in *The Analytical Review* noted in 1793 that it was treated by "every hireling scribbler." The poets concerned themselves with the events of the war in such topical poems as *Nelson's Victory: An Ode*, on Nelson's defeat of the French in Egypt; they treated the effects of the war on individuals, as Amelia Opie's *The Orphan Boy's Tale* or on the country as in*January, 1795*; and frequently poets offered philosophical poems on the subject as in *The Age of War*. Poems were sometimes frankly hortatory as *English, Scots, and Irishmen: A Patriotic Address to the Inhabitants of the United Kingdom, July, 1803*, by John Mayne; they ranged from the satiric *A Modern Ballad* to the unabashedly sentimental *The Generous Soldier* by Mr. Booker, 1800.

Generally poetry columns contained at least one poem on the war and some poems were published and circulated as broadsides as well, such as *The Ploughman's Ditty; Being an Answer to that Foolish Question, What Have the Poor to Lose?* which was printed in at least four periodicals and as a broadside. In addition, periodical verses were occasionally reprinted and circulated in book form: *The Spirit of the Public Journals* was a collection of brief prose passages and verse specifically gathered from newspapers, and *The Anti-Gallican* was a collection of prose and verse gathered from broadsides as well as from newspapers and periodicals.

The Spirit of the Public Journals, unlike most publications of the period, avoided political distinctions or partisan connections in its editorial policy. Instead, it published a cross-section of all jeux d'esprits of the popular journals, although there is a notable absence of material from radical publications. In the early editions of *The Spirit of the Public Journals* such anti-war poems as *The Fruits of the War* and *A Fast Day Hymn* appeared, but by the turn of the century, although selections from both Whig and Tory publications continued to appear, there is no discernable difference in attitude towards the war. By that time, both Whigs and Tories generally agreed that it was a necessity, if not a duty, for Britain to defeat Napoleon and put to rest once and for all the French threat to British liberty.

The Anti-Gallican, on the other hand, was clearly intended to bolster the war morale of its readers. It reproduces approximately two hundred verses, in addition to many prose pieces, on the threatened invasion of Britain by France. Many of the pieces date from before 1803, the year Britain felt that invasion was imminent, but they are consistent in their hostility towards the French and their insistence on the necessity of continuing the struggle to defend Britain. The collection, printed partially for J. Asperne, draws upon many of the broadsides which Asperne printed in 1803—to which he frequently appends the suggestion that they be distributed among the poor by those who could afford to do so in order to rouse the lower classes against the French. Included in *The Anti-Gallican* are Wordsworth's *Anticipation*, Burn's *The Dumfries*

Volunteers, and Campbell's *The Soldier's Dream*. The broadside itself was a popular way of circulating war verses during the war period. It has been noted that although periodicals gained in prestige during the eighteenth century, "the broadside stubbornly held its ground in the service not only of hack writers but of poets of name" and continued to do so into the nineteenth century. In addition to the previously mentioned *Ploughman's Ditty*, poems which appeared in broadsides as well as periodicals or collections include John Mayne's *English, Scots, and Irishmen* and several works by Leigh Hunt which were published in a special form of broadside known as Bellman's verses, verses printed as a broadside and sold to Bellmen or Beadles for distribution as New Year's gifts. Hunt occasionally reprinted these verses in one of his newspapers:*Orange Boven* appeared as a *Bellman's Verse for 1814* and in *The Examiner* on January 23, 1814.

Shelley also made use of the broadside to circulate war verses. His early opposition to the war, as well as to the aristocracy and Napoleon, is demonstrated in his *Esdaile Note-Book* poems, *The Crisis, To the Emperors of Russia and Austria who eyed the battle from the heights whilst Buonaparte was active in the thickest of the fight*, and Henry and Louisa. Influenced by Coleridge's and Southey's *The Devil's Thoughts*, Shelley wrote an anti-establishment, anti-war ballad entitled *The Devil's Walk* and had it printed as a broadside, which resulted in the arrest of Shelley's servant as he was distributing the broadside.

Although the broadside was employed to some effect, the chief medium of publication of war poetry were the magazines and newspapers, which provided poets concerned with the war a steady outlet for their encomiums, their warnings, their arguments. Opposition to the war and acclamation for the war were based on a variety of grounds: political, ethical, religious, economic, humanitarian, nationalistic, moralistic. Content and approach vary not only from poet to poet, but according to the political stance of the medium in which the poems are found. To understand the frequency of particular points of view, it is necessary to examine the influence of politics on the publishing practices of the day.

POLITICS AND POETRY

In the aftermath of the French Revolution, a new term was introduced into British political nomenclature. The term "Jacobin," derived from the French political club established in 1789 to develop and maintain egalitarian government, was found to be a useful pejorative designation and was applied indiscriminately to those who sympathized with the Revolution as well as to British republicans, radicals, and Whigs. In fact, all who opposed the policies of the Tory government found themselves attacked as Jacobins.

The terms designating the two major political parties in Britain during this period, the Tories and the Whigs, had themselves been pejorative appellations used in 1679 during the struggle to exclude James, Duke of York, from succession to the throne. From the Revolution of 1688-89 until the death of Queen Anne in 1714, the Whig and Tory parties maintained a political balance of power and opposition in England. After 1714, however, with the crowning of the Whig nominee George I as king, and the flight of the Tory leader Bolingbroke to France, the Tories declined as a political party. The situation was changed in 1784, when the young Pitt became leader of a new Tory party which represented the interests of the country gentry and the powerful merchant classes. The Whig party, as opposition under the leadership of Charles James Fox, was made up of dissenters, shopkeepers, and the burgeoning industrialists.

Pitt's Tory government was firmly opposed to the Revolution in France and took a position of defending and maintaining the status quo. The Whigs, on the other hand, desired electoral, parliamentary, and philanthropic reform, and were more open to social change. Many Whigs supported the Revolution and opposed the war with France, though the more conservative among them supported the policies of the Pitt government. Thus, the rather imprecise term "Jacobin" was used to suggest all those who sympathized with France and to designate those who opposed Pitt's policies: radicals, republicans, and Whigs alike. Jacobinism was even extended to impute the morals as well as the politics of opponents of the Pitt government. Indeed, the term carried so much negative weight that Wordsworth and Coleridge published the *Lyrical Ballads* anonymously because they were aware that they were "marked out as Jacobins." Coleridge gives the term some precision in an article in *The Morning Post* of October 21, 1802, entitled "Once a Jacobin Always a Jacobin," in which he states that the term has been applied to "all who, from whatever cause, opposed the late war and the late ministry." However, this is a definition of the term by "bigots alarmed and detected culprits." More properly, he maintains, a Jacobin is one who affirms:

that no legislature can be rightful or good which did not proceed from universal suffrage. In the power and under the control of a legislature so chosen he places all and everything, with the exception of the natural rights of man and the means appointed for the preservation and exercise of these rights, by a direct vote of the nation itself—that is to say, by a constitution. Finally, the Jacobin deems it both justifiable and expedient to effect these requisite changes in faulty governments by absolute revolutions, and considers no violences as properly rebellious or criminal which are the means of giving to a nation the power of declaring and enforcing its sovereign will...

Coleridge intended to sum up and at the same time criticize the views of Rousseau which, rather imperfectly understood, were those which the French Revolution had sought to put into practice. The article attempts to define a total Jacobin creed and to indicate that only advocates of despotism did not subscribe to some of the tenets of Jacobinism. While arguing that he was not a

Jacobin, Coleridge tries to dispel the emotion which had become attached to the term.

In the context of the poetry in this collection, "Jacobin" tells less about those who are attacked in satire, or who are impugned in more serious poetry, than it does about the Tory position of those who attack or impugn. Since, throughout the period, the Jacobin label is often used without discrimination, the term "radical" might be substituted as a more appropriate and encompassing designation for those who opposed government policies. The range of opposition was broad—altering as the war progressed —and the term "radical" in this discussion is intended to include all factions which supported the French Revolution as well as those which desired major governmental reform in England.

While there were radical thinkers in Britain before the French Revolution, the radicals were, for the most part, loosely organized and unenfranchised. Those with any political power at all belonged to the tradition of Whig "commonwealthmen," and, in fact, the radicals were not organized into a specific political party until 1820. It was the French Revolution which became a catalystic agent for those in England who were dissatisfied with the British government. The Revolution became synonymous to many with the struggle of the British working class for better living conditions and more representative government. Dr. Richard Price's Sermon, *A Discourse on the Love of Our Country* (November 4, 1789), in support of the Revolution was greeted enthusiastically by a number of radicals and by liberal Whigs.Not all liberal Whigs, however, accepted Price's stand, and Edmund Burke was to take him to task in his*Reflections Upon the Revolution in France*. A significant number of radical thinkers took the opportunity afforded by the French Revolution to press for consideration of the working class and the need for reform. The Second Part of Thomas Paine's *Rights of Man*, in calling the aristocracy into account, effected a bridge between the old tradition of Whig "commonwealthmen" and the radicals.

The strong disapproval of the monarchy and of aristocratic hereditary principles was related to the economic hardships of the poor. Much of the anti-war poetry written during this early phase renders these sentiments in verse, as in *Effects of War* published in *The Cambridge Intelligencer*, February 22, 1794. The opposition was quick to attack those poets who opposed the war on such grounds, and verses in favour of the war linked support of France with destruction of the British establishment.

The argument that the war was being conducted by men "Too high to stoop, too proud to feel,/ For England's bleeding woes" who are disinterested in the "thousands begging at their gates,/ Or welt'ring in their gore," but who are more concerned with "gaudy luxries" and "a scarf or garter blue," is prevalent in the anti-war poetry throughout the war years. In fact, the image of an aristocratic class indifferent to the suffering of the poor became so prevalent that it is used in later years of the war even by poets who do not necessarily oppose government policies. For example, a poet in *The Scots Magazine* in 1802, speaks in the voice of *The Beggar Girl* orphaned by the war:

To the Rich, by whom Virtue's too often
neglected,
I tell my sad story—and crave for relief:
But Wealth seldom feels for a wretch unpro-
tected—
'Tis Poverty only partakes of her grief!
Ah, little they think that the thousands they
squander
On the playthings of Folly and fripp'ries
of Dress,
Would relieve the keen wants of the wretched
who wander,
While the soft tear of pity would soothe
their distress!

Debating societies in which the working man participated were formed sporadically in England from 1776 on. Although there had been such clubs in Sheffield, Derby, and Manchester, it was not until the London Corresponding Society was founded in January 1792 that they were organized into a significant vocal group. This Society, which held meetings at "The Bell" tavern off the Strand, was composed of artisans, small shopkeepers, tradesmen, journeymen, printers, engravers, young attorneys, apothecaries, teachers, journalists, surgeons, and Dissenting clergy. It was a popular radical society, rather than a strictly working-class debating society, and it was formed to discuss the current events and to attempt to influence government. The aristocratic opponents of the radical groups were quick to form "counter-revolutionary" organizations directed against them. "Church and King" clubs proliferated. (It was a "Church and King" club which caused a riot in Birmingham in the summer of 1791 by interrupting a dinner in celebration of the anniversary of the fall of the Bastille.) The position of the "Church and King" groups is enunciated in *Church and King, a Song* of 1793:

True Freedom is a temp'rate treat,
Not savage mirth, not frantic noise;
'Tis the brisk pulse's vital beat;
'Tis not the fever that destroys.
Let Britons then united sing,
Old England's Glory,—Church and King.

The violence and the scare tactics of "Church and King" mobs did not succeed in repressing the early radical groups but on the contrary helped publicize the activities of anti-war factions. Men like John Thelwall, Thomas Spence, Thomas Hardy and other advocates of the rights of the working class voiced their beliefs at meetings and in broadsides and pamphlets. Their work resulted in poetic response both from sympathizers and detractors. The detractors, for the most part, resorted to satire, much of it personal, such as *On Mister Surgeon Thelwall* which implies that Thelwall in his profession as a surgeon has dealings with the illegal "resurrection men," *i.e.* those who stole newly buried bodies to sell for medical experimentation. Since Thelwall is such an unsavory character, the satirist suggests, it is no wonder that he is sympathetic to the democratic ideals of the French Revolution. Other detractors, however, resorted to simple invective, as John Shilettoe in his 1795 *Portrait of a Jacobin*, calling the radicals "a MASS of every FILTH combin'd!/ The horror of the HUMAN KIND!" Those who sympathized with the French ideals attempted to respond in poetic terms to the insinuations of the "Church and King" mobs. The editor of *The Cambridge Intelligencer*, for example, on September 14, 1793 extracted the lines entitled *The Bishop of London's Opinion on War* from a poem which the bishop, Dr. Porteous, had written while a student at Cambridge. The lines suggest a response to Burke and the reaction to the death of the French king:

One murder makes a
Villain,
Millions a Hero: Princes are privileged
To kill, and numbers sanctify the crime.
Ah! Why will Kings forget that they are
men?
And men that they are brethren? Why delight
In HUMAN SACRIFICE?

The author of the *Sonnet to W. Wilberforce* calls upon the philanthropist to:

...teach a guilty Court the Rights of Man;
Not made to suffer only, and to bleed—
Though he has bled of late, and largely too,
At their command,—Tell them that GOD design'd
A nobler object when he made mankind,
And trace the noble purpose to their view.

In the beginning of their existence, the radical artisan groups were supported by the agitation of the ever-increasing manufacturing class and by religious groups such as the Methodist New Connexion, the so-called "Tom Paine Methodists." As the establishment perceived that the reform groups were increasing in strength, the semi-official agency for intimidation of reformers, the Association for Protecting Liberty and Property against Republicans and Levellers, was formed in the 1790's. From 1794 to 1804 there was steady repression of reformers in England: so-called Jacobins were arrested and tried; the London Corresponding Society was outlawed; the *Rights of Man* was banned, and meetings were prohibited. However, as E. P. Thompson points out:

> ... after the success of *Rights of Man*, the radicalism and terror of the French Revolution, and the onset of Pitt's repression, it was the plebian Corresponding Society which alone stood up against the counter-revolutionary wars. And these plebian groups, small as they were in 1796, did nevertheless make up an "underground" tradition which ran through to the end of the Wars.

Both the establishment and the radical opposition attempted to stir up public opinion by means of pamphlets, broadsides, and public meetings, but recognized that the quickest and most effective means of reaching large segments of the public was through newspapers and periodicals. Political bias determined what was published, and it was political consideration rather than artistic merit which was the overriding criterion in the selection of verse.

All the newspapers were committed to a particular party and, more often than not, this commitment was purchased in the form of a regular stipend from a political party or faction which then exercised control over the publication. Lucyle Werkmeister, in summing up the situation as it was in 1789, points out that both the government and the opposition each controlled seven newspapers. The government had*The Daily Advertiser, The Public Advertiser, The Public Ledger, The Times, The World, The Star*, and *The Diary, or Woodfall's Register*; the opposition maintained *The Gazetter, The General Advertiser, The Morning Herald, The Morning Post, The Morning Chronicle,* the "spurious *Star*," and *The Argus*.

The change in ownership of a newspaper could mean a reversal of its political stance and a parallel change in the character of the poetry which it published. One such instance was *The Courier* which, during its Whig years 1792-1799, printed anti-ministerial as well as anti-war poetry. In 1799, however, the paper was purchased by Daniel Stuart and Thomas George Street. Stuart, who already owned the then radical *Morning Post*, left *The Courier* in the hands of Street. Street, a Tory or, as an enemy called him, an "anythingarian," proceeded to make *The Courier* into the chief government organ in London.

The Morning Post, a journal which published Wordsworth and Coleridge as well as a host of other poets, was put on the payroll of Carleton House in 1789 when its editors threatened to make much of the Prince Regent's secret marriage to Mrs. Fitzherbert. However the newspaper did not long remain in government hands. In 1795 it was purchased by Daniel Stuart who made *The Post* a leading Whig-radical journal. Stuart gave his support to Addington's government from 1802 to 1803, and an anti-Napoleonic, pro-ministerial position was maintained by *The Post* after Stuart sold it in 1803.

The leading organ of governmental opposition throughout the war years was *The Morning Chronicle*, edited and owned by James Perry. Unlike so many of the papers of the day, *The Morning Chronicle*remained consistent in its adherence to the Whig position. Initially the paper opposed the war, but it altered its policy during the uneasy peace created by the Treaty of Amiens (1802-1803), as did Charles James Fox, leader of the Whig opposition, to support the war against Napoleon. Nevertheless, *The Morning Chronicle* maintained its staunch condemnation of the Tory party in general, and often printed prose and poetry critical of what it considered to be the war-mongering policies of the Tories. Indeed, after the Battle of Waterloo, *The Morning Chronicle* printed a poem entitled *Napoleon* by P. Cornwall, who prefaced a letter to the editor to his verse complaining that even the most "liberal-minded" men in the ministry were vilifying Buonaparte and stating that *The Morning Chronicle* was "the only corner left in the world of politics where one may hear both sides of the question."

John Walter, editor and proprietor of *The Times*, was in the pay of the Tory government until 1799 when his subsidy stopped. However, from 1801-1804, the Times supported Addington's Tory government not for a subsidy but for a government promise that the Times would be the only paper to have immediate access to government information regarding events on the Continent. Thus, the Times was perhaps the first of the newspapers to cede a financial subsidy in favour of prior intelligence. By 1814 newspapers had become more financially independent of direct government financing, with prior intelligence and the indirect subsidy of government advertising generally taking the place of the more obvious, direct financial control.

The Tory government, in the interest of gaining as much support as possible for its war policy, attempted to control newspapers not only through direct purchase but through restrictive laws. Although the long range effect of the Libel Act of 1792 was beneficial to the press, in that the government could no longer arbitrarily suppress publications and imprison newspapermen, but had to grant them full trial before a jury of their peers, the immediate effect of the act was to increase press prosecutions. The price of newspapers rose throughout the period as the government tried to halt circulation of anti-Tory journals by increasing the fee for the required newspaper stamps. The 1798 Newspaper Act not only raised the cost of stamps; it required that all newspapers be registered with the government.

Despite these measures, newspapers continued to flourish, and the government attempted to find still other methods of control. By 1812 there were at least eighteen Sunday newspapers. These were attacked on the basis of violating the Sabbath, but actually they incurred disfavour because they were mostly democratic in nature and disapproved of governmental positions. As the war continued it became increasingly difficult for newspapers to obtain information from the continent. The government took full advantage of this situation to apply pressure on journals to print only what government policy favoured or run the risk of obtaining no information at all. Attempted control of newspapers by the government reached beyond London into Scotland, Ireland, and the English provinces. Scottish "Jacobins" who were active in pursuit of reform found no support from the press at the beginning of the nineteenth century since newspapers in Scotland were controlled by the government and Scotland did not have a truly independent newspaper until 1817.

The situation in Ireland differed in that most newspapers before the Union of 1800 were anti-English.The French, aware of the hostility between Ireland and England, attempted several landings in Ireland with the aid of Irish radicals. The landings, however, were unsuccessful. After the Union of 1800, the attitude of many Irish newspapers seemed more sympathetic to the British cause, but it has been suggested that this was due to "the lavish bribery resorted to by the government" rather than "any change in the sentiment of the people."

As for the provincial newspapers, in the early years of the war radical or Whig-radical journals were founded in opposition to the war and to the Tory government. Coleridge's *Watchman* (1796), James Montgomery's *Sheffield Iris* (1794-1824), and Benjamin Flower's *Cambridge Intelligencer* (1793-1800) are outstanding examples of the small provincial newspapers that were more than advertising sheets. After 1796, however, these papers found little support, and the provincial newspapers generally consisted of little more than advertisements, many of them governmental, and such poetry and news as the government saw fit to circulate.

Throughout the war, magazines and reviews as well as newspapers were established specifically to treat the war issue. Coleridge founded the *Watchman* to protest against Pitt's war policy and agitate for government reform. In Norwich, a group of anti-war advocates joined together to publish *The Cabinet*(1795), a journal which recalled the ideals of the French Revolution and its initial cause of liberty. On the other side of the political scale were such journals as *The Anti-Gallican Monitor* (1811), *The Tomahawk* (1795-1796), and *The Anti-Jacobin* (1797-1798), whose sole purposes were to publish poetry and prose favouring the war and attack detractors of war policy. One issue of *The Anti-Jacobin*, for example, described *The Cambridge Intelligencer* as "more false than the *Morning Post*, more blasphemous than the *Morning Chronicle*, and more devoted to the cause of Anarchy and Blood than that exploded vehicle of idiot frenzy, the *Courier*."

The Anti-Jacobin was by far the most outstanding of these publications, its reputation based not upon its prose but upon the superior quality of its satiric verse. Organized and contributed to by William Gifford, George Canning, and John Hookman Frere, this weekly was quite popular, and poetry from*The Anti-Jacobin* has been republished at least four times since it was first collected in

1799. The "Introduction" to the poetry section of the first issue of *The Anti-Jacobin* offers a statement explanatory of its policy of publishing mostly satire. Moreover, it gives an ironically candid statement on the quality of Tory vs. radical poetry:

But whether it be that good Morals, and what We should call good Politics, are inconsistent with the spirit of true Poetry—whether "the Muses still with Freedom found" have an aversion to *regular* Governments, and require a frame and system of protection less complicated than King, Lords, and Commons;—

"Whether primordial non-esense springs to life

In the wild *War* of *Democratic* strife," and there only—or for whatever other reason it may be, whether physical, or moral, or philosophical (which last is understood to mean something more than the other two, though exactly *what*, it is difficult to say), We have not been able to find one good and true Poet, of sound principle and sober practice, upon whom we could rely for furnishing us with a handsome quantity of good and approved Verse—such Verse as our Readers might be expected to get by heart and to sing, as MONGE describes the little children of Sparta, and Athens singing the songs of Freedom, in expectation of the coming of *the Great Nation*.

In this difficulty, We have had no choice but either to provide no Poetry at all,—a shabby expedient,—or to go to the only market where it is to be had good and ready made, that of the Jacobíns—an ex-pedient full of danger, and not to be used but with the utmost caution and delicacy.

Crane Brinton's statement that "literature was often blamed as the effective bond between Jacobins" is well underscored by the testimony of the editors of *The Anti-Jacobin*. It is certainly true that literature *qua* literature played an important role in unifying "Jacobin" sentiment, and it is equally true that the literary productions of the "Jacobin" writers were often superior to those of their political adversaries. However, it is well to remember that "Jacobins" were as often Whigs as republicans, and their poetry appeared both in the opposition as well as in the more radical press. Coleridge, who was at first marked out as a Jacobin, contributed poetry on the war to anti-war papers and later to the government press: from 1794 his work appeared in Flower's *Cambridge Intelligencer*; in 1794-1795 his series of sonnets to radical men appeared in *The Morning Chronicle*; from 1797 on he contributed to *The Morning Post.* During the peace created by the Treat of Amiens, Coleridge wrote anti-Napoleonic works for *The Courier* and *The Morning Post*. He believed these contributions were instrumental in the rupture of the treaty, and his belief is supported by the fact that *The Morning Post* "was said by Fox to have helped bring about the renewal of the war in May 1803."

Among the younger generation of poets, Byron, Shelley, Hunt, and Moore were opposed to Pitt and those who carried out his policies. Both Shelley and Byron believed in the necessity of fundamental reform in government, their agitation against the Tories based largely on what they considered to be the immorality of the war. It was clear even before Napoleon's defeat that Britain and her allies intended to restore the Bourbons to the throne of France, thus totally defeating the democratic spirit of the French Revolution. Byron's disappointment and disillusion at the outcome of the war were expressed in two poems printed in periodicals; *The Champion, The European Magazine, The Morning Chronicle*, and *The Examiner* all published his *Ode to Napoleon Buonaparte* in which he gives to the defeated Emperor:

Thanks for that lesson—it will teach
To after-warriors more
Than high Philosophy can preach,
And vainly preach'd before.
That spell upon the minds of men
Breaks never to unite again,
That led them to adore
Those Pagod things of sabre sway,
With fronts of brass and feet of clay.

The only note of hope struck in the poem occurs in the concluding stanza:

Where may the wearied eye repose,
When gazing on the Great;
Where neither guilty glory glows,
Nor despicable state?
Yes—one—the first—the last—the best—
The Cincinnatus of the West,
Whom envy dared not hate,
Bequeath'd the name of Washington,
To make man blush there was but one!

Byron's compassionate *Napoleon's Farewell* (which is discussed in the next section of this introduction) appeared in *The Morning Chronicle* and *The Examiner*. All the journals which published these two poems were Whig affiliated.

Because of the large extent to which politics determined publication, poetic response to the war cannot be measured by a statistical evaluation of the thousands of war verses printed. The radical press, effectively hampered by the vilification campaign launched by the government as well as by restrictive laws, was in a difficult position from the beginning of the war. To oppose the war was to subject oneself to accusations of treason and the violence of "Church and King" mobs. The Whig press, on the other hand, continued and prospered, backed as it was by the established opposition party.

The majority of the verses published favoured the war, but surely this can be attributed to the strong hand of the Tory government as well as to the changes in France's revolutionary and war objectives. The poems in this edition have been gathered from Tory, Whig, and radical publications. In selecting the works, an attempt has been made to draw upon all political viewpoints, and less emphasis has been given to numerical response (Nelson's victory at Trafalgar, for example, evoked hundreds of verses praising the event, all of almost equal dullness) in favour of offering a wide range of poetic response.

THE FLIGHT FOR "LIBERTY" AND "JUSTICE"

From the time of the "Glorious Revolution" throughout the eighteenth century, England, the sole European country governed by a monarchy established as the result of a successful rebellion, regarded itself as the bastion of "liberty" and "justice."

Maintaining this tradition, the poets of the war years were consistent advocates of these two principles. Since poets who supported the war as well as those who opposed it use the same terms, some distinction must be made between them according to the context in which the terms are used. Certainly the use of "liberty" in the lines:

Yet, happy Britain!—with proportion'd
weights
Guard the just balance of thy three Estates;
For, in that balance only, canst thou find
Order and rule, with Liberty combin'd.
Cautions to England

differs greatly from the concept expressed by the author of Ode, Written on the opening of the Last Campaign:

... if on this hour
The fate of Freedom shall depend—
If o'er this earth th' Eternal Pow'r
The scale of Justice now extend.
For then, O Spring, thy sun shall see
The patriot flame triumphant shine;
GALLIA shall bid the world be free,
And WAR his blood-stain'd throne resign!

And, again, from the ironic use of the term in the satiric *The Soldier's Friend* of 1797:

Liberty's friends thus all learn to amalgamate,
Freedom's volcanic explosion prepares itself,
Despots shall bow to the Fasces of Liberty...

And all three differ from that employed by the author of the 1797 *Mutiny at Portsmouth*:

The Genius of Britain went hovering round,
For she fear'd that fair Freedom had fled,
But she found, to her joy that she was

not quite gone,
But remain'd with the Fleet at Spithead.

Although "liberty" and "justice" (and synonymous expressions) are common to much of the war poetry, the principles underlying the terms vary according to the poet's position on the war and on the policies of the government. The author of *Cautions to England* is concerned with maintaining the status quo and is most likely a Tory. The author of the *Ode* is probably a Jacobin. The satire above is opposed to sympathy with France and to democratic notions of any kind. But what of the *Mutiny at Portsmouth*? An author who finds "Freedom" dwelling with the mutinous sailors at Spithead (April 15, 1797) may be considered radical, but in the case of the sailor's widow who is alleged to have written the poem, she may be without political ties altogether. Instead, she may well be continuing in a British tradition of rebellion as a means of obtaining justice.

To the British citizen of the 1790's, the liberty to rebel had historic roots; there had been rebellions in 1753, 1768, and 1780. The right of rebellion against government action of which the citizenry disapproved or "the right of resistance" as it was termed by the lawyers was "an integral part of the national tradition." This national tradition included other freedoms as well. The Revolution of 1688 had confirmed the Saxon laws and the British counted in their heritage freedom from foreign domination, freedom allowed by a constitutional monarchy, "freedom from arbitrary arrest, trial by jury, equality before the law, the freedom of the home from arbitrary entrance and search," and, within limitations, freedom to think, believe, and speak as one liked. The English also believed in the freedom to oppose parliamentary decisions (either by demonstration or by petition), and to participate in elections, even when unenfranchised, through the liberty of "huzzaing at elections."

However, by the end of the eighteenth century, more and more Britons, especially from the middle and working classes, were no longer satisfied with participation in elections by parading and huzzaing. The French Revolution was seen by many Britons as a dramatic representation of citizens of a foreign state attempting to gain liberties which the English already held. In Britain, a wave of democratic agitation broke out, partly in sympathy with the Revolution in France and partly to remind the government at home that long called for electoral reform was due. Although there were those in Britain who were critical of some aspects of their own government, the majority of Britons in 1789 felt as did a writer in *The Edinburgh Review* some eighteen years later, "All civilized Governments may be divided into free and arbitrary: or, more accurately... into the Government of England and the other European Governments."

It is not surprising, then, that at the outset of the French Revolution a wide spectrum of British poets sympathized with its objectives and could write about them comfortably, believing that the British and the French sought the same goals. Advocates of republican doctrine as well as those who believed in limited monarchy (the Whig "commonwealthman") flocked to Paris both before the 1793 declaration of war between Britain and France and during the peace period created by the Treaty of Amiens in 1802-1803. When Wordsworth and his friend Robert Jones went to the continent in 1790, they were welcomed by the French as representatives of liberty. Helen Maria Williams also traveled to Paris in 1790, to remain in France for the rest of her life, retaining her beliefs in the ultimate success of the ideas of the Revolution. Her *Ode to Peace* testifies to her faith in ultimate liberty resultant from the Revolution. This faith remained unbroken despite the fact that she was twice arrested by the French: in 1793 she incurred the disfavour of the Republican regime; in 1802 Napoleon had her arrested in irritation at her not having mentioned him by name in her well-circulated *Ode*.

The initial reaction of many British poets to the Revolution was that it was a means of bringing liberty to France, and the 1789-1792 period is marked by a number of verses written about the destruction of the Bastille as symbolic of new liberty. This initial reaction was not confined to poets alone; Charles James Fox, leader of the Whig opposition, wanted Britain to accept and recognize democratic France.However, the bloodshed involved in establishing the new republic, and the various French internal battles which led to further bloodshed, complicated the issue of French liberty for the British. Some poets, such as Anna Seward in her 1789 *Sonnet to France on Her Present Exertions*, immediately defended the destructive elements of the Revolution as a necessary but temporary condition in the process of the establishment of a new political state:

Thou, that where Freedom's sacred fountains play,
Which spring effulgent, tho' with crimson stains,
On transatlantic shores, and widening plains
Hast, in their living waters, washed away
Those cankering spots, shed by tyrannic sway
On thy long drooping lilies, English veins
Swell with the tide of exultation gay,
To see thee spurn thy deeply-galling chains.

Wordsworth, in the 1850 *Prelude*, gives a more temperate justification of the Revolutionary bloodletting: ...

When a taunt
Was taken up by scoffers in their pride,
Saying, "Behold the harvest that we reap
From popular government and equality,"

I clearly saw that neither these nor aught
Of wild belief engrafted on their names
By false philosophy had caused the woe,
But a terrific reservoir of guilt
And ignorance filled up from age to age,
That could no longer hold its loathsome
Charge,
But burst and spread in deluge through the
land.
(X, 11. 470-480)

Despite attempts to explain and justify the events which followed the Revolution, as the internal tumult in France continued many of those who supported British liberty and who were basically anti-aristocratic came to believe that the result of the Revolution was to substitute one form of tyranny for another. The dilemma presented by France's complete renunciation of monarch and church and the execution of the King and Queen was brought to a head by the British declaration of war with France in 1793. For many British, there was no alternative but to support their own country against what was viewed as the threatened loss of British liberty. Spurred by fear, many Britons came to agree with the sentiments expressed in Dr. Mavor's 1793 *Sonnet to Rational Liberty*:

No tyrant's frown, no traitor's harlot
smile,
My free born soul shall awe, my sense
shall ne'er beguile.
Rais'd on the throne of LAW and RIGHT,
O ever shield thy favourite land!
While Anarchy, with wild affright,
Flies to GALLIA'S frantic strand.
O check these scenes of dire uproar—
Revenge thy prostituted name!
And far, O far, from BRITAIN'S shore
Drive the foul deeds that clothe
thy charms with shame.

Others, in sympathy with the reaction depicted by Thomas Day in *The Disgusted Patriot*, decided to retire to "solitude indignant" and "leave the world to courtiers, priests, and kings."

The war brought a marked increase in the number of poems concerned with both British and French liberty. The mocking satire of *The Humble Petition of the British Jacobins to their Brethren of France*, which hits at the French who "Mirth and murder so merrily blend" and then goes on to attack the British who support the ideals of the Revolution and invite then to spread to Britain, is a prime example of the hostile attitude which became increasingly prevalent as the war continued.

From 1793 it was left to an ever decreasing minority to support the original tenets of the Revolution. Among these was Wordsworth, who was shocked by the war and the fact that he supported not his own country but its enemy. Even in the 1850 *Prelude* Wordsworth portrays the complex emotion he felt when:

... with open
war
Britain opposed the liberties of France.
This threw me first out of the pale of love;
Soured and corrupted, upwards to the
source,
My sentiments; was not, as hitherto,
A swallowing up of lesser things in great,
But change of them into their contraries;
And thus a way was opened for mistakes
And false conclusions, in degree as gross,
In kind more dangerous. What had been a
pride,
Was now a shame; my likings and my loves
Ran in new channels, leaving old ones dry;
And hence a blow that, in maturer age,
Would have but touched the judgement struck
more deep
Into sensations near the heart: meantime,
As from the first, wild theories were
afloat,
To whose pretensions, sedulously urged,
I had but lent a careless ear, assured
That time was ready to set all things
right,
And that the multitude, so long oppressed,
Would be oppressed no more.
(XI, 11. 174-194)

Not until Napoleon assumed the title of Emperor did Wordsworth finally give up his hopes in the ideals of the Revolution. When the Pope was summoned to crown Napoleon, Wordsworth considered it:

This last opprobrium, when we see a
people,
That once looked up in faith, as if to
Heaven
For manna, take a lesson from the dog

Returning to his vomit....
(XI, 11. 361-364)

Coleridge, faced with the same problem of divided allegiance, was less a friend to France than an enemy of his own country's Tory government. Indeed, he accused Pitt, in the pages of *The Watchman*, as Pitt had accused Lord North, of being "at war with a nation of patriots." Furthermore, in his *Religious Musings* (1796) Coleridge indicates that the "Giant Frenzy" of the early days of the French Revolution was a part of divine apocalyptic justice and, as such, was a reaction to "The Great, the Rich, the Mighty Men,/The Kings and Chief Captains of the World." However, as the events in France progressed and when the French took repressive measures against the right of assembly and the printing of political news, Coleridge grew out of sympathy with the French. Napoleon's entry into Switzerland and the pillaging of Italy by the French troops proved the turning point for Coleridge. After 1798 he supported the war against Napoleon.

Much of the poetry written in 1793-1796 against the war with France generally regarded the war as one in which the monarch and the Pitt government of Britain conspired with Austria and Prussia to preserve their own thrones. The resentment on the part of many Britons was two-fold. It was felt that Britain, a constitutional monarchy, should not support a war fought by totalitarian monarchs to reinstate a totalitarian government in France, and also there was sympathy for the Revolution's ideal of liberty.

The twenty-six years from the fall of the Bastille to Waterloo was a period of almost unremitting war. The ideals of the French Revolution were practically forgotten in the course of the Napoleonic Wars. The first generation of romantic poets experienced the fervour of witnessing the establishment of a republican state in Europe, and then suffered the disappointment and disillusionment caused by the turn in France's objectives. The next generation of poets, including Byron and Shelley, had the advantage of historical perspective. Untouched by the genuine threats of invasion (Napoleon kept troops stationed across the Channel until 1805), they were able to regard the ideals of the Revolution with unqualified admiration. They recognized that the Revolution had to struggle for survival from the very beginning against the monarchs of Europe, a view expressed in Shelley's *A Translation of The Marsellois Hymn*:

Tremble, Kings! despised of Man!
Ye traitors to your country—
Tremble! your parricidal plan
At length shall meet its destiny.

....

Frenchmen! on the guilty brave
Pour your vengeful energy.—
Yet in your triumph, pitying save

The unwilling slaves of tyranny;
But let the gore-stained despots bleed.

Shelley was opposed to aristocracy in general and to Napoleon in particular. In *To The Emperors of Russia and Austria who eyed the battle of Austerlitz from the heights whilst Buonaparte was active in the thickest of the fight*, Shelley addresses the Emperors as "Coward Chiefs" and bids them "Think ye on the restless fiend who haunts/ The tumult of yon gory field" concluding:

Yet may your terrors rest secure.
Thou, Northern chief, why starest thou?
Pale Austria, calm those fears. Be sure
The tyrant needs such slaves as you.
Think ye the world would bear his sway
Were dastards such as you away?
No! they would pluck his plumage gay
Torn from a nation's woe
And lay him in the obvious gloom
Where Freedom now prepares your tomb.

Byron, on the other hand, makes it quite clear in his *Ode to Napoleon Buonaparte* that he admired the heroic qualities in Napoleon, but was disappointed that he "forsooth must be a king":

Thine evil deeds are writ in gore,
Nor written thus in vain—
Thy triumphs tell of fame no more,
Or deepen every stain:
If thou hadst died as honour dies,
Some new Napoleon might arise,
To shame the world again—
But who would soar the solar height,
To set in such a starless night?
(91-99)

To both Shelley and Byron the war represented the efforts of a group of tyrants leagued to defeat one tyrant. The poets' radical stand on the war was based on their accurate assessment that Napoleon's defeat would reinstate a Bourbon regime in France and would, on a Continental scale, retard the establishment of government on the basis of liberty and justice.

Byron, Shelley, and other young radicals concerned themselves with international as well as national reform. The majority of Britons, however, had endured the privations of many years of war and were far more concerned with conditions at home. The French were seen by the majority of British citizens as the enemy to be defeated and, perhaps, punished. At the root of this enmity one finds not the bloody aftermath of the Revolution and the subsequent tyranny of Napoleon, but the threat of invasion by the French, potential intrusion on the English freedom. From the declaration of war on France, the British, through the careful propaganda of the Pitt government, were led to expect invasion by the enemy. This propaganda campaign was undoubtedly waged by the Pitt government to lessen the democratic agitation in Britain by uniting Britons against an enemy threat. A "Letter from DAVID DUNGEON to His COUSIN BILLY PIT" in *The Cambridge Intelligencer* of September 7, 1793 presents this viewpoint satirically:

Allow me therefore, dear Cousin, to trespass on your well-known modesty, by congratulating you on the success of that scheme by which you fascinated two-thirds of the inhabitants of Britain, and turned the thoughts of the *Swinish Multitude*, from grunting threats of Reform and complaints against taxes and oppression, to squeaking vengeance on the French for injuries which they never meant, and for plots into which they never entered.

The threatened invasion of Britain by the French served as a stimulus to British nationalism at the outbreak of the war, but the threat came to be a very real one. While France was still under the Republic a small band of Frenchmen landed in Ireland. And in July 1796, plans for the invasion of Ireland were drawn up by the French, with the expectation of aid from the rebellious Irish under Wolfe Tone. At the close of the year, a fleet under the command of the French General Hoche actually embarked for Ireland, but turned back due to inclement weather. In 1797, a small band of Frenchmen reached Wales, only to be quickly captured. Not until February, 1798, when Napoleon turned his "Army of England" from Brest towards Egypt, did the British nave any relief from their fear of invasion. However, this proved to be a respite before the last and most alarming threat of all when the Treaty of Amiens failed in 1803.

Scores of verses appeared with each new sign of invasion and were widely circulated. The repetitive theme of these often satiric verses is the combined threat to King, to God, and to Womanhood. *A Word to the Wise* is an early example of this popular type of warning verse. Not satisfied with picturing the plight of British women should the French succeed, the author sets up a comparison between French and British women. The former are referred to as "fish wives" and of questionable moral fibre:

But our ladies are virtuous, our ladies
are fair,
Which is more than they tell us your French-
women are.

In no year during the war were more of these warning verses produced than in 1803 when it was believed invasion was imminent. Wordsworth's response to the threat was *Anticipation* in which he foresaw a "mighty Victory," where "On British ground the Invaders are laid low." *Anticipation* was one of hundreds of poems written on the subject, and it was common for journals such as *The Gentleman's Magazine* to fill poetry columns almost exclusively with war verses throughout 1803. French troops remained on the coast until August 1805, but by 1804 the general alarm had considerably lessened.

With the immediacy of invasion gone, there yet remained the possibility of French victory on the Continent, and renewed threat of the domination of Europe by the French. This possibility was just as much a threat to British liberty as the immediate prospect of invasion and poets continued to use the threat to King, God, and Womanhood to keep alive the defence of British liberty until the end of the war.

Many of those who objected to the war labeled it a "Church and King" enterprise because the clergy of the Church of England, as part of the establishment, failed to take action by speaking out against the war. As Roland Bartel has pointed out in "English Clergymen and Laymen on the Principle of War, 1789-1802":

Judging by publications announced in contemporary journals, the church remained incredibly silent, for the records fail to show a single pulpit declaration against the war during the first four years of the French Revolution when optimism about world peace was at a peak in England. It is true that after England entered the war a few clergymen denounced the evils of war but then it was too late.

True, *The Bishop of London's Opinion on War*, published in 1793, laments the fact that "Monarchs dream of universal empire, growing up from universal ruin" but these lines were not written in response to the war. They were extracted from a lengthy prizewinning poem, *Death*, written when the bishop, Dr. Porteus, had been a student at Cambridge in 1759. Porteus, far from opposing the war, was a staunch anti-Jacobin and preached against the *Rights of Man*. In general, the Church of England played an active role in supporting the government's policies on war, and clergymen often wrote call-to-arms verses, such as the *War Song* by the Reverend Richard Mant of Oxford. Disappointment in the church's position was voiced both in satire, such as *Impromptu on the Late Fast* and in earnest prayer-like poems such as*Hymn* sung at a meeting of "Friends of Peace and Reform." Most often, those who opposed the war belonged to dissenting religious groups and suffered from limited liberty due to their religious belief. The group which met at Sheffield to observe the official Fast Day during March, 1794 was a group composed of the working class and dissenters. Between five and six thousand persons held an open-air meeting, during which they heard a lecture written by a "labouring mechanic," preceded by a prayer and concluded with the above mentioned *Hymn* in which they called upon God to:

Make bare thine Arm, great King of Kings!
That Arm alone Salvation brings,
That Wonder-working Arm which broke,

From Israel's Neck th' Egyptian Yoke.
Burst every Dungeon, every Chain;
Give injur'd Slaves their Rights again;
Let TRUTH prevail, let Discord cease;
Speak—and the World shall smile in PEACE!

Another important "liberty" which developed during the war years was "Free Trade." Indeed, it was during the Napoleonic Wars that the British commercial interests were converted to the cause of Free Trade. After the destruction of the French fleet at Trafalgar, Napoleon sought to destroy Britain commercially by organizing an economic blockade of the British Isles. In 1806, the Decrees of Berlin prohibited all commerce with Britain and ordered the arrest of British subjects found on French territory as well as the seizure of British vessels and cargoes in Continental waters. More severe decrees followed in a concentrated attempt to bring the British into submission by destroying them financially. The British reaction to the economic boycott was to seek markets elsewhere; to import from the Far East and from the markets in North and South America. The British also responded to Napoleon's blockade by a tariff policy which attempted to prohibit all neutral countries from trade with France unless their ships put in at an English port and paid a high duty to the English Exchequer; the high duty rate applied to English goods as well. British manufacturers were immediately against this policy, and the government bowed before them and opened to Free Trade a number of German and Italian ports. The restrictions put upon neutrals dealing with France, however, was the chief cause of the War of 1812 between Britain and the United States.

A growing number of poems during this period deal with commerce, linking the protection of trade and commerce to the protection of God and Country. This is strikingly represented in an ode written in 1812 by a clergyman, the Reverend John Black, addressed *To the Sons of Britain and America*. In bidding an end to the war between Britain and America, the clergyman argues first in terms of the numbers who will die in the fighting. If this argument does not prevail, he warns:

Reflect, how Commerce must decline,
The loom stand still, and Want assail
The many that must starving pine;
And burdens weigh each nation down,
And wild Despair with fury frown.

It is only in the last stanza that the clergyman-poet mentions religion.

There were those for whom the preoccupation with commerce in Great Britain at this time seemed somewhat of an embarrassment. The author of an article in *The Monthly Mirror* protested:

The present ruler of France has called Great Britain a *nation of shopkeepers*; but if it had been his fortune, instead of gathering together unwilling conscripts, to have superintended the voluntary contributions to the MONTHLY MIRROR, we think he would have denominated us a*nation of poets.*

Not all protests were so mild and good-humored. John Thelwall felt that Commerce was a "monopolizing fiend" which bred inhumane monsters at home and sent abroad the voice of war "to bellow hideous discord through the World." Blake, too, considered the trade expansion, which was heightened by the Napoleonic Wars, "Fiends of Commerce," which led to war and destruction.Scattered throughout the period are poems which accuse those in power—the Tories—of continuing the war for their own profit. *A New Song to an Old Tune* pictures Pitt and his circle as conspiring to beat Napoleon in order to raise prices on the stockmarket; the author of an 1813 poem hits at industries supported by the war and war profiteering in his title *War the Source of Riches*.

However, the majority of war poems on this theme view commerce as the very heart of British greatness. The well-known jibe of Napoleon, noted by the author of the article in *The Monthly Mirror* quoted above, "L'Angleterre est une nation de boutiquiers" had a resounding response in the verse of the day. The verse writers ignored the contempt in Napoleon's statement and, like the author of *To Buonaparte*, refused to "a charge contradict so extremely correct." Furthermore, many poems, such as*The Want*, accused Napoleon and the French of using warfare as a means of developing their own commerce and industry.

Although Napoleon threatened English commerce by his system of embargoes on British goods, he found it necessary to violate his own system. His troops required clothing and boots and in order to supply these wants, Napoleon imported British cloth and leather by way of Hamburg "in perfect safety and at half-price."

The accelerated growth of industry and the development of commerce was a potentially divisive issue between industrialists and the working-class. A strong effort was made to convince British workers that the Revolution had reduced the amount of liberty held by the French under the monarchy and as the war continued, more and more poetry called upon all classes to join forces in order to defeat their common foe. For example, the 1804 *A New Song on the Renewed Threat of Invasion* calls upon farmers, artisans, tailors, blacksmiths as well as merchants and bankers—"For, Trade is our Sheet-anchor"—to unite; taking no chances, it also lists "Quaker, Churchman, Presbyterian."

The universality of this and other call to arms verses represents not so much a political swing towards democracy as a literal call-to-arms to the workingman. In the early years of the war, British troops were commonly gathered through impressment or through a variety of deceitful and devious practices called "crimping." These methods raised a great outcry, and poets wrote of hardships endured both by those kidnapped or otherwise forced into service and by the families of those men. *The Tender's Hold Or, Sailor's*

Complaint was a popular poem on the subject. Wordsworth's *Guilt and Sorrow* (1793-1794) tells the privations of:

A Sailor he, who many a wretched hour
Hath told; for, landing after labour hard,
Full long endured in hope of just reward,
He to an arméd fleet was forced away
By seamen, who perhaps themselves had shared
Like fate; was hurried off, a helpless prey,
'Gainst all that in his heart, or theirs perhaps, say nay.

Shelley's *The Voyage* (1812) concludes with the sailor's return home, only to be impressed again and told:

... "oh! your wife
"Died this time year in the House of Industry
"Your young ones all are dead, except one brat
"Stubborn as you—Parish apprentice now"

In 1793, seventy-five per cent of the crews on British vessels consisted of prisoners of war, convicts, etc. forced into service. In 1794, "crimping houses" in Holborn, the City, Clerkenwell, and Shoreditch were wrecked by rioters. As a result of the public condemnation of government recruiting practices, the government found itself caught between the strong position of those who opposed the prevalent unjust methods of conscription and the ever escalating need for men in the British armed forces, particularly the Navy. The solution resolved upon in 1799 and maintained until 1815 was to offer militiamen bounty money to join the regular British forces. This was considered the most feasible approach since compulsory military service was regarded as out of the question at this time.

Throughout the war period, journals and newspapers published verses in praise of the fighting forces, and considerable anger was aroused when military decisions led to the needless destruction of British troops, as at Walcheren in August 1810. Forty-thousand men sent to the Continent had succeeded in capturing Flushing. Instead of continuing their march towards Antwerp, they remained immobile and plagued by epidemic diseases unrelieved due to lack of provisions, the men perished by the thousands. When, at the end of September, they set sail, they had lost 106 men in battle and 4,000 from disease. The incompetence of the military inspired highly critical poetry, particularly in the Whig press, none more bitter than Leigh Hunt's *Walcheren Expedition; Or, the Englishman's Lament for the Loss of His Countrymen* and Thomas Clio Rickman's *Extempore on the Invasion of Walcheren*. The government was so embarrassed by this expedition that they ordered home Peter Finnerty, the Irish radical journalist, to whom they had granted permission to report on the expedition for *The Morning Chronicle*.

British poetry of the war years demanded liberty and justice not only for themselves but for British allies and neutral nations as well. When the British fleet attacked neutral Denmark in September 1807, many poems appeared deprecating a war policy which led to the deaths of more than two thousand Danish citizens. *The Morning Chronicle* published *Ode On the Big-Endiuns* in 1807, *Song on the New Affair of Copenhagen*, and *A Danish Tale* in 1808, the last a parody of Southey's *The Battle of Blenheim*. Burton R. Pollin notes that Southey in private correspondence considered the act an atrocity, whereas Coleridge defended the attack in *The Friend*. Another poet to respond in the negative was the youthful Shelley, whose *Fragment of a Poem the original idea of which was suggested by the cowardly and infamous bombardment of Copenhagen* leaves no doubt of the author's anguish and his contempt for British war policy.

Even greater was the outcry against the "Convention of Cintra" of August 1808. In March 1808 Spain was invaded by the French under the guise of protecting the coast from the British. The Spanish monarchs, first Charles IV and then his son Ferdinand, abdicated, and Napoleon placed his brother Joseph on the throne. This resulted in a general uprising against the French on the part of the Spanish people, and Britain entered the fray on the side of Spain. The British, commanded by Sir Arthur Wellesley (who had also participated in the attack on Copenhagen), defeated the French at Vimeiro, Portugal. Instead of continuing the war to a complete rout, Wellesley's superior, Sir Hew Dalrymple, agreed to permit the defeated French General Jurot and his troops not only to leave unmolested, but also to carry with them booty as well as supplies. This led to cries of outrage in England, with the strongest protest appearing in the Whig press. *The Morning Chronicle* published scores of poems on the events in Portugal many of which, like *Catch*, are angry satires which hold Wellesley and Dalrymple as well as the entire ministry responsible. *Catch* is written in the form of a song with each verse attributed to the People, Sir Arthur, Sir Hew, and the Ministers. The People conclude:

We heed you not a feather;
You're drivellers altogether!
And we'll hang you altogether up; yes, you,
Sirs, and you!

There are also poetic expressions of sorrow and disappointment at the events surrounding Cintra, such as the simply-worded, ballad-like *An Imitation*:

There, sharing one destiny
Under a nameless stone,
Let the Knights Cintra, three,

Mingle their dust alone.
Shame and dishonour sit,
By their graves ever,
Blessings shall hollow it—
Never—Oh! never!

The Courier, although a strong Tory supporter in 1808, also criticized the Convention, much to the surprise of the ministry.

Byron expressed his view of the Convention of Cintra in *Childe Harold's Pilgrimage*, published in 1812:

And ever since that martial synod met,
Britannia sickens, Cintra! at thy name;
And folks in office at the mention fret,
And fain would blush, if blush they could,
for shame.
How will posterity the deed proclaim!
Will not our own and fellow-nations sneer,
To view these champions cheated of their
fame,
By foes in flight o'erthrown, yet victors
here,
Where Scorn her finger points through many
a coming year?
(Canto I, xxxvi)

But perhaps the most famous protest, although not well known to readers in its day, is Wordsworth's pamphlet *Concerning the Convention of Cintra.* Wordsworth and Coleridge were by then firm supporters of the war against France. The pamphlet, which Coleridge helped write and which Thomas De Quincey saw through the press, regarded the treatment accorded the French troops as unnecessarily kind and detrimental to Spanish and Portuguese nationalism. It suggested that the national feeling of these peoples had to be aroused in order to defeat Napoleon. Thus, Wordsworth and Coleridge who, at the beginning of their careers, had been considered radicals for their pro-revolutionary, anti-war position had become advocates and advisors on methods of waging war.

During the war years the question, in the British press, of any single nation's love of liberty seems almost always to have been decided by that nation's fighting allegiance at the moment, for the period was marked by shifting alliances and separate peace treaties. For example, in 1796-97, Britain sent the Earl of Malmesbury to Lillie to negotiate since its allies Prussia and Austria had already signed treaties with France. Hostilities between Britain and France were initially somewhat diminished, and poems appeared hailing an impending peace. The failure of the negotiations, however, engendered not only an ever-increasing militancy against France; it also evoked hostility towards Austria and Prussia which was voiced in poetry until 1798, at which time an alliance was concluded between Russia and Great Britain to which Austria, Naples, Portugal, and the Ottoman Eire were parties.

To understand the various attitudes of British poetry towards Spain, it is necessary to trace Spain's shifting alliances during the war years.

At war with France from 1793, Spain was defeated and signed a peace treaty in April 1795; in August 1796 Spain became an ally of France. Until the 1808 uprising of the Spanish against the French and the ensuing Peninsular War in which Britain and Spain were allied, Spain was depicted in British poetry as a land governed by a tyrannic monarch and a repressive, corrupt church. After 1808, however, Spain is treated in numerous poems as a nation which defends liberty. This attitude seems to continue throughout the remaining war years, although the end of the war in Spain brought back the Bourbon regime and the Inquisition.

Towards the end of war, a number of poems deal with the continuation of the slave trade in Spain and Portugal, suggesting that nations which seek their own freedom should support freedom for others.

The British ideal of justice occasionally found voice even in the manner of treatment of Napoleon and the French after their defeat. In contrast to the many poems of celebration, there were some like the*Epistle from Tom Cribb to Big Ben* which dealt with the problem of a conqueror's peace and the effect it would have not only on France but on all Europe. However, towards the end of the war it was the unusual poem which expressed dismay at the thought of reinstating the Bourbons in France. Napoleon had become synonymous with tyranny to the British, and he is the principal object of attack in poem after poem. If mercy towards the French is suggested, it is usually after the poet carefully differentiates between the people of France and their leader. When Byron's dramatic monologue*Napoleon's Farewell* was published in *The Examiner*, the editors took the precaution of appending the following explanatory note:

We scarcely need remind our readers, that there are points in the following spirited Lines, with which our opinions do not accord; and indeed the Author himself has told us, that he rather adapted them to what may be considered as the speaker's feelings, than his own.

The poem is unusually sympathetic to Napoleon, "The last single Captive to millions in war":

Farewell to thee, France! when thy diadem
crowned me,
I made thee the gem and the wonder of earth,—
But thy weakness decrees I should leave as I
found thee,

Decay'd in thy glory, and sunk in thy worth.
Oh! for the veteran hearts that were wasted
In strife with the storm, when their battles
were won—
Then the Eagle, whose gaze in that moment
was blasted,
Had still soar'd with eyes fix'd on victory's
sun!

The explanatory note is consistent with *The Examiner*'s view of the war and Napoleon. Although the paper, begun in 1808, was considered liberal in the sense that it was an outspoken medium for criticism of maladministration in Britain, it was firmly committed from its inception to the defeat of Napoleon.

The final defeat of Napoleon at Waterloo made the continental monarchs more powerful than before the Revolution. The *Ancien Regime* under Louis XVIII was restored in France, a Bourbon was again on the Spanish throne, and Napoleon was to spend his days in closely guarded exile on the island of Saint Helena. While British poets jubilantly celebrated the victory and the end of the war, there is also an air of exhaustion in the poetry. Certainly one reason for this was the disappointment and dismay at the failure of the first Treaty of Paris of May 1814. "The Hundred Days" in which Napoleon again waged war forced Britain to reassemble her armies; the long-awaited peace had lasted only until March 1815 and Britain was again at war. After Waterloo, the exile imposed on Napoleon seemed to secure the peace. Wordsworth's 1815 *Ode* suggests that the victory at Waterloo was not sustained because praise was given to men for that victory and not to God:

To THEE—To THEE,
Just God of christianised Humanity,
Shall praises be poured forth, and thanks
ascend,
That Thou has brought our warfare to an end,
And that we need no second victory!

However joyful the British were, there was still the recognition on the part of this nation which cherished its ideals of liberty and justice that these ideals were, at least at that time, restricted to their own nation. Among the Whigs and the radicals there was an uneasiness because Britain had joined Prussia, Austria, and Russia in the Quadruple Alliance to prevent further violations of the Treaty of Paris.

Britons had looked forward to the end of the war for alleviation of economic hardships—the high cost of food and the high income tax particularly. Instead, an economic depression followed. Thousands were out of work, and there was agitation in proportions unknown in Britain before. If the ideals of British liberty and justice—the ideals also of the French Revolution—seemed to have lost hold on the Continent, in Britain they found new support. The end of the war signified the beginning of an unflagging struggle by the working and middle classes for liberty and justice, a struggle which was to continue throughout the nineteenth century.

WAR POETRY AND ROMANTICISM

The *Lyrical Ballads*, published anonymously by Wordsworth and Coleridge in 1798, have long been considered the demarcation line which divides the "romantic age" from the "age of sensibility" as well as from the earlier "Augustan age." In recent years, attempts have been made to reconsider the position and influence of the *Lyrical Ballads* arising from a natural uneasiness about assigning the beginning of any literary movement to a pinpoint in time. Critics, such as Mary Moorman in her biography of Wordsworth and Emile Legouis in "Some Remarks on the Composition of the *Lyrical Ballads* of 1798," have noted but not underscored the fact that the ballad was a popular poetic mode of the day prior to the composition of the *Lyrical Ballads*. The significant study by Robert Mayo on the question of the originality of the *Lyrical Ballads*, which contains a variety of forms including ballad, ode, and blank verse, buttresses its argument that they were neither revolutionary in form nor in content by citing lists of similar poems selected from several periodicals of the 1790's. Mayo's study is confined to the ten year period before the *Lyrical Ballads*, and does not consider the multitude of ballad-like verse written after 1798. Nor does he treat the content of the ballads that appeared in periodicals beyond their similarity to the *Lyrical Ballads.*

A study of British periodicals from 1789 through 1815 makes it readily apparent that the French Revolution and the Napoleonic Wars were a major topic and inspiration for poetry not only for the nine years preceding the *Lyrical Ballads* but for the sixteen war years that followed. The question which arises from this nexus of poetry and war centers on the role of the war poetry in the development of romanticism.

Due to the duration of hostilities, Wordsworth, Coleridge, and their contemporaries had the experience of contributing to a movement which in turn circled back and influenced them. It is not simply that the*Ballads* had been anticipated by earlier newspaper and periodical verse, but that the *Ballads* themselves are part of a larger movement which developed out of the social and political conditions of the period.

To begin with, it is essential to understand what was meant by the term "ballad" during the 1790's. Charles Ryskamp points out that the word carried a far broader definition than is generally realized; that, in fact, "ballad" was then synonymous with "song":

Under "Ballad" in the *Encyclopaedia Brittanica* of 1797 we read only of "a kind of song, adapted to the capacity of the lower class of people; who, being mightily taken with this species of poetry, are thereby not a little influenced in the conduct of their lives. Hence we find, that seditious and designing men never fail to spread ballads among the people, with a view to gain then over to their side."

To this definition add the words of Wordsworth and Coleridge in their Advertisement published with the 1798 edition of the *Ballads*:

The majority of the following poems are to be considered as experiments. They were written with a view to ascertain how far the language of conversation in the middle and lower classes of society is adapted to the purposes of poetic pleasure.

Note that the experiment consists not in "if" middle and lower class conversational language is suited to poetic expression but, rather, "how far" it is suited. The reason for this is evident to anyone who reads the journals and periodicals of the 1790's. Experimentation with every-day language was commonplace; variations on the ballad, blank-verse, and the ode were commonplace. Because of the impact of the Revolution and the subsequent wars, it is not surprising to find that war is central to the many variations in form and language. Indeed, the incorporation of everyday speech patterns stems at least in part from the plethora of nationalistic war ballads and odes that were addressed to the middle and working classes. Furthermore, the favoured subjects of the period—the beggar, the orphan, the widow, the sailor and soldier and veteran, the country cottage—were largely derived from the war experience.

The French Revolution and the romantic era are alike not in their suddenness but in their elemental democracy. Signs of discontent in France were recognized for years before the overthrow of the Bastille and, as the war poetry in this edition indicates, signs of romanticism were quite apparent during the decade preceding the *Lyrical Ballads*. Romantic literature was essentially an evolutionary not a revolutionary process. Its roots are found in the rejection of the heroic couplet of Pope and Johnson by poets of the second half of the eighteenth century. A cursory look at the period recalls Macpherson's*Poems of Ossian* (1762-63), Hurd's *Letters of Chivalry and Romance* (1765), Chatterton's Rowley poems (1777), Cowper's *Olney Hymns* and *The Diverting History of John Gilpin* (1782), Gray's *Elegy Written in a Country Churchyard* (1750) the hymns of Charles and John Wesley which began to appear in 1739 and, perhaps most significantly, Percy's *Reliques* (1765) and the works of Robert Burns. These and other contemporaries rejected the emphasis on clarity, mimesis, objectivity, balance, and the aristocratic in favour of ambiguity, subjectivity, the exotic, the simple, and the sentimental. The seemingly antithetical turn to both the exotic and the simple is explicable when evaluated in terms of their equi-distance from neo-classical aristocratic standards and topics of poetry.

The period of English literature that spanned the latter half of the eighteenth century is generically referred to as "the age of sensibility" or "the age of sentiment." Used as such, the terms are synonymous; they refer to an age that relied on the senses as the means of perceiving all knowledge. This belief in the "quickness and acuteness of apprehension or feeling" was supported by the theory that people are innately good, and, if not led astray by "bad education, false religion, or faulty social institutions," their own senses would lead them to a state of perfect understanding. This perfect understanding would naturally develop sympathetic feelings towards the problems of fellow creatures, and the result is that the ideal human being would feel, weep, and be charitable.

Along with the utilitarian aspect of this extension of brotherhood (and wealth), which was based on Locke and was developed early in the century in the teachings of Collier and Shaftsbury, there developed the need to instruct the "new man," that is, the then-evolving bourgeoisie and trade-aristocracy, how to "properly feel." One outgrowth of the notion of "proper feelings" was sentimentalism in its modern, pejorative sense: "an overindulgence in emotion, especially the conscious effort to induce emotion in order to analyze or enjoy it." Thus, the term "sentimentality" applied to the eighteenth-century refers to a range of emotions, from realistic benevolence to romantic titillation. However, underlying the variable of sentimentalism is a fairly uniform philosophic rationale: the novelists and the poets of the period, including the most sensational, viewed their work as a means of pleasurable moral instruction.

The war poetry of the last decade of the century had much the same principles operative, but there is a noticeable change in authors and audience. What had begun as a response on the part of the wealthy and well-educated to instruct the middle class in sensibility filtered through to the lower class as well. We have already noted the growth of newspapers and periodicals directed towards the working class in the 1790's. So, too, writing poetry became less the exclusive sphere of the upper strata of society. Although there remained remnants of benevolence in the act, it was not uncommon for the well-educated to "discover" and encourage poets among the working class. James Hogg was referred to as "The Ettrick Shepherd;" Burns was regarded and celebrated as an unread rustic, a legend that still clings today despite the many scholarly works that disprove it.

This collection of war poetry includes selected verses by other members of the working â class, for example William Cunningham, whose poem *On the Peace*, appeared in *The Gentleman's Magazine* with a lengthy footnote giving credit to his mentors, the poet T. S. Stott (Hafiz) and the Bishop of Dromore, for encouraging his writing. The footnote reveals that Cunningham's change from loom operator to student in the Diocesan Grammar School was effectuated by the Bishop of Dromore. To the contemporary reader, this note of endorsement carried particular weight for the Bishop of Dromore was Thomas Percy, the one man perhaps most instrumental in introducing the ballad into eighteenth-century literature.

In 1765 Percy published his *Reliques of Ancient English Poetry*, a collection of ballads dating from before Chaucer to the period of Charles I, including verses by Scottish poets. Contained in the *Reliques* are a variety of poetic structures and subject matter. The xaxa four line ballad stanza structure of *Chevy Chase* and *The Battle of Otterbourne* is dominant in the collection, but also there are other stanza forms such as eight line stanzas which rhyme xaxaxbxb, as in *Hardyknute*; three line aaa structures, as in *Verses by King Charles I*; six line ababcc verse such as *My Mind to Me a Kingdom Is*; the abab quatrain doubled, that is abababab as in *Robin and Makyne* and the xaxa quatrain doubled, as in *Plain Truth and Blind Ignorance*, as well as any number of other variations in stanza length and rhyme scheme. These variations, and more, are later found in the war poetry. *To the Tyrants Infesting France* (abab); *The Tender's Hold* (ababcdcd); *[All Hail the Shouting Trumpet]* (xaxaxbxb); *Poor Tom* (xaxa) are a few examples of the many verses which duplicate the variations found in Percy's *Reliques*. The significance of the war poetry is not structural innovation, for there were few poets who were truly experimental at this time. Blake is the great exception; however, his poetry did not reach a contemporary audience, and even Blake was influenced by the ballad revival as his *Songs of Innocence and Songs of Experience* indicate.

Percy's *Reliques* was well-known to the educated eighteenth-century reader, but it was the poetry written in response to the war which was the chief means of popularizing the ballad and its variants. Never before in British literary history had one topic evoked so diverse and so extensive a response. Nor had poetry concerned with one subject ever before reached so wide an audience. Printed in newspapers, magazines, and broadsides, the war verse reached the middle and working classes, and was designed to engage their sentiments and emotions in a language which they could understand. Percy's theory in the*Reliques* that the Saxon bard, speaking to the people in simple poetic forms, was a powerful political and moral force is applicable to the war poets as well in the sense that the poets, in creating a popular poetry, saw themselves as addressing and educating the populace on a vital national question.

While many of the poems in the *Reliques* conform to a generalized description of the ballad as a condensed, objectified narrative containing repetition and elements of the mysterious or the super-natural, there are many works in the collection that do not adhere to this formula. Several of the ballads are personal and use the first-person voice: *An Elegy on Henry, Fourth Earl of Northumberland*; *The Tower of Doctrine*; *The Aged Lover Renounceth Love*; and *Jane Shore* all employ the first-person voice and are concerned more with emotional response to events than objective narration of events. Furthermore, the collection contains a number of explicit dialogues, ranging from *Plain Truthand Blind Ignorance*, fashioned after the traditional Medieval dialogue, to the dramatic *The Nut-Browne Mayd* or the Browningesque *A Ballad of Luther, the Pope, a Cardinal, and a Husbandman*.

Just as the war poetry often utilized rhyme schemes derived from Percy, so, too, it duplicated the traditional objectivity of the ballad, as in *The Soldier*, 1795; the dialogue, *Dialogue Betwixt Peace and War*, 1799; the first person narrative, *The Orphan Sailor-Boy*, 1803. While the forms exist in the *Reliques*and the war poetry alike, there is a notable difference in emphasis. The *Reliques* offer a majority of objective ballads; the war poetry consists far more of verse written from a personalized and frankly emotional point of view. For example, in *Hardyknute*, a poem that passed for some years as "ancient" although it may have been written in the early eighteenth century, the plight of the widow is considered in one stanza of a forty-two stanza ballad:

On Norways coast the widowit dame
May wash the rocks with tears,
May lang luik ow'r the shipless seas
Before her mate appears.
Cease, Emma, cease to hope in vain;
Thy lord lyes in the clay;
The valiant Scots nae revers thole
to carry life away.

During the 1793-1815 period, it is far more common for entire poems to treat the experience of the war widow. In *The Widow*, 1795:

Alternate Hope, alternate Fear,
In NANCY'S constant bosom reign:
In vain she dropp'd the pearly tear—
Hope sooth'd her constant heart in vain:
Her WILLIAM'S fate was told; she heard and sigh'd,
Cast up to Heav'n her eyes—then bow'd and died.

Anna's Complaint, 1795, combines the war widow's sorrow:

On Thanet's rock, beneath whose steep,
Impetuous rolls the foaming deep,
A lowly maid to grief consign'd,
Thus pour'd the sorrow of her mind:
And while her streaming eyes pursue
Of Gallia's cliffs the misty view,
Accurst she cries that guilty shore,
Whence William shall return no more.
Thou, cruel war, what has thou done!

Thro' thee the mother mourns her son,
The orphan joins the widow's cries,
And torn from love—the lover dies.

with anti war-propaganda:

Fair-sounding words my love deceiv'd,
The great ones talk'd, and he believ'd,
That war would fame and treasure bring,
That glory call'd to serve the king.

A more self-evident quality of the ballads included in Percy's collection (and sometimes overlooked because it is obvious) has to do with poetic diction. The ballad by its very nature employs condensed, concise, and simple diction. As a popular form of verse, the ballad is directed to an oral audience, and the diction of the ballad is close to that of common speech. However, the diction employed by the ballads collected by Percy is antiquarian, that is, the simple speech of an earlier age. The effect of this was to encourage poets in two directions: there were poems which sought to imitate archaic language, such as *Imitation of the Ancient Ballad*, 1807, and at the same time, an ever-increasing tendency towards simple speech patterns. Certainly the *Reliques* can be seen as a major influence in the period's turning away from the Latinate diction prescribed by Augustan theorists.

As the century continued, poets inclined more and more towards the dual standards of archaic and modern common speech. In 1786, a key poetic work appeared that seemed to draw at once on the ancient and the simple—Robert Burn's *Kilmarnock* poems. Beginning with Allan Ramsay (1686-1758) and Robert Fergusson (1750-1774), the use of the Scottish vernacular had been revived in Scotland. The publication of the *Reliques* encouraged David Herd, a Scots antiquarian, to publish his excellent collection of Scots ballads *The Ancient and Modern Scots Songs, Heroic Ballads, etc. Now First Collected in One Body* (1769). Burns, inspired by Fergusson's Scots poems, developed a poetic style that incorporated English grammar and syntax with Scottish and English vocabulary. The impact Burns had on the world of British letters in the last decade of the eighteenth-century was extraordinary and dramatic. His poetry was reprinted in English as well as Scottish periodicals. That he was known and admired by English newspaper readers is demonstrated by Peter Stuart's offer to Burns to become a regular contributor to *The Star*. Mary Moorman, in discussing Burns and Wordsworth, suggests: "It is almost impossible to overestimate the effect of Burns's poems on Wordsworth." Critics have also traced Burns's influence on Coleridge, Southey, Campbell, and Scott.

Wordsworth's own testimony to his regard for Burns is expressed in his poem *At the Grave of Burns, 1808*:

I mourned with thousands, but as one
More deeply grieved, for He was gone

Whose light I hailed when first it shone,
And showed my youth
How Verse may build a princely throne
On humble truth.

Leigh Hunt paid homage to Burns in his *Ode to the Memory of Robert Burns* which imitates Burns's use of English syntax with Scottish vocabulary:

But in the grave na wealthy scorn
Frowns on the Muse's blushing morn;
Nor fra' her tear-dew'd brow is torn
The wither'd wreath;
That cherish'd by no dews, forlorn,
Shrunk into death!
Yet shouldst thou scorn a hundred deaths,
On Scotia's wild red-blossom'd heaths,
For Burns they weave immortal wreaths;
Fra' ev'ry grove
His lay each ruby lip soft breaths,
That talks o' love!
Adieu, wi' a' thy wood-notes wild,
Thy rural pipe sae sweetly mild,
Thy song that mony a sigh beguil'd
In Sorrow's breast;
Adieu, Misfortune's tuneful child,
Thou'rt gane to rest!

Burns influenced the well-known poets of the period and the mass of newspaper and periodical verse writers. For example, on February 28, 1804 *The Hull Packet*, a provincial English newspaper, reported the proceedings of a meeting of Burns's admirers and printed an *Ode on the Anniversary of the Birthday of Burns*:

While Gaul's martial Demon, inflated with
pride,
Of Invasion sends threat after threat o'er the
tide,
And the Sons of the Britons with Banners
unfurl'd
By Patience heroic astonish the world:
In wielding our arms, and our glasses by
turns,
We will spend the convivial hours;
And fir'd by the bold independence of
BURNS,
Wake our social, our patriot powers:

And till the loud roar of the battle shall cease,
Round the chaplet of war wreath the garland
of peace.

The 1804 *Anti-Gallican* reprinted a *Parody* of Burns's *For a' that and a' that* along with Burns's 1795 *The Dumfries Volunteers*.

Burns's influence on his contemporaries was due to his ability to write poetry which all classes of society could read and appreciate and to his never-failing celebration of the spirit of the individual. He was an early supporter of the French Revolution until the French became aggressors. In 1792, in his capacity of exciseman, he had purchased a cannon confiscated from a smuggler and sent it to the French legislative body with an encouraging letter. Burns's reversal of attitude towards the French was consistent with his egalitarian ideals. While his 1795 poem to the *Dumfries Volunteers* demonstrates his support of the war against France, it is balanced by his well known democratic song, also written in 1795, *For a' that and a' that* (based on a Jacobite song of the same title) which sets up a comparison between wealthy men of rank and working men:

What though on hamely fare we dine,
Wear hoddin grey, and a' that.
Gie fools their silks, and knaves their
wine,
A Man's a Man for a' that.
For a' that, and a' that,
Their tinsel show, and a' that;
The honest man, though e'er saw poor,
Is king o' men for a' that.

Before the *Religues*, ballads were considered the products of minor and uneducated poets and had been consigned to special collections of antiquarians. The ballad existed as a verbal tradition, as it still does, and in broadside form, but until Percy, David Herd, and their followers, the ballad, in any of its variations, was not regarded as a serious art form. Burns treated the ballad as a serious art form. His was the outstanding example to his contemporaries and to the following generations of poets who used direct realistic diction and dealt with people and places of a real world. His poetry demonstrated a democratic political attitude in an age of political upheaval and reassessment, an age in which the "rights of man" came to be a vital issue.

The influence which brought Burns to his poetic as well as political position—and this is to set aside the fact of his great artistic accomplishment—were also operative on other poets of the age. The French Revolution served as a poetic and a political stimulus to a populace firmly entrenched in concepts of a constitutionally limited monarchy which guaranteed its subjects certain rights and liberties, and who were newly re-evaluating their government as it in fact existed. This re-evaluation did not necessarily lead to the conclusion that Britain required a new form of government or that Britain's position in the war was untenable. In fact, the majority of war verse published in newspapers and periodicals supported Britain's fight against France though, as has been noted, the reasons for this stem from government control as well as political attitude.

Most of the nationalistic war verse imitates one or another variation of ballad structure, for example,*Church and King*, 1793:

Go, democratic Demons, go!
In France your horrid banquet keep!
Feast on degraded Prelates' woe,
And drink the tears that Monarchs weep!
Chorus.—While Britons still united sing,
Old England's Glory,—Church and King.

The 1813 poem *Written the Night of the Illuminations For the Battle of Vittoria*:

"Hark! the loud peal, the thund'ring gun,
"Another glorious field is won,
"Another wreath crowns WELLINGTON,
"And Freedom's sacred cause.

The Soldier's Prayer in the Field of Battle, 1803:

God of my fathers! guide my way
Amidst the Battle's fierce alarms;
Grant me to see, this dreadful day,
The triumph of my Country's arms.

And John Mayne's well-circulated *English, Scots, and Irishmen*, 1803:

ENGLISH, SCOTS, and IRISHMEN,
All that are in VALOUR'S ken!
Shield your KING; and flock agen
Where his sacred Banners fly!
Now's the day, and now's the hour,
Frenchmen would the Land devour—
Will ye wait till they come o'er
To give ye Chains and Slavery?

No doubt the haste required in writing topical verse as well as the desire to reach a broad audience contributed to the popular use of the stanza plus refrain pattern. This type of war song, commonly hawked as broadsheets and popularized through newspapers and periodicals to an ever-increasing working and middle-class readership, furthered the idea, however unintentionally, of the place of unadorned speech in verse.

Since the war verses were written prior to, and after, the *Lyrical Ballads*, the experiment "to ascertain how far the language of conversation in the middle and lower classes of society is adapted to the purposes of poetic pleasure" must be understood in terms of an age that produced a multitude of verse written in the language of the middle and working classes. The prevalence of the war verse in the journals of the day may have even contributed to the experimental notion behind the *Lyrical Ballads.* However, the object of the *Ballads* was not merely to use simple language, it was to use it in a way that gave "poetic pleasure" whereas the emphasis in much of the war verse was less on poetic pleasure than on political motivation.

Before the war, an obvious distance is found between the poet and subject in almost all the poetry which dealt with the common man. This is especially true in the popular sentimental poetry of the latter eighteenth century. Thomas Gray's *Elegy Written in a Country Churchyard*, 1751, presents the rural way of life in almost idyllic terms:

Let not Ambition mock their useful toil,
Their homely joys, and destiny obscure;
Nor Grandeur hear with a disdainful smile
The short and simple annals of the poor.

The poet, however, partakes neither of the "homely joys" nor of the realm of "Grandeur." He recognizes beauty in the simplicity of country-life, but fails to look beyond its apparent calm to the constant struggle for survival which marked the lives of so many of Britain's lower classes. What the poet sees from the country churchyard seems to be those aspects of the "simple" life which might comfort him. Where he is concerned with the actual lives he comments upon, it is in terms of comparison with an urban world which he castigates for its shrines to "Luxury and Pride." George Crabbe (1754-1832) in *The Village*, 1783, is an exception in the period. He depicts village life as one of hardship and frustration, drawing on the experience of his own life as a member of a poor family in the bleak town of Aldeburgh.

The poets of the Revolution and the Napoleonic wars brought closer together the experience of the subject of the poetry, the reader, and the poet. The change that occurred cannot be discussed in terms of a movement from the position that the purpose of poetry was "to instruct" towards a position that poetry was "to delight." Much of the war poetry, as well as other poetry of the period, was clearly didactic in purpose. Neither can the change which occurred be demonstrated by dividing pre-war poets from post-war poets in terms of subject matter. Rather, it is primarily the kind and degree of response which differentiated Romanticism from the age which preceded it.

The change which occurred in poetry was one of intensity combined with a basic discontent for surface appearances. And these were two qualities of the political climate as well. The American colonies had successfully rebelled against Britain; the impoverished French had rebelled against the Bourbons; and in Britain there was growing agitation for government reform by the middle and working classes. The rapidity with which old aristocratic social standards were being questioned brought re-evaluations and demands on all social levels. Poets, stirred by the needs and demands of the common people, began to write in terms of the democratizing spirit of the time. Poetry no longer idealized the condition of the poor but, in a more realistic vein, dealt with the hungry, the weary, the poorly-clothed and housed, the ill.

Writing in an age which combined a penchant for the sentimental with the desire to treat more realistically the problems of ordinary people, it was natural for poets, particularly those who opposed the war, to focus upon the effects of the hostilities on the working classes. The declaration of war called for an immediate increase in the fighting forces, and methods of impressment and crimping (deceitful recruiting methods) became a poetic topic. *The Tender's Hold; Or, Sailor's Complaint*, 1794 is only one of many poems which deplored the impressing of seamen:

While Landmen wander uncontrol'd,
And boast the rights of Freemen,
Oh! view the tender's loathsome hold,
Where droop your injur'd Seamen:
Dragg'd by Oppression's savage grasp,
From ev'ry dear connection;
'Midst putrid air, Oh! see them gasp,
Oh! mark their deep dejection.
Blush then, Oh! blush ye pension'd host,
Who wallow in profusion,
For our foul cell proves all your boast
To be but mere delusion.
If Liberty be ours, Oh! say
Why are not all protected;
Why is the hand of ruffian sway
'Gainst Seamen thus directed?
Is this your proof of British rights?
Is this rewarding bravery?
Oh! shame to boast your Tars' exploits,
Yet doom those Tars to slavery.

The 1813 *Crimp Serjeant* first attacks the heroic image of war:

The bed of honour is a pretty spot,
For heroes to lie down and rot,
And war's a very noble game,
At which Kings play at arms and legs
Of soldiers, who thenceforward walk on pegs,
And Mister CROKER doth such feats proclaim—
So do Crimp Serjeants—'tis their bounden duty

To call grim-visaged carnage, Beauty;

After a narrative in which "poor PAT CLOD" is induced to join the army with lavish promises of rank and honour:

PAT took the shilling, and e'er three
months older,
He died in Portugal—a common soldier.

As has been noted earlier, many poems were written about war widows or lovers parted by war. Quite often, the poems depict a wife or sweetheart searching for her soldier on battle sites, as in *The Field of Battle*, 1794:

Faintly bray'd the battle's roar,
Distant, down the hollow wind;
Panting terror fled before,
Wounds and death were left behind.
The war-fiend curs'd the sunken day,
That check'd his fierce pursuit too soon;
While, scarcely lighting to the prey,
Low hung, and lour'd, the bloody moon:
The field, so late the hero's pride,
Was now with various carnage spread;
And floated with a crimson tide,
That drench'd the dying and the dead!

The heroine of the poem, Maria, searches for her beloved Edgar and finally finds him "Half buried with the hostile dead,/ And bor'd with many a grisly wound;":

She knew—she sunk—the night-bird scream'd,
The moon withdrew her troubled light,
And left the fair, tho' fall'n she seem'd,
To worse than death—and deepest night!

Shelley's 1809 *Henry and Louisa* is written in this vein, with an anti-religious theme added to the anti-war theme. Louisa, too, searches the battlefield:

"Where is my love!—my Henry—is he dead?"
Half-drowned in smothered anguish wildly
burst
From her parched lips—"is my ador'd one
dead?
Knows none my Henry? War! thou source
accurst,
In whose red blood I see these sands immerst,
Hast thou quite whelmed compassion's tear-
ful spring
Where thy fierce tide rolls to slake Glory's

thirst?
(II, 194-200)

Finding Henry wounded and dying, Louisa willingly dies with him. Shelley depicts Louisa's death as an act of virtue based on love, and envisions a new anti-despotic movement as the result:

Shall Virtue perish? No;
Superior to Religion's tie,
Emancipate from misery,
Despising self, their souls can know
All the delight love can bestow
When Glory's phantom fades away
Before Affection's purer ray,
When tyrants cease to wield the rod
And slaves to tremble at their nod.
(II, 295-303)

The Story of *Henry and Louisa* may have been derived from any number of poems which told the same tale, for it was an often used narrative from the outset of the war.

In the 1795 *Thomas and Kitty* the widow is not only far from home "on Batavia's sea-beat shore," she has with her an infant who perishes from starvation:

Now, rage ye winds! 'tis but on me,
Pour on, ye rains—Ye thunders, reel!
My baby sleeps too sound to feel.
Drench'd with the rain,
I'll lay me by my Tom once more,
Tho' louder still the tempests roar,
And all the biting blasts sustain.
—Ah me! my shivering, fainting heart!
My Tom! my Tom! we shall not part.
Far from our home, from friends afar,
My Tom, my little babe, and I
Shall rest in one cold bed—Ah! ruthless War!
My heart!—O Heaven!—I faint, I die.

A child who either perishes with its parents as a result of war, or is left an unprotected orphan is yet another much used theme of the war verse. Wordsworth's *The Female Vagrant*, 1798, tells the story of another woman who, like "Kitty" and "Maria," is the victim of war:

The pains and plagues that on our heads
came down,
Disease and famine, agony and fear,
In wood or wilderness, in camp or town,

It would thy brain unsettle even to hear.
All perished—all, in one remorseless year.
Husband and children! one by one, by sword
And ravenous plague, all perished: every tear
Dried up, despairing, desolate, on board
A British ship I waked, as from a trance restored.
(pp. 47-48)

The best of the war poetry closed the gap that had existed between poet and subject in eighteenth-century poetry before the French Revolution. Benevolence and condescension were swept aside as genuine interest in the subject matter took precedence over interest in creating a poem-experience which would allow the reader to feel "understanding" and "generous".

In his 1800 "Preface to the *Lyrical Ballads*," Wordsworth declared:

Humble and rustic life was generally chosen, because, in that condition, the essential passions of the heart find a better soil in which they can attain their maturity, are less under restraint, and speak a plainer and more emphatic language; because in that condition of life our elementary feelings co-exist in a state of greater simplicity, and consequently, may be more accurately contemplated, and more forcibly communicated; because the manners of rural life germinate from those elementary feelings, and, from the necessary character of rural occupations, are more easily comprehended, and are more durable; and, lastly, because in that condition the passions of men are incorporated with the beautiful and permanent forms of nature.

Wordsworth made Burns's democratic attitude an official tenet of a poetic creed. The poet as "a man speaking to men" was a democratic ideal; "to keep the Reader in the company of flesh and blood" was a poetic ideal. Both ideals give voice to principles underlying the war poetry which dealt compassionately and far more realistically with the common man. Poems like *The Soldier* 1795 juxtaposed individual conscience and religious fealty with the aims of war:

Tell me now thou gallante soldier,
Now thy lockes with age be hoarie,
Can'st thou praise thy wilde carriere,
Can'st thou call thy madnesse glorie?
To upholde some lordlinge proud,
Or king with curst ambition,
What soule murders hast thou done!
Sweet Christ, give thee contrition.

Amen, amen, thou reverent priest,
Thy Counsaile is most holie;
Thy wordes do teache repentante age,
To curse its manhood's follie.
But doubly curst be kinglie pride,
Makinge erthe one charnel,
Millions of masses dailie sayde
Stay not Hell's payees eternal.

Published in the anti-war *Cabinet* (1795), this poem vehemently expresses its opposition to war in terms of the responsibility of the individual for his acts, whether he be soldier or king. The romantic tendency to regard nobility not as an inherited condition but rather as an individual quality found in all ranks of society was bolstered by the war poetry which often placed the common man and the nobleman on the same plane.

To counter the war poetry which emphasized the agonies and deprivations of war and the injustice permitted, even sanctioned by government, an opposite kind of poetry developed. Thousands of call-to-arms verses were written which celebrated the willingness of the common man to join the armed services:

Bob Rusty, who ne'er a rupee got
(He roundly swears that he ought not,)
Is in his hammock pent.
Safe moor'd, he hugs his swinging-bed,
Without a rag to bind his head,
Bob's night cap is CONTENT.

The heroism of the common man in battle:

From the main-deck to the quarter,
Strew'd with limbs and wet with blood,
Poor Tom Halliard, pale and wounded,
Crawl'd where his brave Captain stood.
"O, my noble Captain! tell me
Ere I'm borne a corpse away,
Have I done a Seaman's duty
On this great and glorious day?
"Tell a dying Sailor truly,
For my life is fleeting fast;
Have I done a Seaman's duty?
Can there aught my mem'ry blast?"
"Ah! brave Tom!" the Captain answer'd,
"Thou a Sailor's part hast done!
I revere thy wounds with sorrow—
Wounds by which our glory's won."

And the willing sacrifice of the working classes to defend their rights and property:

Because I'm but poor,
And slender my store,
That I've nothing to lose is the cry;
Let who will declare it,
I vow I can't bear it,
I give all such praters the lie.
Tho' my house is but small,
Yet to have none at all,
Would sure be a greater distress, Sir;
Shall my garden so sweet,
And my orchard so neat,
Be the pride of a foreign oppressor?

....

Now do but reflect,
What I have to protect;
Then doubt if to fight I shall choose—
King, Church, Babes and Wife,
Laws, Liberty, Life,—
Now tell me I've nothing to lose.

To a large extent, the image of the common man presented in these verses is fictional. The common soldier generally had no property, and it was property which determined the right to vote. The object of many of these verses was to gain allegiance to the government's war policy (and so induce men to join the services) and generally to keep the war spirit of the populace at a pitch sufficient to offset the deprivations and suffering caused by the war.

These poems, however, had an effect quite apart from what was intended. In their effort to enhance the role of the common man as soldier and citizen, they glorified the image of the individual as much as did the anti-war poetry. The epithets once reserved only for officers of the army and navy were applied to ordinary fighting men. They were ennobled not only in their military role, but given credit for excellent, albeit rough, intelligence, and sensitivity as well. In *The British Soldier*, 1813 for example, a soldier, having disobeyed his officer's command to shoot an enemy officer, argues:

"Chide not my chief, the gallant soldier
cries,
"Knit not your brows, oh cast that frown
away;
"Your wishes to my feelings sacrifice,
"Nor harshly judge me if I disobey.
"Oh, I have seen the day when thousands

fell,
"Have join'd in th' inspiring battle cry;
"These scars, more eloquent than words,
can tell
"I did my part towards the victory.
"Then pardon, chieftain, if this once
I dare,
"Refuse performing the too harsh decree;
"Oh pardon then, and in my feelings share,
"Unsoldier like I am, unchristian cannot
be."

The officer perceives "beneath a rough war-beaten form,/ Nature's affections, and best virtue lie," and so he "could not punish, where reward was due."

Ironically, the result of the effort to ennoble the position of the fighting man was less to bind him to notions of status quo, that is servitude and obedience without question, then to further democratize the working and middle classes. If the ordinary man demonstrated the capacity to respond intelligently and bravely in the defence of his nation why then might not the same ordinary man have a voice in government and a greater share of the national wealth.

The war poetry, then, is an extensive body of verse which deals compassionately and sympathetically with the common man. The lyricism, emotionalism, simplicity of language and subject matter are the basic elements of Romanticism. This is true of war poetry both before and after the *Lyrical Ballads* and Wordsworth and Coleridge can be placed within this larger poetic movement.

The many varieties of war verses are, to a great extent, imitations within the Percy-Burns ballad revival. The poets of the *Lyrical Ballads*, however, broke through what might have become a static poetic mode. They re-shaped and re-directed the qualities found in the war poetry in a way which evoked in the reader the emotional as well as the intellectual experience of the poem. Wordsworth and Coleridge, Shelley and Byron celebrated the individuality of the common man, but it was the popular war poetry that, for the first time in British literary history, put the common man center-stage.

3

World War I Poets

WAR POET

A war poet is a poet in time of and on the subject of war. The term, which is applied especially to those in military service during World War I, was documented as early as 1848 in reference to German revolutionary poet, Georg Herwegh.

WORLD WAR I

In England

For the first time, a substantial number of important English poets were soldiers, writing about their experiences of war. A number of them died on the battlefield, most famouslyEdward Thomas, Isaac Rosenberg, Wilfred Owen, and Charles Sorley. Others including Robert Graves, Ivor Gurney and Siegfried Sassoon survived but were scarred by their experiences, and this was reflected in their poetry. Robert H. Ross characterised the English "war poets" as a subgroup of the *Georgian Poetry* writers.

Many poems by British war poets were published in newspapers and then collected into anthologies. Several of these early anthologies were published during the war and were very popular, though the tone of the poetry changed as the war progressed. One of the wartime anthologies was *The Muse in Arms*, published in 1917. Several anthologies were also published in the years after the war had ended.

In November 1985, a slate memorial was unveiled in Poet's Corner commemorating 16 poets of the Great War: Richard Aldington, Laurence Binyon, Edmund Blunden, Rupert Brooke, Wilfrid Gibson, Robert Graves, Julian Grenfell, Ivor Gurney, David Jones, Robert Nichols, Wilfred Owen, Herbert Read, Isaac Rosenberg, Siegfried Sassoon, Charles Sorley and Edward Thomas.

In other countries

Canadian war poets of this period included John McCrae, who wrote *In*

Flanders Fields, and Robert W. Service who worked as an ambulance driver for the Canadian Red Crossand was a war correspondent for the Canadian government.

Russia also produced a number of significant war poets including Nikolay Gumilyov (whose war poems were assembled in the collection *The Quiver* (1916)), Alexander Blok, Ilya Ehrenburg (who published war poems in his book "On the Eve"), and Nikolay Semenovich Tikhonov (who published the book *Orda* (The horde) in 1922).

THE SPANISH CIVIL WAR

The Spanish Civil War produced a substantial volume of poetry in English (as well as in Spanish). There were English-speaking poets serving in the Spanish Civil War on both sides. Among those fighting with the Republicans as volunteers in the International Brigades were Clive Branson, John Cornford, Charles Donnelly, Alex McDade and Tom Wintringham. On the Nationalist side, the most famous English language poet of the Spanish Civil War remains South African bard Roy Campbell.

AMERICAN WORLD WAR I POETS

FLORENCE EARLE COATES

Florence Van Leer Earle Nicholson Coates (July 1, 1850 – April 6, 1927) was an American poet.

Biography

She was born in Philadelphia, Pennsylvania. Granddaughter of noted abolitionist and philanthropist Thomas Earle, and eldest daughter of Philadelphia lawyer George H. Earle, Sr. and Mrs. Frances ("Fanny") Van Leer Earle, Mrs. Coates gained notoriety both at home and abroad for her works of poetry—nearly three-hundred of which were published in literary magazines such as the*Atlantic Monthly, Scribner's Magazine, The Literary Digest, Lippincott's, The Century Magazine, and Harper's*. Many of her poems were set to music by composers such as Mrs. H. H. A. Beach (Amy Cheney Beach), Clayton Johns, and Charles Gilbert Spross. She attended school in Lexington, Massachusetts sometime between 1864 and 1867 under the instruction of abolitionist and teacher Theodore Dwight Weld, who had "charge of Conversation, Composition, and English Literature," and would further her education abroad at the Convent of the Sacred Heart in Paris (Rue de Varenne), and by studying music in Brussels under noted instructors of the day.

Literary and social critic Matthew Arnold both encouraged and inspired Mrs. Coates' writing of poetry. He was a guest at the Coates' Germantown home when his lecture tours brought him to Philadelphia. Coates and Arnold first met in New York—during Arnold's first visit and lecture tour of America—at the home of Andrew Carnegie, "where they formed a lasting friendship." The tour (which lasted from October 1883 to March 1884) brought Arnold to Philadelphia in December 1883, where he lectured at Association Hall on the topics of the "Doctrine of the Remnant" and on "Emerson." His second visit and tour of America took place in 1886, and brought him to Philadelphia in early June where he was again hosted by Mr. and Mrs. Coates and spoke on the topic of "Foreign Education" at the University of Pennsylvania chapel. Arnold wrote to Mrs. Coates in 1887 and 1888 from his home at Pains Hill Cottage in Cobham, Surrey, England describing his remembrance of and fondness for her "tulip-trees and maples." Rarely did Mrs. Coates write or publish prose work, but in April 1894 and again in December 1909, she dedicated her pen to remembrances of her mentor in issues of the *Century* and *Lippincott's* magazines respectively.

The Coates' often spent their summer months in the Adirondacks, where they maintained "Camp Elsinore"—their summer camp by the Upper St. Regis Lake. It was there that they entertained, rested and escaped the humidity of Philadelphia summers. In the early 1900s (decade), the Coates' seasonally opened their camp to Anna Roosevelt Cowles ("Bamie")—elder sister of Theodore Roosevelt. Among Mrs. Cowles' visitors during her stays at Elsinore was Alice Roosevelt, President Theodore Roosevelt's daughter. Many of Mrs. Coates' nature poems were inspired by the flora and fauna of the Adirondacks. Of her "spot in the mountains," Mrs. Coates sings:

There's a cabin in the mountains, where the fare, dear,
Is frugal as the cheer of Arden blest;
But contentment sweet and fellowship are there, dear,
And Love, that makes the feast he honours—best!

In the March 1913 issue of *Lippincott's Monthly Magazine*, noted anthologist and poet, William Stanley Braithwaite (1878–1962), gives a detailed 9-page review of Mrs. Coates' poetry, relating how "she draws from the Olympian world figures that typify some motive or desire in human conduct, and in the modern world the praise of men and women, heroic in attainment or sacrifice; or laments events that effect social and ethical progress, showing how beneficently she has brought her art, without modifying in the least its abstract function as a creator of beauty and pleasure, into the service of profound and vital problems."Much of Mrs. Coates' later published work was written during the years spanning World War I and showcased her concern for such "profound and vital problems" as her voice joined the chorus of 'singers' in support of American involvement in the war—evidenced in her privately published pamphlet of war poetry, *Pro Patria* (1917). Mrs. Coates also penned several other works of fugitive verse, much of which is patriotic and war-related, describing the selfless sacrifices made by soldiers and citizens alike for the cause of freedom and liberty. Florence was a founder of the Contemporary Club of Philadelphia in 1886; one of twenty founders of the Society of Mayflower Descendants in the Commonwealth of Pennsylvania in 1896—herself being a ninth generation descendant of Pilgrim John Howland; and twice president of the Browning Societyof Philadelphia from 1895 to 1903, and again from 1907 to 1908. In 1915, Florence was unanimously elected poet laureate of Pennsylvania by the state's Federation of Women's Clubs.

She married first, William Nicholson—who died in 1877 after only five years of marriage. On 7 January 1879, she married Edward Hornor Coates at Christ Church in Philadelphia. Mr. Coates would eventually adopt Florence's daughter from her first marriage—Alice Earle Nicholson. Florence and Edward had one child together in 1881, but the baby—Josephine Wisner Coates—died in infancy. Mr. Coates was president of the Pennsylvania Academy of the Fine Arts from 1890 to 1906. He died on 23 December 1921. In 1923, Mrs. Coates presented *The Edward H. Coates Memorial Collection* to the Pennsylvania Academy of the Fine Arts in Philadelphia. The exhibition included 27 paintings and 3 pieces of sculpture, and was displayed from 4 November 1923 to 10 January 1924. Florence died at Hahnemann Hospital in Philadelphia on 6 April 1927. She is buried at the Church of the Redeemer churchyard in Bryn Mawr, Pennsylvania alongside her husband and her brother George Howard Earle, Jr. and many of his descendants, including his son, former Pennsylvania Governor, George Howard Earle III—Florence's nephew.

LENA GUILBERT FORD

Lena Gilbert Brown Ford (1870 – March 7, 1918) was a lyricist, best known for "Keep the Home Fires Burning" which she wrote during the First World War.

She was born Lena Gilbert Brown in Venango County, Pennsylvania and attended Elmira College, graduating in 1887. She married physician Harry Hale Ford and settled in Elmira, later divorcing him and relocating, with her mother and son, to London, England, where they would remain for twenty years. During World War I, Ford opened her home to soldiers and took care of them.

While in Britain she met Ivor Novello, with whom she collaborated to produce "Keep the Home Fires Burning" in 1914. It was the first major success for Novello and the only one for Ford. Among Ford's other published musical works are "When God Gave You to Me", "We Are Coming, Mother England", and "God Guard You" (with Westell Gordon).

Ford and her thirty-year-old son Walter were the first United States citizens to become fatalities of a German air raid on London, their home being hit by one of two bombs that fell on the city on 7 March 1918. Mrs. Brown, Ford's mother, was only hurt in the bombing. Their remains were returned to and interred in the United States.

HARRY ELMORE HURD

Harry Elmore Hurd (1889 - August 21, 1958 Haverhill, Massachusetts) was an American poet, and minister.

Life

He graduated from Boston University in 1916, and Harvard University in 1922. He was a Chaplain, First Lieutenant with the 33rd Engineers during World War I. He was a minister in Methodist and Congregational churches for eighteen years, in Haverhill, Quincy, and Reading.

His work was publisher in *Prairie Schooner*, *Overland Monthly*, *Voices*, *Saturday Review*,

HERBERT KAUFMAN

Herbert Kaufman (March 6, 1878 – September 6, 1947) was an American writer and newspaperman whose editorials were widely syndicated in both the United States and Canada. During World War I, Kaufman regularly contributed articles and editorials to the *Evening Standard*, *The Times*, and other leading British periodicals, along with more than 50 war poems, including the classic *The Hell-Gate of Soissons*.

His work

Kaufman is the author of several books, including:

- *The Stolen Throne* (c. 1907; co-authored with May Isabel Fisk and illustrated by Howard Chandler Christy and Herman Rountree)
- *The Winning Fight* (c. 1910) being perhaps his most popular work
- *Do Something! Be Something!* (c. 1912)
- *The Efficient Age* (c. 1913)
- *The Song of Guns* (1914, reissued in 1915 as "The Hell-Gate of Soissons And Other Poems")
- *The Clock that Had No Hands* (c. 1912; a compilation of essays on the value of advertising)
- *Neighbours* (c. 1914)

Kaufman is known for his essays on success, war poetry, and "Kaufmanisms." A "Kaufmanism" is the persuasive rhetorical juxtaposition of words that reverses the subject andobject of a phrase often meant to change its context and meaning, typically used to add additional emphasis to both nouns.

Select Kaufmanisms:

- *A coward can't conquer anything, because he can't conquer himself.*
- *The man who won't go through to the finish has finished at the start.*
- *They who fight in the dark do not shine in the light.*
- *Mind your own business and in time you'll have a business of your own to mind.*

Selected magazine bibliography

- "The Stainless Banner", *Everybody's Magazine*, June 1909.
- "America (pm)" *Everybody's Magazine*, January 1910.
- "The Song of the Man", *Hampton's*, August 1910.
- "The Living Dead", *Everybody's Magazine*, November 1911.
- "Fool's Gold", *Everybody's Magazine*, March 1913.
- "To Wilhelm the Mad", *Nash's Magazine*, September 1914.

JOYCE KILMER

Joyce Kilmer (born as Alfred Joyce Kilmer; 6 December 1886 – 30 July 1918) was an American writer and poet mainly remembered for a short poem titled "Trees" (1913), which was published in the collection *Trees and Other Poems* in 1914. Though a prolific poet whose works celebrated the common beauty of the natural world as well as his Roman Catholic religious faith, Kilmer was also a journalist, literary critic, lecturer, and editor. While most of his works are largely unknown, a select few of his poems remain popular and are published frequently in anthologies. Several critics—including both Kilmer's contemporaries and modern scholars—have disparaged Kilmer's work as being too simple and overly sentimental, and suggested that his style was far too traditional, even archaic. Many writers, including notably Ogden Nash, have parodied Kilmer's work and style—as attested by the many parodies of "Trees".

At the time of his deployment to Europe during World War I, Kilmer was considered the leading American Roman Catholic poet and lecturer of his generation, whom critics often compared to British contemporaries G. K. Chesterton (1874–1936) and Hilaire Belloc(1870–1953). He enlisted in the New York National Guard and was deployed to France with the 69th Infantry Regiment(the famous "Fighting 69th") in 1917. He was killed by a sniper's bullet at the Second Battle of the Marne in 1918 at the age of 31. He was married to Aline Murray, also an accomplished poet and author, with whom he had five children.

Biography

Early years and education: 1886–1908

Kilmer was born 6 December 1886 in New Brunswick, New Jersey, the fourth and youngest child, of Annie Ellen Kilburn (1849–1932), a minor writer and composer, and Dr. Frederick Barnett Kilmer (1851–1934), a physician and analytical chemist employed by the Johnson and Johnson Company and inventor of the company's baby powder. He was named Alfred Joyce Kilmer after two priests at Christ Church in New Brunswick: Alfred R. Taylor, the curate; and the Rev. Dr. Elisha Brooks Joyce (1857–1926), the rector. Christ Church is the oldest Episcopal parish in New Brunswick and the Kilmer family were parishioners.Rector Joyce, who served the parish from 1883 to 1916, baptised the young Kilmer. Kilmer's birthplace in New Brunswick, where the Kilmer family lived from 1886 to 1892, is still standing, and houses a small museum to Kilmer, as well as a few Middlesex Countygovernment offices.

Kilmer entered Rutgers College Grammar School (now Rutgers Preparatory School) in 1895 at the age of 8. During his years at the Grammar School, Kilmer was editor-in-chief of the school's paper, the *Argo*, and loved the classics but had difficulty with Greek. He won the first Lane Classical Prize, for oratory, and obtained a scholarship to Rutgers College which he would attend the following year. Despite his difficulties with Greek and mathematics, he stood at the head of his class in preparatory school.

After graduating from Rutgers College Grammar School in 1904, he continued his education at Rutgers College (now Rutgers University) from 1904 to 1906. At Rutgers, Kilmer was associate editor of the *Targum*, the campus newspaper, and a member of the Delta Upsilon fraternity. However, he was unable to complete the curriculum's rigorous mathematics requirement and was asked to repeat his sophomore year. Under pressure from his mother, Kilmer transferred to Columbia University in New York City.

At Columbia, Kilmer was vice-president of the Philolexian Society (a literary society), associate editor of *Columbia Spectator* (the campus newspaper), and member of the Debating Union. He completed his Bachelor of Arts (A.B.) degree and graduated from Columbia on 23 May 1908. Shortly after graduation, on 9 June 1908, he marriedAline Murray (1888–1941), a fellow poet to whom he had been engaged since his sophomore year at Rutgers. The Kilmers had five children: Kenton Sinclair Kilmer (1909–1995); Michael Barry Kilmer (1916–1927); Deborah ("Sister Michael") Clanton Kilmer (1914–1999) who was a Catholic nun at the Saint Benedict's Monastery; Rose Kilburn Kilmer (1912–1917); and Christopher Kilmer (1917–1984).

Years of writing and faith: 1909–1917

In the autumn of 1908, Kilmer was employed teaching Latin at Morristown High School in Morristown, New Jersey. At this time, he began to submit essays to *Red Cross Notes* (including his first published piece, an essay on the "Psychology of Advertising") and his early poems to literary periodicals. Kilmer also wrote book reviews for *The Literary Digest*, *Town and Country*, *The Nation*, and *The New York Times*. By June 1909, Kilmer had abandoned any aspirations to continue teaching and relocated to New York City, where he focused solely on developing a career as a writer.

From 1909 to 1912, Kilmer was employed by Funk and Wagnalls, which was preparing an edition of *The Standard Dictionary* that would be published in 1912. According to Hillis, Kilmer's job "was to define ordinary words assigned to him at five cents for each word defined. This was a job at which one would ordinarily earn ten to twelve dollars a week, but Kilmer attacked the task with such vigour and speed that it was soon thought wisest to put him on a regular salary."

In 1911, Kilmer's first book of verse was published, entitled *Summer of Love.* Kilmer would later write that "...some of the poems in it, those inspired by genuine love, are not things of which to be ashamed, and you, understanding, would not be offended by the others."

In 1912, Kilmer became a special writer for the *New York Times Review of Books* and the *New York Times Sunday Magazine* and was often engaged in lecturing. He moved toMahwah, New Jersey, where he resided until his service and death in World War I. By this time he had become established as a published poet and as a popular lecturer. According to Robert Holliday, Kilmer "frequently neglected to make any preparation for his speeches, not even choosing a subject until the beginning of the dinner which was to culminate in a specimen of his oratory. His constant research for the dictionary, and, later on, for his New York Times articles, must have given him a store of knowledge at his fingertips to be produced at a moment's notice for these emergencies."

When the Kilmers' daughter Rose (1912–1917) was stricken with poliomyelitis (also known as infantile paralysis) shortly after birth, they turned to their religious faith for comfort. A series of correspondence between Kilmer and Father James J. Daly led the Kilmers to convert to Roman Catholicism, and they were received in the church in 1913. In one of these letters Kilmer writes that he "believed in the Catholic position, the Catholic view of ethics and aesthetics, for a long time," and he "wanted something not intellectual, some conviction not mental – in fact I wanted Faith." Kilmer would stop "every morning for months" on his way "to the office and prayed for faith," claiming that when "faith did come, it came, I think, by way of my little paralyzed daughter. Her lifeless hands led me; I think her tiny feet know beautiful paths. You understand this and it gives me a selfish pleasure to write it down."

With the publication of "Trees" in the magazine *Poetry* in August 1913, Kilmer gained immense popularity as a poet across the United States. He had established himself as a successful lecturer—particularly one seeking to reach a Catholic audience. His close friend and editor Robert Holliday wrote that it "is not an unsupported assertion to say that he was in his time and place the laureate of the Catholic Church." *Trees and Other Poems* (1914) was published the following year. Over the next few years, Kilmer was prolific in his output, managing an intense schedule of lectures, publishing a large number of essays and literary criticism, and writing poetry. In 1915 he became poetry editor of*Current Literature* and contributing editor of *Warner's Library of the World's Best Literature*. In 1916 and 1917, before the American entry into World War I, Kilmer would publish four books: *The Circus and Other Essays* (1916), a series of interviews with literary personages entitled *Literature in the Making* (1917),

Main Street and Other Poems (1917), and *Dreams and Images: An Anthology of Catholic Poets* (1917).

War years: 1917–1918

In April 1917, a few days after the United States entered World War I, Kilmer enlisted in the Seventh Regiment of the New York National Guard. In August, Kilmer was assigned as a statistician with the U.S. 69th Infantry Regiment (better known as the "Fighting 69th" and later re-designated the 165th Infantry Regiment), of the 42nd "Rainbow" Division, and quickly rose to the rank of sergeant. Though he was eligible for commission as an officer and often recommended for such posts during the course of the war, Kilmer refused, stating that he would rather be a sergeant in the Fighting 69th than an officer in any other regiment.

Shortly before his deployment to Europe, the Kilmers' daughter Rose had died, and twelve days later, their son Christopher was born. Before his departure, Kilmer had contracted with publishers to write a book about the war, deciding upon the title *Here and There with the Fighting Sixty-Ninth*. The regiment arrived in France in November 1917, and Kilmer wrote to his wife that he had not written "anything in prose or verse since I got here—except statistics—but I've stored up a lot of memories to turn into copy when I get a chance." Kilmer did not write such a book; however, towards the end of the year, he did find time to write prose sketches and poetry. The most notable of his poems during this period was "Rouge Bouquet" (1918) which commemorated the deaths of two dozen members of his regiment in a German artillery barrage on American trench positions in the Rouge Bouquet forest north-east of the French village of Baccarat. At the time, this was a relatively quiet sector of the front, but the first battalion was struck by a German heavy artillerybombardment on the afternoon of 7 March 1918 that buried 21 men of the unit, killing 19 (of which 14 remained entombed).

Kilmer sought more hazardous duty and was transferred to the military intelligence section of his regiment, in April 1918. In a letter to his wife, Aline, he remarked: "Now I'm doing work I love – and work you may be proud of. None of the drudgery of soldiering, but a double share of glory and thrills." According to Hillis, Kilmer's fellow soldiers had accorded him much respect for his battlefield demeanour—"He was worshipped by the men about him. I have heard them speak with awe of his coolness and his nerve in scouting patrols in no man's land. This coolness and his habit of choosing, with typical enthusiasm, the most dangerous and difficult missions, led to his death."

Death and burial

During the Second Battle of Marne there was heavy fighting throughout the last days of July 1918. On 30 July 1918, Kilmer volunteered to accompany

Major William "Wild Bill" Donovan (later, in World War II, the founder of the Office of Strategic Services, forerunner to the Central Intelligence Agency) when Donovan's battalion (1–165th Infantry) was sent to lead the day's attack.

During the course of the day, Kilmer led a scouting party to find the position of a German machine gun. When his comrades found him, some time later, they thought at first that he was peering over the edge of a little hill, where he had crawled for a better view. When he did not answer their call, they ran to him and found him dead. According to Father Francis P. Duffy: "A bullet had pierced his brain. His body was carried in and buried by the side of Ames. God rest his dear and gallant soul." A sniper's bullet likely killed him immediately. According to military records, Kilmer died on the battlefield near Muercy Farm, beside the Ourcq River near the village of Seringes-et-Nesles, in France, on 30 July 1918 at the age of 31. For his valor, Kilmer was posthumously awarded the Croix de Guerre (War Cross) by the French Republic.

Kilmer was buried in the Oise-Aisne American Cemetery and Memorial, near Fere-en-Tardenois, Aisne, Picardy, France. A cenotaph erected to his memory is located on the Kilmer family plot in Elmwood Cemetery, in New Brunswick, New Jersey. A Memorial Mass was celebrated atSt. Patrick's Cathedral in Manhattan on 14 October 1918.

Criticism and influence

Trees

Joyce Kilmer's reputation as a poet is staked largely on the widespread popularity of one poem—"Trees" (1913). It was first published in the August 1913 issue of *Poetry: A Magazine of Verse* which had begun publishing the year before in Chicago, Illinois and was included as the title poem in a collection of poems *Trees and Other Poems* (1914). According to Kilmer's oldest son, Kenton, the poem was written on 2 February 1913 when the family resided in Mahwah, New Jersey.

It was written in the afternoon in the intervals of some other writing. The desk was in an upstairs room, by a window looking down a wooded hill. It was written in a little notebook in which his father and mother wrote out copies of several of their poems, and, in most cases, added the date of composition. On one page the first two lines of 'Trees' appear, with the date, February 2, 1913, and on another page, further on in the book, is the full text of the poem. It was dedicated to his wife's mother, Mrs. Henry Mills Alden, who was endeared to all her family.

Many locations including Rutgers University (where Kilmer attended for two years), University of Notre Dame, as well as historians in Mahwah, New Jersey and in other places, have boasted that a specific tree was the inspiration for Kilmer's poem. However, Kenton Kilmer refutes these claims, remarking that, Mother and I agreed, when we talked about it, that Dad never meant his poem to apply to one particular tree, or to the trees of any special region. Just any trees or all trees that might be rained on or snowed on, and that would be suitable nesting places for robins. I guess they'd have to have upward-reaching branches, too, for the line about 'lifting leafy arms to pray.' Rule out weeping willows."

The popular appeal of this simple poem is likely the source of its endurance despite the continuing negative opinion of the poem's merits from scholars and critics. According to Robert Holliday, Kilmer's friend and editor, "Trees" speaks "with authentic song to the simplest of hearts" and that "(t)he exquisite title poem now so universally known, made his reputation more than all the rest he had written put together. That impeccable lyric which made for immediate widespread popularity." Its popularity has also led to parodies of the poem—some by noted poets and writers. The pattern of its first lines (*I think that I shall never see/ A poem lovely as a tree.*) is of seemingly simple rhyme and meter and easy to mimic along with the poem's choice of metaphors. One of the best known parodies is "Song of the Open Road" by American humorist and poet Ogden Nash (1902–1971):

I think that I shall never see
A billboard lovely as a tree.
Indeed, unless the billboards fall,
I'll never see a tree at all.

Influences upon Kilmer's verse

Kilmer's early works were inspired by, and were imitative of, the poetry of Algernon Charles Swinburne, Gerard Manley Hopkins, Ernest Dowson, Aubrey Beardsley, and William Butler Yeats (and the Celtic Revival). It was later through the influence of works by Coventry Patmore, Francis Thompson, and those of Alice Meynell and her children Viola Meynell and Francis Meynell, that Kilmer seems to have become interested in Catholicism. Kilmer wrote of his influences:

I have come to regard them with intense admiration. Patmore seems to me to be a greater poet than Francis Thompson. He has not the rich vocabulary, the decorative erudition, the Shelleyan enthusiasm, which distinguish the *Sister Songs* and the *Hound of Heaven,* but he has a classical simplicity, a restraint and sincerity which make his poems satisfying.

Because he was initially raised Episcopalian (or Anglican), Kilmer became literary editor of the Anglican weekly, *The Churchman*, before his conversion to Catholicism. During this time he did considerable research into 16th and 17th century Anglican poets as well as metaphysical, or mystic poets of that time, including George Herbert, Thomas Traherne, Robert Herrick, Bishop Coxe, and Robert Stephen Hawker (the eccentric vicar of the Church of Saint

Morwenna and Saint John the Baptist at Morwenstow inCornwall)—the latter whom he referred to as "a coast life-guard in a cassock." These poets also had an influence on Kilmer's writings.

Critics compared Kilmer to British Catholic writers Hilaire Belloc and G. K. Chesterton—suggesting that his reputation might have risen to the level where he would have been considered their American counterpart if not for his untimely death.

Criticism of Kilmer's work

Kilmer's death at age 31 removed from him the opportunity to develop into a more mature poet. Because "Trees" is often dismissed by modern critics and scholars as simple verse, much of Kilmer's work (especially his literary criticism) has slipped into obscurity. Only a very few of his poems have appeared in anthologies, and with the exception of "Trees"—and to a much lesser extent "Rouge Bouquet" (1917–1918)—almost none have obtained lasting widespread popularity.

The entire corpus of Kilmer's work was produced between 1909 and 1918 when Romanticism and sentimental lyric poetry fell out of favour and Modernism took root—especially with the influence of the Lost Generation. In the years after Kilmer's death, poetry went in drastically different directions, as is seen especially in the work of T. S. Eliot and Ezra Pound. Kilmer's verse is conservative and traditional, and does not break the formal rules of poetics—he can be considered as one of the last poets of the Romantic era. His style has been criticized for not breaking free of traditional modes of rhyme, meter, and theme, and for being too sentimental to be taken seriously.

ALAN SEEGER

Alan Seeger (22 June 1888 – 4 July 1916) was an American poet who fought and died in World War I during the Battle of the Sommeserving in the French Foreign Legion. Seeger was the uncle of American folk singer Pete Seeger, and was a classmate of T.S. Eliot at Harvard. He is most well known for having authored the poem, *I Have a Rendezvous with Death*, a favourite of President John F. Kennedy. A statue modeled after Seeger is found on the monument honouring fallen Americans who volunteered for France during the war, located at thePlace des États-Unis, Paris. He is sometimes called the "American Rupert Brooke."

Early life

Born in New York on June 22, 1888, Seeger moved with his family to Staten Island at the age of one and remained there until the age of 10. In 1900, his family moved to Mexico for two years, which influenced the imagery of some of his poetry. His brother Charles Seeger, a noted pacifist and musicologist, was the father of the American folk singers Peter "Pete" Seeger, Mike Seeger, and Margaret "Peggy" Seeger.

Seeger entered Harvard in 1906 after attending several elite preparatory schools, including Hackley School.

Writing

At Harvard, he edited and wrote for the *Harvard Monthly*. Among his friends there (and afterwards) was the American Communist John Reed, though the two had differing ideological views, and his Harvard class also included T.S. Eliot and Walter Lippmann, among others. After graduating in 1910, he moved to Greenwich Village for two years, where he wrote poetry and enjoyed the life of a young bohemian. During his time in Greenwich Village, he attended soirées at the Mlles. Petitpas' boardinghouse (319 West 29th Street), where the presiding genius was the artist and sage John Butler Yeats, father of the poet William Butler Yeats.

Having moved to the Latin Quarter of Paris to continue his seemingly itinerant intellectual lifestyle, on August 24, 1914, Seeger joined the French Foreign Legion so that he could fight for the Allies in World War I (the United States did not enter the war until 1917).

Death

He was killed in action at Belloy-en-Santerre on July 4, 1916, famously cheering on his fellow soldiers in a successful charge after being hit several times by machine gun fire.

Poetry

Seeger's poetry was published by Charles Scribner's Sons in December 1916 with a 46 page introduction by William Archer. *Poems*, a collection of his works, was relatively unsuccessful, due, according to Eric Homberger, to its lofty idealism and language, qualities out of fashion in the early decades of the 20th century.

Poems was reviewed in *The Egoist*, where the critic—T. S. Eliot, Seeger's classmate at Harvard—commented that,

Seeger was serious about his work and spent pains over it. The work is well done, and so much out of date as to be almost a positive quality. It is high-flown, heavily decorated and solemn, but its solemnity is thorough going, not a mere literary formality. Alan Seeger, as one who knew him can attest, lived his whole life on this plane, with impeccable poetic dignity; everything about him was in keeping.

One of his more famous poems was *I Have a Rendezvous with Death,* published posthumously. A recurrent theme in both his poetic works and his personal writings was his desire for his life to end gloriously at an early age.

This particular poem, according to the JFK Library, "was one of John F. Kennedy's favourite poems and he often asked his wife (Jacqueline) to recite it."

Memorial

On 4 July 1923, the President of the French Council of State, Raymond Poincaré, dedicated a monument in the Place des États-Unis to the Americans who had volunteered to fight in World War I in the service of France. The monument, in the form of a bronze statue on a plinth, executed by Jean Boucher, had been financed through a public subscription.

Boucher had used a photograph of Seeger as his inspiration, and Seeger's name can be found, among those of 23 others who had fallen in the ranks of the French Foreign Legion, on the back of the plinth. Also, on either side of the base of the statue, are two excerpts from Seeger's *"Ode in Memory of the American Volunteers Fallen for France"*, a poem written shortly before his death on 4 July 1916. Seeger intended that his words should be read in Paris on 30 May of that year, at an observance of the American holiday, Decoration Day (later known as Memorial Day):

They did not pursue worldly rewards; they wanted nothing more than to live without regret, brothers pledged to the honour implicit in living one's own life and dying one's own death. Hail, brothers! Goodbye to you, the exalted dead! To you, we owe two debts of gratitude forever: the glory of having died for France, and the homage due to you in our memories.

AMOS WILDER

Amos Niven Wilder (September 18, 1895 Madison, Wisconsin - May 4, 1993) was an American poet, minister, and theology professor.

Life

He studied two years at Oberlin College (1913–1915), but volunteered in the Ambulance Field Service; he was awarded the *Croix de Guerre.* In November 1917, he enlisted in the U.S. Field Artillery as a corporal.

In 1920, he graduated from Yale University. In college, he was an inter-collegiate doubles champion tennis player, and he played at Wimbledon in 1922, with his partner, Lee Wiley. He served as secretary to Albert Schweitzer lecturing at Oxford University, where he was studying at Mansfield College, (1921–1923). He completed his study for the ministry at Yale in 1924.

Ministry

He was ordained in 1926, and served in a Congregationalist church in North Conway, New Hampshire He received his doctorate from Yale in 1933. He taught for 11 years at the Chicago Theological Seminary and the University of

Chicago, and served as president of the Chicago Society of Biblical Research in 1949-1950. Wilder joined Harvard University in 1954 as Hollis Professor of Divinity. In 1962 he was part of the first board of directors for the Society for the Arts, Religion and Contemporary Culture. In 1963, Wilder was named *emeritus* faculty. His papers are held at Andover-Harvard Theological Library of Harvard Divinity School.

Literature

Battle Retrospect, was a volume of verse he wrote about his experiences in World War I; it was reprinted in 1971 by AMS Press.

Family

His father was a journalist with a doctorate from Yale, worked at the U.S. consulate in China. His mother was the daughter of a Presbyterian minister. His brother was Thornton Wilder, and sisters, were Charlotte Wilder and Janet Wilder Dakin.

He married Catharine Kerlin in 1935. They had a daughter, Catharine Wilder Guiles, and a son, Amos Tappan Wilder.

CANADIAN WORLD WAR I POETS

WILLIAM WILFRED CAMPBELL

William Wilfred Campbell (15 June 1860 – 1 January 1918) was a Canadian poet. He is often classed as one of the country'sConfederation Poets, a group that included fellow Canadians Charles G.D. Roberts, Bliss Carman, Archibald Lampman, andDuncan Campbell Scott; he was a colleague of Lampman and Scott.

By the end of the 19th century, he was considered the "unofficial poet laureate of Canada." Although not as well known as the other Confederation poets today, Campbell was a "versatile, interesting writer" who was influenced by Robert Burns, the English Romantics, Edgar Allan Poe, Ralph Waldo Emerson,Henry Wadsworth Longfellow, Thomas Carlyle, and Alfred Tennyson. Inspired by these writers, Campbell expressed his ownreligious idealism in traditional forms and genres.

Life

William Wilfred Campbell was born around 15 June 1860 in Newmarket, Upper Canada (present-day Ontario). There is some doubt as to the date and place of his birth. His father, Rev. Thomas Swainston Campbell, was an Anglican clergyman who had been assigned the task of setting up several frontier parishes in "Canada West", as Ontario was then called. Consequently, the family moved frequently.

The Campbell family settled in Wiarton, Ontario in 1871, where Wilfred grew up, attending high school (which was later renamed theOwen Sound Collegiate and Vocational Institute) in nearby Owen Sound. Campbell would look back on his childhood with fondness:

As a boy, I always enjoyed the campfires we built in the woods or on the shingly beach of some lone lake shore, when the stars came out and peered down on the windy darkness and swallowed up the sparks and flames from the crackling logs and dry branches we heaped up while the local warmth and radiance added a contrast to the outside vastness of darkness and cold.

Campbell taught in Wiarton before enrolling in the University of Toronto's University College in 1880, Wycliffe College in 1882, and at the Episcopal Theological School in Cambridge, Massachusetts, in 1883.

Campbell married Mary DeBelle (née Dibble) in 1884. They had four children, Margery, Faith, Basil, and Dorothy. In 1885 Campbell was ordained to the Episcopal priesthood, and was soon appointed to a New England parish. In 1888 he returned to Canada and became rector of St. Stephen, New Brunswick. In 1891, after suffering a crisis of faith, Campbell resigned from the ministry and took a civil service position in Ottawa. He received a permanent position in the Department of Militia and Defence two years later.

Living in Ottawa, Campbell became acquainted with Archibald Lampman—his next door neighbour at one time—and through him with Duncan Campbell Scott. In February 1892, Campbell, Lampman, and Scott began writing a column of literary essays and criticism called "At the Mermaid Inn" for the *Toronto Globe*. As Lampman wrote to a friend:

Campbell is deplorably poor.... Partly in order to help his pockets a little Mr. Scott and I decided to see if we could get the *Toronto Globe* to give us space for a couple of columns of paragraphs and short articles, at whatever pay we could get for them. They agreed to it; and Campbell, Scott and I have been carrying on the thing for several weeks now.

The column ran only until July 1893. Lampman and Scott found it difficult to "keep a rein on Campbell's frank expression of his heterodox opinions." Readers of the *Toronto Globe* reacted negatively when Campbell presented the history of the cross as a mythic symbol. His apology for "overestimating their intellectual capacities" did little to resolve the controversy.

In the 20th century, Campbell became a strong advocate of British imperialism, for example telling Toronto's Empire Club in 1904 that Canada's only choice lay "between two different imperialisms, that of Britain and that of the Imperial Commonwealth to the south." It was the principles of Imperialist that guided his work in *Poems of loyalty by British and Canadian authors* (London, 1913) and for *The Oxford Book of Canadian Verse* (Toronto, 1913).

As editor of *The Oxford book of Canadian Verse*, Campbell devoted more pages to his own poetry than to others'. But by choosing mostly from his longer work—including an excerpt from *Mordred* (one of his verse dramas)—he did not choose his best work. In contrast, the poems he selected from his fellow Confederation Poets reflected some of their best work.

Campbell was transferred to the Dominion Archives in 1909. In 1915 he moved his family to an old stone farmhouse on the outskirts of Ottawa, which he named "Kilmorie". He died of pneumonia on New Year's morning, 1918. He was buried in Ottawa's Beechwood Cemetery.

Writing

Campbell's first chapbook, *Poems!*, "seems to have been printed at a newspaper office sometime around 1879 or 1880." He placed poetry in the University of Toronto *Varsity* in 1881.

As a theology student in Massachusetts, Campbell met Oliver Wendell Holmes, who recommended his poetry to *Atlantic Monthly* editor Thomas Bailey Aldrich. Aldrich published Campbell's "Canadian Folk Song" in the January 1885 issue, launching his career in the American magazines.

In 1888 *Snowflakes and Sunbeams* was printed at Campbell's expense in St. Stephen, New Brunswick. The book "was favourably reviewed in Canada and the United Statesfor its lovely nature lyrics, one of which, 'Indian summer' (it starts with 'Along the line of smoky hills/ The crimson forest stands'), remains among the most beloved of Canadian poems." The entire volume, including "Indian Summer," was incorporated into *Lake Lyrics*, published the following year. "The poems in *Lake lyrics and other poems* (1889), with their intense rhythms, dramatic imagery, and ardent spirituality, express Campbell's devotion to nature as the revelation of God's presence; this book established his reputation as 'laureate of the lakes.'" Notable new poems in the book included "Vapor and Blue" and "The Winter Lakes".

Campbell's poem "The Mother" was printed in *Harper's New Monthly* in April 1891; a traditional ballad, the poem tells of a dead mother who rises from the grave to claim her still-living baby. It "created a sensation in the literary press and was reprinted in newspapers such as the *Week* and the *Globe* in Toronto. In September 1881, the House of Commons (and, in 1892, the Senate) debated whether Campbell should receive a permanent civil service position in recognition of his literary abilities. The proposal was defeated, ostensibly for practical reasons, and the decision established a precedent for withholding patronage from artists. Nevertheless, in 1893 he was quietly given a permanent position in the Department of Militia and Defence, and he would remain a civil servant until his death."

Campbell's third book of poetry, *The Dread Voyage Poems* (1893), was darker than the earlier two. "In this volume, his poetry began to show the preoccupation with harmonizing religion, science, and social theory that had started while he was still a clergyman and would continue through his middle age." The book contains some of Campbell's best-known poems, such as "How One Winter Came in the Lake Region" and the 'surprise ending' sonnet, "Morning on the Shore."

"In 1895 he published two versified tragedies, *Mordred* and *Hildebrand*, and these were included, with two others, *Daulac* and *Morning*, in a volume entitled *Poetical tragedies*(1908)." Also in 1895, Campbell sparked a literary controversy by accusing Bliss Carman of plagiarism, an incident documented in Alexandra Hurst's 1994 book, *The War Among the Poets* (Canadian Poetry Press).

Campbell published a new book of lyrics, *Beyond the Hills of Dream*, in 1899. "Included in the book was his jubilee ode 'Victoria,' written for the Queen's diamond jubilee in 1897. Eleven of its thirty-five other poems were reprinted from *The Dread Voyage*, thus perpetuating the dark tone of the earlier volume. Sombre also was "Bereavement of the Fields," one of the better new poems, written in memory of Archibald Lampman, who died on 10 February 1899."

"The early years of the twentieth century saw a prolific outpouring of prose from Campbell. In addition to numerous pamphlets, he wrote five historical novels and three works of non-fiction. Only two of his novels ever appeared in book form: *Ian of the Orcades* (1906)... and *A Beautiful Rebel* (1909). Another novel was never re-printed after its appearance in *The Christian Guardian*, and two novels still remain only in manuscript form. Two of his works of non-fiction were labours of love: a book about the Great Lakes (1910, reprinted and enlarged 1914), and an account of the Scottish settlements in Eastern Canada (1911). The title of the former is quite a mouthful: *The Beauty, History, Romance, and Mystery of the Canadian Lake Region*. Campbell intersperses these descriptive sketches, which appeared originally in *The Westminster* magazine, with selections of his lake lyrics to give the reader a very personal tour of the region. Subjective, also, is the bias of *The Scotsman in Canada*, which credits Scots with laying the foundation of nearly everything that is admirable in Canada."

In 1914, with war threatening, Campbell published a book of imperialistic verse, *Sagas of a Vaster Britain*. "Many of its seventy poems were recycled from previous collections, patriotic effusions like "England" ("Over the freedom and peace of the world/ Is the flag of England flung"), and some of his best work like "How One Winter Came to the Lake Region". The new poems, like "Life's Ocean" and "The Dream Divine," have the old weaknesses of displeasing sound ("large-mooned waters") and awkward structure ("And of all love's far, dim dawnings of hope unborn/ God's latest are best")." "*Sagas*... was his last book, but each New Year's from 1915 to 1918 he distributed pamphlets of poems relating to World War I."

When Campbell died in 1918, his "popularity died with him. Technically, his work is usually conservative, and his ideas have become unfashionable. His poetry has been compared with the more polished works" of the four major Confederation poets. "In fact," though, as the *DCB* sums up his career, "Campbell worked hard to achieve naturalness, sincerity, and simplicity of expression, rather than polish; he tried to convey universal truths in order to inspire his readers to strive towards their noblest ideals. Within this framework, the artistic merit of many of his poems becomes evident."

Campbell was elected a Fellow of the Royal Society of Canada in 1894. He was declared a Person of National Historic Significance in 1938.

JOHN MCCRAE

Lieutenant Colonel John McCrae, MD (November 30, 1872 – January 28, 1918) was a Canadian poet, physician, author, artist and soldier during World War I, and a surgeon during the Second Battle of Ypres, in Belgium. He is best known for writing the famous war memorial poem "In Flanders Fields". McCrae died of pneumonia near the end of the war.

Biography

McCrae was born in McCrae House in Guelph, Ontario to Lieutenant-Colonel David McCrae and Janet Simpson Eckford; he was the grandson of Scottish immigrants. His brother, Dr. Thomas McCrae, became professor of medicine at Johns Hopkins Medical School in Baltimore and close associate of Sir William Osler.

He attended the Guelph Collegiate Vocational Institute. He was eventually promoted to Captain and commanded the company. He took a year off his studies at the university due to recurring problems with asthma.

Among his papers in the John McCrae House in Guelph is a letter he wrote on July 18, 1893 to Laura Kains while he trained as an artilleryman at the Royal Military College of Canada inKingston, Ontario. "I have a manservant.. Quite a nobby place it is, in fact.. My windows look right out across the bay, and are just near the water's edge; there is a good deal of shipping at present in the port; and the river looks very pretty."

He was a resident master in English and Mathematics in 1894 at the Ontario Agricultural College in Guelph.

He returned to the University of Toronto and completed his B.A. McCrae returned again to study medicine on a scholarship. While attending the university he joined the Zeta Psi Fraternity (Theta Xi chapter; class of 1894) and published his first poems.

While in medical school, he tutored other students to help pay his tuition. Two of his students were among the first woman doctors in Ontario.

He graduated in 1898, and was first a resident house-officer at Toronto General Hospital, and then in 1899, at Johns Hopkins Hospital in Baltimore, Maryland. In 1902, he was appointed resident pathologist at Montreal General

Hospital and later became assistant pathologist to the Royal Victoria Hospital in Montreal. In 1904, he was appointed an associate in medicine at the Royal Victoria Hospital. Later that year, he went to England where he studied for several months and became a member of the Royal College of Physicians.

In 1905, he set up his own practice although he continued to work and lecture at several hospitals. The same year, he was appointed pathologist to the Montreal Foundling and Baby Hospital. In 1908, he was appointed physician to the Royal Alexandra Hospital for Infectious Diseases. In 1910, he accompanied Lord Grey, the Governor General of Canada, on a canoe trip to Hudson Bay to serve as expedition physician.

McCrae served in the artillery during the Second Boer War, and upon his return was appointed professor of pathology at the University of Vermont, where he taught until 1911; he also taught at McGill University in Montreal, Quebec.

McCrae was the co-author, with J. G. Adami, of a medical textbook, *A Text-Book of Pathology for Students of Medicine* (1912; 2nd ed., 1914).

World War I

When Britain declared war on Germany at the start of World War I, Canada, as a Dominion within the British Empire, was at war as well. McCrae was appointed as a field surgeon in the Canadian artillery and was in charge of a field hospital during the Second Battle of Ypres in 1915. McCrae's friend and former student, Lt. Alexis Helmer, was killed in the battle, and his burial inspired the poem, "In Flanders Fields", which was written on May 3, 1915 and first published in the magazine *Punch*.

From June 1, 1915, McCrae was ordered away from the artillery to set up No. 3 Canadian General Hospital at Dannes-Camiers near Boulogne-sur-Mer, northern France. C.L.C. Allinson reported that McCrae "most unmilitarily told [me] what he thought of being transferred to the medicals and being pulled away from his beloved guns. His last words to me were: 'Allinson, all the goddamn doctors in the world will not win this bloody war: what we need is more and more fighting men.'"

"In Flanders Fields" appeared anonymously in *Punch* on December 8, 1915, but in the index to that year McCrae was named as the author. The verses swiftly became one of the most popular poems of the war, used in countless fund-raising campaigns and frequently translated (a Latin version begins *In agro belgico...*). "In Flanders Fields" was also extensively printed in the United States, which was contemplating joining the war, alongside a 'reply' by R. W. Lillard, ("...Fear not that you have died for naught,/ The torch ye threw to us we caught...").

For eight months the hospital operated in Durbar tents (donated by the Begum of Bhopal and shipped from India), but after suffering storms, floods and frosts it was moved in February 1916 into the old Jesuit College in Boulogne-sur-Mer. McCrae, now "a household name, albeit a frequently misspelt one", regarded his sudden fame with some amusement, wishing that "they would get to printing 'In F.F.' correctly: it never is nowadays"; but (writes his biographer) "he was satisfied if the poem enabled men to see where their duty lay."

On January 28, 1918, while still commanding No. 3 Canadian General Hospital (McGill) at Boulogne, McCrae died of pneumonia with "extensive pneumococcus meningitis". He was buried the following day in the Commonwealth War Graves Commission section of Wimereux Cemetery,just a couple of kilometres up the coast from Boulogne, with full military honours. His flag-draped coffin was borne on a gun carriage and the mourners – who included Sir Arthur Currie and many of McCrae's friends and staff – were preceded by McCrae's charger, "Bonfire", with McCrae's boots reversed in the stirrups. McCrae's gravestone is placed flat, as are all the others in the section, because of the unstable sandy soil.

"In Flanders Fields"

A collection of his poetry, *In Flanders Fields and Other Poems* (1918), was published after his death.

'In Flanders Fields'
In Flanders fields the poppies blow
Between the crosses, row on row,
That mark our place; and in the sky
The larks, still bravely singing, fly
Scarce heard amid the guns below.
We are the Dead. Short days ago
We lived, felt dawn, saw sunset glow,
Loved and were loved, and now we lie
In Flanders fields.
Take up our quarrel with the foe:
To you from failing hands we throw
The torch; be yours to hold it high.
If ye break faith with us who die
We shall not sleep, though poppies grow
In Flanders fields.

Though various legends have developed as to the inspiration for the poem, the most commonly held belief is that McCrae wrote "In Flanders Fields" on May 3, 1915, the day after presiding over the funeral and burial of his friend Lieutenant Alex Helmer, who had been killed during the Second Battle of Ypres. The poem was written as he sat upon the back of a medical field ambulance near an advance dressing post at Essex Farm, just north of Ypres. The poppy, which was a central feature of the poem, grew in great numbers in the spoiled earth of the battlefields and cemeteries of Flanders. In 1855, British historian Lord Macaulay, writing about the site of the Battle of Landen (in modern Belgium, 100 miles from Ypres) in 1693, wrote "The next summer the soil, fertilised by twenty thousand corpses, broke forth into millions of poppies. The traveller who, on the road from Saint Tron to Tirlemont, saw that vast sheet of rich scarlet spreading from Landen to Neerwinden, could hardly help fancying that the figurative prediction of the Hebrew prophet was literally accomplished, that the earth was disclosing her blood, and refusing to cover the slain."

The Canadian government has placed a memorial to John McCrae that features "In Flanders Fields" at the site of the dressing station which sits beside the Commonwealth War Graves Commission's Essex Farm Cemetery.

Legacy

McCrae was designated a Person of National Historic Significance in 1946.

McCrae was the great-uncle of former Alberta MP David Kilgour and of Kilgour's sister Geills Turner, who married former Canadian Prime Minister John Turner.

In 1918, Lieut. John Philip Sousa wrote the music to "In Flanders Fields the poppies grow" words by Lieut.-Col John McCrae.

The Cloth Hall of the city of Ieper (*Ypres* in French and English) in Belgium has a permanent war museum called the "In Flanders Fields Museum", named after the poem. There are also a photograph and a short biographical memorial to McCrae in the St George Memorial Church in Ypres. In May 2007, to commemorate the 90th anniversary of the writing of his best-known poem with a two-day literary conference.

Several institutions have been named in McCrae's honour, including John McCrae Public School (in Guelph), John McCrae Public School(part of the York Region District School Board in Markham), John McCrae Senior Public School (in Scarborough) and John McCrae Secondary School (part of the Ottawa-Carleton District School Board in Barrhaven).

A bronze plaque memorial dedicated to Lt. Col. John McCrae was erected by the Guelph Collegiate Vocational Institute.

McCrae House was converted into a museum. The current Canadian War Museum has a gallery for special exhibits, called *The Lieutenant-Colonel John McCrae Gallery*.

A line from his poem ("To you from failing hands...") was painted on the wall of the Montreal Canadiens dressing room at the Forum in Montreal, a blunt reminder to each team that they have much to live up to.

E. J. PRATT

Edwin John Dove Pratt, FRSC (February 4, 1882 – April 26, 1964), who published as E. J. Pratt, was "the leading Canadianpoet of his time." He was a

Canadian poet originally from Newfoundland who lived most of his life in Toronto, Ontario. A three-time winner of the country's Governor General's Award for poetry, he has been called "the foremost Canadian poet of the first half of the century."

Early life

EJ Pratt was born Edwin John Dove Pratt in Western Bay, Newfoundland, on February 4, 1882. He was brought up in a variety of Newfoundland communities as his father John Pratt was posted around the colony as a Methodist minister. John Pratt was originally a lead miner from Old Gang mines in Gunnerside - a village in North Yorkshire, England. In 1850's he became a Methodist pastor and immigrated to Newfoundland and settled down with Fanny Knight, a daughter of Capt. William Chancey Knight. EJ Pratt and his seven siblings were under strict control of their father, who had high expectations of all of them. While John was strict and stern father, who had firm authority with which he ruled his family, Edwin and his siblings got a bit of a break when his father was gone on pastoral rounds, since their mother was very different in temperament from her husband. "Fanny Pratt was easy-going and unpunctilious where John was careful and exacting, lenient and forbearing where he was strict and inflexible, soft hearted where he was hard-headed – she inevitably had a closer, more comradely relationship with the children. Raised in a less rigoristic household than he, she was prepared to take her children for what they were, make allowances for their fallen natures, and generally overlook their innocent iniquities" E.J. Pratt's brother, Calvert Pratt, became a Canadian Senator.

E.J. Pratt graduated from St. John's, Newfoundland's Methodist College in 1901. Like his father he became a candidate for the Methodist ministry, in 1904, and served a three-year probation before entering Victoria College of the University of Toronto. He studied psychology and theology, receiving his BA in 1911 and his Bachelor of Divinity in 1913.

Pratt married fellow Victoria College student Viola Whitney, herself a writer, in 1918, and they had one daughter, Claire Pratt, who also became a writer and poet. Pratt was ordained as a minister, in 1913, and served as an Assistant Minister in Streetsville, Ontario, until 1920. Also in 1913, he joined the University of Toronto as a Lecturer in psychology. As well, he continued to take classes, receiving his PhD in 1917.

Pratt was invited by Pelham Edgar in 1920 to switch to the University's faculty of English, where he became a professor in 1930 and a Senior Professor in 1938. He taughtEnglish literature at Victoria College until his retirement in 1953. He served as Literary Adviser to the college literary journal, *Acta Victoriana*. "As a professor, Pratt published a number of articles, reviews, and introductions (including those to four Shakespeare plays), and edited Thomas Hardy's *Under the greenwood tree* (1937)."

Writing

Pratt's first published poem was "A Poem on the May examinations," printed in *Acta Victoriana* in 1909 when he was a student. In 1917 he privately published a long poem,*Rachel: A Sea Story of Newfoundland*. He then spent two years working on a verse drama, *Clay*, which he ended by burning (except for one copy which Mrs. Pratt managed to save).

It was only in 1923 that Pratt's first commercial poetry collection, *Newfoundland Verse*, was released. It contains "A Fragment of a Story," the only piece of *Clay* that Pratt ever published, and the conclusion to *Rachel.* "*Newfoundland verse* (1923), is frequently archaic in diction, and reflects a pietistic and sometimes preciously lyrical sensibility of late-Romantic derivation, characteristics that may account for Pratt's reprinting less than half these poems in his *Collected poems* (1958). The most genuine feeling is expressed in humorous and sympathetic portraits of Newfoundland characters, and in the creation of an elegiac mood in poems concerning sea tragedies or Great War losses. The sea, which on the one hand provides 'the bread of life' and on the other represents 'the waters of death' ('Newfoundland'), is a central element as setting, subject, and creator of mood."

With illustrations by Group of Seven member Frederick Varley, *Newfoundland Verse* proved to be Pratt's "breakthrough collection." He would publish 18 more books of poetry in his lifetime. "Recognition came with the narrative poems *The Witches' Brew* (1925), *Titans* (1926), and *The Roosevelt and the Antinoe* (1930), and though he published a substantial body of lyric verse, it is as a narrative poet that Pratt is remembered."

"Pratt's poetry frequently reflects his Newfoundland background, though specific references to it appear in relatively few poems, mostly in *Newfoundland Verse*," says *The Canadian Encyclopaedia*. "But the sea and maritime life are central to many of his poems, both short (*e.g.*, "Erosion," "Sea-Gulls," "Silences") and long, such as "The Cachalot" (1926), describing duels between a whale and its foes, a giant squid and a whaling ship and crew; *The Roosevelt and the Antinoe* (1930), recounting the heroic rescue of the crew of a sinking freighter in a winter hurricane; *The Titanic* (1935), an ironic retelling of a well-known marine tragedy; and *Behind the Log* (1947), the dramatic story of the North Atlantic convoys during World War II."

Another constant motif in Pratt's writing was evolution. "Pratt's work is filled with images of primitive nature and evolutionary history," wrote literary critic Peter Buitenhuis. "It seemed instinctive to him to write of molluscs, of cetacean and cephalopod, of Java and Piltdown Man. The evolutionary process early became and always remained the central metaphor of Pratt's work." He added that evolution provided Pratt "the solid framework within which he could achieve an epic style," and also "gave him the themes for his best lyrics" (such as his much-anthologized "From Stone to Steel," from 1932's *Many Moods*.)

Pratt founded *Canadian Poetry Magazine* in 1935, and served as its first editor until 1943. He published 10 poems in the 1936 "milestone selection of modernist verse," *New Provinces*, edited by F.R. Scott.

In 1937, with war on the horizon, Pratt wrote an anti-war poem, "The Fable of the Goats," which became the title poem of his next volume. *The Fable of the Goats and Other Poems*, which included his classic free-verse poem "Silences," won him his first Governor General's Award.

Pratt returned to Canadian history in 1940 to write *Brébeuf and his Brethren*, a blank-verse epic on the mission of Jean de Brébeuf and his seven fellow Jesuits, the North American Martyrs, to the Hurons in the 17th century; their founding of Sainte-Marie-among-the-Hurons; and their eventual martyrdom by the Iroquois. "Pratt's research-oriented methodology is made clear in the precise diction and detailed, documentary-style recounting of events and observation in this, his first attempt to write a national epic; but in his ethnocentrism Pratt presents the Jesuit priests as an enclave of civilization beleaguered by savages." Canadian literary critic Northrop Frye has said that *Brébeuf* expresses "the central tragic theme of the Canadian imagination."

Expounding on that theme in 1943, in a review essay of A.J.M. Smith's anthology *The Book of Canadian Poetry*, Frye stated that, in Canadian poetry:

The unconscious horror of nature and the subconscious horrors of the mind thus coincide: this amalgamation is the basis of symbolism on which nearly all Pratt's poetry is founded. The fumbling and clumsy monsters of his "Pliocene Armageddon," who are simply incarnate wills to mutual destruction, are the same monsters that beget Nazism and inspire The Fable of the Goats; and in the fine "Silences," which Mr. Smith includes, civilized life is seen geologically as merely one clock-tick in eons of ferocity. The waste of life in the death of the Cachalot and the waste of courage and sanctity in the killing of the Jesuit missionaries are tragedies of a unique kind in modern poetry: like the tragedy of Job, they seem to move upward to a vision of a monstrous Leviathan, a power of chaotic nihilism which is "king over all the children of pride."

By the time *Brébeuf* was published the war had begun; and "in his next four volumes, Pratt returned to themes of patriotism and violence. Sea poetry merges with war poetry in*Dunkirk* (1941), which recounts the epic rescue of British forces while also emphasizing its democratic nature.... Language plays a pivotal role as Churchill's call inspires the miraculous deliverance. The title poem in *Still Life and Other Verse* (1943) satirizes poets who ignore the destruction, the still life, all about them in wartime.... Other poems include 'The Radio in the Ivory Tower,' which shows isolation from world events to be impossible... 'The Submarine,' which highlights the atavism of modern warfare by treating the submarine as a shark; and 'Come Away, Death,' which personifies death to show its new horrors in modern times."

Still Life and Other Verse included another poem, "The Truant," which Frye later called "the greatest poem in Canadian literature." In "The Truant," a "somewhat comic deity, who speaks in evolutionary terms and metaphors, has man hauled before him to be punished for messing up the grand evolving scheme of things. Cheeky *genus homo*, instead of being duly cowed by the Great Panjandrum, points out that He is largely man's invention in any case." Says Buitenhuis: "The poem is too simplistic to be convincing, but is essential reading for anyone who seeks to understand Pratt's thought."

Pratt's next book, "*They are Returning* (1945) celebrates the anticipated end of the war, but also introduces one of the first treatments in literature of the concentration camps. And retrospectively, *Behind the Log* (1947) commemorates the wartime role of the Royal Canadian Navy and the merchant marine."

By 1952, Frye was calling Pratt one of "Canada's two leading poets" (the other being Earle Birney). In that year Pratt published *Towards the Last Spike*, his final epic, on the building of Canada's first transcontinental railroad, the Canadian Pacific Railway. "Presenting an anglo/central-Canadian perspective, the poem interweaves the political battles between Sir John A. Macdonald and Edward Blake with the labourers' physical battles against mountains, mud, and the Laurentian Shield. In a metaphorical method typical of his style, Pratt characterizes the Shield as a prehistoric lizard rudely aroused from its sleep by the railroad builders' dynamite."

Pratt's reputation as a major poet rests on his longer narrative poems, "many of which show him as a mythologizer of the Canadian male experience; but a number of shorter philosophical works also command recognition. 'From stone to steel' asserts the necessity for redemptive suffering arising from the failure of humanity's spiritual evolution to keep pace without physical evolution and cultural achievements; 'Come away, death' is a complexly allusive account of the way the once-articulate and ceremonial human response to death was rendered inarticulate by the primitive violence of a sophisticated bomb; and 'The truant' dramatically presents a confrontation in a thoroughly patriarchal cosmos between the fiercely independent 'little genus homo' and a totalitarian mechanistic power, 'the great Panjandrum'.

Pratt's choices of forms and metrics were conservative for his time; but his diction was experimental, reflecting in its specificity and its frequent technicality both his belief in the poetic power of the accurate and concrete that led him into assiduous research processes, and his view that one of the poet's tasks is to bridge the gap between the two branches of human pursuit: the scientific and artistic."

The Canadian Encyclopaedia adds of Pratt: "A major poet, he is, nevertheless, an isolated figure, belonging to no school or movement and directly influencing few other poets of his time."

Recognition

Pratt won Canada's top poetry prize, the Governor General's Award, three times: in 1937 for *The Fable of the Goats and other Poems*; in 1940 for *Brébeuf and his Brethren*; and in 1952, for *Towards the Last Spike*.

He was elected to the Royal Society of Canada in 1930, and was awarded the Society's Lorne Pierce Medal in 1940. In 1946, he was made a Companion of the Order of St. Michael and St. George by King George VI.

He was awarded a Canada Council Medal for distinction in literature in 1961.

He was designated a Person of National Historic Significance in 1975.

The University of Toronto's Victoria University library currently bears his name, as do the University's E.J. Pratt Medal and Prize for poetry. Winners of the award includeMargaret Atwood in 1961 and Michael Ondaatje in 1966.

The E. J. Pratt Chair in Canadian Literature was created in his name by the University of Toronto in 2003. The chair has been held since its founding by George Elliot Clarke.

CHARLES G. D. ROBERTS

Sir Charles George Douglas Roberts, KCMG FRSC (January 10, 1860 – November 26, 1943) was a Canadian poet and prose writer who is known as the Father of Canadian Poetry. He was "almost the first Canadian author to obtain worldwide reputation and influence; he was also a tireless promoter and encourager of Canadian literature.... He published numerous works on Canadian exploration and natural history, verse, travel books, and fiction." "At his death he was regarded as Canada's leading man of letters."

Besides his own body of work, Roberts is also called the "Father of Canadian Poetry" because he served as an inspiration and a source of assistance for other Canadian poets of his time.

Roberts, his cousin Bliss Carman, Archibald Lampman and Duncan Campbell Scott are known as the Confederation Poets.

Life

Roberts was born in Douglas, New Brunswick in 1860, the eldest child of Emma Wetmore Bliss and Rev. George Goodridge Roberts (an Anglican priest). Rev. Roberts was rector of Fredericton and canon of Christ Church Cathedral, New Brunswick. Charles's brother Theodore Goodridge Roberts and sister, Jane Elizabeth Gostwycke Roberts, would also become authors.

Between the ages of 8 months and 14 years, Roberts was raised in the parish of Westcock, New Brunswick, near Sackville, by the Tantramar Marshes. He was homeschooled, "mostly by his father, who was proficient in Greek, Latin and French." He published his first writing, three articles in *The Colonial Farmer,* at 12 years of age.

After the family moved to Fredericton in 1873, Roberts attended Fredericton Collegiate School from 1874 to 1876, and then the University of New Brunswick (UNB), earning his B.A. in 1879 and M.A. in 1881. At the Collegiate School he came under the influence of headmaster George Robert Parkin, who gave him a love of classical literature and introduced him to the poetry of Dante Gabriel Rossetti and Algernon Charles Swinburne.

Roberts was principal of Chatham High School in Chatham, New Brunswick, from 1879 to 1881, and of York Street School in Fredericton from 1881 to 1883. In Chatham he met and befriended Edmund Collins, editor of the Chatham *Star* and the future biographer of Sir John A. Macdonald.

Early Canadian career

Roberts first published poetry in the *Canadian Illustrated News* of March 30, 1878, and by 1879 he had placed two poems in the prestigious American magazine, *Scribner's*.

In 1880 Roberts published his first book of poetry, *Orion and Other Poems*. Thanks in part to his industry in sending out complimentary review copies, there were many positive reviews. *Rose-Belford's Canadian Monthly* proclaimed: "Here is a writer whose power and originality it is impossible to deny — here is a book of which any literature might be proud." The *Montreal Gazette* predicted that Roberts would "confer merited fame on himself and lasting honour on his country." As well, "several American periodicals reviewed it favourably, including the *New York Independent*, which described it as 'a little book of choice things, with the indifferent things well weeded out.'"

On December 29, 1880, Roberts married Mary Fenety, who would bear him five children.

The biography by Roberts's friend Edmund Collins, *The Life and Times of Sir John A. Macdonald*, was published in 1883. The book was a huge success, going through eight printings. It contained a long chapter on "Thought and Literature in Canada," which devoted 15 pages to Roberts, quoting liberally from *Orion*. "Beyond any comparison," Collins declared, "our greatest Canadian poet is Mr. Charles G.D. Roberts." "Edmund Collins is probably responsible for the early acceptance of Charles G.D. Roberts as Canada's foremost poet."

From 1883 to 1884 Roberts was in Toronto, Ontario, working as the editor of Goldwin Smith's short-lived literary magazine, *The Week*. "Roberts lasted only five months at*The Week* before resigning in frustration from overwork and clashes with Smith."

In 1885 Roberts became a professor at the University of King's College in Windsor, Nova Scotia. In 1886, his second book, *In Divers Tones*, was published by a Boston publisher. "Over the next six years, in addition to his academic duties, Roberts published more than thirty poems in numerous American periodicals, but mostly in *The Independent* while Bliss Carman was on its editorial staff. During the same period, he published almost an equal number of stories, primarily for juvenile readers, in periodicals like *The Youth's Companion*. He also edited *Poems of Wild Life* (1888), completed a 270-page *Canadian Guide Book* (1891), wrote about a dozen articles on a variety of topics, and gave lectures in various centres from Halifax to New York."

Roberts was asked to edit the anthology, *Songs of the Great Dominion*, but that position eventually went to W.D. Lighthall. Lighthall included a generous selection of Roberts's work, and echoed Collins's assessment of six years earlier: "The foremost name in Canadian song at the present day is that of Charles George Douglas Roberts."

Roberts resigned from King's College in 1895, when his request for a leave of absence was turned down. Determined to make a living from his pen, in 1896 "he published his first novel, *The Forge in the Forest*... his fourth collection of poetry, *The Book of the Native*... his first book of nature-stories, *Earth's Enigmas*... and a book of adventure stories for boys, *Around the Campfire*."

Move to New York

"Determining to work free-lance, Roberts separated from his wife, daughter, and sons in 1897, leaving Canada for New York City." During 1897 and 1898 he worked for *The Illustrated American* as an associate editor.

In New York Roberts wrote in many different genres, but found that "his most successful prose genre was the animal story, in which he drew upon his early experience in the wilds of the Maritimes. He published over a dozen such volumes between *Earth's Enigmas* (1896) and *Eyes of the Wilderness* (1933).... Roberts is remembered for creating in the animal story, along with Ernest Thompson Seton, the one native Canadian art form."

Roberts also wrote historical romances and novels. "*Barbara Ladd* (1902) begins with a girl escaping from an uncongenial aunt in New England in 1769; it sold 80,000 copies in the US alone." He also wrote descriptive text for guide books, such as *Picturesque Canada* and *The Land of Evangeline and Gateways Thither* for Nova Scotia's Dominion Atlantic Railway.

Roberts famously became involved in a literary debate known as the nature fakers controversy after John Burroughs denounced his popular animal stories, and those of other writers, in a 1903 article for *Atlantic Monthly*. The controversy lasted for nearly six years and included important American environmental and political figures of the day, including President Theodore Roosevelt.

Europe and return to Canada

In 1907 Roberts moved to Europe. First living in Paris, he moved to Munich in 1910, and in 1912 to London, where he lived until 1925. During World War I he enlisted with the British Army as a trooper, eventually becoming a captain and a cadet trainer in England. After the war he joined the Canadian War Records

Office in London. Roberts returned to Canada in 1925 which "led to a renewed production of verse." During the late 1920s he was a member of the Halifax literary and social set, The Song Fishermen.

He married his second wife Joan Montgomery on October 28, 1943, at the age of 83, but became ill and died shortly thereafter in Toronto. The funeral was held in Toronto, but his ashes were returned to Fredericton, where he was interred in Forest Hill Cemetery.

Poetry

Orion and Other Poems

Roberts's first book, *Orion and Other Poems* (1880), was a vanity book for which he had to "pay an advance of $300, most of which he borrowed from George E. Fenety, theQueen's Printer for New Brunswick, soon to become his father-in-law." *Orion* was "a collection of juvenilia, written while the poet was still a teenager."

Critic Desmond Pacey wrote in 1958 that "when we remind ourselves that it was published when the poet was twenty... we realize that it is a remarkable performance. It is imitative, naively romantic, defective in diction, the poetry of books rather than life itself, but it is facile, clever, and occasionally distinctly beautiful.... It is the work of an apprentice, who is quite frankly serving under a sequence of masters from whom he hopes to learn his art."

In Divers Tones

The title of Roberts's second book, *In Divers Tones*, "aptly describes the hodgepodge of its contents. The selections vary greatly, not only in style and subject matter, but also in quality.... Among those written between 1883 and 1886... there is evidence of a maturing talent. In fact, it might be argued that at least three of these poems, 'The Tantramar Revisited,' 'The Sower,' and 'The Potato Harvest," were never surpassed by any of his subsequent verse."

Songs of the Common Day

By the time of *Songs of the Common Day, and Ave* (1893), Roberts "had reached the height of his poetic powers.... It is the sonnet sequence of *Songs of the Common Day*that has established Roberts' reputation as a landscape poet.... Evidence of the Tantramar setting occurs in lines like "How sombre slope these acres to the sea' ('The Furrow"), 'These marshes pale and meadows by the sea' ('The Salt Flats'), and 'My fields of Tantramar in summer-time' ('The Pea-Fields'). The descriptions are full of evocative details."

Middle period

After Roberts turned to free-lance writing in 1895, "Financial pressure forced him to turn his main attention to fiction." He published two more books of poetry by 1898, but managed only two more in the following 30 years.

"As their titles often indicate, the numerous seasonal poems in *The Book of the Native* (1897) were written with an eye on the monthly requirements of the magazines: 'The Brook in February,' 'An April Adoration,' 'July,' and 'An August Woodroad.' Roberts "is generally at his best in the poems in which he depicts these seasonal stages of nature with the palette of a realistic landscape painter." However, the book also "signalled a shift in his poetic oeuvre away from descriptive, technically tight Romantic verses to more mystical lyrics."

"Most of the nature poetry in Roberts's *New York Nocturnes and Other Poems* (1898) was written before he moved to New York. It belongs to a period of upheaval, desperation and overwork, which may at least partly account for its disappointing slackness.... Even 'The Solitary Woodsman,' much anthologized and frequently praised, is a series of unremarkable images made tedious by fifty-two lines of irritating rhythm and rhyme.... Roberts seldom looks at New York with the eye of a painter, and never captures its essence with the effectiveness he displays in his best pictures of rural landscape.... Instead of turning an enquiring eye upon urban conditions, he is inclined to retreat from "'he city's fume and stress' and 'clamour' ('The Ideal').".

The first and title section of *The Book of the Rose* (1903) was a collection of love poetry. "Roberts handling of the symbol sounds artificial at best and sometimes downright fatuous.... Although most of the poems in the second section are unimpressive, there are a few exceptions. "Heat in the City," noteworthy for being the best poem he ever wrote about city life, effectively evokes the distress and despair of the tenement-dwellers.... The final poem in the book, "The Aim," is remarkable for its frank self-analysis."

"*New Poems*, a slim volume published in 1919, shows the drop in both the quantity and quality of Roberts' poetry during his European years. At least half of the pieces had been written before he left America, some as early as 1903."

Later poems

Roberts's "return to Canada in 1925 led to a renewed production of verse with *The Vagrant of Time* (1927) and *The Iceberg and Other Poems* (1934)." Literary criticDesmond Pacey calls this period "the Indian summer of his poetic career."

"Among the best of the new poems" in *The Vagrant of Time* "is the one with this inspired opening line: 'Spring breaks in foam along the blackthorn bough.' In another love poem, 'In the Night Watches,' written in 1926, his command of free verse is natural and unstrained, unlike the laboured language and forced rhymes of his earlier love poetry. Its synthesis of lonely wilderness setting with feelings of separation and longing is harmonious and poignant." "Most critics rank 'The Iceberg' (265 lines), the title poem of the new collection" published in 1934, "as one of Roberts' outstanding achievements. It is almost as ambitious as 'Ave!' in conception; its cold, unemotional images are as apt and precise in their detached way as the warmly-remembered descriptions in 'Tantramar Revisited.'

Animal Stories

The Canadian Encyclopaedia says that "Roberts is remembered for creating in the animal story, along with Ernest Thompson Seton, the one native Canadian art form." A typical Roberts animal story is "The Truce".

In his introduction to *The Kindred of the Wild* (1902), Roberts called the animal story "a potent emancipator. It frees us for a little from the world of shop-worn utilities, and from the mean tenement of self of which we do well to grow weary. It helps us to return to nature, without requiring that we at the same time return to barbarism. It leads us back to the old kinship of earth, without asking us to relinquish by way of toll any part of the wisdom of the ages, any fine essential of the 'large result of time.' (Kindred 28)"

Critical interest in Roberts's animal stories "emerged in the 1960s and 70s in the growth of what we now know as Canadian Literary Studies.... But these critics tended as a group to see in the animal stories a masked reference to Canadian nationhood: James Polk 'attempts to subsume the animal genre entirely within the identity crisis of an emerging nation [...seeing] the sympathetic stance of Seton and Roberts towards the sometimes brutal fate of the "lives of the hunted" as a larger political allegory for Canada's "victim" status as an American satellite. (Sandlos 74)'"

Margaret Atwood devotes a chapter of her 1971 critical study *Survival: A Thematic Guide to Canadian Literature* to animal stories, where she states the same thesis: "*the stories are told from the point of view of the animal*. That's the key: English animal stories are about the 'social relations,' American ones are about people killing animals; Canadian ones are about animals being killed, as felt emotionally from inside the fur and feathers. (qtd. in Sandlos 74; *emphasis in original*)."

Recognition

Charles G. D Roberts was elected a Fellow of the Royal Society of Canada in 1893.

Roberts was elected to the United States National Institute of Arts and Letters in 1898.

He was awarded an honorary LLD from UNB in 1906, and an honorary doctorate from Mount Allison University in 1942.

For his contributions to Canadian literature, Roberts was awarded the Royal Society of Canada's first Lorne Pierce Medal in 1926. On June 3, 1935, Roberts was one of three Canadians on King George V's honour list to receive a knighthood (Knight Commander of the Order of St. Michael and St. George). Roberts was honoured by a sculpture erected in 1947 on the UNB campus, portraying him with Bliss Carman and fellow poet Francis Joseph Sherman.

"In the 1980s — a hundred years after his first volumes appeared — a major Roberts revival took place, producing monographs, a complete edition of his poems, a new biography, a collection of his letters, etc. A Roberts Symposium at Mount Allison University (1982) and another at the University of Ottawa (1983) included several scholarly reappraisals of his poetry." Roberts was declared a Person of National Historic Significance in 1945, and a monument to him was erected by the Historic Sites and Monuments Board of Canada in Westcock in 2005.

Publications

Poetry

- *Orion, and Other Poems*. Philadelphia: J.B. Lippincott, 1880.
- *In Divers Tones*. (Boston: Lothrop, 1886).
- *AVE! An Ode for the Shelley Centenary*. Toronto: Williamson, 1892.
- *Songs of the Common Day and, AVE! An Ode for the Shelley Aentenary*. Toronto: William Briggs, 1893. Montreal: C.W. Coates, 1893. London: Longman's Green, 1893.
- *The Book of the Native*. (Toronto: Copp Clark, 1896) (Boston: Lamson, Wolfe, 1896).
- *New York Nocturnes and Other Poems*. (Boston: Lamson Wolffe, 1898).
- *Poems*. New York: Silver, Burdett, 1901.
- *The Book of the Rose*. (Toronto: Copp, Clark, 1903) (Boston: L.C. Page, 1903).
- *New Poems*. (London: Constable, 1919).
- *The Sweet o' the Year and Other Poems*. (Toronto: Ryerson, 1925).
- *The Vagrant of Time*. (Toronto: Ryerson, 1927).
- *The Iceberg and Other Poems*. (Toronto: Ryerson, 1934).
- *Selected Poems of Sir Charles G.D. Roberts*. Toronto: Ryerson, 1936.
- *Flying Colours.* Miami: Granger Books, 1942. Toronto: Ryerson P, 1942.
- *Selected Poems of Charles G.D. Roberts.* Desmond Pacey ed. Toronto: Ryerson, 1955.
- *Selected Poetry and Critical Prose.* W.J. Keith ed. Toronto: U of Toronto P, 1974.
- *Collected Poems of Sir Charles G.D. Roberts.* Desmond Pacey and Graham Adams, ed. Wolfville, NS: Wombat P, 1985.

Fiction

- *The Raid from Beauséjour and How the Carter Boys Lifted the Mortgage*.

New York, Cincinnati: Hunt and Eaton, Cranston and Curts, 1894. Toronto: Musson, 1900. – 2 novelettes

- *Reube Dare's Shad Boat: a tale of the tide country.* New York, Cincinnati: Hunt and Eaton, Cranston and Curts, 1895. – novelette
- *Around the Campfire.* Toronto: Musson Book Co., 1896. Toronto: William Briggs, 1896. New York: Thomas Y. Crowell and Co., 1896.
- *Earth's Enigmas*. Boston: Lamson, Wolffe, 1896.
- *The Forge in the Forest*. Boston: Lamson, Wolffe, 1896. New York: Grosset and Dunlap, 1896. Toronto: William Briggs, 1897.
- *By the Marshes of Minas.* Boston, New York: Silver, Burdett, 1900.
- *A Sister to Evangeline.* Boston, New York: Silver, Burdett, 1900.
- *The Feet of the Furtive*. London: Ward, Lock, 1900.
- *The Heart of the Ancient Wood.* Toronto: Copp Clark, 1900.
- *The Haunters of the Silences*. London: Thomas Nelson, 1900.
- *Barbara Ladd*. Boston: L.C. Page, 1902. New York: Grosset and Dunlap, 1902. – novel set in New York and Connecticut
- *The Kindred of the Wild* Boston: L.C. Page, 1902.
- *The Prisoner of Mademoiselle*. Boston: L.C. Page, 1904.
- *The Watchers of the Trails*. Toronto: Copp Clark, 1904.
- *Red Fox*. Boston: L. C. Page/Toronto: Copp Clark, 1905. – short story
- *The Watchers of the Campfire.* Boston: L.C. Page, 1906.
- *The Heart That Knows*. Boston: L.C. Page, 1906. Toronto: Copp, Clark, 1906.
- *The Cruise of the Yacht "Dido".* Boston: L.C. Page, 1906.
- *The Little People of the Sycamore*. Charles Livingston Bull illus. Boston: L.C. Page, 1906.
- *The Return to the Trails.* Charles Livingston Bull illus. Boston: L.C. Page, 1906.
- *In the Deep of the Snow*. Toronto: Musson Book Co., 1907. New York: T.Y. Crowell, 1907.
- *The Young Acadian*. Boston: L.C. Page, 1907.
- *The Haunters of the Silences. Boston: L.C. Page, 1907.*
- *Kings in Exile*. London: Ward, Lock, 1908. – novel
- *The House in the Water.* Boston: L. C. Page/London: Ward, Lock, 1908.
- *The Backwoodsmen. New York: Macmillan, 1909.*
- *More Kindred of the Wild.* London: Ward, Lock, 1911.
- *Neighbours Unknown*. London: Ward, Lock, 1910. New York: Macmillian, 1911. – short stories
- *Babes of the Wild.* Warwick Reynolds illus. London: Cassell, 1912.
- *Children of the Wild.* Paul Bramson illus. New York: Macmillan, 1913.
- *Hoof and Claw*. London: Ward, Lock, and Co., 1913. New York: Macmillan, 1914. – short stories

- *The Secret Trails.* New York: Macmillan, 1916.
- *The Ledge on Bald Face.* London: Ward, Lock, and Co., 1918.
- *In the Morning of Time*. London: Hutchinson, 1919. New York: Frederick A. Stokes, c1919.
- *The Secret Trails*. New York: Macmillan, 1921. – short stories
- *Wisdom of the Wilderness*. London, Toronto: J.M. Dent, 1922. New York: Macmillan, 1923.
- *They Who Walk in the Wilds.* New York: Macmillan, 1924.
- *Further Animal Stories* (1936) – short stories
- *When Twilight Falls on the Stump Lots* (1945) – short stories
- *The Last Barrier and Other Stories.* Alec Lucas ed. Toronto: McClelland and Stewart, 1958.
- *The Vagrants of the Barren and Other Stories of Charles G.D. Roberts.* Martin Ware ed. Ottawa: Tecumseh, 1992.

Non-fiction

- *A History of Canada.* Toronto: G.N. Morang, 1898.
- *The Canadian Guide-Book.* New York: D. Appleton, 1898.
- *Discoveries and Explorations in the Century. London, Philadelphia: Linscott, 1904.*
- *Canada in Flanders* (1918) – non-fiction

Edited

- *Poems of Wild Life.* London: W. Scott, 1888.
- *Canada Speaks of Britain and Other Poems of the War*. Toronto: Ryerson, 1941.

Papers

- *Sir Charles G. D. Roberts papers.* Charles George Douglas Roberts; Linda Dumbleton; Rose Mary Gibson. Kingston: Queen's University Archives, {c.1983}.
- *The Collected Letters of Sir Charles G.D. Roberts.* Fredericton, NB: Goose Lane, 1989.

W.W.E. ROSS

William Wrightson Eustace Ross (June 14, 1894 – August 26, 1966) was a Canadian geophysicist and poet. He was the first published poet in Canada to write Imagist poetry, and later the first to write surrealist verse, both of which have led some to call him "the first modern Canadian poet."

Life

Ross was born in Peterborough, Ontario, to Ralph and Nellie Creighton

Ross. He grew up in Pembroke, Ontario. He studied geophysics at the University of Toronto.,supporting his studies with summer work on geological surveys in Northern Ontario.

Ross served with the Canadian Expeditionary Force in World War I as a private in the signal corps. On his return, he worked until his retirement as a geophysicist at the Dominion Magnetic Observatory at Agincourt, Ontario (now part of Toronto). On June 3, 1924, he married Mary Lowrey, "the well-known journalist." They had two children, Mary Loretto and Nancy Helen. The family bought a house on Delaware Ave. in Toronto, where Ross lived for the rest of his life.

Ross began writing poetry in or around 1923. His earliest works "are written in free verse and reflect a knowledge of both imagism and Japanese poetry." In 1925 Ross developed the 'laconic' as a distinctly Canadian verse form, "one that would be 'native' and yet not 'free verse,' one that would be unrhymed and yet definitely a 'form.'"

One night in April 1928, after an evening's discussion of Canadian nationalism among friends, Ross wrote "practically all" of his most famous work, "North." "It never 'clicked' so well before or since as that night in 1928," he later wrote. "North" was a series of laconics based on Ross's memories of his summers in Northern Ontario years earlier. Ross submitted some of its poems to Harriet Moore's Chicago magazine *Poetry* and to Marianne Moore's magazine *The Dial*, and was published in both.

In 1930 Ross published a book of *Laconics,* privately and only under the initials 'E.R.'. ("North" was the first section of the book.) Ross mailed his own review copies to periodicals that he respected. He received "an admiring review by Marianne Moore (*Poetry* 35, 1931)",

Ross's next book, in 1932, was a volume of *Sonnets*. It was meant as a companion volume to *Laconics*, the subject matter of the sonnets "mirroring the subject matter and imagery of the modernist poems" in the earlier book. Once again, the book was published privately, and signed only 'E.R.'. "After *Sonnets*, a work that he considered a failed book, Ross's disdain for publication increased."

In the 1930s Ross translated work by the surrealist Max Jacob. He also wrote prose poems influenced by Jacob and Franz Kafka, some of which were published in *New Directions in Prose and Poetry for 1937*. "His work in this period incorporates elements of automatic writing, transcendentalism, mysticism, and archetypal imagery." The above were the first published prose poems written in Canada.

Ralph Gustafson included Ross's work in his 1942 *Anthology of Canadian Verse*, bringing his works before a large reading public in Canada for the first time. By then, though, Ross had ceased to write new poetry. Through the next two decades he "revised and polished poems begun much earlier and experimented with some new poetry." He "confined his often brilliant verse-parodies to his letters and with the exception of Margaret Avison generally disliked the younger poets beginning to publish in the 'fifties.

In 1944 Ross wrote an article in the *Canadian Forum*, "On Canadian Poetry," as part of the ongoing nationalist/cosmopolitan debate, calling for a poetry that is "distinctly located" in a geographic "locale."

Ross contributed poems "sporadically to literary periodicals and anthologies until his death in 1966. Most of what he published after 1930 was solicited by anthologists or magazine editors. Critic Barry Callaghan suggests that Ross wrote 'only when strenuously urged by an anthologist or literature student.'" Urging by poet Raymond Sousterresulted in previously unpublished poetry in the mimeographed collection *Experiment 1923-29*, published in 1956 by Souster's Contact Press, at which time Ross began to be recognized as Canada's first Imagist poet. However, "Ross felt this collection misrepresented him in its emphasis on his imagist work." Later encouragement by Callaghan led to Ross's composing new poetry included in the posthumously published *Shapes and Sounds* (1968). *Shapes and sounds* is a selection of Ross's poems edited by Souster and John Robert Colombo, with a memoir by Callaghan.

Ross died of cancer in 1966.

Writing

"Though never widely read outside academic circles... Ross had clearly thought out his attitudes towards poetry early on and diverged little from his initial position." "He objected to both difficult and ornate verse and found the conventional romanticism of Canada's Confederation poets particularly unappealing." He "was disapprovingly detached from what was happening in Canadian poetry in general and disliked Pratt's 'pretty expert word-juggling and rhyming' in particular.... He felt more enthusiastic about poems by Pickthall, Knister and Patrick Anderson than Pratt, and Tom MacInnes 'quite hypnotized' him." His chief American influences were E.E. Cummings and Marianne Moore.

Ross distrusted the cosmopolitanism of the Montreal Group. In "On Canadian Poetry" he "wrote that a poet is inevitably associated with a place and that the cosmopolitan doctrine as espoused by Smith was not tenable. 'I have a horrid suspicion,' he said, 'that the "Cosmopolis" will turn out to be not "world city" in general but one of London, New York, [or] Paris.'"

Laconics

His first book,*Laconics,* "ratified Ross's claim as an innovative poetic craftsman by establishing an aesthetic bridgehead on the modern world, and the conditions under which poetry could be written in order to be reconciled with the modern world." It "collects the imagist poems Ross is best known for:" "The Fish," "The Diver," "The Dawn; the Birds," "The Snake Trying,"

"Gum," "The Creek," "The Walk": mostly, the poems of "North" that he had written that one night in April 1928.

"In Ross's spare... narrow poems, the enquiring spirit of the New World seeks release from old sentiments, customs, and poetic conventions.... Ross seeks 'something of the sharper tang of Canada' in the surface reflections and dark shadows of pine-surrounded lakes, where reality is recognized as profound and mysterious. The modern poet of the New World seeks illumination by objectifying the ordinary sensations of sight and sound. His explorations of the land of lake and loon thereby serve as metaphors for illumination and rejuvenation."

"In an early draft for his 'Introduction' to *The Penguin Book of Canadian Verse* (1958), Ralph Gustafson explained what these poems meant to him: 'A modern awareness, with its concomitant experimentation with technique, a reduction of Canada, of the quality of Canada, were entering into Canadian verse. W.W.E. Ross' "northern" poems were written almost entirely in one night in April 1928.... They captured precisely, with wonder and freshness, a distinct Canada."

It has been said that the poems of "North" "present the northern Ontario landscape in the stark manner of the Group of Seven. His strongest work is undoubtedly this early imagist-oriented poetry, work that derives its strengths from his restrained, skeptical personality, from his scientist's preference for objective, factual material, and from his affection for the Canadian wilderness landscape." This is poetry which, as he wrote in 'On National Poetry' (*Canadian Forum*, 1944), is 'distinctly located' in a geographic 'locale.'

Sonnets

"Exhilarated by the knowledge that he had succeeded" in *Laconics* — "a knowledge that came to him from inner self-realization rather than popular success" — Ross next "turned his new-found strength, in *Sonnets*, to the conditions under which poetry had been written in the past. His purpose was... to reduce tradition to the structures of the method that had tested out in *Laconics*."

The book "reveals a lesser-known side of Ross — the classicist and traditional metricist concerned not only with factual reality but also with spiritual truth." *Sonnets* was meant to be more overtly philosophical than *Laconics* — which Ross thought would be better suited by the traditional form's longer lines — but ultimately he considered the book an experiment that failed:

The general idea was to employ the 'clean' language of free verse without the lack of rhythm or pattern which offended me in all the latter except some of Pound etc. As regards *Sonnets* I had the notion that longer lines were needed to express ideas adequately and the sonnet form seemed suited to this purpose. I was ditched by my inability to carry over into them — the prestige of the models being so great — the aforesaid 'cleanness.'

Legacy

"Ross's private and somewhat trenchant nature, together with his diffidence towards publishing and the publicly lived literary life, caused him to be little known during his lifetime except to fellow poets." He "was never fully accepted into the company of the 'moderns' — Livesay, Smith, Gustafson and so forth — because unlike them he was not interested in propagating the future any more than he was interested in perpetuating the past.... Ross was well-read in Canadian, European and American poetry, yet he cut his own work free from any direction that this reading might have suggested for his verse. His poetry is unique in its timelessness."

"Ross's writing became of special importance in the 1950s and 1960s when new generations of Canadian poets sought their precursors in the modernist goals of restraint, precision, organic rhythm, and the factual image."

DUNCAN CAMPBELL SCOTT

Duncan Campbell Scott (August 2, 1862 – December 19, 1947) was a Canadian bureaucrat, Canadian poet and prose writer. With Charles G.D. Roberts, Bliss Carman, and Archibald Lampman, he is classed as one of Canada's Confederation Poets.

Scott was a Canadian lifetime civil servant who served as deputy superintendent of the Department of Indian Affairs from 1913 to 1932, and is better known today for advocating the assimilation of Canada's First Nations peoples in that capacity.

Life

Scott was born in Ottawa, Ontario, the son of Rev. William Scott and Janet MacCallum. He was educated at Stanstead Wesleyan College.

Early in life, he became an accomplished pianist.

Scott wanted to be a doctor, but family finances were precarious, so in 1879 he joined the federal civil service. As the story goes, "William Scott might not have money [but] he had connections in high places. Among his acquaintances was the prime minister, SirJohn A. Macdonald, who agreed to meet with Duncan. As chance would have it, when Duncan arrived for his interview, the prime minister had a memo on his desk from the Indian Branch of the Department of the Interior asking for a temporary copying clerk. Making a quick decision while the serious young applicant waited in front of him, Macdonald wrote across the request: 'Approved. Employ Mr. Scott at $1.50.'"

Scott "spent his entire career in the same branch of government, working his way up to the position of deputy superintendent of Indian Affairs in 1923, the highest non-elected position possible in his department. He remained in this post until his retirement in 1932."

Scott's father also subsequently found work in Indian Affairs, and the entire family moved into a newly built house on 108 Lisgar St., where Duncan Campbell Scott would live for the rest of his life.

In 1883 Scott met fellow civil servant, Archibald Lampman. "It was the beginning of an instant friendship that would continue unbroken until Lampman's death sixteen years later.... It was Scott who initiated wilderness camping trips, a recreation that became Lampman's favourite escape from daily drudgery and family problems. In turn, Lampman's dedication to the art of poetry would inspire Scott's first experiments in verse." By the late 1880s Scott was publishing poetry in the prestigious American magazine, *Scribner's*. In 1889 his poems "At the Cedars" and "Ottawa" were included in the pioneering anthology, *Songs of the Great Dominion.*

Scott and Lampman "shared a love of poetry and the Canadian wilderness. During the 1890s the two made a number of canoe trips together in the area north of Ottawa."

In 1892 and 1893, Scott, Lampman, and William Wilfred Campbell wrote a literary column, "At the Mermaid Inn," for the Toronto *Globe*."Scott... came up with the title for it. His intention was to conjure up a vision of The Mermaid Inn Tavern in old London where Sir Walter Raleigh founded the famous club whose members included Ben Jonson, Beaumont and Fletcher, and other literary lights.

In 1893 Scott published his first book of poetry, *The Magic House and Other Poems.* It would be followed by seven more volumes of verse: *Labour and the Angel* (1898), *New World Lyrics and Ballads* (1905), *Via Borealis* (1906), *Lundy's Lane and Other Poems* (1916), *Beauty and Life* (1921), *The Poems of Duncan Campbell Scott* (1926) and *The Green Cloister* (1935).

In 1894, Scott married Belle Botsford, a concert violinist, whom he had met at a recital in Ottawa. They had one child, Elizabeth, who died at 12. Before she was born, Scott asked his mother and sisters to leave his home (his father had died in 1891), causing a long-time rift in the family.

In 1896 Scott published his first collection of stories, *In the Village of Viger*, "a collection of delicate sketches of French Canadian life. Two later collections, *The Witching of Elspie*(1923) and *The Circle of Affection* (1947), contained many fine short stories." Scott also wrote a novel, although it was not published until after his death (as *The Untitled Novel*, in 1979).

After Lampman died in 1899, Scott helped publish a number of editions of Lampman's poetry.

Scott "was a prime mover in the establishment of the Ottawa Little Theatre and the Dominion Drama Festival." In 1923 the Little Theatre performed his one-act play, *Pierre*; it was later published in *Canadian Plays from Hart House Theatre* (1926). His wife died in 1929. In 1931 he married poet Elise Aylen, more than 30 years his junior. After he retired the next year, "he and Elise spent much of the 1930s and 1940s travelling in Europe, Canada and the United States." He died in December 1947 in Ottawa at the age of 85 and is buried in Ottawa's Beechwood Cemetery.

Indian Affairs

Prior to taking up his position as head of the Department of Indian Affairs, in 1905 Scott was one of the Treaty Commissioners sent to negotiate Treaty No. 9 in Northern Ontario. Aside from his poetry, Scott made his mark in Canadian history as the head of the Department of Indian Affairs from 1913 to 1932.

Even before Confederation, the Canadian government had adopted a policy of assimilation. "The Canadian government's Indian policy had already been set before Scott was in a position to influence it, but he never saw any reason to question its assumption that the 'red' man ought to become just like the 'white' man. Shortly after he became Deputy Superintendent, he wrote approvingly: 'The happiest future for the Indian race is absorption into the general population, and this is the object and policy of our government.'... Assimilation, so the reasoning went, would solve the 'Indian problem,' and wrenching children away from their parents to 'civilize' them in residential schools until they were eighteen was believed to be a sure way of achieving the government's goal. Scott... would later pat himself on the back: 'I was never unsympathetic to aboriginal ideals, but there was the law which I did not originate and which I never tried to amend in the direction of severity.'"

" *I want to get rid of the Indian problem. I do not think as a matter of fact, that the country ought to continuously protect a class of people who are able to stand alone... Our objective is to continue until there is not a single Indian in Canada that has not been absorbed into the body politic and there is no Indian question, and no Indian Department, that is the whole object of this Bill.* "

—Duncan Campbell Scott,

In 1920, under Scott's direction, and with the concurrence of the major religions involved in native education, an amendment to the Indian Act made it mandatory for all native children between the ages of seven and fifteen to attend school.

Attendance at a residential school was made compulsory. Although a reading of Bill 14 states that no particular kind of school was stipulated. Scott was in favour of residential schooling for aboriginal children, as he believed removing them from the influences of home and reserve would hasten the cultural and economic transformation of the whole aboriginal population. See Canada's Residential Schools. In cases where a residential school was the only kind available, residential enrollment did become mandatory, and aboriginal children were compelled to leave their homes, their families and their culture, with or without their parents' consent. However, in 1901, 226 of the 290 Indian schools across Canada were day schools, and by 1961, the 377 day schools far outnumbered the 56 residential institutions.

CBC has reported that "In all, about 150,000 aboriginal, Inuit and Métis children were removed from their communities and forced to attend the schools." The 150,000 enrollment figure is an estimate not disputed by Aboriginal Affairs and Northern Development, but it is not clear what percentage were "removed from their communities and forced to attend the schools." A percentage of the residential schools were in or close by the children's communities.

Moreover, while many aboriginal parents distrusted the residential schools or preferred to raise and educate their children in a traditional manner, other parents willingly enrolled their children, partly from a belief that the schooling of the "white man" would benefit them, and partly from a knowledge that schools would provide shelter, food and clothing which dire conditions on the reserve could not provide. Harsh criticism has been leveled at Scott and the residential school system, as children who attended some of the more poorly maintained or administered schools lived in terrible conditions; in some cases the mortality rate exceeded fifty per cent due to the spread of infectious disease.

This situation was made worse by the federal policy that tied funding to enrollment numbers, which resulted in some schools enrolling sick children in order to boost their numbers. Echoing Scott's desire to absorb aboriginals into the wider Canadian population, many residential and day schools strongly discouraged students from speaking their native language, and harsh punishments were administered.Corporal punishment was sometimes justified by the belief that it was the only way to "save souls", "civilize" the native children and, in the residential schools, punish runaways who might make the school responsible for injury or death while trying to return home. Many reports of physical, sexual and psychological abuse in the residential schools have surfaced over the years. Because any kind of scandal coming out of the residential schools would have caused Indian Affairs, the churches and the government of the day much embarrassment, incidents of abuse were often discounted or covered up.

When Scott retired, his "policy of assimilating the Indians had been so much in keeping with the thinking of the time that he was widely praised for his capable administration."At the time, Scott was able to point to evidence of success in increasing enrollment and attendance, as the number of First Nations children enrolled in any school rose from 11,303 in 1912 to 17,163 in 1932. Residential school enrollment during the same period rose from 3,904 to 8,213. Actual attendance figures from all schools had also risen sharply, going from 64 per cent of enrollment in 1920 to 75 per cent in 1930, and Scott attributed this rise partly to Bill 14's section on compulsory attendance but also to a more positive attitude among First Nations people towards education. However, despite the encouraging statistics, Scott's efforts to bring about assimilation through residential schools could be judged a failure, as many former students retained their language, went on to maintain and preserve their tribe's culture, and refused to accept full Canadian citizenship when it was offered. Moreover, over the long history of the residential system, only a minority of all enrolled students went beyond the elementary grades, and many former students found themselves lacking the skills that would enable them to find employment on or off the reserve.

One summing-up of his Indian Affairs legacy from an aboriginal viewpoint states that Scott "took a romantic interest in Native traditions, he was after all a poet of some repute (a member of the Royal Society of Canada), as well as being an accountant and a bureaucrat. He was three people rolled into one confusing and perverse soul. The poet romanticized the whole 'noble savage' theme, the bureaucrat lamented our inability to become civilized, the accountant refused to provide funds for the so-called civilization process. In other words, he disdained all 'living' Natives but "extolled the freedom of the savages."

Writing

Scott's "literary reputation has never been in doubt. He has been well represented in virtually all major anthologies of Canadian poetry published since 1900."

In *Poets of the Younger Generation* (1901), Scottish literary critic William Archer wrote of Scott:

He is above everything a poet of climate and atmosphere, employing with a nimble, graphic touch the clear, pure, transparent colours of a richly-furnished palette.... Though it must not be understood that his talent is merely descriptive. There is a philosophic and also a romantic strain in it..... There is scarcely a poem of Mr. Scott's from which one could not cull some memorable descriptive passage.... As a rule Mr. Scott's workmanship is careful and highly finished. He is before everything a colourist. He paints in lines of a peculiar and vivid translucency. But he is also a metrist of no mean skill, and an imaginative thinker of no common capacity.

The Government of Canada biography of him says that: "Although the quality of Scott's work is uneven, he is at his best when describing the Canadian wilderness and Indigenous peoples. Although they constitute a small portion of his total output, Scott's widely recognized and valued 'Indian poems' cemented his literary reputation. In these poems, the reader senses the conflict that Scott felt between his role as an administrator committed to an assimilation policy for Canada's Native peoples and his feelings as a poet, saddened by the encroachment of European civilization on the Indian way of life."

"There is not a really bad poem in the book," literary critic Desmond Pacey said of Scott's first book, *The Magic House and Other Poems*, "and there are a number of extremely good ones." The 'extremely good ones' include the strange, dream-like sonnets of "In the House of Dreams." "Probably the best known poem from the collection is 'At the Cedars,' a grim narrative about the death of a young man and his sweetheart during a log-jam on the Ottawa River. It is crudely melodramatic... but its style — stark understatement, irregular lines, and abrupt rhymes — makes it the most experimental poem in the book."

His next book, *Labour and the Angel*, "is a slighter volume than *The Magic House* in size and content. The lengthy title poem makes dreary reading.... Of greater interest is his growing willingness to experiment with stanza form, variations in line length, use of partial rhyme, and lack of rhyme." Notable new poems included "The Cup" and the sonnet "The Onandaga Madonna." But arguably "the most memorable poem in the new collection" was the fantasy, "The Piper of Arll." One person who long remembered that poem was future British Poet Laureate John Masefield, who read "The Piper of Arll" as a teenager and years later wrote to Scott:

I had never (till that time) cared very much for poetry, but your poem impressed me deeply, and set me on fire. Since then poetry has been the one deep influence in my life, and to my love of poetry I owe all my friends, and the position I now hold.

New World Lyrics and Ballads (1905) revealed "a voice that is sounding ever more different from the other Confederation Poets... his dramatic power is increasingly apparent in his response to the wilderness and the lives of the people who lived there." The poetry included "On the Way to the Mission" and the much-anthologized "The Forsaken," two of Scott's best-known "Indian poems."

Lundy's Lane and Other Poems (1916) seemed "to have been cobbled together at the insistence of his publishers, who wanted a collection of his work that had not been published in any previous volume.". The title poem was one that had won Scott, "in the *Christmas Globe* contest of 1908... the prize of one hundred dollars, offered for the best poem on a Canadian historical theme.". Other notable poems in the volume include the pretty lyric "A Love Song," the long meditation, "The Height of Land," and the even longer "Lines Written in Memory of Edmund Morris." Anthologist John Garvin called the last "so original, tender and beautiful that it is destined to live among the best in Canadian literature."

"In his old age, Scott would look back upon *Beauty and Life* (1921) as his favourite among his volumes of verse," E.K. Brown tells us, adding: "In it most of the poetic kinds he cared about are represented." There is a great diversity, from the moving war elegy "To a Canadian Aviator Who Died For His Country in France," to the strange, apocalyptic "A Vision."

The Green Cloister, published after Scott's retirement, "is a travelogue of the sites he visited in Europe with Elise: Lake Como, Ravelllo, Kensington

Gardens, East Gloucester, etc. — descriptive and contemplative poems by an observant tourist. Those with a Canadian setting include two Indian poems of near-melodrama — 'A Scene at Lake Manitou' and 'At Gull Lake, August 1810' —that are in stark contrast to the overall serenity of the volume." More typical is the title poem, "Chiostro Verde."

The Circle of Affection (1947) contains 26 poems Scott had written since *Cloister*, and several prose pieces, including his Royal Society address on "Poetry and Progress." It includes "At Delos," which brings to mind the poet's approaching death:

There is no grieving in the world
As beauty fades throughout the years:
The pilgrim with the weary heart
Brings to the grave his tears.

Reputation

Scott was honoured for his writing during and after his lifetime. He was elected a Fellow of the Royal Society of Canada in 1899 and served as its president from 1921 to 1922. The Society awarded him the second-ever Lorne Pierce Medal in 1927 for his contributions to Canadian literature.

In 1934 he was made a Companion of the Order of St. Michael and St. George.

He also received honorary degrees from the University of Toronto (Doctor of Letters in 1922) and Queen's University (Doctor of Laws in 1939).

In 1948, the year after his death, he was designated a Person of National Historic Significance.

However, as the *Encyclopædia Britannica* points out, Scott is "best known at the end of the 20th century," not for his writing, but "for advocating the assimilation of Canada's First Nations peoples."

As part of their Worst Canadian poll, a panel of experts commissioned by Canada's National History Society named Scott one of the Worst Canadians in the August 2007 issue of *The Beaver*.

Arc Poetry Magazine renamed the annual "Archibald Lampman Award" (given to a poet in the National Capital Region) to the Lampman-Scott Award in recognition of Scott's enduring legacy in Canadian poetry, with the first award under the new name given out in 2007.

The 2008 winner of the award, Shane Rhodes, turned over half of the $1,500 prize money to the Wabano Centre for Aboriginal Health, a First Nations health centre. "Taking that money wouldn't have been right, with what I'm writing about," Rhodes said. The poet was researching First Nations history and found Scott's name repeatedly referenced. Rhodes felt "Scott's legacy as a civil servant overshadows his work as a pioneer of Canadian poetry", in the words of a CBC News report.

Anita Lahey, editor of *Arc Poetry Magazine*, responded with a statement that she thought Scott's actions as head of Indian Affairs were important to remember, but did not eclipse his role in the history of Canadian literature. "I think it matters that we're aware of it and that we think about and talk about these things," she said. "I don't think controversial or questionable activities in the life of any artist or writer is something that should necessarily discount the literary legacy that they leave behind." However, "This partnership came to an end in 2010, and the prize returned to its former identity as the Archibald Lampman Award for Poetry."

FREDERICK GEORGE SCOTT

Frederick George Scott (7 April 1861 – 19 January 1944) was a Canadian poet and author, known as the Poet of the Laurentians. He is sometimes associated with Canada's Confederation Poets, a group that included Charles G.D. Roberts, Bliss Carman,Archibald Lampman, and Duncan Campbell Scott. Scott published 13 books of Christian and patriotic poetry. Scott was a British imperialist who wrote many hymns to the British Empire—eulogizing his country's roles in the Boer Wars and World War I. Many of his poems use the natural world symbolically to convey deeper spiritual meaning. Frederick George Scott was the father of poet F. R. Scott.

Life

Frederick George Scott was born 7 April 1861 in Montreal, Canada. He received a B.A. from Bishop's College, Lennoxville, Quebec, in 1881, and an M.A. in 1884. He studied theology at King's College, London in 1882, but was refused ordination in the Anglican Church of Canada for his Anglo-Catholic beliefs. In 1884 he became a deacon. In 1886 he was ordained an Anglican priest atCoggeshall, Essex. He served first at Drummondville, Quebec, and then in Quebec City, where he became rector of St. Matthew's Anglican Church.

In April 1887, Scott married Amy Brooks, who would bear him six surviving children. In 1889, anthologist W.D. Lighthall included two of his poems in his anthology, *Songs of the Great Dominion*, and as well used a quotation from Scott, "All the future lies before us/ Glorious in that sunset land", on the title page as the book's epigraph.

In 1914, well over the age of 50, Scott enlisted to fight in World War I. He held the rank of Major and served as the Senior Chaplainto the 1st Canadian Division. After the war he became chaplain of the army and navy veterans.

During the Quebec Conference of 1943, Scott was invited by Winston Churchill and Franklin Roosevelt to a private meeting where he read some of his poetry.

Frederick George Scott died on 19 January 1944 in Quebec City, leaving a daughter and four sons.

Writing

In 1885, Scott printed his first chapbook, *Justin and Other Poems*, later included in *The Soul's Quest and Other Poems* (London 1888). "Several of Scott's early narrative poems, and his later didactic novel *Elton Hazelwood* (1891), describe typically Victorian crises of faith and the recognition of 'life and death as they are'.... Scott's many religious poems and his novel offer a more explicit rendering of the Victorian pessimism underlying the poetry of his more significant contemporaries, Charles G.D. Roberts and Archibald Lampman."

John Garvin, who included Scott's poems in his 1916 anthology *Canadian Poets*, wrote of him: "Frederick George Scott, 'The Poet of the Laurentians,' has this supreme gift as a writer: the art of expressing noble, beautiful and often profound thoughts, in simple, appropriate words which all who read can understand. His poems uplift the spirit and enrich the heart." "The Unnamed Lake" has been called his best-known poem.

Garvin included a quotation from M.O. Hammond writing in the Toronto *Globe*: "Frederick George Scott's poetry has followed three or four well-defined lines of thought. He has reflected in turn the academic subjects of a library, the majesty of nature, the tender love of his fellowmen, and the vision and enthusiasm of an Imperialist. His work in any one field would attract attention; taken in mass it marks him as a sturdy, developing interpreter of his country and of his times. Whether he writes of 'Samson' and 'Thor,' of the 'Little River,' or whether he expands his soul in a 'Hymn of Empire,' his lines are marked by imagination, melody, sympathy and often wistfulness. Living on the edge of the shadow-flecked Laurentians, he constantly draws inspiration from them, and more than any other has made articulate their lonely beauties. His pastoral relations with a city flock give colour and tenderness to not a few of his poems of human relationships. His ardent love of the Empire gives rein to his restless, roving thoughts and has finally drawn him to the battle-front as a chaplain."

The Canadian Encyclopaedia calls him "an Anglican priest, minor poet and staunch advocate of the civilizing tradition of imperial Britain, who instilled in his son a commitment to serve mankind, a love for the regenerative balance of the Laurentian landscape and a firm respect for the social order."

ROBERT W. SERVICE

Robert William Service (January 16, 1874 – September 11, 1958) was a British-Canadian poet and writer who has often been called "the Bard of the Yukon". He is best known for his poems "The Shooting of Dan McGrew" and "The Cremation of Sam McGee", from his first book, *Songs of a Sourdough* (1907; also published as *The Spell of the Yukon and Other Verses*). His vivid descriptions of the Yukon and its people made it seem that he was a veteran of the Klondike gold rush, instead of the late-arriving bank clerk he actually was.

"These humorous tales in verse were considered doggerel by the literary set, yet remain extremely popular to this day."

Life

Early life

Service was born in Preston, Lancashire, England, the first of ten children. His father, also Robert Service, was a banker fromKilwinning, Scotland, who had been transferred to England.

When he was five, Service was sent to live in Kilwinning with his three maiden aunts and his paternal grandfather, the town'spostmaster. There he is said to have composed his first verse, a grace, on his sixth birthday:

God bless the cakes and bless the jam;
Bless the cheese and the cold boiled ham:
Bless the scones Aunt Jeannie makes,
And save us all from bellyaches. Amen

At nine, Service re-joined his parents who had moved to Glasgow. He attended Glasgow's Hillhead High School.

After leaving school, Service joined the Commercial Bank of Scotland which would later become the Royal Bank of Scotland. He was writing at this time and reportedly already "selling his verses". He was also reading poetry: Browning, Keats, Tennyson, andThackeray.

When he was 21, Service travelled to Vancouver Island, British Columbia, with his Buffalo Bill outfit and dreams of becoming a cowboy. He drifted around western North America, "wandering from California to British Columbia," taking and quitting a series of jobs: "Starving in Mexico, residing in a California bordello, farming on Vancouver Island and pursuing unrequited love in Vancouver." This sometimes required him to leech off his parent's Scottish neighbours and friends who had previously emigrated to Canada.

In 1899, Service was a store clerk in Cowichan Bay, British Columbia. He mentioned to a customer (Charles H. Gibbons, editor of the Victoria *Daily Colonist*) that he wrote verses, with the result that six poems by "R.S." on the Boer Wars had appeared in the *Colonist* by July 1900 – including "The March of the Dead" that would later appear in his first book. (Service's brother, Alick, was a prisoner of the Boers at the time. He had been captured on November 15, 1899, alongside Winston Churchill.)

The *Colonist* also published Service's "Music in the Bush" on September 18, 1901, and "The Little Old Log Cabin" on March 16, 1902.

In her 2006 biography, *Under the Spell of the Yukon*, Enid Mallory revealed that Service had fallen in love during this period. He was working as a "farm labourer and store clerk when he first met Constance MacLean at a dance in Duncan B.C., where she was visiting her uncle." MacLean lived in Vancouver, on the mainland, so he courted her by mail. Though he was smitten, "MacLean was looking for a man of education and means to support her" so was not that interested. To please her, he took courses at McGill University's Victoria College, but failed.

In 1903, down on his luck, Service was hired by a Canadian Bank of Commerce branch in Victoria, British Columbia, using his Commercial Bank letter of reference. The bank "watched him, gave him a raise, and sent him to Kamloops in the middle of British Columbia. In Victoria he lived over the bank with a hired piano, and dressed for dinner. In Kamloops, horse country, he played polo. In the fall of 1904, the bank sent him to their Whitehorse branch in the Yukon. With the expense money he bought himself a raccoon coat."

Throughout this period, Service continued writing and saving his verses: "more than a third of the poems in his first volume had been written before he moved north in 1904."

Yukon period

Whitehorse was a frontier town, less than ten years old. Located on the Yukon River at the White Horse Rapids, it had begun in 1897 as a campground for prospectors on their way to Dawson City to join the Klondike Gold Rush. The railroad that Service rode in on, the White Pass and Yukon Route, had reached Whitehorse only in 1900.

Settling in, "Service dreamed and listened to the stories of the great gold rush." He also "took part in the extremely active Whitehorse social life. As was popular at the time he recited at concerts – things like 'Casey at the Bat' and 'Gunga Din', but they were getting stale."

One day (Service later wrote), while pondering what to recite at an upcoming church concert he met E.J. "Stroller" White, editor of the*Whitehorse Star*. White suggested: "Why don't you write a poem for it? Give us something about our own bit of earth. We sure would appreciate it. There's a rich paystreak waiting for someone to work. Why don't you go in and stake it?"

Returning from a walk one Saturday night, Service heard the sounds of revelry from a saloon, and the phrase "A bunch of the boys were whooping it up" popped into his head. Inspired, he ran to the bank to write it down (almost being shot as a burglar), and by the next morning "The Shooting of Dan McGrew" was complete.

"A month or so later he heard a gold rush yarn from a Dawson mining man about a fellow who cremated his pal." He spent the night walking in the woods composing "The Cremation of Sam McGee", and wrote it down from memory the next day.

Other verses quickly followed. "In the early spring he stood above the heights of Miles Canyon... the line 'I have gazed on naked grandeur where there's nothing else to gaze on' came into his mind and again he hammered out a complete poem, "The Call of the Wild". Conversations with locals led Service to write about things he had not seen (some of which had not actually happened) as well. He did not set foot in Dawson City until 1908, arriving in the Klondike ten years after the Gold Rush when his renown as a writer was already established.

After having collected enough poems for a book, Service "sent the poems to his father, who had emigrated to Toronto, and asked him to find a printing house so they could make it into a booklet. He enclosed a cheque to cover the costs and intended to give these booklets away to his friends in Whitehorse" for Christmas. His father took the manuscript to William Briggs in Toronto, whose employees loved the book. "The foreman and printers recited the ballads while they worked. A salesman read the proofs out loud as they came off the typesetting machines." An "enterprising salesman sold 1700 copies in advance orders from galley proofs." The publisher "sent Robert's cheque back to him and offered a ten per cent royalty contract for the book."

Service's book, *Songs of a Sourdough*, was "an immediate success." It went through seven printings even before its official release date. Ultimately, Briggs "sold fifteen impressions in 1907. That same year there was an edition in New York, Philadelphia, and London. The London publisher, T. Fisher Unwin, struck a twenty-third printing in 1910, and thirteen more by 1917." "Service eventually earned in excess of $100,000 for *Songs of a Sourdough* alone (Mackay 14, 408n19)" (equal to about $2.5 million today after inflation).

(In the United States, the book would be given the more Jack London-ish title, *The Spell of the Yukon and Other Verses*).

"When copies of the book reached Whitehorse, Robert's own minister took him aside to let him know how wicked were his stories. Service hung his head in shame.... But, that summer, tourists from the south arrived in Whitehorse looking for the famous poet; and he autographed many of his books."

"In 1908, after working for the bank for three years in Whitehorse, he was sent outside on mandatory paid leave for three months, a standard practice for bank employees serving in the Yukon." According to Enid Mallory, he went to Vancouver and looked up Constance MacLean. Now that he was a successful author, she agreed to become engaged to him.

Following his leave, in 1908 the bank transferred Service to Dawson, where he met veterans of the Gold Rush, now ten years in the past: "they loved to reminisce, and Robert listened carefully and remembered." He used their tales to write a second book of verse, *Ballads of a Cheechako*, in 1908. "It too was an overwhelming success."

In 1909, when the bank wanted Service to return to Whitehorse as manager, he decided to resign. "After quitting his job, he rented a small two-room cabin on Eighth Avenue in Dawson City from Mrs. Edna Clarke and began his career as a full-time author." He immediately "went to work on his novel.... He went for walks that lasted all night, slept till mid-afternoon, and sometimes didn't come out of the cabin for days. In five months the novel, called *The Trail of '98*, was complete and he took it to a publisher in New York." Service's first novel also "immediately became a best-seller."

Newly wealthy, Service was able to travel to Paris, the French Riviera, Hollywood, and beyond. He returned to Dawson City in 1912 to write his third book of poetry, *Rhymes of a Rolling Stone* (1912). During that time he became a freemason, being initiated into Yukon Lodge No. 45 in Dawson.

It is unclear what happened between Service and Constance MacLean as no known letters between them exist after Service's departure for Dawson City. In 1912 she "married Leroy Grant, a surveyor and railroad engineer based in Prince Rupert."

Later life

Service left Dawson City for good in 1912. From 1912 to 1913 he was a correspondent for the *Toronto Star* during the Balkan Wars.

In 1913, Service moved to Paris, remaining there for the next 15 years. He settled in the Latin Quarter, posing as a painter. In June 1913, he married Parisienne Germaine Bourgoin, daughter of a distillery owner, and they purchased a summer home at Lancieux, Côtes-d'Armor, in the Brittany region of France. Thirteen years younger than her husband, Germaine Service survived him by 31 years, dying aged 102 in 1989.

Service was 41 when World War I broke out; he enlisted, but was turned down "due to varicose veins." He briefly covered the war for the *Toronto Star* (from December 11, 1915, through January 29, 1916), but "was arrested and nearly executed in an outbreak of spy hysteria in Dunkirk." – then "worked as a stretcher bearer and ambulance driverwith the Ambulance Corps of the American Red Cross, until his health broke." Convalescing in Paris, he wrote a new book of mainly war poetry, *Rhymes of a Red Cross Man*, in 1916. The book was dedicated to the memory of Service's "brother, Lieutenant Albert Service, Canadian Infantry, Killed in Action, France, August 1916." Robert W. Service has been honoured by three medals for his war engagement: 1914–15 Star, British War Medal and the Victory Medal.

With the end of the war, Service "settled down to being a rich man in Paris.... During the day he would promenade in the best suits, with a monocle. At night he went out in old clothes with the company of his doorman, a retired policeman, to visit the lowest dives of the city". During his time in Paris he was reputedly the wealthiest author living in the city, yet was known to dress as a working man and walk the streets, blending in and observing everything around him. Those experiences would be used in his next book of poetry, *Ballads of a Bohemian* (1921), "The poems are given in the persona of an American poet in Paris who serves as an ambulance driver and an infantryman in the war. The verses are separated by diary entries over a period of four years." In the 1920s, Service began writing thriller novels. *The Poisoned Paradise, A Romance of Monte Carlo* (New York, 1922) and *The Roughneck. A Tale of Tahiti* (New York, 1923) were both later made into silent movies. During the winter season, Service used to live in Nice with his family where he met Anglo-Saxon writers such as H.G. Wells, A.K. Bruce, Somerset Maugham, Rex Ingram, Franck Scully, James Joyce, Franck Harris, Frieda Laurence who all spent their winter in the French Riviera and he wrote to have been lucky to have lunch with Colette.

In 1930, Service returned to Kilwinning, to erect a memorial to his family in the town cemetery. He also visited the USSR in the 1930s and later wrote a satirical "Ballad of Lenin's Tomb". For this reason his poetry has never been translated into Russian in the USSR and he was never mentioned in Soviet encyclopaedias.

Service's second trip to the Soviet Union "was interrupted by news of the Hitler-Stalin pact. Service fled across Poland, Latvia, Estoniaand the Baltic to Stockholm. He wintered in Nice with his family, then fled France for Canada." Not long after, the Nazis invaded France, and "arrived at his home in Lancieux... looking specifically for the poet who had mocked Hitler in newspaper verse."

During World War II, Service lived in California, "and Hollywood had him join with other celebrities in helping the morale of troops – visiting US Army camps to recite his poems. He was also asked to play himself in the movie *The Spoilers* (1942), working alongsideMarlene Dietrich, John Wayne and Randolph Scott.

"He was thrilled to play a scene with Marlene Dietrich." After the war, Service and his wife returned to his home in Brittany, to find it destroyed. They rebuilt, and he lived there until his death in 1958, though he wintered in Monte Carlo on the French Riviera. Service's wife and daughter, Iris, travelled to the Yukon in 1946 "and visited Whitehorse and Dawson City, which by then was becoming a ghost town. Service could not bring himself to go back. He preferred to remember the town as it had been."

Service wrote prolifically during his last years, publishing six books of verse from 1949 to 1955. One that he wrote the following year was published posthumously. It was at Service's flat in Monte Carlo that Canadian broadcaster Pierre Berton recorded, over a period of three days, many hours of autobiographical television interview, for theCanadian Broadcasting Corporation, in the spring of 1958, not long before Service died. At this occasion, Robert Service recited The Shooting of Dan McGrew and The Cremation of Sam McGee

Service wrote two volumes of autobiography – *Ploughman of the Moon* and *Harper of Heaven*. He died in Lancieux and is buried in the local cemetery.

Writing

Robert Service wrote the most commercially successful poetry of the century. Yet his most popular works "were considered doggerel by the literary set."During his lifetime, he was nicknamed "the Canadian Kipling." – yet that may have been a double-edged compliment. As T. S. Eliot has said, "we have to defend Kipling against the charge of excessive lucidity," "the charge of being a 'journalist' appealing only to the commonest collective emotion," and "the charge of writing jingles." All those charges, and more, could be levelled against Service's best known and best loved works.

Certainly Service's verse was derivative of Kipling's. In "The Cremation of Sam McGee", for instance, he uses the form of Kipling's "The Ballad of East and West".

In his E. J. Pratt lecture "Silence In the Sea," critic Northrop Frye argued that Service's verse was not "serious poetry," but something else he called "popular poetry": "the idioms of popular and serious poetry remain inexorably distinct." Popular poems, he thought, "preserve a surface of explicit statement" – either being "proverbial, like Kipling's 'If' orLongfellow's 'Song of Life' or Burns's 'For A' That'," or dealing in "conventionally poetic themes, like the pastoral themes of James Whitcomb Riley, or the adventurous themes of Robert Service."

Service himself did not call his work poetry. ""Verse, not poetry, is what I was after... something the man in the street would take notice of and the sweet old lady would paste in her album; something the schoolboy would spout and the fellow in the pub would quote. Yet I never wrote to please anyone but myself; it just happened. I belonged to the simple folks whom I liked to please."

In his autobiography, Service described his method of writing at his Dawson City cabin. "I used to write on the coarse rolls of paper used by paper-hangers, pinning them on the wall and printing my verses in big charcoal letters. Then I would pace back and forth before them, repeating them, trying to make them perfect. I wanted to make them appeal to the eye as well as to the ear. I tried to avoid any literal quality."

One remarkable thing about both of Service's best-known ballads is how easily he wrote them. When writing about composing "The Shooting of Dan McGrew", 'easy' was exactly the word he used: "For it came so easy to me in my excited state that I was amazed at my facility. It was as if someone was whispering in my ear." And this was just after someone had tried to shoot him. He continued: "As I wrote stanza after stanza, the story seemed to evolve itself. It was a marvelous experience. Before I crawled into my bed at five in the morning, my ballad was in the bag."

Similarly, when he wrote "The Cremation of Sam McGee", the verses just flowed: ""I took the woodland trail, my mind seething with excitement and a strange ecstasy.... As I started in: There are strange things done in the midnight sun, verse after verse developed with scarce a check... and when I rolled happily into bed, my ballad was cinched. Next day, with scarcely any effort of memory I put it on paper."

In 1926, Archibald MacMechan, Professor of English at Canada's Dalhousie University, pronounced on Service's Yukon books in his *Headwaters of Canadian Literature*:

The sordid, the gross, the bestial, may sometimes be redeemed by the touch of genius; but that Promethean touch is not in Mr. Service. In manner he is frankly imitative of Kipling's barrack-room balladry; and imitation is an admission of inferiority. 'Sourdough' is Yukon slang for the provident old-timer... It is a convenient term for this wilfully violent kind of verse without the power to redeem the squalid themes it treats. *The Ballads of a Cheechako* is a second installment of sourdoughs, while his novel *The Trail of '98* is simply sourdough prose.

MacMechan did give grudging respect to Service's World War I poetry, conceding that his style went well with that subject, and that "his *Rhymes of a Red Cross Man* are an advance on his previous volumes. He has come into touch with the grimmest of realities; and while his radical faults have not been cured, his rude lines drive home the truth that he has seen."

Reviewing Service's *Rhymes of a Rebel* in 1952, Frye remarked that the book "interests me chiefly because... I have noticed so much verse in exactly the same idiom, and I wonder how far Mr. Service's books may have influenced it. There was a time, fifty years ago," he added," when Robert W.Service represented, with some accuracy, the general level of poetic experience in Canada, as far as the popular reader was concerned.... there has been a prodigious, and, I should think, a permanent, change in public taste."

Service has also been noted for his use of ethnonyms that would normally be considered offensive "slurs", but with no insult apparently intended. Words used in Service's poetry include *jerries* (Germans), *dago* (Italian), *pickaninny* (in reference to a Mozambican infant), *cheechako* (newcomer to the Yukon and Alaska gold fields, usually from the U.S.),*nigger* (black person), *squaw* (Aboriginal woman), and *Jap* (Japanese).

Recognition

Robert W. Service has been honoured with schools named for him including Service High School in Anchorage, Alaska, Robert Service Senior Public School (Middle/ Jr. High) in Toronto, Ontario and Robert Service School in Dawson City.

He was also honoured on a Canadian postage stamp in 1976. The Robert Service Way, a main road in Whitehorse, is named after him.

Additionally, the Bard and Banker public house in Victoria is dedicated to him, the building having at one time been a Canadian Bank of Commerce branch where Service was employed while residing in the city. In 2010 Phillips Brewery in Victoria released the Service 1904 Scottish Stone Fired Ale, available only on tap in three Victoria locations: The Bard and Banker, Irish Times, and Penny Farthing public houses.

Service's first novel, *The Trail of '98*, was made into a movie by Metro-Goldwyn-Mayer, directed by Clarence Brown. "*Trail of '98*starring Dolores del Río, Ralph Forbes and Karl Dane in 1929... was the first talking picture dealing with the Klondike gold rush and was acclaimed at the time by critics for depicting the Klondike as it really was."

Folksinger Country Joe McDonald set some of Service's World War I poetry (plus "The March of the Dead" from his first book), to music for his 1971 studio album, *War War War*.

The town of Lancieux, where he used to come every summer organized several recognitions to the memory of Robert W. Service. One of the street of Lancieux has been called Robert Service street. On July 13, 1990, a commemorative tablet has been unveiled at the Lancieux Office du Tourism by the daughter of the poet: Iris Davies-Service. An evening of celebration was organized after with a dinner. A few years later, on May 18, 2002 the school of Lancieux in Brittany took the name of "Ecole Robert W. Service". At the dedication ceremony was present the granddaughter and great granddaughter of the poet.

Dawson City cabin

Robert Service lived from 1909 to 1912 in a small two-room cabin on 8th Avenue which he rented from Edna Clarke in Dawson City. His prosperity allowed him the luxury of a telephone. Service eventually decided he could not return to Dawson, as it would not be as he remembered it. He wrote in his autobiography:

"Only yesterday an air-line offered to fly me up there in two days, and I refused. It would have saddened me to see dust and rust where once hummed a rousing town; hundreds where were thousands; tumbledown cabins, mouldering warehouses."

After Service left for Europe, the Imperial Order of the Daughters of the Empire (I.O.D.E.) took care of the cabin until 1971, preserving it. In 1971 it was taken over by Parks Canada, which maintains it, including its sod roof, as a tourist attraction.

Irish-born actor Tom Byrne created *The Robert Service Show* which was presented in the front yard of the cabin, starting in 1976. This was very popular for summer visitors and set the standard for Robert Service recitations. A resurgence in sales of Service's works followed the institution of these performances. Byrne discontinued the show at the cabin in 1995, moving it to a Front Street storefront. Since 2004 the show has been held at the Westmark

Hotel in Dawson City at 3:00 p.m. every day during the summer months. Byrne collects Robert Service first editions, and corresponded with Service's widow for years.

At the Service Cabin, local Dawson entertainers dressed in period costumes and employed by Parks Canada offer biographical information and recite Service's poetry for visitors sitting on benches on the front lawn. Johnny Nunan performed this role through 2006. Following the presentation, visitors can view Service's home through the windows and front door. The fragility of the house, and the rarity of the artifacts, precludes any possibility of allowing visitors to enter the house itself.

4

Reframing First World War Poetry

In some papers found in his kit after his death in the Battle of Loos on 13 October 1915, the twenty-year-old Charles Hamilton Sorley had scribbled in pencil what would become one of the most celebrated sonnets of the First World War:

When you see millions of the mouthless dead
Across your dreams in pale battalions go,
Say not soft things as other men have said,
That you'll remember. For you need not so.
Give them not praise. For, deaf, how should they know
It is not curses heaped on each gashed head?
Nor tears. Their blind eyes see not your tears flow.
Nor honour. It is easy to be dead.
Say only this, 'They are dead.' Then add thereto,
'Yet many a better one has died before.'
Then, scanning all the o'ercrowded mass, should you
Perceive one face that you loved heretofore,
It is a spook. None wears the face you knew.
Great death has made all his for evermore.

Repeatedly anthologised, yet forever startling. The power of this bleak, disturbing sonnet partly lies in the way the insistent rhythm and the desolate imagery of the octave reach some sort of climax in the opening lines of the sestet with the exhortation and the classical allusion (the quotation in line 10 refers to Patroclus's death in the *Iliad*), only to be intensified by the haunting gaze ('Then, scanning...') and the sudden, ominous, darkly comic shock of 'It is a spook'. The eeriness of the image is enhanced by the poignant circumstances of the poem's posthumous discovery. Sorley's poem operates on that fine threshold where poetic form and personal tragedy meet.

Often regarded as the 'transitional' figure between the early and later soldier-poets, Sorley, like his poem, was unusual for the time. Yet, the poem provides one of the earliest examples of what we now regard as the classic features of First World War poetry: the lyric testimony of the broken body –

mouth, eyes, the 'gashed' head – set against the abstract rhetoric of honour; the address to the reader ('you') that we associate with the poetry of Wilfred Owen and Siegfried Sassoon, as opposed to the egotistical 'I' of Rupert Brooke; the 'pale battalions' haunting the shell-shocked dreams of veterans, John Singer Sargent's dream-like *Gassed* (1919) and Sigmund Freud's *Beyond the Pleasure Principle* (1920), and becoming the iconic image of the war. Robert Graves found Sorley's poetry so powerful that he introduced it to Sassoon, who in turn introduced it to Wilfred Owen.

And spook-like, First World War poetry knows no habitation or rest. Mixing cultural memory with linguistic desire, First World War poetry has ranged far beyond the covers of the book. It appears on postcards, posters and in politicians' speeches, in memorials and epitaphs, and has inspired every art form, from Sean O'Casey's play *The Silver Tassie* (1928) and Benjamin Britten's musical tribute *War Requiem* (1962) to the BBC TV series *Blackadder Goes Forth* (1989) and Pat Barker's novel *Regeneration* (1991).

Over the last hundred years, the image of the First World War soldier as damaged but resilient has remained etched on British cultural consciousness, partly formed and periodically reinforced by the reading of a handful of soldier-poets, particularly Owen and Sassoon. Other important soldier-poets include Edmund Blunden, Ivor Gurney, Robert Graves, Edward Thomas, David Jones, Francis Ledgwidge, and Isaac Rosenberg, and of course the golden-haired young man whose 'begloried' war sonnets they all opposed and yet one who haunts their work: Rupert Brooke. More than any other genre – fiction, memoir or film – it is the poetry of the trenches, as represented by a small group of 'anti-war' soldier-poets, that has come to dominate First World War memory. We seldom read such poetry; it is usually a matter of re-reading, remembering, returning – with familiarity, surprise, sometimes resistance. We associate it with a part of our former selves. Today, the poetry of the soldier-poets has coalesced, beyond literary history and cultural memory, into a recognisable structure of feeling. Herein lies an undeniable part of its power and some of the larger critical problems.

For the scope of First World War poetry is much wider than that of the trench lyric. There is a substantial and distinguished body of war poetry by male civilian poets, including Thomas Hardy, Rudyard Kipling and D.H. Lawrence, as well as by women-poets such as Charlotte Mew, Mary Borden, Vera Brittain, Rose Macaulay and Margaret Postgate Cole. The poetry of the First World War is often regarded as peculiarly 'English', but many of the soldier-poets had a conflicted relation to 'Englishness': Sorley was Anglo-Scottish, Rosenberg and Sassoon (on his father's side) were Jewish, Ledwidge was Irish, while Owen, Jones and Thomas could trace their recent family history to Wales. Moreover, war poetry was produced across Europe, by poets as diverse as Giuseppe Ungaretti, Georg Trakl, Guillaume Apollinaire and Anna Akhmatova, and further afield from countries such as Australia and New Zealand, Canada, India, the West Indies and Turkey.

FORM SAND HISTORY

One of the achievements of war poetry has been to democratise poetry itself. Its centrality in the school curriculum means that, for many, it represents their first encounter with poetry – and not just in Great Britain. When I was a student in Kolkata, the former capital of British India, the figures of the two 'Tommies' standing guard by the city's Cenotaph-like First World War memorial always blended in my mind with Owen and Sassoon whom we read at Presidency College, which claimed to have the oldest English department in the world.

In India, as in many other countries, First World War poetry spoke with a British accent. And of all the literary genres, it was one that remained most tightly cling-filmed around an event, and conjured up the iconic images – trenches, barbed wire, gas, rats, mud. The anthropologist Claude Lévi-Strauss has argued that the substance of myth 'does not lie in its style, its original music, or its syntax, but in the story which it tells'.

In the classroom, First World War poetry often ceases to be poetry and begins to look like history by proxy. Neither the transparent envelope of experience nor just language whispering to itself about itself, First World War poetry represents one of those primal moments when poetic form bears most fully the weight of historical trauma. Art and testimony are often yoked together by real-life violence, leading to formal realignment, invention or dissonance. Categories such as 'pro-war' and 'anti-war' often prove inadequate, when tested against the complexity of individual poems. Similarly, combatant, non-combatant and women's poetry operated within a larger poetic field and shared common ground.

For many scholars, the very term 'war poetry' is problematic: indeed, a 'war poem' contains much besides the war. As Simon Featherstone has noted, the label may confine the poem, artificially, within the parenthesis of the war years. War is crucial to the poetry and its intensities of meaning, but it is not the only – or isolated – focus of attention or analysis. First World War poetry looks before and after the war, joining past and future, and combatant and civilian zones; it speaks in varying cadences not just of combat, but also of life at large – of beauty, longing, religion, nature, animals, intimacy, historical change, poetic responsibility, Europe and Englishness, race, democracy and empire, or what it is for women to have 'years and years in which we shall still be young' – all touched directly or indirectly by the war.

A constant tension in writings on First World War poetry is whether the accent should fall on war or on poetry, on cultural history or on literary form. If the surrounding material world was important to the soldier-poets, so was a sense of poetic tradition. Investigation into the literary culture of the trenches

– from Paul Fussell's *The Great War and Modern Memory* (1972) to Jon Stallworthy's *Survivors' Songs: From Maldon to the Somme* (2008) – shows the intense engagement of this group of soldier-poets with a vast range of literature, from the Iliad through Shakespeare, Milton and the Romantics to Hardy and Housman. The finest trench poetry revels in the meeting of tradition and innovation: in Gurney's exquisite handling of meter, punctuation and sibilance in the terrifying image of 'Darkness, shot at: I smiled, as politely replied –' ('The Silent One'); in Sassoon's powerful rhymes which compact visceral horror and religious blasphemy while conjuring up the commonest trench expletive – 'And someone flung his burden in the muck/Mumbling: 'O Christ Almighty, now I'm stuck' ('Redeemer'); or in Owen's intricate negotiation with Keats's 'To a Nightingale' as he relocates sensuousness in the frozen landscape of the Western Front: 'Our brains ache, in the merciless iced east winds that knife us...' ('Exposure'). Similarly, a number of women-poets both inherit and interrogate different traditions of lyric verse with remarkable power as they try to represent the war and its effects on civilian spaces and minds. Consider the following poem 'Afterwards' by Margaret Postgate Cole – at once a poignant elegy, a powerful critique of the war and a negotiation with the pastoral tradition – as it moves beyond the battlefields or the actual years of the war to a postwar sense of futility and desolation:

And peace came. And lying in Sheer
I look round at the corpses of the larches
Whom they slew to make pit-props
For mining the coal for the great armies.

...

And if these years have made you into a pit-prop,
To carry the twisting galleries of the world's reconstruction
(Where you may thank God, I suppose,
That they set you the sole stay of a nasty corner)
What use is it to you?

THE CANON: ITS FORMATION AND EXPANSION

The 'war poet' and 'war poetry', observed Robert Graves in 1942, were 'terms first used in World War I and perhaps peculiar to it'. From Anglo-Saxon times to the Boer War, war poetry in English was written largely by civilians and did not have a clearly defined identity; with the extraordinary outpouring between 1914 and 1918, it established itself as a genre and the soldier-poet became a species. On Easter Sunday 1915, when Dean Inge read out 'The Soldier' by Brooke from the pulpit at St Paul's Cathedral, he was at once creating and anointing a secular saint: the 'poet soldier'.

Over the next three years, the 'poet soldier' would morph into 'soldier-poet', and by the 1930s he had become, according to Edmund Blunden, 'as familiar as a ration card'. The term 'war poetry' or 'war verse', by contrast, starts gaining currency from 1917 and crests in popularity in the post-war years. In her 1917 essay 'Contemporary British War Poetry, Music and Patriotism', Marion Scott – friend and music teacher of Ivor Gurney – noted an 'enormous increase in poetic output' related to the war, ranging 'from genius to doggerel'. This was partly the result of a conjunction of particular historical factors: a late Victorian culture of heroism and patriotism and a dominant public school ethos among the officer classes, as well as the more general spread of education.

Above all, the processes of recruitment – first voluntary and then the Conscription Acts of 1916 – meant that the British army included an enormous number of highly educated young men. According to Catherine Reilly's exhaustive bibliography, some 2,225 poets from Britain and Ireland alone wrote war poetry; only a handful among them are remembered today. In his letters of 1917, Owen refers to 'war impressions', 'war poem' and 'War Poetry', but in the celebrated Preface (1918) to his intended collection of poems, he eschewed the term 'war poet': 'That is why the true War Poets must be truthful'. The conflation of First World War poetry with the trench lyric was encouraged by the soldier-poets and anthologists, and consolidated with the publication of memoirs such as Graves's *Good-Bye to All That* (1929) and Sassoon's *Memoirs of an Infantry Officer* (1930).

Rapidly, the trench poets claimed centre-stage; civilian poets such as Hardy and Kipling moved to the margins. In the politicized climate of the 1930s, Owen and Sassoon became cultural icons. Both figured prominently along with other combatant poets in Frederick Brereton's *Anthology of War Poems* (1930) and Robert Nichols's *Anthology of War Poetry, 1914–18* (1943). However, it was with the renewed swell of interest in the group in the 1960s, with the musical *Oh! What A Lovely War* (1963) and anthologies such as Brian Gardner's *Up the Line to Death* (1964) and I.M. Parsons's *Men Who March Away* (1965), that the canon began to take shape more firmly. The process was completed by, among others, two literary critics: Paul Fussell, with his enormously influential *The Great War and Modern Memory* (1975), and Jon Silkin, with the *Penguin Book of First World War Poetry* (1979).

Over the last 30 years, the First World War and its literature have been powerfully reconfigured. The recovery in recent years of poetry by women, civilians, dissenters, working-class and non-English (particularly Irish, Scottish, Welsh and American) writers in anthologies has led both to an expansion and a rethinking of the canon. Moreover, developments in the general critical field – cultural studies, queer theory, work on testimony and trauma – have left their mark. The frameworks and critical idiom used to understand the popular soldier-poets have accordingly shifted: we have moved from a moral register of the 'truth of war' to an exploration of textual complexity and wider socio-cultural contexts; there is closer interrogation of the relationship between poetic form and historical, political and psychic processes; and far greater attention is being paid to questions of difference (class, nationality, gender and sexuality, among others).

In spite of this, however, colonial war poetry remains barely visible even in the recently expanded canon. Colonial war poetry, coming out of different political, social and cultural contexts, is a remarkably copious and varied body of work: it ranges from volumes by individual soldier-poets to anthologies such as *Soldier Songs from Anzac* (1915), *Indian Ink* (1915–16) and *Canada in Khaki* (1917) to poems by established figures such as Rabindranath Tagore in India, Robert Service in Canada and Clarence Dennis in Australia. For a variety of reasons, such poetry – with the exception of John McCrae's ubiquitous 'In Flanders Fields' – has proved resistant to assimilation within the war canon. Indeed, the project of recovering colonial or non-white First World War verse is not so much a matter of trying to find an Indian Owen or an Arab Sassoon, but trying to understand how the war affected the colonial poetic cultures more widely,

In his poem, 'The War Graves', Michael Longley writes, 'There will be no end to cleaning up after the war'. The war's debris – both physical and metaphorical – will be inspected afresh in the next four years. War poetry is often too neatly aligned with a political and moral agenda. While it is crucial to recognise the political force of First World War poetry, individual poems can be more complex and disturbing. Indeed, why does that strange word 'ecstasy' ('Gas! Gas! An ecstasy of fumbling/Fitting the clumsy helmets just in time') appear in the most grimly realistic of war poems – Owen's 'Dulce Et Decorum Est'? Indeed, 'strange' remains one of the most recurring words in First World War poetry, perhaps testifying to the strange fact that the traumatic debris of war would inspire, energise and even excite poetic language. Powerful war poems, such as Owen's 'Dulce' or Hardy's 'I looked Up from My Writing' often ask the most difficult ethical questions. As we approach the centennial commemoration of the war with ceremony, and young men and women continue to get killed in action, these poems bring us no immediate hope or assurance or comfort, but in their combination of pity, anger, moral complexity and linguistic pleasure, remind us as readers what it is to be idealistic, thoughtful, mortal, guilty – and make us question what it is to be human.

5

British Poetry of the Great War

INTRODUCTION

The Great War, which took place between 1914-1918, changed many aspects of British literature. Literature during the Great War reflects the changes society was undergoing and provides a drastic transition between pre and post war work. Many social, political and economic shifts occurred during the war. Many of the writers of the time felt the need to speak out against the flaws they saw in their society. Their poetry became an act of dissidence in a terrible time in our world's history. Women became key economic supporters in the absence of men and men suffered the physical and psychological stress of war. Women and men alike turned to writing as a means of emotional outlet. Women had to take on a role that was considered to be a more masculine job, most women got jobs working in factories in order to provide for their children. Additionally, women were forced to care for their family while the men were off at war. As a result many women began to speak out, discussing their view on the war and the impact it was placing on their families. The new style of war allowed soldiers an exorbitant amount of time to ponder the battles which they fought; writers and poets of the Great War attempted to distinguish how this war was different than anything the world had seen before.

THE GREAT WAR (1914-1918)

"Masses of dead bodies strewn upon the ground, plumes of poison gas drifting through the air, hundreds of miles of trenches infested with rats—these are but some of the indelible images that have come to be associated with World War I (1914-18). It was a war that unleashed death, loss, and suffering on an unprecedented scale." - The Norton Anthology of English Literature; Online Topics: Intro to 20th Century

Intro film on WWI, authentic footage and images

The Great War started on June 28, 1914, after a chain of events that followed the assassination of Francis Ferdinand, the Archduke of Austria-Hungary, and his wife. The war was fought by two separate sides, the Central Powers and the Allies.

- Central Powers: Germany, Austria-Hungary, the Ottoman Empire and Bulgaria
- Allies: United Kingdom, France, and the Russian Empire

Britain was an ally of France and it fell on the Britain to defend France against Germany. Also, due to the 1839 Treaty of London, Britain had a treaty with Belgium that required the defence of the neutral country after Germany's invasion on August 4th, 1914. On that day the Prime Minister, Herbert Asquith declared war on Germany. By default they went to war with the rest of the Central Powers.

The Great War brought about a new type of warfare that the world had never seen before. This is known as trench warfare.

- Trench warfare
  - Fighting from a network of fortifications dug or constructed at or below ground level.
  - Machine gun range and firing power made it impossible for troops to move to new positions
  - Trenches dug along battlefield fronts to fight without mobility
  - Resulted in stalemate, especially on Western Front, that lasted most of the war
  - Provided place and time for soldiers to get to know one another
  - Connected through networks; resting and off duty trenches
  - Soldier would eat, sleep, fight, rest in trenches
  - Area between trenches of opposing forces know as "No Man's Land"
  - Significant to literature because Trench Poetry was produced; soldiers needed to pass time during long periods in trenches
- Battle of the Somme (July 1 - Nov. 18, 1916):
  - Main allied attack on the Western Front
  - First British attack in war
  - 58,000 British troops lost in 1 day, remains record
  - 420,000 British troops lost total
  - Significant to British literature:
    a. Loss of men during first attack brought morale of soldiers down immensely
    b. Provided inspiration to utilize poetry as outlet for their emotions

Germany Crumbles

Gemany lost the war due to its people becoming tired of war. The sailors of the German Navy did not want to go back to see and began to mutiny. As a result, on November 9th, 1918, the Kaiser escaped across German lines into the Netherlands. On November 11th an armistice was signed and there was finally peace.

Treaty of Versailles

- June 28, 1919
- Peace treaty at the end of the war between Germany and the Allied Powers
- Negotiations took 6 months at the Paris Peace Conference

BRITISH POETRY OF THE GREAT WAR

THE TRENCH POETS

Wilfred Owen 1893-1918

"My subject is War, and the pity of War. The Poetry is in the pity." - Wilfred Owen, 1916

- British Soldier
- Known for realistic style
- Wrote on horrors of trench and gas warfare
- Endured many war injuries, resulting in "shell-shock"
- Intended to publish book of poetry, but killed in action on November 4, 1918
- Most of his poetry published after his death
- "His poetry often graphically illustrated both the horrors of warfare, the physical landscapes which surrounded him, and the human body in relation to those landscapes. His verses stand in stark contrast to the patriotic poems of war written by earlier poets of Great Britain, such as Rupert Brooke." - poets.org

ISAAC ROSENBERG 1890-1918

"I am determined that this war, with all its powers for devastation, shall not master my poeting; that is if I am lucky enough to come through it alright" - Isaac Rosenberg, 1916

- British Soldier
- Heavily influenced by Keats and other Romantics
- Enlisted in war because he was out of work poet
- Killed in action, 1918
- All works published after death
- "Rosenberg's poems, such as 'Dead Man's Dump' or the often-anthologized 'Break of Day in the Trenches,' are characterized by a profound combination of compassion, clarity, stoicism, and irony" - poets.org

LITERATURE THROUGH OTHER MEDIA

Trench Songs and Poetry

- Trench songs were poems written by both every-day soldiers and those who had previous literary backgrounds. They created short songs or poems which had a sing-song rhyme and often became known throughout the writers barrack. Some songs were notorious throughout certain regions. The language in many of the works is vulgar, after-all, soldiers put their feelings towards the war, fellow soldiers, and their superiors in writing. They used writing as an outlet for emotions which could not be honorably be spoken. Often trench songs were only sung among lower ranked soldiers. Their songs and poems revolve along such topics as their desire to go home, their personal lack of support for the war, problems with superiors, and other general annoyances in the camp.
  - "I Want to go Home"
  - I want to go home, I want to go home.

I don't want to go in the trenches no more,
Where whizzbangs and shrapnel they whistle and roar.
Take me over the see, where the Alleyman can't get at me.
Oh my, I don't want to die, I want to go home.

  - "Good-bye-ee"
  - "Never Mind"
  - "Bombed Last Night"
  - " I don't want to join the Army"
  - "Oh its a Lovely War"

WOMEN IN THE WAR

Gender Role Change and the Fatherless Family

Due to the absence of men on the home front, typically domestic British women occupied jobs that men usually did. Approximately two million women replaced men employment between 1914-1918. Many jobs were in factories that required heavy physical work, creating a new image of the woman worker. In addition to their masculine occupations, women had to care and provide for their families while their husbands were serving in the war. The change in gender role for women helped women suffrage in the future, however, the woman worker image was unfortunately only a temporary one. Immediately after the war, women resumed being the housewives they were prior to the Great War, even though it was not entirely voluntary on the woman's part.

Expression through Literature

Although the men were more physically affected by the Great War, women were also emotionally affected. Between their high level of stress from assuming the role of men in the workplace and home life and their sadness from being separated from their husbands, women found writing as a means of expressing their feelings and drastic situations. Women who became nurses used their exposure to and observations of wounded soldiers and hospital life as the main subjects of their writing.

SELECT WOMEN WRITERS

Vera Brittain (1893-1970)

During the war, Vera Brittain left Oxford to become a VAD nurse for four years. She married quartermaster-sergeant Roland Leighton, whose writing also played a major role in British literature during the war. They wrote letters and poems to each other while he was away before his untimely death in the war.

Her works include:

- *Verses of a VAD* (1918)
- *The Dark Tide* (1923) - first novel
- *Not Without Honour* (1924)
- *Testament of Youth* (1933)
- *Testament of Friendship* (1940)
- *Testament of Experience* (1957)

Eva Dobell (1867-1963)

Eva Dobell drew from her experiences as a volunteer nurse for inspiration when writing. She wrote to boost the morale of the wounded soldiers and was known to write about specific patients. A fan of sonnets, Eva was deeply affected by the war, which is easily visible in her poetry.

Eva Dobell's "Advent, 1916"

I dreamt last night Christ came to earth again
To bless His own. My soul from place to place
On her dream-quest sped, seeking for His face
Through temple and town and lovely land, in vain.
Then came I to a place where death and pain
Had made of God's sweet world a waste forlorn,
With shattered trees and meadows gashed and torn,
Where the grim trenches scarred the shell-sheared plain.
And through that Golgotha of blood and clay,
Where watchers cursed the sick dawn, heavy-eyed,
There (in my dream) Christ passed upon His way,
Where His cross marks their nameless graves who died
Slain for the world's salvation where all day
For others' sake strong men are crucified.

THEMATIC OUTCOMES AND TRENDS

"The excitement, however, came to a terrible climax in 1914 with the start of the First World War, which wiped out a generation of young men in Europe, catapulted Russia into a catastrophic revolution, and sowed the seeds for even worse conflagrations in the decades to follow. By the war's end in 1918, the centuries-old European domination of the world had ended and the "American Century" had begun. For artists and many others in Europe, it was a time of profound disillusion with the values on which a whole civilization had been founded. But it was also a time when the avante-garde experiments that had preceded the war would, like the technological wonders of the airplane and the atom, inexorably establish a new dispensation, which we call modernism."

THE POETRY OF WORLD WAR I

From poems written in the trenches to elegies for the dead, these poems commemorate the Great War.

Roughly 10 million soldiers lost their lives in World War I, along with seven million civilians. The horror of the war and its aftermath altered the world for decades, and poets responded to the brutalities and losses in new ways. Just months before his death in 1918, English poet Wilfred Owen famously wrote, "This book is not about heroes. English Poetry is not yet fit to speak of them. Nor is it about deeds, or lands, nor anything about glory, honour, might, majesty, dominion, or power, except War. Above all I am not concerned with Poetry. My subject is War, and the pity of War."

To mark the WWI centenary, we've put together a sampling of poems written in English by both soldiers and civilians, chosen from our archive of over 250 poems from WWI. We've also compiled a sampler showcasing the poets who served and volunteered in World War I.

While many of these poems do not address a particular war event, we've listed them by year, along with a selection of historical markers, to contextualize the poems historically. You may notice that more poems in 1914 and 1915 extoll the old virtues of honour, duty, heroism, and glory, while many later poems after 1915 approach these lofty abstractions with far greater skepticism and moral subtlety, through realism and bitter irony. Though horrific depictions of battle in poetry date back to Homer's *Iliad*, the later poems of WWI mark a substantial shift in how we view war and sacrifice.

1914

Archduke Ferdinand assassinated. Outbreak of war in July/August. Germany invades Belgium. First Battle of the Marne, First Battle of Ypres. United States remains neutral. Trench warfare begins. The Siege of Antwerp. The Christmas truce.

"Channel Firing" by Thomas Hardy

"On Receiving News of the War" by Isaac Rosenberg

"Peace" by Rupert Brooke (published in Poetry)
"The Soldier" by Rupert Brooke (published in Poetry)
"The Dead" by Rupert Brooke
"Joining the Colours" by Katherine Tynan
"Men Who March Away" by Thomas Hardy
"War Girls" by Jessie Pope
"On Heaven" by Ford Madox Ford (published in Poetry)
"To Germany" by Charles Sorley
"For the Fallen" by Laurence Binyon
"Phases" by Wallace Stevens (published in Poetry)
"Iron" by Carl Sandburg (published in Poetry)
"The Bombardment" by Amy Lowell (published in Poetry)
"War Yawp" by Richard Aldington (published in Poetry)
"Fallen" by Alice Corbin Henderson (published in Poetry)
"August 1914" by Mary Wedderburn Cannan
"August 1914" by Isaac Rosenberg
"August, 1914" by Vera Mary Brittain

1915

Germans sink RMS Lusitania*. The Dardenelles campaign. Battle of Gallipoli. Second Battle of Ypres. First use of poison gas.*

"In Flanders Fields" by John McCrae
"Absolution" by Siegfried Sassoon
"Home" by Edward Thomas
"Champagne, 1914-15" by Alan Seeger
"Belgium" by Edith Wharton
"Before Marching and After" by Thomas Hardy
"In Memoriam (Easter, 1915)" by Edward Thomas
"The Owl" by Edward Thomas
"A Lament" by Katherine Tynan
"The Spring in War-Time" by Sara Teasdale
"Into Battle" by Julian Grenfell
"On Being Asked for a War Poem" by William Butler Yeats
"Rouen" by Mary Wedderburn Cannan
"Marching" by Isaac Rosenberg (published in Poetry)
"Such, Such is Death" by Charles Sorley
"The Falling Leaves" by Margaret Postgate Cole
"When You See Millions of the Mouthless Dead" by Charles Sorley
"This is No Case of Petty Right or Wrong" by Edward Thomas

1916

Battle of Verdun, Battle of the Somme. President Wilson re-elected with campaign slogan, "He kept us out of the war." Rasputin is murdered.

"Rain" by Edward Thomas
"Break of Day in the Trenches" by Isaac Rosenberg (published in Poetry)
"The Troop Ship" by Isaac Rosenberg
"The Kiss" by Siegfried Sassoon
"The Poet as Hero" by Siegfried Sassoon
"As the Team's Head Brass" by Edward Thomas
"Sonnet 9: On Returning to the Front after Leave" by Alan Seeger
"In Time of 'The Breaking of Nations'" by Thomas Hardy
"Easter, 1916" by William Butler Yeats
"The Trumpet" by Edward Thomas
"The Messages" by Wilfrid Wilson Gibson
"The Death Bed" by Siegfried Sassoon
"Lights Out" by Edward Thomas
"The Night Patrol" by Arthur Graeme West
"The War Films" by Henry Newbolt
"The Twins" by Robert Service
"Ode in Memory of the American Volunteers Fallen for France" by Alan Seeger
"At the Movies" by Florence Ripley Mastin

1917

Germans issue Zimmerman Telegram to Mexico, United States declares war on Germany, draft begins. U.S. troops land in France. Third Battle of Ypres. Bolshevik uprising in Russia, led by Lenin, headed by Trotsky.

"Dulce et Decorum Est" by Wilfred Owen
"I Have a Rendezvous with Death" by Alan Seeger
"Blighters" by Siegfried Sassoon
"Two Fusiliers" by Robert Graves
"Anthem for Doomed Youth" by Wilfred Owen
"Returning, We Hear the Larks" by Isaac Rosenberg
"The Dead Kings" by Francis Ledwidge
"Servitude" by Ivor Gurney
"from Battle of the Somme: The Song of the Mud" by Mary Borden
"Dead Man's Dump" by Isaac Rosenberg
"Counter-Attack" by Siegfried Sassoon
"Sergeant-Major Money" by Robert Graves
"The Work" by Gertrude Stein
"To His Love" by Ivor Gurney
"After the War" by Mary Wedderburn Cannan
"To Any Dead Officer" by Siegfried Sassoon
"Photographs" by Ivor Gurney
"Breakfast" by Wilfrid Wilson Gibson

1918

U.S. President Wilson issues Fourteen Points to peace. Germany launches Spring Offensive, bombs Paris. United States launches attacks at Belleau Wood and Argonne Forest. Bolsheviks murder Tsar Nicholas II and Romanov family. Kaiser Wilhelm II abdicates, Germany signs armistice on November 11. Paris Peace Conference.

"Strange Meeting" by Wilfred Owen
"Futility" by Wilfred Owen
"Attack" by Siegfried Sassoon
"The Veteran" by Margaret Postgate Cole (published in Poetry)
"Repression of War Experience" by Siegfried Sassoon
"Grass" by Carl Sandburg
"Dawn on the Somme" by Robert Nichols
"God! How I hate you, you young cheerful men" by Arthur Graeme West
"Lettres d'un Soldat" by Wallace Stevens (published in Poetry)
"Ypres" by Laurence Binyon
"Spring Offensive" by Wilfred Owen
"Epitaph On My Days in Hospital" by Vera Mary Brittain
"Roundel" by Vera Mary Brittain
"War Mothers" by Ella Wheeler Wilcox
"Glory of Women" by Sigfried Sassoon
"Smile, Smile, Smile" by Wilfred Owen
"S. I. W." by Wilfred Owen
"And There Was a Great Calm" by Thomas Hardy

1919 and After

Armies demobilize, return home. Peace Treaty of Versailles ratified by Germany; U.S. Senate votes to reject treaty and refuses to join League of Nations. Proposal and constitution for League of Nations. The Cenotaph unveiled in London. Treaty of Sevres in 1920 ends war on Eastern Front.

"January 1919" by Christopher Middleton (1919)
"Everyone Sang" by Siegfried Sassoon (1919)
"The Cenotaph" by Charlotte Mew (1919)
"First Time In" by Ivor Gurney (1919)
"from Epitaphs of the War, 1914-18" by Rudyard Kipling (1919)
"Gethsemane" by Rudyard Kipling (1919)
"Hugh Selwyn Mauberley (Part I)" by Ezra Pound (1920)
"A.E.F." by Carl Sandburg (1920)
"To E.T." by Robert Frost (1920)
"In Memory of George Calderon" by Laurence Binyon (1920)
"War and Peace" by Edgell Rickword (1921)
"Trench Poets" by Edgell Rickword (1921)

"Soldier-Poet" by Hervey Allen (1921)
"For a War Memorial" by G.K. Chesterton (1921)
"Festubert, 1916" by Edmund Blunden (1921)
"Elegy in a Country Churchyard" by G.K. Chesterton (1922)
"Epitaph on an Army of Mercenaries" by A.E. Housman (1922)
"Soldier from the wars returning" by A.E. Housman (1922)
"I Saw England — July Night" by Ivor Gurney (1922)
"Champs d'Honneur" by Ernest Hemingway (1923) (published in Poetry)
"Laventie" by Ivor Gurney (1925)
"A War Bride" by Jessie St. John (1928) (published in Poetry)

6

Literary Views of the Great War 1914-1918

INTRODUCTION

The First World War or Great War was the first military conflict in history that evoked the widest possible spectrum of literary responses, ranging from enthusiastic patriotic affirmation to disillusioned *reductio ad absurdum*. The poets Rupert Brooke, Robert Nichols, Julian Grenfell, and Charles Sorley hailed the War as a renewal and purification, in time-hallowed terms and forms. The traditional commonplace metaphors gained new life from the feeling that the sickly sluggishness and suicidal subversionism of the Decadent Movement and the Fin de Siècle had to be overcome: a sick organism must be radically purged, foul weather must be cleared by a purifying thunderstorm or "stahlgewitter", wintry stagnation must be broken up to yield to regenerative vitality. Thus Robert Nichols proclaimed in 'The Day's March':

Heads forget heaviness,
Hearts forget spleen,
For by that mighty winnowing
Being is blown clean.

SACRIFICIAL BENEFITS OF THE WAR

The poets Rupert Brooke and Rudyard Kipling praised the sacrificial benefits of the War, with more or less strong evocations of the biblical doctrine of the *imitatio Christi* in faithfulness and self-sacrifice. The posthumous soldier-speaker of Kipling's lyric prayed in Picardy, like Christ in the Garden of Gethsemane, that his "cup might pass"; but the cup would not pass, and he met his death in a gas attack, like Christ on the cross upon Golgotha, beyond Gethsemane:

It didn't pass - it didn't pass
It didn't pass from me.
I drank it when we met the gas
Beyond Gethsemane.

Kipling also gave voice to an even more apocalyptic Christian view of the War current in Britain, based on the Anglo-Israel parallel. God's own chosen people, the British, and their Allies, fought the Battle of Armageddon against the Germans or "Huns", prophesied to lead to the final victory of good over evil upon the earth (Revelation 16. 16). King George and his true "God" would overcome Kaiser Wilhelm and his idol "Gott" just as the Kings of Israel and their true Jehovah overcame the heathens and their Baal:

Emmanuel's vanguard dying
For right and not for rights,
My Lord Apollyon lying
To the State-kept Stockholmites,
The Pope, the swithering Neutrals,
The Kaiser and his Gott

The neutrality, which Kipling here denounces, found a strong supporter in the dramatist G. B. Shaw. In such plays as *Heartbreak House* (1919) and *Saint Joan*(1923), Shaw diagnosed a number of low motives for the outbreak of the War: the Death Force (as opposed to the Life Force), the cupidity of capitalists, the inefficiency or greed and ambition of political leaders, the Pharisaism of patriots, and, last but not least, an animal mixture of stupidity and cruelty. The latter is especially stressed in St Joan's very modern plea for the abolition of the traditional chivalrous rules of warfare and the introduction of more effective armament, glancing at the radical innovations of the Great War. Both in his Essay *Commonsense About the War* (1914) and in various prefaces to his plays Shaw called upon the British and the Germans to mutually respect their cultural and scientific achievements, in the evolutionist's hope that progress in political science would lead to a victory over war just as progress in medicine would lead to a victory over certain diseases. Shaw's numerous suggestions that Britain had been no better than Germany were resented as subversive:

At all events it is clear that the kingdom of the Prince of Peace has not yet become the kingdom of this world. His attempts at invasion have been resisted far more fiercely than the Kaiser's.

It was exactly that fierceness of a "half-drunk or whole-mad soldiery" which W. B. Yeats criticized both in the Irish Easter Rising of 1916 and in the death in action of Major Robert Gregory in 1918, a false heroism prefigured in the myth of Cuchulain. Yeats's pacifism was not fundamental, but mystical and aesthetic, advocating an elegant, dance-like, balanced management of conflicts.

Another argument of a more radical aesthetic pacifism was, with varying emphasis, advanced by D. H. Lawrence and A. E. Housman, who regarded the War as a destruction of the male youth and beauty of rural old England, chiefly in the interest of money. As also in the case of Wilfred Owen, traditionalism and homoeroticismcombined into disgust of the War. In many homoerotic War poems, however, death in action was oddly welcomed as providing a remedy both against old age and against homophobic prejudice, fixing male beauty in the speakers' memories (in a Keatsian moment of highest bloom) and relieving its erotic enjoyment of all worldly encumbrance.

At the extreme subversive end of that wide spectrum of literary responses to the Great War stood those War poets who would more properly be called trench poets: Edward Thomas (born 1878), Frederic Manning (born 1882), Siegfried Sassoon (born 1886), Ivor Gurney and Isaac Rosenberg (both born 1890), Richard Aldington andOsbert Sitwell (both born 1892), Wilfred Owen and Herbert Read (both born 1893), Robert von Ranke Graves (born 1895), and Edmund Blunden (born 1896). Beside these major trench poets and conscious artists, scores of other names of trench soldiers could be added, whose shock erupted into verse, and whose poems are either still in manuscript or were printed in cheap rare editions. Some of them have been recently (and more or less deservedly) salvaged from oblivion.

These soldier poets were the first to experience the radical innovations, the breakdown of the old forms and norms of warfare as mirroring the final breakdown of all the crumbling forms and norms, that 'Crisis of European Civilization' which shattered all the brittle traditional beliefs. They experienced the War as a meaningless gap in time and history, raising their very personal and subjective experience to the rank of a general philosophy. They belonged to what Gertrude Stein and Ernest Hemingway called "the lost generation". Their pitiful or angry exposure of the absurdity of the Great War, as revealing the absurdity of life and death in general, proved a signal contribution to the breakthrough of literary 'Modernism'.

Trench poetry proper could only be written under the shock of the immediate experience of that radically new kind of warfare: either in the trenches themselves (as in the case of Isaac Rosenberg, who had only one brief leave in his twenty months at the Front), or in hospital (as in the case of Siegfried Sassoon and Wilfred Owen, who were wounded in the trenches and sent home for recovery, where they met), or immediately after the War (as in the case of Edmund Blunden, who survived sane), or in mental homes (as in the case of Ivor Gurney, who survived insane and relived his experience until his death in 1937). The freshness of this shock did not allow the trench poets to gain distance to their experience of total chaos, to relate it to new metaphysical or anthropological concepts, to discern new purposes in self-sacrifice and war, to re-establish a theodicy.

Such distance could only be either in time, after the immediate experience, or in space, removed from the immediate experience. Thus, Robert Graves later overcame the absurd view of life and death expressed in his trench poetry, *Over the Brazier* (1916) and *Fairies and Fusiliers* (1917), and elimitated these poems from later collections of his poetry. Thus, after a lapse of almost twenty years, the Welsh poet David Jones could rediscover a secret universal meaning in his very personal suffering in the trenches. His long epic of mixed poetry and prose, *In Parenthesis* (1937), written on the model of T. S. Eliot's *Waste Land*(1922) with its conglomeration of archetypes of ritual and mystery, succeeded in unbracketing the individual trench experience and relating it to previous noble wars and their epics of heroic self-sacrifice (such as *La Chanson de Roland* and *Y Gododdin*). Thus, the poetess May Wedderburn Cannan, who was a volunteer nurse behind the lines, and the poetess Jessie Pope and the popular novelist Mrs Humphry Ward, who never came near the front line, could write affirmative poems and tales restating Christian sacrifice and Britain's just cause.

On the whole, the most varied contemporary sources inform us that all those who had no immediate trench experience were quite incapable of believing the horrors of the chaos that trench soldiers (writing letters or wounded or on leave) reported. Small wonder that such trench soldiers were taken either for cowards, braggarts, or madmen. Thus, H. G. Wells could only write his shockingly realistic war novel *Mr Britling Sees It Through* (1916) in the context of a visit to the Western Front. The home-leave episodes in War memoirs and War novels, Robert Graves's *Goodbye to All That* or Erich Maria Remarque's *Im Westen nichts Neues* (both 1929), give us lively portraits of an irreconcilable clash. On the one hand, civilians and back area soldiers desperately clung to an already shaken belief in an orderly world where war was a natural season of divinely sanctioned and calculated conflict; on the other hand, trench soldiers shattered that shaken belief altogether. Wilfred Owen wrote one of his angriest poems on reading Jessie Pope's *War Poems* (1915), published to instil English children with a Horatian sense of patriotism. Had Jessie ever seen the chaos of the trenches, Owen scolded,

My friend, you would not tell with such high zest
To children ardent for some desperate glory,
The old Lie: Dulce et decorum est
Pro patria mori.

CRIMEAN WAR AND THE BOER WAR

The Crimean War and the Boer War could still be imagined at home; the Great War surpassed the imagination of all those who had no immediate trench experience. Never before in history had war so radically changed its face and turned into what seemed an autonomous *urchaos*. Camouflage and steel helmets replaced shining uniforms, tanks replaced horses, machine guns forced armies into immobile dirty trenches, aeroplanes and gas were other quite new weapons threatening the mass destruction of soldiers who had themselves become masses instead of individual combatants. The newness was registered on both sides, in Thomas Hardy's poem 'Then and Now' (1915) and in Karl Kraus's satire on "der chlorreiche Krieg". Paintings of War scenes, such as Stanley

Spencer's *Travoys* or John Singer Sargent's*Gassed*, show numbers of soldiers without individual faces. The impossibility of conventional individual heroism in that infernal chaos was obvious, and a favourite subject in the poetry and prose of the trench soldiers. The fallen enemy in Robert Graves's poem 'A Dead Boche' (1917) has no face, no name, no heroic attribute, not even any human attributes any more. The illusion of the hero's blood and fame gradually yields to a real vision of ugly black blood dribbling out of a stinking dehumanized clump of flesh (reminiscent of Benn's *Morgue* poems):

TO you who'd read my songs of War
And only hear of blood and fame,
I'll say (you've heard it said before)
"War's Hell!" and if you doubt the same,
Today I found in Mametz Wood
A certain cure for lust of blood:
Where, propped against a shattered trunk,
In a great mess of things unclean,
Sat a dead Boche: he scowled and stunk
With clothes and face a sodden green,
Big-bellied, spectacled, crop-haired,
Dribbling black blood from nose and beard.

George Winterbourne,the young protagonist of Richard Aldington's War novel *Death of a Hero*(1929), loses the heroic illusions of his traditional upbringing and civilian imagination in the mass-murderous battles of matériel, where he dies a quite unheroic death. Paul Bäumer, the young protagonist of Erich Maria Remarque's War novel *Im Westen nichts Neues* (1929), goes through a similar experience, in a similarly inverted *bildungsroman*. Christopher Tietjens, the progressively failing hero of Ford Madox Ford's novel tetralogy *Parade's End* (1924-1928), survives as an Edwardian Don Quixote in a disillusioned and profoundly unheroic and unaristocratic post-War England. Neither were "the impermanence of trench life and the sordidness of life in billets" and the "primitive filth, lice, boredom and death" compatible with conventional concepts of heroism. The maddening noise and mass slaughter in the trenches proved so unbearable that trench soldiers had to spend most of their time recovering and waiting behind the lines, in a boredom that was felt to be just as unheroic as death in action. When, at the end of a day of somewhat less mass slaughter on which Paul Bäumer dies, the army report summarizes that "all is quiet on the Western Front", the individual combatant counts for nothing, and all *post-mortem* heroicization is a no less insolent lie. Ten years after the end of the war, Sassoon wrote an angry sonnet on the heroicizing lies of War memorials, with tens of thousands of engraved individual names:

Who will remember, passing through this Gate,
The unheroic Dead who fed the guns?

Who shall absolve the foulness of their fate -
Those doomed, conscripted, unvictorious ones?
...
Here was the world's worst wound. And here with pride
"Their name liveth for ever," the Gateway claims.
Was ever an immolation so belied
As these intolerably nameless names?
Well might the Dead who struggled in the slime
Rise and deride this sepulchre of crime.

Modern armour and modern warfare had paradoxically reduced man to his nakedness, his ignoble savagery, both in his passive vulnerability and in his active aggressiveness, foreshadowing the characters of Tennessee Williams's plays. The illusion of safety behind armour-plated tanks and protecting walls had restored soldiers to a sense of human fragility, and consequently of a new brotherly "humanity" uniting and outliving the trenches, as in the Imagist verse of the Italian trench poet Giuseppe Ungaretti. But that sense of fragility paradoxically alternated with animalistic outbreaks of ferocity. Thus, Herbert Read's two volumes of trench poems were entitled *Songs of Chaos* (1915) and *Naked Warriors* (1919). His ironic Imagist poem 'The Happy Warrior' describes a soldier in a state of murderous frenzy, reminiscent of Lawrence of Arabia:

Bloody saliva
dribbles down his shapeless jacket.
I saw him stab
and stab again
a well-killed Boche.
This is the happy warrior,
this is he...

On the less shocking Eastern Front, the collapse of the old order of war was also obvious. In *Seven Pillars of Wisdom* (1926 and 1935), T. E. Lawrence described the first guerilla war that a civilized country (Britain) organized against another civilized country (Turkey), and his own frantic officer's orders to slaughter beaten and defenceless Turkish soldiers and prisoners. Both happened in open violation of the traditional chivalrous rules of warfare which Lawrence well knew and very highly respected as an expert in ancient and medieval war literature, carrying Malory's *Morte Darthur* in his saddle-bags throughout the Arabian campaign.

The maddening tension of his fascinating book lies in its Conradian dichotomy between involvement and judgement, honest confessions of the pleasures of slaughter alternating with stern moral assessments of human failure under tragic necessities. Such honest confessions, implicitly admitting the similarity of English, Turkish, and German War crimes, brought the excellently written book and its author much critical and personal hostility. Thomas Hardy's complaint of the loss of "knightlihood" in the Great War, though primarily aimed at Germany (for lack of immediate frontline experience), applied to the Eastern as well as the Western Front on both sides, and also to the unrestricted and murderous submarine war:

But now, behold, what
Is warfare wherein honour is not!
Rama laments
Its dead innocents:
Herod breathes:'Sly slaughter
Shall rule! Let us, by modes once called accurst,
Overhead, under water,
Stab first.'

THE RADICAL CHANGES IN CIVILIZATION

The awareness of the radical changes in civilization, which the War had made apparent, did not dawn upon the population of Britain until the years after the end of the War. One of the most comprehensive artistic accounts of that growing sense of historical discontinuity is George Orwell's novel *Coming Up for Air* (1939), written in the shadow of the unavoidably imminent Second World War. George Bowling, the novel's first-person narrator, a bourgeois and quite unheroic protagonist, looks back upon his life from 1938 against a background of new grotesquely bungled bomber and gas-mask exercises to 1893 (the year of his birth before the outbreak of the Boer War). This narrative device not only allowed Orwell to present the Boer War as Britain's last 'normal' war.

The protagonist's very personal and subjective stream of consciousness takes us, Proust-like, back into the *temps perdu* before 1914, into the War years 1914-1918, into the years following the peace, and time and again into 1938. These frequently shifting memories build up a contrast between "those days" of rural old England (before the Great War) and "these days" of lost identities (after the Great War).

"Those days" were not ideal times. There existed social injustice and poverty, there occurred private and commercial catastrophes. But in "those days" men were still individuals who had social as well as local roots. The cobbler and the grocer had been cobblers and grocers in one village for generations, their children had hidden playgrounds in the surrounding landscape, their food still had identity and taste. Men and women had their assigned gender roles, and churches were frequented. Signs of the decline of that old order appeared with the turn of the century: trade went down, bankruptcies forced more and more honest tradesmen out of their traditional professions into other jobs and out of their traditional villages into other places. Agnosticism and woman's suffrage added to the increasing decay of the old order.

Then came the Great War, experienced as a disruptive watershed in the history of European civilization, and the crumbling old order broke down completely. After the Great War, the chaos appeared to be complete, all identities lost. It was the England that Ezra Pound and D. H. Lawrence left in disgust, in 1919. Soldiers returning from the front had to find new jobs in new places, often as travelling salesmen, and went hunting for customers (in inversion of the old order). Analogously, shops and food lost their identities. General stores sold the most varied articles, restaurant chains sold generic food, fresh food was replaced by preserves, where fish and meat exchanged their taste.

Masses (of men and products), devoid of individual or corporate identity, revealed a cult of falseness: false teeth (with which the novel begins), false packing, false food, false playgrounds for children, false names, false grammar. "Ersatz" replaced the real thing. Gigantically disproportionate houses, where false replaced true Tudor, and gigantically disproportionate factories flattened villages and landscapes, providing mass housing and mass products for deracinated men. George Bowling's unsuccessful *recherche du temps perdu* anticipates Winston Smith's insofar as it is at the same time a displaced person's unsuccessful *recherche de l'identite perdue*.

George Bowling's view of deteriorating and identity-crippling post-War civilization is obviously George Orwell's. It was this mass civilization which, in Orwell's view, led to the dictatorships of Hitler and Stalin who could easily replace lost identities by new ones, as analysed in *Animal Farm* (1945) and *Nineteen Eighty-Four* (1949), with Big Brother as "Ersatzgott". George Bowling's *recherche du temps perdu*, first mental and then physical, ends in disappointment and the signs of a new imminent war. Sunk in the dump of modern civilization, more and more deprived of their genetic and acquired identities, neither fish nor men can any longer "come up for air". George Bowling's stream-of-consciousness evocation of his wartime experiences, as a young 'involuntary volunteer' wounded in the trenches, makes him realize how the absurdity of modern life broke out with the absurdity of the Great War:

It's very strange, the things the war did to people.... It was like an enormous machine that had got hold of you. You'd no sense of acting of your own free will, and at the same time no notion of trying to resist.... Why had I joined the army? Or the million other idiots who joined before conscription came in?... The machine had got hold of you and it could do what it liked with you. It lifted you up and dumped you down among places and things you'd never dreamed of...

Not only did soldiers realize that things just "happened" to them, and that they "found themselves" in unwanted situations, both when they volunteered and when bombs lifted them from one place to another. The traditional *homo ludens*, who steered his own fortunes, had been replaced by a *homo lusus*, a marionette that fortune played with. Soldiers also realized that the War machine itself was no longer under reasonable control and began to follow its own absurd dynamism, much like the wheels of machines and bicycles in the pre-War novels of H. G. Wells:

It was like a great flood rushing you along to death, and suddenly it would shoot you up some backwater where you'd find yourself doing incredible and pointless things and drawing extra pay for them. There were labour batallions making roads across the desert that didn't lead anywhere. There were chaps marooned on oceanic islands to look out for German cruisers which had been sunk years earlier...

Incompetent officers, mostly members of an obsolete aristocracy, gave stupid orders, until the whole chain of command was as disconnected as the torn bodies of their victims in their own armies. The disconnectedness and fragmentation of post-War life, already realized by 'modern' pre-War artists and magnified in the Great War itself, is symbolized in a grammatically crippled (pre-Dada) newspaper headline on a murder: "LEGS. FAMOUS SURGEON'S STATEMENT."

Orwell's novel raises the old Hobbesian question which the novels of Joseph Conrad and H. G. Wells as well as the psychoanalysis of Sigmund Freud raised before and after the War, and which is central to the verse of the trench poets. Possibly the war of everybody against everybody was the atavic human condition, *homo homini lupus*. Possibly all civilization was a mere crust, based upon a fragile social contract, ready to dissolve upon a call to arms. Possibly the relapsing of modern civilization into the primordial jungle had already begun, and Conrad was right in imagining that the jungle would finally be victorious: "The horror!" Possibly all historiography and mythography had told abject lies about the reality of past conflicts, and weak man had never had a chance against the brutal strength of a malevolent and godless fate, as in Robert Graves's poem 'Goliath and David' (1916). Possibly religious hold in life was a pious lie, and not even a Romantic prophetic child (Wordsworth's mighty prophet and seer blest) could detect a sanctuarium anywhere, as in Robert Graves's poem 'A Boy in Church' (1917). Or, in modern terms, life and death possibly were intrinsically absurd and circular, devoid of divine nature and aim and sense and order.

Similarly in Wells's War novel *Mr Britling Sees It Through* (1916), the protagonist asks himself whether the War had done more than merely "unmask reality." And Graves cast doubt upon the truth of all myths of creation:

Here now is chaos once again,
Primeval mud, cold stones and rain.

In their pessimistic view of man, however, Orwell's novels went a step beyond Wells's *The Island of Dr Moreau* (1896) and Conrad's *Heart of Darkness* (1902), with the War experience behind their back. Beyond evincing the anthropophagic and predatory nature of man chiefly from the natural cruelty of 'culturally unspoilt' children, they stressed their herding and hoarding instincts. George Bowling's Black Hand Gang and Big Brother's Young Spies are described in term of animal (especially wolf) packs that delight in hunting, roaming, creeping, torturing, and killing. The hunting instinct, which European civilization had only domesticated, would break all bounds when men and animals alike herded for war, Huns as well as non-Huns. The game would shed its rules and become brutal murder. In Siegfried Sassoon's fictionalized war memoirs, the George Sherston Trilogy, *Memoirs of a Fox-Hunting Man* (1928) was succeeded by *Memoirs of an Infantry Soldier* (1930). The transition appears natural, in George Sherston as well as his comrades in the trenches: "Dick's father was a very good man with a gun, so Dick used to say..." In Ford Madox Ford's novel *The Good Soldier* (1915), a study of the society that produced the Great War, the titular hero is Edward Ashburnham, a landowner of a redundant and useless aristocracy in search of a renewal of its traditional sphere of activity: war. There is chaos lurking behind the conservative façade, ending in suicide, and the bookcase holds a gun instead of books.

Not only hunting, but all games could be seen as temporarily domesticated battles. In the introduction to his best-selling anthology of War poems, *The Muse in Arms*(1917), E. B. Osborn called attention to the fact that "this stout old nation persists in thinking of war as a sport". In Wilfred Owen's poem 'Disabled' (MS 1917-18), a crippled soldier hears the voices of playing boys and remembers how he liked being cheered with a blood-smear down his leg after football, before a shell tore away both his legs. And the emotionally crippled soldier-speaker of Edward Thomas's poem 'Tears' (MS 1915) would cry, if cry he still could, when he remembers his former delight in watching a fox-hunt or a splendid military parade. Their sporting instincts had obviously driven both to volunteer for a War which cost the one his leg and the other his feelings.

With regard to the masses of volunteers on both sides and the triumph of the Death Force over the Life Force in the Great War, G. B. Shaw wrote in the preface to his War drama *Heartbreak House*:

What really happened was that the impact of physical death and destruction... tore off the masks of education, art, science, and religion from our ignorance and barbarism, and left us glorying grotesquely in the licence suddenly accorded to our vilest passions and most abject terrors.

Even the most sceptical of the trench poets, Isaac Rosenberg and Siegfried Sassoon and Wilfred Owen, and even the half-German poet Robert von Ranke Graves, as well as the half-German novelist Ford Madox Hueffer (later Ford), had volunteered, driven by an irresistible instinct. And those among them who were wounded and sent home longed to go back into the trenches, in spite of the insight that they had gained from their trench experience. Robert Graves, who records that absurdly inconsistent behaviour observed both in himself and others, attests that even Siegfried Sassoon "varied between happy warrior and bitter pacifist", and that he later offered a poem in praise of war as an ironical satire. And Graves slyly suggests that intellectuals and pacifists like Aldous Huxley and Bertrand Russell did not volunteer for the simple reason that they were rejected for being too ill or too old. It should be added that even Isaac Rosenberg, one of the bitterest trench poets, initially wrote patriotic poems in praise of the War. Rosenberg's later shamefaced statement, that he had been poor and volunteered for the money, must be regarded as an anti-myth and *post festum* excuse.

Orwell's George Bowling summarizes the absurdity and confusion of such helpless, senseless, and incoherent *geworfensein.* Dumped down in the muck of a ditch by a shell and then back into civilian life by the same "enormous hand" or "enormous machine", George Bowling realizes that post-War existence with its reckless fight for jobs and housing is much more warlike than "those days" before the War. The new mass civilization with its brittle Peace of Versailles had imposed a thinner crust and poorer domestication upon that predatory animal, man. *Vivere militare est.* The Second World War would soon follow the First, as its natural result.

But, retrospectively, pre-War life had also already shown closer affinities to the Great War than tradition would allow to admit. There was the same social hierarchy, with the same stupid and obsolete aristocrats in command of university dons, who were in command of the death-doomed privates. The trenches bore the names of well-known streets, squares, and junctions. And the soldiers, bored in a War stuck in the mud due to new machine guns, alternately played games, killed enemies, and read or wrote literary texts. *C'était une drôle de guerre.*

Retrospectively, the Great War proved to be the result not only of a fatal network of alliances, but as the historically and psychologically unavoidable *mise en scène* of feelings and convictions of a death-doomed world that had lost both its sense and support. War had been in the air, which well before it broke out was a subject of the poetry and painting of all the European countries involved. The Austrian poets Georg Heym (died 1912) and Georg Trakl (died 1914) described it in terms of their inherited *fin-de-siècle* imagery of autumnal decay.

The German poet Gottfried Benn refashioned Baudelaire in his *Morgue* cycle (1912), reducing human existence to hollow bodies rattling themselves into life and again out of life after having been moved round an absurd circle of mere incoherent coincidences, a confused mass of fragmentarily perceived or amputated limbs, in a life or death where (as in the later poetry of the trenches) rats and flowers have more individuality and command more sympathy than men. The German painters Otto Dix and George Grosz (later soldiers of the trenches) and Ernst Ludwig Kirchner painted street scenes with hollow houses and hollow men in chaotic cities that show waste-land scenes of barrenness, war chaos, war devastation, war fire, and death years before the outbreak of the War, claiming war to be the condition of modern man even in what was misnamed 'peace'. In pre-War paintingsJames Ensor, Egon Schiele and Emil Nolde, human beings appear as faceless fragments or histrionic masks in a mere circus world, a theme later insistently taken up by Max Beckmann. The mask is no longer a temporary and ritual alter ego for a divinely created unique and distinctive individual that can (and must) again unmask itself, but the arbitrarily interchangeable husk of hollowness and emptiness. It is typical of these paintings that their hollow-eyed men and women move on unstable, slippery ground. Any metaphysical or physical individuality or security in life is implicitly denied. Their hollowness, their waste-land situation, and their lack of an individual core reflect similar images of man in the earlier novels of H. G. Wells,anticipating central themes in the early poetry of T. S. Eliot, *Prufrock* (1915), *The Waste Land* (1922) and *The Hollow Men* (1925). Thus, the War made apparent that absurdity of human existence to which 'Modern' artists had already given expression, in various movements and styles characterized by a multiplicity of -isms, itself a manifestation of the sense of disconnectedness and fragmentariness: Imagism, Vorticism, Divisionism, Expressionism, Cubism, Futurism, Cubo-Futurism, Constructivism, etc.

Wilfred Owen's poem 'Apologia Pro Poemate Meo' (MS 1917), an *ars poetica* of trench poetry, poses the question of the absurdity of all existence in view of the physical experience of such chaotic confusion:

Merry it was to laugh there -
Where death becomes absurd and life absurder.
For power was on us as we slashed bones bare
Not to feel sickness or remorse of murder.

The poem is a plea for the aesthetics of ugliness and chaos, in rejection of any literary rule of reason or decorum as well as any theology. After a short perversion of Henry Cardinal Newman's experience of God in its first line, the poem proceeds to an ironical hymnification of trench life as the human condition. Where mud and excrement replace biblical clay, the absurdity of life and death becomes apparent, just as in the disorderly confusion of established categories. Where hell is but trench life and heaven but the trajectory of a shell, fair and foul become indiscriminate and merge into wry laughter. Owen describes a mixture that was later elaborated in the theatre of the absurd:

I have perceived much beauty
In the hoarse oaths that kept our courage straight;
Heard music in the silentness of duty;
Found peace where shell-storms spouted reddest spate.

War poems, War novels, and War memoirs frequently describe scenes of misplaced, mad mirth. There was the infernal grin in the faces of soldiers who died in greatest pain, and there was the frequent dementia due to shell-shock and gas-raids. But these appeared as mere related symptoms of a more universal disease, the total loss of order. Isaac Rosenberg, the most visionary of all the trench poets, wrote consciously uncoordinated poems evoking scenes of trench life as "a demons' pantomime" with men "flung on the shrieking pyre", with "grinning faces" and "yelling in lurid glee". In 'Dead Man's Dump', the speaker wildly addresses a merely mad earth, which had formerly been seen as the divine seedground of the dialectics of birth, death, and resurrection:

Maniac Earth! howling and flying, your bowl
Seared by the jagged fire, the iron love,
The impetuous storm of savage love.
Dark Earth! dark Heavens! swinging in chemic smoke,
What dead are born...?

Small wonder that shrieking madness was perceived and formulated everywhere, both literally and metaphorically. Robert Graves's War memoirs *Goodbye to All That* (1929), his farewell to the old life in an old world, describes frequent scenes of madness, such as the "nightmare" when the inmates of a lunatic asylum were "caught between two fires, broke out and ran all over the countryside". In Wells's *Mr Britling Sees It Through*, the protagonist's son Hugh, a volunteer in Flanders, sends disappointed letters about the War's madness and absurdity. So, he reports the senseless prolonged shelling of an empty village, misaimed with the destruction of only one or two houses "just as though they had been kicked to pieces by a lunatic giant". And in Orwell's *Coming Up for Air,* George Bowling finds that after the War the old feudal Binfield House has been converted into a "loony bin".

God, it was said, died in the trenches of the Great War, after the increasing doubt that atheists and agnostics had for more than a century cast upon His existence. And with Him died the belief in the *harmonia mundi* as the expression of the sanity of the world. The trench poets' harping on the mad shrieks of battles of materiél as modern harmony coincided with Arnold Schönberg's composition of atonal music. The "maniac blast" of barrage-fire was felt to be the concert of a modern world torn and undermined by war, as in Edmund Blunden's poem 'Concert Party: Busseboom':

To this new concert, white we stood;
Cold certainty held our breath;
While men in the tunnels below Larch Wood
Were kicking men to death.

The soldiers listen to that maniac blast as they would formerly have listened to a tonal symphony. This imaginative pattern, the observance of old forms filled with new opposite contents, is also that of literary parody. Parody, especially of church anthems, hymns, and Georgian pastorals, easily offered itself to the trench poets. Robert Graves reports how spontaneously soldiers perceived a mess of officers as "a caricature of the Last Supper", and how readily they exchanged the words of hymns so as to discredit the biblical message of any church- or field-service. Where "the last trump" of the Apocalypse became "the last crump" (a German shell) of the Great War, any metaphysical perspective was denied and ridiculed. Wilfred Owen's 'Anthem for Doomed Youth' (MS 1917) is perhaps the most consistent and best-known exercise in techniques of perversion, typical of trench poetry. Thundering guns replace harmonious passing-bells, rattling rifles replace prayers, the mad noise of shells replaces choirs, the tears of boys and the pallor of girls replace candles and palls. The deconstruction of the *Missa Pro Defunctis* is underlined by pararhymes:

What passing-bells for these who die as cattle?
- Only the monstrous anger of the guns.
Only the stuttering rifles' rapid rattle
Can patter out their hasty orisons.

There existed other - inherited and radicalizable - literary techniques to discredit conventional faith. One was the *reductio ad absurdum* of the dialogue between man and God, and, analogously, man and God's alleged representatives upon earth, divines and officers. The soldier asking questions underneath a cross, or being sermonized by a preacher or instructed by an officer, is offered ready-made clichés instead of answers: purification, regeneration, sacrifice. Underlining the disruption of communication, the soldiers' questions are in modern dialect, and their superiors' answers in obsolete Authorized Version or Book of Common Prayer English. Sassoon's poems 'They' and 'Christ and the Soldier' are typical instances of this pre-absurd technique. Another, related technique of discrediting was the negation of the redemptive power of Christian symbols, in the literary tradition of Romantic disillusionism (Byron, Heine, Leopardi). The cross, like the charred trees, shows unregenerative death; the sun wakes the seeds, but not the dead; the rain and the wind do not "quicken a new birth", but soak the trenches in mud and cold; "bitter stars" and "withered suns" stare indifferently down upon a "Devil's Mass" of a War instead of conferring biblical peace and consolation. Richard Aldington's 'Battlefield' is a 'Waste Land', though without T.S. Eliot's later hope of regeneration:

The wind is piercing chill
And blows fine grains of snow
Over this shell-rent ground;
Every house in sight
Is smashed and desolate.
But in this fruitless land,
Thorny with wire
And foul with rotting clothes and sacks,
The crosses flourish -
Ci-gît, ci-gît, ci-gît...

'Ci gît 1 soldat Allemand,
Priez pour lui.'

The grave is not a solemn promise of *resurrectio mortuorum*, but a most unholy dead and anonymous man's dump. Either the frozen earth would not admit a burial of the dead, or falling bombs would fling the buried corpses up again and again, as a modern circular form of the resurrection. Wells's novel *Mr Britling Sees It Through*imagines such a scene of repeated piecemeal resurrection by shelling:

And as luck would have it, he was spun up again. In pieces. The trench howled with laughter...

This is the same absurd laughter described in Owen's 'Apologia Pro Poemate Meo'.

All the major trench poets, including the self-taught Isaac Rosenberg, were conscious artists, steeped in pre-War English literature, philosophy, and theology. Late Victorian and Edwardian epistemological scepticism, relativism and perspectivism, the reduction of the world to an indvidual's experience of disrupted sensations, was quite familiar to them. It prefigured their later very personal and narrow trench-view of war and peace, death and life. The saying that the trench experience made them poets is a similar terrible simplification as the saying that they went into the War like Rupert Brooke and came out like Siegfried Sassoon. Their reading, especially in Romantic and neo-Romantic literature, was enormous, so that they knew the religious and literary conventions which they alternately followed and undermined. They had published poems, written poems, or at least cultivated literary connections before the War, and they continued doing so in the trenches. Isaac Rosenberg, though delighting in the Romantic image of an untaught child of nature, carried on a sophisticated literary correspondence with Edward Marsh, editor of *Georgian Poetry* (1912-1922). And Rosenberg might also have become a professor of poetry specializing in the Romantics, like Edmund Blunden and Herbert Read, had he survived the War like them.

Georgian poetry, often misunderstood as a pastoral escape from 'Modernism', was the starting point of most trench poets. Georgian poetry was one of several attempts at overcoming the literature of the *décadence* and*fin de siècle*, in this case by a recourse to the beauty and vitality of English landscape. But unprejudiced readers of the pre-War Georgian poetry and prose of Rupert Brooke or Edmund Blunden or Edward Thomas will notice the modern undertone of doubt, just as viewers of the pre-War Georgian landscape paintings of the later trench painter Paul Nash will note the menacing quality of seeming idylls. Rupert Brooke's poem 'The Old Vicarage, Grantchester' (MS 1912) ends on too many question marks, and his 'Five War Sonnets' (MS 1914) contain too many subtle satirical lunges at established rites of war to be read as pure confirmations of man's vital regeneration by England's landscapes and England's wars. Had Brooke not died in 1915, on his way to the Eastern Front and without the trench experience, he might well have come to write trench poems like Sassoon's or Owen's. In 1917, with the disillusioning experience of the trenches of the Western Front, Ivor Gurney wrote 'Five War Sonnets' in critical imitation of Rupert Brooke's. In these he consciously darkened Brooke's shades of doubt, while minimizing his belief in the sense of the War for rural old England:

So the dark horror clouds us, and the dread
Of the unknown....But if it must be, then
What better passing than to go out like men
For England, giving all in one white glow?
Whose bodies shall lie in earth as on a bed,
And as the Will directs our spirits may go.

GEORGIAN POETRY

Firstly, Georgian poetry was neo-Romantic poetry of a seemingly "spontaneous overflow of powerful feelings" or "emotions recollected in tranquillity", quite distinct from Imagist poetry with its 'early Modern' insistence on formal precision and emotional detachment. Occasional attempts at writing Imagist trench poems, as was done by Herbert Read and Isaac Rosenberg, were quickly dropped because they could not adequately convey the trench experience. Secondly, Georgian poetry with its elements of doubt easily offered the techniques of a destruction of pastoral illusion, especially with a background knowledge of William Blake's *Songs of Innocence*(1789) and *Songs of Experience* (1794). Insofar, Edward Thomas's 'As the Team's Head Brass' (MS 1916) may be read as an ironical counterpart to Rupert Brooke's 'The Old Vicarage, Grantchester'. Georgian pastoralism is progressively unmasked as an illusion, when Thomas's speaker watches a ploughman with his team of horses and the flashing brass on their harness. The elm, symbol of vitality, was felled by a natural disaster, a blizzard, analogous to the War in which the other horses and the ploughman's mate were conscripted and killed. The information is conveyed in a dialogue between the speaker and the ploughman, and ends on the sceptical reflection that a peaceful world "might seem good" if "we could see all". The dialogue is just as torn as the poem's metre and rhyme-scheme. Again, peace is no real alternative to war. Lovers, who disappear at the poem's beginning, emerge out of the wood again, the short idyll is past, *post coitum homo tristis*. And the disappointed speaker sees the initially idyllic scene in terms of toil and torn earth:

Then
The lovers came out of the wood again:
The horses started and for the last time
I watched the clods crumble and topple over
After the ploughshare and the stumbling team.

A study of Edmund Blunden's landscape-centred War poems reveals a similar progression from illusions of innocence to experience of earthly reality, though without Blake's millenarian synthesis. As in 'Thiepval Wood', there is no regeneration for the charred stalks of trees in a shell- and gas-defiled earth:

Ember-black the gibbet trees like bones or thorns protrude
*From the poisonous smoke - past all impulses.*85

Byronic negative Romanticism is here driven to its extreme, using Byron's literary techniques. The extreme consists in the suggestion that ugliness and deformity are the beauty and natural order of the modern world, deprived of its former cultural varnish. Blackened trees that looked like pillars or gibbets, or that were artificial traps to hide snipers; the above-mentioned atonal symphony of shelling; faces covered by soot or grotesque gas-masks; zeppelins or planes or tanks or submarines that looked like strange and ugly additions to the old creation; the whole War stuck in the mud of trenches due to monstrous machine-guns; and the breakdown of the traditional chivalrous rules of warfare by land and water; - all that seemed to confirm H. G. Wells, whose novel *The Island of Dr Moreau* (1896) had doubted the existence of 'natural' forms and norms, both physical and moral.

Analogous to this was the above-mentioned denial of a divine natural core in individual man, identity as opposed to mask. It constituted a reversion from the Judaeo-Christian doctrine of the individual soul to former polytheism, which (as cultural anthropology has shown) had known no such difference between *persona* (the inner individual) and *persona* (the outer mask). Scepticism towards physical verities found its parallel in scepticism towards psychological verities. Man had begun sacrilegiously to understand himself as an amalgam of exchangeable masks (which could be peeled like the rings of an onion), a Proteus varying between peacefulness and aggressiveness, refinement and vulgarity, deceit and honesty.

Thus, in André Gide's novel *Les caves du vatican* (1914) or Wells's novel *The History of Mr Polly* (1910), characters like Protos or Polly can alternately be stupid and brilliant, moral and criminal, courageous and cowardly, reckless and conscience-ridden, believers or unbelievers. The denial of natural individuality and identity preceded the denaturation and de-individualization of man in the trenches of the Western Front. Again, the shocks of the War blew up beliefs that pre-War scepticism had already shaken.

The Island of Dr Moreau, Wells's nominalistic and perspectivistic nightmare of the possible arbitrariness of all physical and psychological fixities, as well as of the possible fraudulence of all ethical and aesthetical norms, corresponded to the nightmarish confusion of the trench soldiers. Everything that had been dear to the Romantic and Georgian lovers of nature, - love, fresh spring, red dawn, green trees, rain showers, the song of birds, the beauty of butterflies -, was suddenly either false or deadly. In Isaac Rosenberg's poems 'Spring 1916'

(MS 1916) and 'Returning, We Hear the Larks' (MS 1917) spring, song, lark, and love are divested of their Romantic Shelleyan symbolism of regeneration and metaphysical certainty. The larks appear as mocking harbingers of death, their song "showering" down at uncertain moments upon blind soldiers who can no longer see the sky, any more than lovers can see the serpent hiding to destroy them. In Remarque's *Im Westen nichts Neues*, young Paul Bäumer is shot dead when thinking of beautiful autumnal trees (in the novel of 1929) or while observing a beautiful butterfly (in the film version of 1930). And Edmund Blunden's poem 'Trench Raid Near Hooge' visualizes false untimely dawns with false thunders which are, in reality, caused by deadly gunfire, bombs, and shells. The traditional Homeric epithet is discredited:

At an hour before the rosy-fingered
Morning should come
To wonder again what meant these sties,
These wailing shots, these glaring eyes,
These moping mum,
Through the black reached strange long rosy fingers;
All at one aim
Protending and bending...

This alienation of nature and beauty was the more nightmarish for its breaking of assumed units. The mass of dismembered bodies and the distorted vision of the battlefield upon a torn earth shaking under heavy bombing and obscured by nebelwerfer weirdly confirmed the truth of the fragmented view of things in the pre-War prose of Wells and Conrad, the poetry of Pound and Eliot, the Cubist paintings of Braque and Picasso. The surface of earth and civilization, broken in peace and finally rent up by the War, revealed a nightmarish inferno. Surrealistic techniques and fantasies of dreamlike subterraneous adventures, developed in Horace Walpole's Gothic Novel and Coleridge's Mystery Poems and Poe's Tales, combined with reports of the new nineteenth-century sciences psychiatry and psychoanalysis and found their way into trench poetry - and via trench poetry into post-War surrealism. The modern entropic assumption that hell is not a place of the world beyond, but the chaos within and without man, is here anticipated. The Hindenburg Line and the Maginot Line, with their long, maddening, dark tunnels above and below ground, naturally recalled both Romanticism and psychoanalysis. Sassoon's poem 'The Rear-Guard' (MS 1917) imagines a soldier staggering through a tunnel up on his way to the battleground:

Groping along the tunnel, step by step,
He winked his prying torch with patching glare
From side to side, and sniffed the unwholesome air.

The tunnel's narrowness suggests fatalism, tragic necessity, its chaos and stench and animality and dead bodies suggest hell. The soldier's *ascensio* is not a dignified man's traditionally expected escape from hell to heaven, but a sniffing, creeping, groping, staggering, grabbing and climbing creature's movement underground. The biblical creature man is the heaven-orientated crown of creation, endowed with a *natura humana separata*; by contrast, the soldier of trench poetry is re-bestialized, even, as in Rosenberg's poem 'Break of Day in the Trenches' (MS 1916), below the rats who are at least cosmopolitan. The biblical people that walked in darkness have seen a great light; by contrast, the soldier who gropes his way in darkness sees nothing but "dawn's ghost", "the rosy gloom of battle overhead", and "twilight air", and even that is nothing but the artificial light of gunfire. Here was a troglodyte world where soldiers felt they had relapsed from the illusory dignity of civilization into the pristine company of the omnipresent rats, a fact noted in numerous War poems, memoirs, and novels.

Sassoon's soldier is not identified with regard to his nationality, implying the poet's quite unpatriotic awareness of the universality of the experience. Much the same applies to the speakers of Owen's poems 'Miners' and 'Strange Meeting' (both MSS 1918). Both speakers are soldiers who have dreamy visions of their enemies and of imminent unavoidable death. The first speaker listens to the sounds of his fireplace which spark off Coleridgean musings, of pristine earth before civilization, of miners suffering in pits and soldiers suffering in tunnels. The pristine human condition is the same in peace and war. All life is war, and peace is found in death alone:

I thought of all that worked dark pits
Of war, and died
Digging the rock where Death reputes
Peace lies indeed.

The second speaker tells a dream of his escape from battle down "some profound dull tunnel". But, instead of peace, he found a pristine inferno where he met the ghost of an enemy soldier whom he had recently killed. The ghost's concluding speech, coined by the omniscience of the dead, forms the longest part of the poem and reveals the enemy soldier to be the speaker's *alter ego*. He speaks "truths that lie too deep for taint", of the hopelessness of a civilization relapsing into barbarity, of the war poet's commitment to the cathartic pity of the war. Tragedy ends in death, and the ghost invites the speaker, Hamlet-like, to follow him: "Let us sleep now... " A few months after the composition of his visionary poem, Owen was killed in action, a week before the end of the War.

Wells's Mr Britling realizes more and more, not least through the letters and final death in action of his shocked son Hugh (initially an enthusiastic volunteer), that the War has become a "bickering futility" and a "nightmare vision". This realization shatters Mr Britling's inherited Christian theodicies, and he becomes fragmentary and discontinuous in his search for new explanations of this suffering world. Was the world created by a malignant spirit, as in Gnosticism? Is the War a step in the scale of evolution towards higher things, such as a future federal world republic? Is God finite instead of omnipotent, Himself subject to a blind fate? All these heretical explanations have one thing in common: a sense of fatalism and helplessness in view of an absurd and bungled War which ran out of human control. When, at the end of the novel, Mr Britling forces his way back into orthodoxy in a desperate rage of traditional theodicy, both his style and the symbolism of the surrounding landscape discredit the possibility that the old order - and its philosophy and theology - could ever be genuinely recovered. The Christian symbol of the cock upon the spire, announcing the break of the dawn of mankind, is undermined by sights and sounds of scythes und guns:

It was as if there was nothing but morning and sunrise in the world. From away towards the church came the sound of some early worker whetting a scythe.

The Crisis of European Civilization may, from a historian's point of view, be a myth engendered by the perspectivism and relativism of pre-War philosophy and literature, as Samuel Hynes claims, "the myth of disruption and fragmentation that is the Myth of the War". In the history of ideas, however, it marked a further advance of the philosophy and literature of the absurd (often inadequately identified with 'Modernism'), a philosophy and literature under way ever since Byronic negative Romanticism. But 'modernism' is an unoriginal make-shift and omnibus term for various innovating ideological and stylistical tendencies in twentieth-century arts, which had their roots in the nineteenth century. As such, 'Modernism' is definable rather as the period or movement that was obliged to come to terms with the absurd, not only as a monolithic ideological formation accepting the absurd and giving it artistic forms. Later poets, the David Jones of *In Parenthesis* (1937) and the T.S. Eliot of *Four Quartets* (1943) and the Robert Graves of *Collected Poems* (1955), succeeded in overcoming Wilfred Owenism. Their works reformulate 'the circuitous journey of Ulysses', the Modern dialectical and melioristic recovery of their lost religious identity out of the bomb-rubble of their shattered belief in the sense of human suffering in wars, and out of their idolatry of the very Unholy and Absurd Trinity of Fate, Accident, and Nature's Blind Will.

LITERATURE AND THE GREAT WAR

CONFLICT, CULTURE, LANGUAGE, AND LITERATURE 1914-1918

Literature and the Great War is a study of the relationship between language, literature, and the events of the conflicts that took place between 1914 and 1918. It also addresses the fact that quite a lot of what we call 'war poetry' and 'first world war memoirs' was not produced during that period, but many years later – for very good reasons. With the exception of poetry, which can quickly capture impressions and emotions on the fly, most writing about major events in other genres such as stories, novels, documentaries, histories, and autobiographies require a period of reflection and digestion before they can be properly expressed. This is especially true of events as cataclysmically disruptive as the first world war – which turned the whole world's view of itself upside down.

There were memorable and enduring works written during the conflict — Henri Barbusse's *Under Fire*(1916) and the poetry of Wilfred Owen and Edward Thomas. However, the majority of works which seem to encapsulate both the horrors of the war and the almost universal sense of disillusionment which followed were produced almost a decade later — Robert Graves*Goodbye to All That* (1929), Ernest Hemingway *A Farewell to Arms* (1929), Richard Aldington, *Death of a Hero* (1929), Siegfried Sassoon *Memoirs of a Fox-Hunting Man* (1928), R.C. Sheriff*Journey's End*(1929), Erich Maria Remarque *All Quiet on the Western Front* (1929)

There are a number of explanations for this delay. Many people felt that the horrors of the war were almost too shocking to write about at the time – especially when official propaganda and the newspapers were telling everybody about 'heroic' victories and not mentioning the vast number of men slaughtered (the hundreds of thousands killed were described as 'wastage').

After the war very few combatants wanted to talk about their experiences, and those who had survived understandably wanted to simply get back to normal life, often feeling guilty about those they had left behind on the Somme, Passchendale, and Gallipoli.

Because everyone had been persuaded that it had been a 'war to end all wars' there was a general sense that optimism would prevail. But then in the 1920s came a period of economic collapse, austerity, and poverty throughout most of Europe. Instead of having fought a war to achieve a better world, it appeared that nothing had been achieved at all, and the huge sacrifice of lost lives had been wasted..It was the period from late 1920s onward when the spate of angry, critical, and anti-establishment narratives concerning 1914—1918 were produced

Nor should it be thought that during the war itself the public were eager for critical accounts of the carnage, the gassings, and the colossal numbers of people killed. Some of the most popular publications at the time were patriotic and religious works speaking to 'heroism', 'sacrifice'. and 'victory'.

Stevenson's (persuasive) argument is that society in the post-war period felt saturated by this sort of language, and writers purged their vocabularies of these now-corrupted abstract generalisations. They used instead a language of concrete nouns, in which only that-which-can-be-known was named. Hence the rise in popularity in the 1920s of writers such as Ernest Hemingway, whose terse and pared-down literary prose style had been shaped by his experience of the first world war:

I was always embarrassed by the words sacred, glorious, and sacrifice and the expression in vain ... I had seen nothing sacred, and the things that were glorious had no glory and the sacrifices were like the stockyards at Chicago .... Abstract words such as glory, honour, courage or hallow were obscene beside the concrete names of villages, the numbers of roads, the names of rivers, the numbers of regiments and the dates.

The Sun Also Rises (1926) and *A Farewell to Arms* (1929) were enormously popular at the time, and went on to influence two or three generations of writers (particularly writers of thrillers and crime fiction) until the fashion for this sort of writing faded (following Hemingway's suicide) in the 1960s.

Stevenson argues that the war produced a fracturing of time and language. Events began to be described as 'pre-war' and post-war'; double summer-time was introduced; and ordinary men and women were plunged into a linguistic vortex in which official language in no way reflected the reality they faced every day in the trenches.

An interesting point he makes about the *language* of the war is that many of the volunteers and conscripts who took part from the early days of 1914 onwards would be young men (almost boys) who at that time had probably never travelled more than a few miles beyond their own towns and villages. Consequently, since there was at that time, no national broadcasting system, they would never have heard speech other than their own regional accents.

In addition to this, they were plunged into Picardy, where the vast majority of them had never heard the French language spoken before. It is not surprising that towns such as Ypres and Auchonvillers were translated into 'Wipers and 'Ocean Villas' and indeed the satirical newspaper produced by the troops was called the *Wipers Times*. Newly conscipted men also had to grapple with enormous amounts of army slang and jargon – some of it remnants of the imperial past. Words such as *cushy*, *blighty*, and *dekko* were Hindi or Urdu in origin.

The latter part of the book is devoted largely to the reception and evaluation of poetry produced *during* the war and in the years since, reminding us that at the time religious and patriotic poetry was far more highly regarded, whereas the critical reputation of writers such as Owen, Thomas, and Sassoon has taken much longer to establish

I was glad to see that he put the reputation of Rupert Brooke into perspective. Brooke had glorified a jingoistic sense of Englishness and war prior to 1914 but didn't actually have any first-hand experience of combat – dying of a rather inglorious flea bite before he reached Gallipoli.

Stevenson does his best to be fair to modernists such as T.S.Eliot and Virginia Woolf, but he misses the opportunity to note that almost the whole of theBloomsbury Group and its adherents were *pacifists* during 1914-1918. And this was not based simply on an unwillingness to fight, but on a genuine sense of internationalism and the belief that the war was a huge *mistake* which need not have taken place. Indeed, before the war had even ended Leonard Woolf helped set up the League of Nations (which went on to become the United Nations) with the sole aim of preventing any further conflicts of its size and kind between nations.

This was an extremely unpopular view to hold at the time – though it has become increasingly sane with hindsight. People were jailed for 'conscientious objection' and of course this is a period when young men were executed and crucified in no-man's-land for crimes of 'cowardice' and falling asleep on duty. The only other people to oppose the war on internationalist grounds were figures such as Trotsky and Lenin.

Stevenson's final chapter considers revisionist histories of the war which have been produced in recent years. He gives their defence of the blundering generals and the gigantic carnage a fair hearing, but eventually undermines their arguments with a few well chosen quotations that emphasise his concluding argument – that we need to read closely and not be swayed by rhetoric and false metaphors.

Revisionist history cannot be accused of ignoring the war's loss and mutilation. [Gary Sheffield's] *Forgotten Victory* is regularly attentive to the 'callous arithmetic of battle' and the 'butcher's bill' that resulted. Yet Sheffield also suggests that at one stage that the Canadians' capture of Vimy Ridge in 1917 was achieved 'with relatively little difficulty, although at the cost of 11,000 casualties'. Such remarks cast doubt on his promise of 'analysis based on firm grasp of the facts'. Avoidance of difficulty, even relatively, at the cost of 11,000 casualties, is not fact but interpretation, the kind of interpretation the generals were apt to make themselves.

BRITISH WOMEN'S LITERATURE OF WORLD WAR I

For much of the twentieth century, a deep ignorance was displayed towards British women's literature of World War I. Scholars reasoned that women had not fought combatively, thus, did not play as significant a role as men. Accordingly, only one body of work, Vera Brittain's autobiographical, *Testament of Youth*, was added to the canon of Great War literature. Conversely, anthologies published mid-century such as Brian Gardner's, *Up the Line to Death: The War Poets of 1914-1918*, contained no mention of contributions made by women. Similarly, Jon Silkin's 1979 anthology, *Penguin Book of First World War Poetry*, included the work of only two women, Anna Akhmatova andMarina Tsvetaeva. However, new research has changed ideological beliefs about the role women assumed in producing authentic accounts of war. More specifically, in Britain, research attends to an explanation of how women's war literature shaped feminist discourse during and immediately following the war. Catherine Reilly has closely studied women's literature from World War I and its resulting impact on the relationship between gender, class, and society.

Reilly's 1981 anthology,*Scars Upon my Heart: Women's Poetry and Verse of the First World War*, is the first work strictly dedicated to examining women's poetry and prose from World War I. In it, she demonstrates the existence of a strong female narrative. She argues that women's writing was overshadowed by the false belief that male writing was of greater importance.Scholar Vincent Sherry agrees, noting that women had a strong and powerful literary voice, that until recently had been ignored.

WOMEN ON THE HOME FRONT

According to Millicent Fawcett, founder of Newnham College, Cambridge and president of the National Union of Women's Suffrage Societies, women transitioned from domestic serfdom to social freedom by the end of World War One. This is due to the fact that women moved from domestic life into the industrial realm of society. During the war, industrial factories often transitioned into munitions factories. The women that worked in this field were referred to as munitionettes. There was an increase of opportunities in the job market, as two million women replaced men in the workplace. Women became active in the roles that were previously occupied by men. Furthermore, 37 per cent of women were employed by the end of the war. British women were brought out of the household and traditional domestic life and thrust into industrial factory work.

Women also began working in hospitals. More specifically, the Scottish Women's Hospital was founded in 1914 and began working in relation with the Royal Army Medical Corps. By the end of the war, women were partaking in tasks throughout war ravaged Europe, including Serbia, Russia, and Germany.

Although women began working in the same sector as men, there remained a significant difference in rights. Unable to unionize as uniformly as men during this period, women faced struggles to acquire similar work hours and wages. Even throughout the post-war years, women's unions did not increase wages.

The emergence of the term 'home front' carried a gendered aspect that defined the theatre of war as masculine and the home as feminine. While problematic, this gendered identification worked to support the traditional male and female paradigm in Britain. Scholar Susan Kingsley Kent argues that, "women at the front represented the war with a tone and imagery "markedly dissimilar" from those at home." This was reflected in women's writing.

SPACES OF WOMEN'S WRITING

During the War, women were being published in anthologies, newspapers, periodicals, factory newspapers, and women's magazines. Therefore, women's writing from this time was more extensive than was previously thought. Claire Buck asserts that more than 2000 poets were published during the war. However, only one-fifth of all published work was written by active service members. Alternatively, Nosheen Khan estimates that over one quarter, or 500 women wrote on war at this time. This is a significant development because British women actively documented the war experience from home and on the battlefield. These works chronicled firsthand accounts of interaction with wounded soldiers, life in the trenches, and the difficulties of maintaining moral support from mainland Britain. They are important documents as they provide a new perspective on issues concerning Britain's role. Thus, poetry and prose produced by women between 1914 and 1918 contributed to a richer and more accurate textual experience of the war effort.

A great fear arose amongst women who believed their writing would fall into obscurity. In 1949, Brittain noted that she was anxious that most female literature would not survive because it was overshadowed by the male experience of war (Smith, 105). This theory was proven correct, as interest in Women's writing did not gain prominence until the early 1980s when, as part of the larger feminist conversation, critics began examining the politics of gender and war.

SOCIAL CLIMATE OF WOMEN'S WRITING

World War I challenged Britain's entrenched societal hierarchy. The First World War required the British populous to reassess their historical precedence in international involvement and domestic issues concerning class and gender. By the start of the First World War, the role of women in Britain changed rapidly. While men were shipped to the frontlines, women remained on the home front, ensuring that Britain and its vast Empire continued to operate.

The outbreak of World War I brought substantial unemployment. Some of the worst hit industries were those that traditionally employed women during peacetime. For instance, fabrication and associated industries such as, "traditional 'women's trades'- cotton, linen, silk, lace, tailoring, dressmaking, millinery, hat-making, pottery, and fish-gutting" saw drastic employment decline. As the war dragged on and conscription was instituted women entered the workforce in significant numbers.

FICTION

The British government strongly advocated the use of women's literature for propagandist means. Images and prose combined to sway popular opinion before conscription became mandatory. These ideas manifested gendered beliefs that would often inspire or shame men into joining the war effort. Posters would often be used with captions to the effect of, "Women of Britain say: Go!". Likewise, women's poetry asserted the patriotism and fortitude of women in wartime. Women's writing used traditional symbols of male heroism to reinforce the power of women writers' poetic voices in contrast to the perceived cowardice of men who failed to enlist. In contrast, posters and literature were aimed at women with the intention of reinforcing positive attitudes. For example, writing and images featured depictions of cheerful munitions workers and homemakers in aprons whose kitchens provided the "key" to victory.

Women's Prose

Feminist historians have claimed that women's writing from the front gave access to a more authentic representation of the war. Literary historian David Trotter asserts that the addition of women's writing helps provide a more encompassing, and thus, stronger picture of Britain's involvement in the First World War. The women who served in non-combative roles such as ambulance drivers, nurses, and munitions workers all provided a unique perspective of life during this time. As a result, women's wartime writing reflected many of the overarching themes of early twentieth century feminist discourse. Women who wrote about war shared themes of patience, loss, and grief, and their experiences at the front. The result was a sense of liberation and freedom that had not previously been explored within British female authorship.

Rebecca West

Authors such as Rebecca West used her work to produce literature that supported revolution. For instance, her 1916 novel, *The Return of the Soldier*, examined the psychoanalytical conditions of war and the resulting impact on returning soldiers. Furthermore, it provided a strong commentary on feminist discourse that allowed women to reimagine Britain as a space where they could gain cultural capital and privilege.

POETRY

According to Paul Fussell, many soldiers relied on poetry as a method to cope with the atrocities and horrors of the First World War. British male poetry often promoted the idea that women stayed at home to support the war with 'undying love.' Poetry was not strictly composed by men on the battlefield, but it was also written by women in different areas of conflict. This includes women at home in the factories, at the front lines, or in military hospitals. The poems written by women were often taken from person experiences including romance, heroism, outrage, or suffering. In addition to these central themes, many female writers of this era believe that women's writing will be overshadowed by the stories of war told my men. John Buchan and J.G. Wilson believed that the First World War was the greatest period in England for poetry. This can be attested to the fact that over five-hundred women wrote poetry about the Great War during its time.

There are numerous female poets that remain popular today. Dissimilar to the idea that their writings would be overshadowed by war stories told by men, these poets have many publications. Vera Brittain has written poems and stories about the Great War. Not only was Brittain a writer, she was a nurse in the Voluntary Aid Detachment. This shows the support women had for the war and the importance they played in a non-combative manner. In addition, Lady Margaret Sackville refers to the women during the Great War as life-savers. More specifically, Sackville believes that women are supporting a war that is unnecessary in her poem *The Pageant of War*. Rupert Brookeattributed women with more credit than had previously been given in his poem *There's Wisdom in Women* which he published in *1914 and Other Poems*.

The bombing of England during World War One by the zeppelin raids provided citizens at home to see first-hand the devastation of war. Rose MaCaulay explains this in her poem *The Shadow*. There was an attempt to show the relationship between the sufferings of soldiers on the battlefield with the suffering of British citizens at home. *The Shadow* was not MaCaulay's only poem on the Great War. *Many Sisters to Many Brothers* expresses her distaste to the fact that the societal norm was to determine that women were more disabled than men in the war effort. More specifically, there was an idea that the war was specifically fought and won by soldiers on the battlefield. Women played an important role in supporting the war, both at home and abroad. Vera Brittain's poem *The Sisters Buries at Lemnos* is a poem about the heroics displayed by women during the war. The role that women played in supporting the war must be remembered because many women were killed during the conflict. Brittain's poem expresses disappointment that there is no memorial to remember the women that fell alongside the soldiers.

The following is a list of a few popular female British poets writing about or during the Great War:

- Vera Brittain
- May Wedderburn Cannan
- Margaret Postaget Cole
- Rose MaCaulay
- Alice Meynell
- Jessie Pope
- Margaret Sackville

Poetry and gender roles

Poetry provided female writers an opportunity to express their views through metaphor and allusion. Consequently, wartime writing allowed women to challenge prevailing societal beliefs by arguing in favour of extended social and political rights such as enfranchisement. Women writers reimagined Britain's post-war social landscape by using their writing as a way to evoke sharp criticism of masculine British hegemony. Even while confined to the trenches, men held to intrinsic beliefs about gender. For instance, correspondence between men in the trenches and women at home provided insight into the way men viewed the role of women. Men saw home as reflecting the prescribed gender roles, where women were responsible for nurturing and caring for the man. In return, men received letters that remind them of the domesticity at home.

Poetry was a literary outlet that had traditionally been more accessible to British women. For instance, "women were a substantial part of the poetic tradition in wartime Britain, as writers and readers, and their wartime works offer an opportunity to examine how women writers positioned their sex as central to the War effort." Poems allowed women to express feminist discourse concerning ideas of nationalism and sacrifice, and provided a space in which they could inform their desire to contribute more prominently in post-war Britain. Even women who opposed the war on moral and philosophical grounds argued that they played an important role in the British war effort.

USES OF WWI FEMALE LITERATURE

World War I challenged Britain's entrenched societal hierarchy. The First World War required the British populous to reassess their historical precedence in international involvement and domestic issues concerning class and gender. By the start of the First World War, the role of women in Britain changed rapidly. While men were shipped to the frontlines, women remained on the home front, ensuring that Britain and its vast Empire continued to operate.

The outbreak of World War I brought substantial unemployment. Some of the worst hit industries were those that traditionally employed women during peacetime. For instance, fabrication and associated industries such as, "traditional 'women's trades'- cotton, linen, silk, lace, tailoring, dressmaking, millinery, hat-making, pottery, and fish-gutting" saw drastic employment decline. As the war dragged on and conscription was instituted women entered the workforce in significant numbers.

The emergence of the term 'home front' carried a gendered aspect that defined the theatre of war as masculine and the home as feminine. While problematic, this gendered identification worked to support the traditional male and female paradigm in Britain. Scholar Susan Kingsley Kent argues that, "women-at the front represented the war with a tone and imagery "markedly dissimilar" from those at home." This was reflected in women's writing.

7

World War II Poets

INTRODUCTION

The various sections of Voices in Wartime's, *The World at War: World War II* are filled with the poetry of hundreds of poets. In the "case study" section, poets who were directly linked to a specific event are highlighted. For example, an excerpt from Edna St. Vincent Millay's long poem, "Lidice," recounts a horrendous massacre in that Czech village at the hands of the Nazis; and Anna Akhmatova recalls the 900-Day Siege of Leingrad in the case study of the same name. In the study on the dropping of the first atomic bomb on Hiroshima, the witness poetry of Toge Sankichi and Shinoe Shoda recount that catastrophic event.

This section features more than 130 poets, from both sides of the Atlantic and Pacific who write about the Second World War. The majority of these writers are professional poets coming from different sides of the war, many of them intimately involved in the struggle to survive the war. Some never lived to see the liberation, or an end to their concentration camp lives, or the signing of the armistice. Others who write of the horrors of the battlefields do so because of their sense of history, of recalling stories they heard, or in fear that the world may once again lose its sanity and embark on still another war.

WORLD WAR II

IN BRITAIN

By World War II the role of "war poet" was so well-established in the public mind that "Where are the war poets?" became a topic of discussion.. Robert Graves gave a radio talk 'Why has this War produced no War Poets?' in October 1941 and Stephen Spender also addressed the question at about the same time (as did T. S. Eliot a year later). Alun Lewis and Keith Douglas are the standard critical choices amongst British war poets of this time.

In America

The American poet Karl Shapiro made a reputation based on poetry that he wrote during the war and published in his debut book of verse, *V-Letter and Other Poems* (1945). His book won the Pulitzer Prize that same year. Also, while serving in the U.S. Army, the American poet Randall Jarrell published his second book of poems, *Little Friend, Little Friend* (1945) based on his wartime experiences. The book includes one of Jarrell's best known war poems, "The Death of the Ball Turret Gunner." In his follow-up book, *Losses*(1948), he also focused on the war. The poet Robert Lowell stated publicly that he thought Jarrell had written "the best poetry in English about the Second World War."

LATER AMERICAN WAR POETS

The Korean War produced the American war poets Rolando Hinojosa and William Wantling.

The Vietnam war produced a number of war poets, including Michael Casey whose début collection, *Obscenities*, drew on his work as military police officer in Vietnam's Quang Nga province. The book won the 1972 Yale Younger Poets Award. Other prominent Vietnam War poets include W. D. Ehrhart, Yusef Komunyakaa, and Bruce Weigl.

Most recently, the Iraq War has produced some notable war poets including Brian Turner whose début collection, *Here, Bullet*, is based on his experience as an infantry team leader with the 3rd Stryker Brigade Combat Team from November 2003 until November 2004 in Iraq. The book won numerous awards including the 2005 Beatrice Hawley Award, the 2006 Maine Literary Award in Poetry, and the 2006 Northern California Book Award in Poetry. The book also was an Editor's Choice in *The New York Times*and received significant attention from the press including reviews and notices on NPR and in *The New Yorker, The Global and Mail*, and the *Library Journal*. In *The New Yorker*,Dana Goodyear wrote that, "As a war poet, [Brian Turner] sidesteps the classic distinction between romance and irony, opting instead for the surreal."

POETRY OF THE SECOND WORLD WAR

In August a group of us veterans from the Northamptonshire Yeomanry go to Normandy to the site of our most notable tank battle (Operation Totalize).

We make the normal visits to cemeteries, stand at graves of remembered pals and recite*'They shall grow not old...'*

However we are always aware of other comrades who suffered what would eventually prove fatal injuries but because they survived a while, yet died young, are not remembered on official gravestones or memorials.

This is particularly poignant for us because we crewed the notorious 'Tommy Cooker' Sherman which often exploded in a volcano of fire and cremated one or other of the crew as they sat, with another crew member emerging bodily on fire. Due to the pollution of the soil caused by the inferno these places are still discernable.

In August at least one son of our regiment will stand where his father came out of his tank on fire and then endured a brief but useless life after discharge. As I saw the event, joined in destroying the German self-propelled gun and later commanded the replacement tank I have a very personal interest. For our August event I have written a short alternative verse to the traditional one for such tragic spots -

Honour them who may have woken
to know the battle's grim tomorrow;
yet equally whose youth was broken
by living death of pain and sorrow:
they shared the pulling down of blinds
on their own shattered limbs and minds.

Ken Tout,
(Dr Ken Tout, OBE)

A TRIBUTE TO THE ILLUMINATED WOMAN OF WORLD WAR II

(The poet's notes follow the poem.)

Our humble tribute to you
The illuminated woman
Of Word War II
Oh! The courageous Miss Noor Inayat Khan
Great grand daughter
Of the Sufi king Tipu Sultan
The Tiger of Mysore
You were bestowed
With the highest military awards
For your splendid valor
Oh! The most charismatic heroine
Of World War II
Oh! The beloved daughter
Of the legendary Sufi master
From whom you learned
The jewels of spirituality
Love, joy, harmony,
Endurance and beauty
And when he passed away
You nurtured your mother
And siblings with benevolence
We truly cherish your munificence
Oh! The kind hearted woman
Of World War II
Oh! The emblem of

Purest beauty and grace
You, the poet and musician
You, the writer and champion of languages
Your stunning tales of inspiration
Now captivating the children's attention
You, the amazing air force lady
You, the brilliant wireless operator
You are Madeleine and Nora
The master of disguises and aura
Oh! The dynamic spy
Of World War II
Oh! The incredible tigress
You were betrayed
And tortured with the high level of severity
Yet you stood firm and never gave up
For the sake of humanity
You challenged the wicked hegemony
Fighting heroically
Against the horrendous evils
You sacrificed your precious life
Uttering the last single word, "Liberte!"
Oh! The Freedom Fighter
Of World War II
Oh! The Sufi princess
You are the sweetest martyr
That we all madly admire
You are the icon of integrity
Dwelling in our hearts for eternity
You are now the radiant star
In this glorious universe
May God, The Almighty, All-Compassionate and All-Loving
Bless your gentle soul, rest you in peace
And grant you the highest place in heaven
Oh! The most magnificent woman
Of World War II

Irfanulla Shariff

POET'S NOTES ABOUT THE POEM

The language of poetry is a metaphor. Here the word, "illuminated" is a metaphor. The readers should not take this literally. Miss Noor Inayat Khan's first full name was, "Noor-un-Nisa". For short, people used to call her Noor. The meaning of "Noor-un-Nisa" is the divine light of womanhood". Her name speaks for her great spiritually illuminated qualities. That is the reason I gave her the title, "The Illuminated Woman". This is not the ordinary light, but the light of enlightenment.

The poem, "The Illuminated Woman Of World War II" is dedicated to Miss Noor Inayat Khan, the heroic woman of World War II. This poem fully illustrates her remarkable life story.

Miss Noor Inayat khan was a British national. She was an extremely talented lady. This brave woman fought against German fascism during World War II. She was a part of British Air Force and worked as a wireless operator. She was later recruited by British Special Operations Executive (SOE). As a SOE agent, she performed her duties very efficiently in Nazi occupied France and gave Gestapo agents a very hard time. During her operations in France, she was betrayed by a double agent and then arrested by Gestapo agents. She made two dramatic escape attempts, but was recaptured and sent to Germany. Here she was interrogated, tortured and finally sent to the Dachau Concentration Camp, where she was again severely tortured. At last, when Gestapo agents found that they were not making any progress in getting the classified information out of her, she was executed on September 13, 1944 and her body was cremated. The only word she said before she was executed was, "Liberte!" For her remarkable gallantry, she was posthumously awarded a British George Cross and a French Croix de Guerre.

BIO OF IRFANULLA SHARIFF

Irfanulla Shariff has been writing poetry for years. He has a great passion for writing inspirational poetry. His work has been published in various poetry magazines and anthologies. His poems were selected to appear in "The Sound of Poetry", a special audio CD and tape collection. He was presented an International Poet of Merit Award by the International Society of Poets in 2002. Irfanulla's poetic influences are Rumi, Robert Frost and Maya Angelou. He is also a member of Illinois State Poetry Society. By profession, he is a Computer Scientist and Telecommunication Engineer. He is married, lives in South Elgin, Illinois, USA and has three children.

THE PARTY

Here's a poem I felt compelled to write shortly after my father (James Thomas Walker) passed away in May 2011. He rarely spoke of his war days. *I expect he chose to not dwell on them. However, this poem is from a story he told me about forty years ago.*

Rob Walker

Three months was the least we would sail,
From Fort St. John to St. Ives,
And we set out again with one hundred-six men

In hopes we would come home alive.
The able on both sides enlisted,
To wage the Great War on their foe,
And the safety of those who were loved and held close
Was the force that compelled them to go.
This was my fourth tour of duty,
With more than our fair share of nubs,
But they would return with the lessons they'd learn,
As long as we stymied the subs.
Two ounces of rum was our issue,
To be drunk before bed for our nerves,
But we stored it away for that most fateful day
No ninety-day wonder deserves.
We checked on our stockpile of foxers
That were saving our lives by their sound,
Whenever we missed with the DCs we dished,
And the Jerry's torpedoes came round.
The Third Reich developed a missile
To skim slightly under our wake
And alter its path to deliver its wrath
To the noise the ship's engine would make.
Our Corvette could never stop moving,
For the noise from the foxer would fail,
And the racket that kept us alive would be still
And the 'fish' would be right on our tail.
The Captain had given us orders,
For whenever the engine was down,
To slip off our shoes - so we'd break out the booze
And we'd binge without making a sound.
Two weeks out of port, in the crossing,
When the spray of mid-April still bit,
In spite of the engineers' efforts,
The engine decided to quit.
The subs kept on ringing the radar,
And now we were waiting to die.
As we prayed, the mechanics, who couldn't make noise,
Had no other choice but to try.
As they laboured to fix what was broken,
The men up above faced their fear,
And no one would sleep for three days on the deep
With the prospect of drowning so near.
I saw the crew stagger and stumble

As the waves and the booze took effect,
But they knew that their eyes never would see St. Ives
If they so much as spoke on the deck.
The carryings on and the binging,
With an absolute absence of noise
Caused a fear so intense it turned boys into men
And some of the men into boys.
And somewhere above me a seabird
Looked down upon miles of sea
Where the sun on the whitecaps and wind in its wings
Must have made it feel glorious and free.
As it spotted our speck of a vessel
And thought how men must be at peace,
With forty-eight million warriors killed
And no plan to surrender or cease,
It spied this superior species
From its vantage point, miles above
And watched as the speck slowly sank out of site,
Out of hatred and fear, out of love.
Rob Walker
Received October 2012

THE ENSIGN AND THE PLANK

You've pulled a man from the freezing sea all black with ship's oil fuel
You've cleaned him off, and see his wounds and wondered what to do,
You see the whiteness of his ribs where steam has skinned him too.
The guilt you feel when you look at him feeling glad it isn't you
And all you have to ease his pain is aspirin and 'goo.'
You fear to look him in the eye for the question you know will be there
The answer you know is certain death, and there's nothing more you can do.
You light him a fag, and give him your tot as he looks for the rest of his crew.
Then you lay him out on the iron deck knowing that's his lot
Briefly wondering if you did aright by giving him your tot.
For the rest of the watch, with a sail maker's palm with needle and with
thread You sew him up in canvas with the rest of that night's dead.
With a dummy shell between their feet, making certain that they will sink
You sit and sew till the morning's glow, amid the mess and stink.
By dawn's grey light you carry them aft, to the ensign and the plank.
And the hands off watch gather round all bleary eyed and dank.
Then the skipper with his bible says a sailor's prayer
Our father which art in heaven (we hope you're really there).
One by one the dead are gone slid from the greasy plank

A second's pause and then a splash, they sink beneath the main.
The hands go forward, feeling chill, thinking of those that were slain
with a certain knowledge in a while we'll do it all again.
Each one being still alive, breathes a silent prayer of thanks
Wondering, with a cold dark fear, will I be next on the plank?

Petty Officer Stanley Kirby

This poem was introduced to me by his nephew at the launch of *Heroes*. (From a new book of war poems, *Heroes*. - November 2011) - DR

A POEM IN MEMORY OF PIPER BILL MILLIN

Tony Church writes occasional verse and is a member of the St. Andrews Pipe Band of Hamble Le Rice. [Hampshire, UK]

On 4th/5th June this year [2011] there is a "Pipefest" on Sword Beach,Normandy, to commemorate Bill Millin, the D Day Piper who died last year, raising funds for a statue in his memory.

Tony Church composed this verse, partly because Bill, piper to Brigadier Lord Lovat, embarked for the D-Day Landings from the Hamble river.

PIPER BILL

(The legend of Bill Millin, the D-Day Piper)

The sighing surf on sand abounds, and seabirds call, the only sounds
At break of summers day, and yet, within the hour men will have met
Their destiny as war's shrill chatter ends this tranquil scene. The clatter
Of machine guns spit their hate, as landing craft nose in to grate
Against the shingle to disgorge their human load who wait to charge
Into oncoming deathly hail, but never faltering, nerves taut, pale
Faced, leaping down into the cold wet breakers, seeking firm foothold.
Struggling forward, arms raised clear to gain refuge ahead, so near
And yet seeming so far away as spiteful guns traverse and spray
The killing ground that lies ahead, already littered with the dead
And dying who would never see this bitter, bloody victory.
Then faintly, through the deafening din, an alien sound is heard, the thin
Melodious wailing cry of highland pipes, though bullets fly
Around him, he is unscathed still. Thus starts the tale of Piper Bill.
Bill, who piped for Brigadier Lord Lovat, raised a special cheer
When, leaving on the previous day, took up his pipes, began to play
"Road to the Isles", as, leaving Hamble river for this costly gamble,
Lifting spirits of the men, calling, cheered and cheered again,
Who as the Solent slipped away, all knew that on the following day
They'd face their own worst fears and doubts, prayed that when it came about
They would stand firm and conquer fear to face the perils that appeared.
And now, amid the smoke and roar of high explosives, Bill endures

The hail of death, which all around leaves him untouched, while yet the sound
Of "Highland Laddie" fills the air as fingers on the chanter dare
To still defy the lethal storm, this awesome hell in all its forms.
Yet death and wholesale demolition, backdrop to this exhibition
Of the art of Scottish piping, even with the bullets sniping,
Will not quiet this hardy Scot, surviving mortar shell and shot.
He marches at the waters edge, still playing, able still to dredge
From deep within his mortal soul the courage to maintain and hold
Himself upright despite the urge to run for safety, then emerge
When all is still and quiet again, escape the trauma and the pain.
But Bill is made of sterner stuff, clutching his pipes he starts to puff
And fill the bag, then with a squeeze, his hands again with practiced ease
Launch into yet another air, lifting spirits everywhere.
And so the legend now is born, as Bill continues to perform
Beyond this strip of golden sand known as Sword Beach, where many men
Have fallen, sacrificed their all in answering their country's call,
But in this page of history this part of France will always be
Where Highland Bagpipes did their part with inspiration, and gave heart
To all who witnessed Bill that day, who, when he crossed that beach to play,
With all his great panache and poise, gave the Highland Pipes their voice.
Tony Church

ODE TO THE FULL MOON DURING AN "ALERT", 1942

Full moon, brilliant, all-revealing, quiescent,
Spirit of silver silence, soul of night,
I have waited since the first pale crescent
Of your nascent beauty touched the world with light;
I have watched the envious stars grow dimmer;
Orion's girdle faintly glimmer,
Fading beyond your fair translucency.
And, now, the earth, resplendent, caught in dreams,
The incarnation of those long desires,
Her woods aflame with lambent fires,
Her diaphanous streams
Transcended by a deep tranquillity....
Thus I, the poet, extol with eloquence
The full moon's loveliness
And light,
Her calm magnificence;
Dreams of a happy lover!
How, then, can I confess
The beauty hides a cold malevolence,

A hideous, furtive hate?
That, in the myriad pathways of the night,
Soon Death will hover,
Death indiscriminate?
Bodies, fearful now, will cringe and press
Close to the heart of earth;
That Hell will burst through Heaven, the wild, mad cry,
A devil's scream of terrifying mirth,
As foul destruction thunders down the sky;
A crashing, cataclysmic violence
That shatters babies at their hour of birth,
Dispassionately, age and innocence!
Moon, ally of hate and man's vile desecrations,
No more the world will know your madrigals,
But, be the symbol of the shame of nations
Until the last star falls.
Namur King

NAMUR KING 1915-68

NAMUR KING was born in Blackwood (South Wales) on the day British Army won the battle at theBelgian town of Namur. Hence the name. (5 of his brothers all named John had previously died of TB.)

In 1939, at 24 years old, he volunteered for the British Expeditionary Force to France. he saw action as Da dispatch rider and driver, coming under enemy fire. He was vacuated at Dunkirk. Subsequently he was stationed in the Falkland Islands, as S.America was under threat of Japanese attack.

BLOODY WAR - THE CAUSE

Tom Walker, now almost 90 (June 2010), served in the Royal Navy in World War Two. He wrote many poems and is particularly proud of this one since few war poems address the causes of war.

When greed sups with the devil
And principles are shed
When power is corrupted
And truth stands on its head
When fear pervades the confused mind
And fools are easy led
When reason is a prisoner
The bell tolls for the dead.

TOM WALKER

George Fraser Gallie – Poems discovered amongst his papers in 2009

It's rare to find a war poem, such as this first poem, expressing pleasure. George Fraser Gallie 1922-2006 wrote a number of poems whilst serving in Italy and North Africa with the Royal Engineers around 1943 when he was 21. They have recently been discovered amongst his papers by his son. The poems below are two of several that were mailed home to his mother who lived in Penmaenmawr, North Wales. In the first poem there is a reference to 'Craig Mor'. This was the family home, and the 'Hut' was the seaside hut in the area where his peacetime holidays were spent.

A Voyager's Song

I drove through the desert of dusty tracks
Through many a Sicilian street.
Past acres of vineyards and Orchards and flax
And mile after mile of red poppies and wheat.
I drove past the Sphinx and the Cairo zoo,
And remembered the trips that I used to do.
And I thought of my friends
And I thought of 'Craig Mor'
And the old Austin 10
And the hut on the shore.
I lay on the sands of Syracuse
in the heat of a Mediterranean noon
I nakedly swam in the crystal hues
Of the silvery sea by the August moon.
I dived in the foam of the breaking wave
And remembered the spots where I used to bathe.
And I thought of my friends
And I thought of 'Craig Mor'
Of the rattling stones
And the hut on the shore.
I sauntered down the rutted track
Which wound its way past white-washed farms,
I felt the sun on my naked back
The Italian sun on my face and arms,
I smoked my pipe as I went my way
And remembered the pleasures of yesterday.
And I thought of my friends
And the hut on the shore,
And I thought of 'Craig Malin'
'Cregneish' and 'Craig Mor'

George Fraser Gallie 1943 aged 21.

Rocca San Giovanni

It is quiet here now, the valley is silent.

Only the birds and the stream have their noise,
The twittering, bubbling sweet sounds of nature.
Apart from this – silence which nothing destroys.
The smell is a faint one of morning and pine trees,
Of bracken and water, of woodland and stream,
The sight is of rushes, of mill house and lime trees.
The feel is of peacefulness sweet as a dream.
But at one time this valley, this valley of heaven,
Became a most torturous valley of hell.
For the fighting was bitter, the Hun held on grimly,
Regardless of losses, and many men fell.
For the British came north and the silence was shattered,
By rifle – machine gun – trench mortar – grenade.
The Messerschmitt diving bought sickening terror,
The valley vibrated with Death's serenade.
But the British advanced and the valley was taken,
The fighting moved northward as Gerry moved back,
And the only remains to give proof of the fighting,
Are freshly dug graves at the side of the track.
Again it is peaceful, the valley is silent,
Only the birds and the stream have their noise,
The twittering, bubbling sounds of nature.
Apart from this – silence which nothing destroys.

George Fraser Gallie, November, 1943.

LEON ADAMS: THE GOD OF WAR

Thoughts on the Italian Invasion of Ethiopia
Mars has again descended from his throne
To ravage earth with bloody human strife;
To break away the bonds of peace and love
And send one nation warring with another,
As sparrows combat o'er a trifling crumb;
To wash the verdant earth with sickening blood
And herald death into a million homes.
The fields are strewn with reeking, dying men
Filled with the thoughts and hopes of worlds gone mad.
The future? Famine! Poverty! And Strife!
Wars are made by men who seek to line
Their itchy pockets with dishonoured loot.
God sighs. Life goes on.
—Leon Adams (St. Catharines, Ontario, 11 November, 1935)

THRENODY OF THE NATIONS

We have hated and fought,
We have murdered and fled,
But the peace that we sought
Is alone with the dead.
We have offered ourselves
On the altar of greed;
We have poisoned our sons
With our venomous creed.
We have bombed and destroyed;
We have raped and diseased,
Till the earth has grown dark
With our war-obsequies.
We have sung our wild song
In the ghouls' jubilee,
And, O Love, once again
We have crucified Thee.
Leon Adams
Lennoxville, Quebec, May 16, 1940.
Tea at Olivier's
We shall have tea at Olivier's and eat
patisserie francaise
served by a waitress
in blue dress,
white apron, and
white cap.
We shall sip hot tea
and chat about
the battle of Britain,
the latest German move,
our men,
our lovers,
and our hopes.
We shall drink tea
while bombs tear out the hearts
of twisted men;
we shall eat
patisserie francaise
while they are tasting
Death.
—Leon Adams (Sherbrooke, Quebec, 29 November 1940.)

CURTIS D. BENNETT: HARBINGERS

(From Normandy)
Frail, old men with weathered hands stand,
Alone, lost on the wide sandy beaches,
Each turning back his rusty mind clock
Piercing the veil of memories
When they were young, anxious and terrified,
Boy-soldiers in battle fighting for their lives,
Experiencing the gamut of fear and death
Watching friends died horribly,
Scarring their young minds.forever.
Blue beaches murmur waves
Splashing old, rusted war remnants.
A sea bird flaps wet beaches
Where the sea swells and crashes gently on wet sand,
Retreating back erasing all footprints.
The men stare the distance,
At blurred memories through tears.
Trickling down their cheeks dripping softly,
To merge with the sea like before.
They came to say good-bye to their friends,
To a confused past which has no answers.
The graveyard crosses watch in stony silence,
Stoically from tree shadows on soft meadows,
In eternal military formation fronted by small, flags,
Wind-shivering in the hush of silence.
Marching the stillness in quiet precision
Protecting the young soldiers buried there,
Frozen in time and death
The old veterans stand awkward, unsure with the dead.
Experiencing those familiar, dreaded, sick feelings
Of remorse, regret, blame, and fault for what happened
To their generation who gave so much for their country.
They have gathered one final time
To share history, blame and guilt for all eternity
Banding together as one, they embrace the moment,
Experiencing once more, this terrible place of
memories.
And the same salt sea air, still blows up from the beach
Once inhaled in panic by all the young fighting men
Mired in the beach mud conducting the senseless slaughter of children,
Trapped forever in the obscenity and vulgarity of war,

The pain returns for a moment, overwhelming them,
It hangs suspended, as real as yesterday, then drifts away and mellows away.
Now time, history, and denial blessedly blur the horror and inhumanity
Of what they did; of what was done to them.
The War President from America
Mounts the podiums to prattle the virtues of war,
Attempting to rewrite history, to deny war's reality,
He exploits the moment for selfish means,
To justify his war as a noble cause, ignoring its brutality,
Thoughtlessly attempting to validate, substantiate, and authenticate,
War's vicious crimes against civilization
Turning the senseless slaughter of innocents
Into a righteous cause, to be proud of and condone..
Turning war into a sound-bite of empty words
Of praise, blessing, glory, and accomplishment.
Something to be proud of, to revel in,
To relish with sacred, biblical rhetoric
From a shallow, self-centered political opportunist.
Whose meanings and oratory become quickly lost,
His words floating away with the wind, out of relevance, out of touch
Out of context, drifting, beyond the restive crowds.
To fall useless and disappear, in the cold, impassionate mud.
Falling deaf on the ears of the dead warriors
The ultimate, wasted sacrifice, from another generation
It is at this moment, the old veterans
Eyes mist up, overflow, and tears flow shamelessly
As they at last comprehend all their sacrifice, all their pain,
All their sorrow, all their suffering, all the death,
Did not change or alter a thing, was not a lesson learned
Nor an experience not to be repeated..
Realizing their friend's painful, brutal, ultimate sacrifice
Was only a necessary evil of Mankind's political process
Which has never changed, and never will,
For each generation brings anew to the world
Its own self-styled madness of universal death, tragedy and suffering,
In wars to be fought by the young, bright-eyed children of the world
Unknowingly raised as sacrificial lambs of slaughter,
To be killed and gone forever, for nothing.
That is why, all Veterans cry.
In this hallowed place of the dead
The lonely graves of war's youthful victims
Who died for a thought,

an idea, for a cause
Promulgated by selfish, insane men in power
These war graves and cemeteries are Harbingers
Of the eternal, mindless death cycle of war.
Young men killed by politicians' words and mindless acts,
Their promise and existence forever ended too soon.
Now, forever sleep beneath the green muffled grass
Sharing the earth with the youth and victims of past wars,
Too numerous to count, to numbing to contemplate,
The dead, as powerless and impotent as the now living
To change or alter, or detour the inexorable course of madmen,
They patiently wait for the next generation to join them.
—Curtis D. Bennett

Stalag Zehn B

the feldwebel became a general
the campdoctor, a professor
and we the jews - it's banal
we stayed jewish - no error.
—Jan Theuninck

Shoa

wandering jew,damned jew
and no words on them are forbidden
suspected of crimes and treason
they have been put in jail
they have been tortured and murdered
in the name of an insane idea
and now - more than ever -
who is next, please ?

—Jan Theuninck

Mauthausen 186

Stone by stone
we made a step
Step by step
we went to heaven.

—Jan Theuninck

Zuydcote

the sun shines
on the dune

the bunkers hide
the undesirable
all of them lose
their innocence
lost blood
on the beach
the sea...
guilty !

—Jan Theuninck

Papirac

The real post-war power
is still the one of the "Uebermenschen"
and this "democracy" can't be realized
but on the back of the "Untermenschen" !

—Jan Theuninck

CLARE STEWART ("WISH ME LUCK...")

She waits
In the late twilight,
Shivering in the wind
That scoops up
Over the lip
Of the chalk cliff.
She waits,
Listening to the
Throb of the
Wimpy's engines
As the squadron nears
Her look-out post.
She waits
For a glimpse of a
Gauntleted hand
Waving at her eye level,
The hand that caressed
Now ready to trigger the tail guns.
She waits,
Keeping watch
Ears straining to catch
The returning flight,
Waiting to count the returned
And the missing.

She waits
Past the dawn...
Waits for the missing...
Waits...
And waits...
And waits.
Clare Stewart
20 October, 2002

Clare Stewart is the daughter of a Second World War Canadian soldier and a British War Bride, and was born in Canada after the war. She is very proud of the service her family has given to their countries since the time of the American Revolution.

May Hill (1891-1944)

May Hill was a modest Lincolnshire seaside villager who maintained eloquent comprehensive 'Home Front' diaries during World War Two and also expressed many of her thoughts and prayers in poetry. A compilation of her poetry, with a selection of related diary excerpts, edited by two grandchildren, has been published as 'The Casualties Were Small by Ambridge Books.. Readings of several poems and extracts can be heard on 'The Casualties Were Small' – on Deben Radio. Anyone interested in the life of country folk during the Second World War will find the interviews in this radio programme of interest.The war affected them in many ways: they even came under attack.

May Hill's Home Front Poetry and Diaries One of the major themes running through May Hill's writing was her care and concern for her only son Ron who had joined the RAF just before his 20th birthday in November 1940. 'The Click of the Garden Gate' was the first poem showing a mother's sentiments. Rene, in the poem, was May's elder daughter who lived elsewhere in the village.

The Click of the Garden Gate

I hear the click of the garden gate
But it is not he
He comes no more either early or late
To his dinner or tea
He is far away in an Air Force Camp
Learning to fight
(I wonder if his blankets are damp
And if he sleeps well at night)
Not twenty years when went away
Just a boy
He may never again come back to stay

To delight and annoy
Will what he has gained balance what he has lost?
He will change
Will his growth to manhood improve him most?
Or make him change?
I open the casement into his room
So tidy and neat
And the sun shines in and chases the gloom
And the wind blows sweet
Ready for him when, early or late
He comes back home to the sea
I hear the click of the garden gate
But it is not he.
(Perhaps it is Rene coming to tea!)

—May Hill, December 1940

During the following year Ron had been exposed to danger even during his local training as an aircraft instrument mechanic before being posted abroad. Two incidents of mis-handling of bombs by ground crews could easily have resulted in explosions and his death. In fact he was lucky to survive both incidents. 'The Casualties Were Small' was an expression of May's worst fears.

"The Casualties Were Small"

When Winton Aerodrome was bombed
The "Casualties were small"
Just your son, and my son, and little widow Brown's son,
The youngest of them all.
And your son was your eldest lad,
Handsome and straight and tall.
A model for your younger sons,
Beloved by you all.
And Mrs Brown's, her youngest boy
Her sole support, and stay.
So like his father, all her joy
Was quenched, on that dark day.
And mine, my only son and pride
So loved and dear to all.
The blast of bombs spread far and wide
Tho' "the casualties were small".

—May Hill, September 1941

May recorded and gave her views on many happenings, nationally and overseas, which were reported in newspapers and on the BBC wireless. For example she was very moved by the news, in January 1943, of the bombing of a school where many lives were lost when air-raid sirens had not sounded. She recorded this in her diary and wrote a poem: 'Bombing at Noon of School at Lewisham'.

Bombing at Noon of School at Lewisham

Flowers were blooming at noonday
In a city garden on earth.
Children fair, happy and gay,
Laughing aloud in their mirth.
Out of the skies above them
With never a warning wail
Swept a storm of thunder and lightning,
With murderous steel for hail,
It mowed them down like a reaper,
And thunder-bolts crashed and crushed,
Bruising, and killing, and maiming,
Wherever the storm-clouds brushed.
Christ walked in the garden at eventide,
And in wrath beheld the wreck;
He said "It were better for him who did this deed
That he were drowned in the deepest sea
A millstone about his neck
For he hath offended my little ones
In their innocent happy play.
But leave to Me the Vengeance,
It is mine, I will repay."
We buried the broken blossoms
In a grave in the warm brown earth
But Christ gathered up the plantlets,
And took them to Paradise
He planted them all in a garden fair
Where flows the River of Life.
They are growing there and will bloom again
In the loving Father's care.
Where no storms come near, or death or fear,
They will wait for those they left,
And will welcome them in at the garden gate
United for evermore.

—May Hill, January 1943

May's later poems went on to relate to wartime weddings, her son's active RAF service in North Africa and Italy, concern for others on both sides of the conflict, losses of young men from the family and community and a very personal loss.

HITLER WAS A KILLER

(I do not know what you think of this but wrote it as a child, for my granddad, it has always stuck in my mind it was written in 1987 I thought I would finally share it with someone.)

Hitler was a Killer, who killed our British men
Upon the Beaches of Dunkirk He killed so Many Men
Upon the mighty Battlefield he never showed a tear
He sent them off to prison camps which filled them full of fear
He Whipped the Jew he gassed the Jew until so many were dead
He fought to be the Führer but his path was hell instead.

WORLD WAR 2 POEMS

HIGH FLIGHT

Oh! I have slipped the surly bonds of Earth
And danced the skies on laughter-silvered wings;
Sunward I've climbed, and joined the tumbling mirth
Of sun-split clouds - and done a hundred things
You have not dreamed of - wheeled and soared and swung
High in the sunlit silence. Hov'ring there,
I've chased the shouting wind along, and flung
My eager craft through footless halls of air.
Up, up the long delirious burning blue
I've topped the wind-swept heights with easy grace
Where never lark, or even eagle flew.
And while with silent lifting mind I've trod
The high untrespassed sanctity of space,
Put out my hand and touched the face of God.

- John Magee

UBIQUE

There is a word you often see, pronounce it as you may -
'You bike,' 'you bikwe,' 'ubbikwe' - alludin' to R.A.
It serves 'Orse, Field, an' Garrison as motto for a crest,
An' when you've found out all it means I'll tell you 'alf the rest.
Ubique means the long-range Krupp be'ind the low-range 'ill -
Ubique means you'll pick it up an', while you do stand, still.
Ubique means you've caught the flash an' timed it by the sound.
Ubique means five gunners' 'ash before you've loosed a round.
Ubique means Blue Fuse1, an' make the 'ole to sink the trail.
Ubique means stand up an' take the Mauser's 'alf-mile 'ail.
Ubique means the crazy team not God nor man can 'old.
Ubique means that 'orse's scream which turns your innards cold.

Ubique means 'Bank, 'Olborn, Bank - a penny all the way -
The soothin' jingle-bump-an'-clank from day to peaceful day.
Ubique means 'They've caught De Wet,
an' now we sha'n't be long.'
Ubique means 'I much regret, the beggar's going strong!'
Ubique means the tearin' drift where,
breech-blocks jammed with mud,
The khaki muzzles duck an' lift across the khaki flood.
Ubique means the dancing plain that changes rocks to Boers.
Ubique means the mirage again an' shellin' all outdoors.
Ubique means 'Entrain at once for Grootdefeatfontein'!
Ubique means 'Off-load your guns' - at midnight in the rain!
Ubique means 'More mounted men. Return all guns to store.'
Ubique means the R.A.M.R. Infantillery Corps!
Ubique means the warnin' grunt the perished linesman knows,
When o'er 'is strung an' sufferin' front
the shrapnel sprays 'is foes,
An' as their firin' dies away the 'usky whisper runs
From lips that 'aven't drunk all day:
'The Guns! Thank Gawd, the Guns!'
Extreme, depressed, point-blank or short, end-first or any'ow,
From Colesberg Kop to Quagga's Poort - from Ninety-Nine till now
By what I've 'eard the others tell an' I in spots 'ave seen,
There's nothin' this side 'Eaven or 'Ell Ubique doesn't mean!

- Rudyard Kipling (South African War)

ECHO GUN

Bring it into Action!
Spin those trails around!
There's grunts up the sharp end,
screaming out for rounds.
Set the elevation!
Traverse on for line!
Stratton's just a'loaded,
there's still a little time.
Me, I'm on the left side!
Bob, he's on the right!
Dingus yells "You Ready Subs?"
the method's "Battery Right".
When the mission's over!
"Detachments to the Rear!"
"A little slow that time Subs",

John whispers in my ear.
- Mike Subritzky 161 Battery

ANZAC EXCHANGE

Sarge I think I'm buggered,
I'm bitten on me back,
a bloody snakes bin crawlin' thru the grass.
So call the Medic quick,
to give me arm a prick,
and take away the pain until I pass.
Yer mate the Bombardier,
can have me 'ish' of beer,
I won't be drinkin' Fosters when I go.
I've wrote me mum a note,
and I've put it in me pack,
she's livin' down near Kunga-munga-mo.
So tell me Aussie mates,
you'ze Kiwi bloody skates,
have caused the death of one of Anzac's finest.
And when I pass away,
don't put me in the clay,
the bloody dingo's here are rife as goats.
What's that you bloody say,
the choppers on its way,
it won't be here in time to save this Digger.
The Doc he said it's what?
Now how did that get there?
A tear tab from a beer can caused this wound?
Well, the pain will pass away,
and I'll fight another day,
*but PLEEZE you'ze Kiwi's keep this to yourselve*s!
- Mike Subritzky 1986 161 Battery at Enoggora

THE LONELY HILL

Wild grow the poppies in Tunisian vale
Gracing the green of a fertile land
And here comes "Peace" to lay her veil
On the hill of the foes last stand..
Out of the Plain reared the lonely hill
Like a breast bared to the sky
Its slopes clasped the fallen ever still
And its bosom echoed the swallow's cry..

Small sanctuary of a fallen dream
Last bastion to Enfidaville
Your crumbled fort is a desolate scene
Where all but the winds are still..
The winds will rise and the tall grass bend
To ripple like waves of the sea
And time will take the scars to mend
On the lonely hill of the free.

- RA Harris

THE SOLDIER'S CHRISTMAS POEM

T'was the night before christmas.
He lived all alone,
In a one bedroom house.
Made of plaster and stone.
I had come down the chimney
With presents to give
And to see just who
In this home did live
I looked all about
A strange sight I did see
No tinsel no presents
Not even a tree
No stocking by mantle
Just boots filled with sand
On the wall hung pictures
Of far distant lands
With medals and badges
Awards of all kinds
A sober thought
Came through my mind
For this house was different
It was dark and dreary
I found the home of a soldier
Once I could see clearly
The soldier lay sleeping
Silent alone
Curled up on the floor
In this one bedroom home
The face was so gentle
The room in such disorder
Not how i pictured

A new zealand soldier
Was this the hero
Of whom I'd just read?
Curled up on a poncho
The floor for a bed?
I realized the families
That I saw this night
Owed their lives to these soldiers
Who were willing to fight
Soon round the world
The children would play
And grownups would celebrate
A bright christmas day
They all enjoyed freedom
Each month of the year
Because of the soldiers
Like the one lying here
I couldn't help wonder
How many lay alone
On a cold christmas eve
In a land far from home
The very thought brought
A tear to my eye
I dropped to my knees
And started to cry
The soldier awakened
And I heard a rough voice
"Santa don't cry,
This life is my choice;
I fight for freedom
I don't ask for more
My life is my god
My country, my corps
The soldier rolled over
And drifted to sleep
I coundn't control it
I continued to weep
I kept watch for hours
So silent and still
And we both shivered
From the cold night's chill
I didn't want to leave

On that cold dark night
This guardian of honour
So willing to fight
Then the soldier rolled over
With a voice soft and pure
Whispered "carry on santa
It's christmas day all is secure."
One look at my watch
And I knew he was right
"Merry Christmas my friend
And to all a good night."

\- Grant Hays

THE JACKET

Through the Plagues of Egyp'
we was chasin' Arabi,
Gettin' down an' shovin' in the sun;
An' you might 'ave called us dirty,
an' you might ha' called us dry,
An' you might 'ave 'eard us
talkin' at the gun.
But the Captain 'ad 'is jacket,
an' the jacket it was new -
('Orse Gunners, listen to my song!)
An' the wettin' of the jacket
is the proper thing to do,
Nor we didn't keep 'im waitin' very long.
One day they gave us orders
for to shell a sand redoubt,
Loadin' down the axle-arms with case;
But the Captain knew 'is dooty,
an' he took the crackers out
An' he put some proper liquor in its place.
An' the Captain saw the shrapnel,
which is six-an'-thirty clear.
('Orse Gunners, listen to my song!)
"Will you draw the weight,"
sez 'e, "or will you draw the beer?"
An' we didn't keep
'im waiting very long.
For the Captain, etc.
Then we trotted gentle,

not to break the bloomin' glass,
Though the Arabites 'ad
all their ranges marked;
But we dursn't 'ardly gallop,
for the most was bottled Bass,
An' we'd dreamed of it
since we was disembarked.
So we fired economic with
the shells we 'ad in 'and,
('Orse Gunners, listen to my song!)
But the beggars under cover
'ad the impidence to stand,
An' we couldn't keep 'em
waitin' very long.
And the Captain, etc.
So we finished 'arf the liquor
(an' the Captain took champagne),
An' the Arabites was shootin'
all the while;
An' we left our wounded
'appy with the empties on the plain,
An' we used the bloomin'
guns for projectile!
We limbered up an' galloped —
there were nothin' else to do —
('Orse Gunners, listen to my song!)
An' the Battery came a-boundin'
like a boundin' kangaroo,
But they didn't watch us comin' very long.
As the Captain, etc.
We was goin' most extended —
we was drivin' very fine,
An' the Arabites were loosin'
'igh an' wide,
Till the Captain took the glassy
with a rattlin' right incline,
An' we dropped upon
their 'eads the other side.
Then we give 'em quarter —
such as 'adn't up and cut,
('Orse Gunners, listen to my song!)
An' the Captain stood a limberful

of fizzy — somethin' Brutt,
But we didn't leave it fizzing very long.
For the Captain, etc.
We might ha' been court-martialled,
but it all come out all right
When they signalled us to join the main command.
There was every round expended,
there was every gunner tight,
An' the Captain waved a corkscrew in 'is 'and.
But the Captain 'ad 'is jacket, etc.

- Rudyard Kipling

GALATOS

Steadfast they faced the foe at Galatos,
Selfless and true, their spirit did not quail
Until with heavy hearts and heavy loss,
They fell back lest the hun-hordes should prevail.
But steadfast still, with courage undismayed,
And stubborn strength that could not know defeat,
Calm in calamity, a fierce defence displayed,
Which knew no weakening in their retreat.
Forced from the town, their line a shattered shell,
But intact yet, though thin and thinning still.
Where shrapnel scarred and gashed and warrior fell,
They lacked the means, they did not lack the will.
Steadfast their name, the gallant twenty-third,
The Maori men who valiantly fought back.
Swift came the night, but swifter came the word
Which launched four hundred bayonets in attack.
Reversed the scene and irresistible,
The onward rush that thrust resistance down.
Awful the flashing steel, and terrible
The battle cries which echoed through the town.
Avenged the silent comrades now at rest,
Who fully played their part and fighting died,
Man versus man, an equal, epic test,
Which proved the hun defenceless in his pride.
So victory was theirs, this gallant band.
The hun had gone except where hun dead lay.
And thus was covered by that steadfast stand
Our troops evacuation from the bay.

- Lin Rowell, 'A' Troop, 27 Bty, 5 Fd Regt, NZA

SNARLEYOW

This 'appened in a battle
to a batt'ry of the corps
Which is first among the women an'
amazin' first in war;
An' what the bloomin' battle
was I don't remember now,
But Two's off-lead 'e answered*
to the name o' Snarleyow.
Down in the Infantry, nobody cares;
Down in the Cavalry, Colonel 'e swears;
But down in the lead
with the wheel at the flog
Turns the bold Bombardier
to a little whipped dog!
They was movin' into action,
they was needed very sore,
To learn a little schoolin'
to a native army corps,
They 'ad nipped against an uphill,
they was tuckin' down the brow,
When a tricky, trundlin' roundshot
give the knock to Snarleyow.
They cut 'im loose an' left 'im -
'e was almost tore in two -
But he tried to follow after
as a well-trained 'orse should do;
'E went an' fouled the limber, an'
the Driver's Brother squeals:
"Pull up, pull up for Snarleyow -
'is head's between 'is 'eels!"
The Driver 'umped 'is shoulder,
for the wheels was goin' round,
An' there ain't no "Stop, conductor!"
when a batt'ry's changin' ground;
Sez 'e: "I broke the beggar in,
an' very sad I feels,
But I couldn't pull up, not for you -
your 'ead between your 'eels!"
'E 'adn't 'ardly spoke the word,
before a droppin' shell
A little right the batt'ry an'

between the sections fell;
An' when the smoke 'ad cleared away,
before the limber wheels,
There lay the Driver's Brother
with 'is 'ead between 'is 'eels.
Then sez the Driver's Brother, an'
'is words was very plain,
"For Gawd's own sake get over me,
an' put me out o' pain."
They saw 'is wounds was mortial,
an' they judged that it was best,
So they took an' drove the limber
straight across 'is back an' chest.
The Driver 'e give nothin'
'cept a little coughin' grunt,
But 'e swung 'is 'orses
'andsome when it came to "Action Front!"
An' if one wheel was juicy,
you may lay your Monday head
'Twas juicier for the niggers
when the case begun to spread.
The moril of this story,
it is plainly to be seen:
You 'aven't got no families
when servin' of the Queen -
You 'aven't got no brothers,
fathers, sisters, wives, or sons -
If you want to win your battles
take an' work your bloomin' guns!
Down in the Infantry,
nobody cares;
Down in the Cavalry,
Colonel 'e swears;
But down in the lead with
the wheel at the flog
Turns the bold Bombardier
to a little whipped dog!

- Rudyard Kipling

NAMING OF PARTS

Today we have naming of parts. Yesterday,
We had daily cleaning. And tomorrow morning,

We shall have what to do after firing. But today,
Today we have naming of parts. Japonica
Glistens like coral in all of the neighbouring gardens,
And today we have naming of parts.
This is the lower sling swivel. And this
Is the upper sling swivel, whose use you will see,
When you are given your slings. And this is the piling swivel,
Which in your case you have not got. The branches
Hold in the gardens their silent, eloquent gestures,
Which in our case we have not got.
This is the safety-catch, which is always released
With an easy flick of the thumb. And please do not let me
See anyone using his finger. You can do it quite easy
If you have any strength in your thumb. The blossoms
Are fragile and motionless, never letting anyone see
Any of them using their finger.
And this you can see is the bolt. The purpose of this
Is to open the breech, as you see. We can slide it
Rapidly backwards and forwards: we call this
Easing the spring. And rapidly backwards and forwards
The early bees are assaulting and fumbling the flowers:
They call it easing the Spring.
They call it easing the Spring: it is perfectly easy
If you have any strength in your thumb: like the bolt,
And the breech, and the cocking-piece,
and the point of balance,
Which in our case we have not got; and the almond-blossom
Silent in all of the gardens
and the bees going backwards and forwards,
For today we have naming of parts.

- by Henry Reed

THE GLORY OF THE GUNS

When the Battle Cry is spoken,
And the Voice of War is heard,
The soldiers of the Allies,
To battlefields do move.
The enemy is silent,
As if waiting for the sun,
Then they hear that awesome sound,
The booming of the Guns.
They shudder in their trenches

Within a gnawing fear,
Of knowing the Battery
Of 1-6-1 is here.
The shells come whilstling all around,
And wreck and break and knock things down,
Creating havoc among the lines
And all that it surrounds.
The enemy has broken
In torn and tired dismay,
Those so inclined
Get down on knees and pray.
The Allies are victorious,
The enemy is on the run,
Once again they have been beaten
By the Glory of the Guns.

- Gunner MR Duncan

AFTER THE WAR

When the tale is told in text books
Of the battle in the west,
Where the desert meets a desert
And the pasture ain't the best.
When the story's set and stated,
Written down in black and white
For the up and coming soldier
To peruse from left to right.
When the printed pulp is published,
Page on page of lettered lines,
And its dispositioned forces
And its places, points and times.
When the book is there before us,
Full of tactical defeats,
And technical advantages
And strategical retreats.
When the past is put on paper,
Telling why and when and where,
It'll curb the curiosity
Of the thousands that were there.
For the folks that fought this warfare,
On the home front or at the base,
Can peruse their penny papers
And see such and such took place,

But the bloke amidst the battle
Sees his own small, sticky sphere,
And hasn't heard what happened
Further forward or down rear.
He doesn't know the northern news,
The southern state's the same,
And he hopes to hell that convoy
Coming closer turns out tame.
So when those books see daylight
And meet him face to face,
He can pick 'em up and so find out
What actually took place.

- Lin Rowell, A Troop, 27 Bty

SOLDIER'S FAREWELL

I've saddled up, and dropped me hooch,
I'm going to take the gap,
my Tour of Duty's over mates,
and I won't be coming back.
I'm done with diggin' shell scrapes
and laying out barbed wire,
I'm sick of setting Claymore Mines,
and coming under fire.
So no more Fire Support Base,
and no more foot patrols,
and no more eating ration packs,
and sleepin' in muddy holes.
I've fired my last machine gun,
and ambushed my last track,
I'm sick of all the Army brass,
and I sure ain't coming back.
I'll hand my bayonet to the clerk,
he ain't seen one before,
and clean my rifle one more time,
and return it to the store.
So no more spit and polish,
and make sure I get paid,
and sign me from the Regiment,
today's my last parade.

- Mike Subritzky, 161 Bty RNZA

KIWI PEACEKEEPERS

There's death all around me, there's death in the air,

I can smell it and feel it - and I know now the fear.
The road could be mined, or an ambush await,
It may be the end - our appointment with fate.
The escorts have left us, we're now on our own,
I'm as frightened as hell - and we're all so alone.
Our armour is moving, we're leaving the town,
Rhodesians are waving, yelling - "Keep your heads down!"
I look at the Gunner, his face is all drawn,
His machine gun is loaded - and the safety catch on.
We drive through the war zone, on dirt roads blood red,
Past African Kraals - with children unfed.
Expecting a tank mine, or bullet to tell,
Or a Russian made rocket - to take us to hell.
At Assembly "Lima", the site of an old Kraal,
We finally halt - and put our backs to the wall.
Raise the stars of our Nation, raise the Brit's Union Jack,
Put the dread right behind us - for there's no turning back.
Not there for the fighting, not there for the fall,
We are the friend of no-one - and the enemy of all.
...We are the Peacekeepers.

- Mike Subritzky NZATMC Lima 1979

THE RHYME OF THE ANCIENT BOMBARDIER

Come gather round 'me hearties',
I've a salty tale to tell,
of Gunners sailin' dinghies,
Thru' foaming, surging, hell.
Of 'Ahab' Mac, and Maori Joe,
old bos'n Bev Culhane,
and Matt Tepou was there as well,
four boats and gentle rain.
Chorus:
"So it's paddle down the river
and don't be slow,
we're gonna take the boats
where a duck won't go...
Floatsam! Jetsam! Gunners in the tide;
the Whakatane river, is deep and fast, and wide. "
The river flows, the wind it blows,
the rain comes fast and thunder,
White capped rocks and waterfalls,
the first boat goes asunder.

There's four men in the river,
"I'm drown'in" what they yell,
then Snow he pulls the others out,
the waters cold as hell.
Chorus
We can't give up, we just won't stop,
for it's nay been done a'fore,
the first boat she's a'floundered,
but we've still got three boats more.
So on we sail, past 'Ahabs' boat,
just twelve men left are we,
there's 'Radar' eating chocolate,
his paddle on his knee.
Chorus
Young Maori Joe, his boat is next,
it's sinking by the stern.
Was it the rocks that claimed his craft?
I guess we'll never learn.
There's 'water water everywhere',
and not a drop to succor,
into the tide went all their gear,
followed by their tucker.
Chorus
The river rushes onward,
there's cliffs on either side,
a log, it blocks the way 'me lads',
the gorge is ten foot wide.
'Hey Mita!' push the bow down,
and Wally raise the stern,
we've got to fit her thru' the gap,
there's death at every turn.
Chorus
Well it's eight bells ringin',
and it's two boats still afloat...
Is that a banjo playin'?
or do I hear a goat.
A tearing sound, a boats gone down,
it's hull is torn wide open,
old bosun' Bev, his one boat left,
he'll sail on I'm a'hopin.
Chorus
There's Bev and 'Radar', Pete and Wally;

in the last canoe.
There's a waterfall that's comin' up...
'Ye Gods!' what should I do???
So: Leave the sailin' to the Navy,
the walking to the Grunts,
get back to Papakura...
and clean those bloody guns!

- Mike Subritzky 161 Battery

FAMOUS POETS OF WORLD WAR II

ALAMEIN TO ZEM ZEM

Alamein to Zem Zem is a military memoir of the Western Desert campaign of World War II written by the British soldier-poet Keith Douglas shortly before his death in action in Normandy in June 1944. It was first published in 1946.

The book is mainly a personal account of Douglas's experiences as a young tank commander in the Sherwood Rangers Yeomanrywith the British Eighth Army at the Second Battle of El Alamein in October–November 1942. Zem Zem is the name of a wadi inTunisia where Douglas was wounded in early 1943.

Desmond Graham, Douglas's biographer and editor, wrote: "This narrative, like his poems of the Desert War, is unique in the literature of its period, in that no other British poet of Douglas's quality had battle experience and survived long enough to write of it."

Alamein to Zem Zem was first published by Editions Poetry London in 1946 and republished by Faber and Faber (1966), Penguin Modern Classics (1969), Oxford University Press (1979) and again by Faber and Faber (1992).

TIMOTHY CORSELLIS

Timothy Corsellis (1921–1941) was an English poet of World War II.

Early life

Timothy John Manley Corsellis was born on January 27, 1921 in Eltham, London, the third of the four children of Helen (née Bendall) and Douglas Corsellis. His father had lost a fore-arm at Gallipoli, but went on to become a prosperous barrister and learnt to fly his own light aircraft. Timothy went to St. Clare preparatory school in Walmer, Kent, where John Magee, the author of "High Flight" was a contemporary and Henry Bentinck became a friend. After his father's death in an air crash in 1930, Timothy was sent to Winchester College, where he contributed poems to the school magazine and fenced.

Leaving school to start work as an articled clerk in the Town Clerk's office in Wandsworth, he divided his evenings between work as a resident volunteer at the Crown and Manor Club, a Winchester College Settlement in Hoxton,

East London and entertainment inFitzrovia, where he earned money for drinks by "conjuring", a talent which earned him the right of entry into the exclusive Magic Circle.

Wartime experience

Strongly marked by the failure of the Munich Agreement, Corsellis registered in April 1939 as a conscientious objector on religious grounds. When war broke out he became an ARP warden. After Dunkirk, he volunteered for training as a fighter pilot. His initial training in Torquay and Carlisle did not prepare him for his assignment to Bomber Command, an assignment which in January 1941 he refused, on the grounds that his conscience would not permit him to take part in the indiscriminate bombing of civilians.His request to join Fighter Command was met with an honourable discharge from the RAF and his application to join the Fleet Air Arm was ignored, but he was accepted by the Air Transport Auxiliary, which ferried aircraft from factory to operational squadrons. From January to July 1941, at the height of the Blitz, he worked as a full-time ARP warden, and then he began his ATA training at White Waltham in September 1941. On 10 October 1941 the aircraft Corsellis was flying stalled and crashed over Annan in Dumfriesshire, Scotland. He was 20 years old.

Literary life

At the time of his death Corsellis was just beginning to break into London literary circles, and in death he was not forgotten. Keidrych Rhys and Patricia Ledward wroteelegies for him, and included some of his poems in their anthologies, *Poems from the Forces,' More Poems from the Forces* and *Poems of This War by Younger Poets*.As John Sutherland recounts, Stephen Spender, for whom Corsellis had found war work in Wandsworth, was haunted by his sudden disappearance, and his penultimate poem, dated 1941/1995 was dedicated to "Timothy Corsellis". The American anthologist Oscar Williams championed his work, and an American poet and former war pilot,Simon Perchik, has paid him tribute. In 2004 the Oxford Dictionary of National Biography took a first step in establishing a literary canon of World War 2 poets by including nine: Keith Douglas, Sidney Keyes, Alun Lewis, Gavin Ewart, Roy Fuller, John Pudney, Henry Reed, Frank Thompson and Corsellis. Ronald Blythe wrote a moving account of his life for the *Oxford Dictionary of National Biography*, while critics as well known as Andrew Sinclair and D.S.R. Welland have singled out his work.

In 2012 Helen Goethals's *The Unassuming Sky: The Life and Poetry of Timothy Corsellis* made available for the first time a hundred of his poems, arranged to bring out their "unique literary and historical interest". Two reviews put them into context: those of Martyn Halsall in the Church Times – "This study assists the debate on war poetry from 1939 to 1945" – and Ralph

Townsend in The Trusty Servant – "The place of Corsellis among the Second War poets of England is established in the anthologies. Here additional poems... which have not before gone into print present him as an example of a young man whose education led him to take an independent moral view of things...".

In 2014 the introduction to a War Words poetry reading by Andrew Eaton stated that "The First and Second World Wars inspired gifted writers from Wilfred Owen to Timothy Corsellis to commit to paper their personal wartime narratives. These texts, often graphic and harrowing, have gone on to become parts of the world's cultural fabric.".

Also in 2014 the Poetry Society, supported by the War Poets Association and the Imperial War Museums, launched its Timothy Corsellis Prize Competition for a poem responding to the Second World War. This was directed at young poets all over the world aged 14-25, and was for a poem responding to the life and/or work of Keith Douglas, Sidney Keyes, Alun Lewis, John Jarmain, Henry Reed or Timothy Corsellis, with a short comment (300 words) explaining how the competitor responded to one or more of them. The competition will be repeated annually for at least 5 years.

Excerpts from poems

When I was a civilian I hoped high
Dreamt my future cartwheels in the sky
Almost forgot to arm myself
Against the boredom and the inefficiency
The petty injustice and the everlasting grudges
The sacrifice is greater than I ever expected.

—*from* "What I never saw" (January 24, 1941)

Under this pile of fallen masonry
Under those spillikins of beams
Where number thirty two lies shattered
There may be a body
Dig
For there may be a body.
Distorted corpse once breathed slum air
Lived in the grey dust where it died;
Is it for this that bending we strived
And fought in other's blood and other's sorrow
To reach these wretched mangled remains?
Is it for this that we ached in the darkness
Not knowing that nearby
Another house had fallen
To the blast of that same bomb.
Sweat fell, we were not the strong and young

They were out training, preparing,
We are the best of those remaining
We are the mellow and the hardened
And though our backs are hard of bending
Under aloofness our souls bend rending
The sorrow out of the bereaved father's breast
Tearing it out and holding it in our own hands
Adopting it to our own bodies
Caring for the children we had never seen
Sometimes we pray to be hardened and callous
But God turns a deaf ear
And we know hate and sorrow,
Intimately
And we do not mind dying tomorrow.

—*from* "Dawn after the raid" (April 20, 1941)

I will not sing the song of others
In other people's words;
I will not see the world of others
Through other people's eyes.
But blue, far into space,
I'll hurl my judgement of the human race
Upwards to the unassuming sky,
Farther than any bird can fly.

—*from* "It is not you, pale lonely star" (August 22, 1941)

And for the gifts that you can proffer
Hope and love and power and pride
Take from me all I can offer
Weakness and some words beside.

—*from* "The gifts" (August 28, 1941)

KEITH DOUGLAS

Keith Castellain Douglas (24 January 1920 – 9 June 1944) was an English poet noted for his war poetry during World War II and his wry memoir of the Western Desert campaign, *Alamein to Zem Zem*. He was killed in action during the invasion of Normandy.

Poetry

Douglas described his poetic style as 'extrospective'; that is, he focused on external impressions rather than inner emotions. The result is a poetry which, according to his detractors, can be callous in the midst of war's atrocities. For others, Douglas's work is powerful and unsettling because its exact descriptions eschew egotism and shift the burden of emotion from the poet to the reader. His best poetry is generally considered to rank alongside the twentieth-century's finest soldier-poetry.

In his poem, "Desert Flowers" (1943), Douglas mentions World War I poet Isaac Rosenberg, claiming that he is only repeating what Rosenberg has already written.

Early life

Douglas was born in Tunbridge Wells, Kent, the son of Capt. Keith Sholto Douglas, MC (retired) and Marie Josephine Castellain. His mother became unwell and collapsed in 1924 of encephalitis lethargica, never to fully recover. By 1926, the chicken farm set up by his father had collapsed. Douglas was sent to a preparatory school (Edgeborough School in Guildford) the same year. The family became increasingly poor, and his father had to leave home in early 1928 to seek better employment in Wales. The persistent ill-health of Marie led to the collapse of the marriage of his parents by the end of that year, and his father remarried in 1930. Douglas was deeply hurt by his father not communicating with him after 1928, and when Capt. Douglas did write at last in 1938, Keith did not agree to meet him. In one of his letters written in 1940 Douglas looked back on his childhood: "I lived alone during the most fluid and formative years of my life, and during that time I lived on my imagination, which was so powerful as to persuade me that the things I imagined would come true."

Education

Marie Douglas faced extreme financial distress, so much so that only the generosity of the Edgeborough headmaster Mr. James permitted Douglas to attend school in 1930–1931, his last year there. Douglas sat in 1931 for the entrance examination to Christ's Hospital, where education was free and there was monetary assistance to cover all other costs. He was accepted, and joined Christ's Hospital, near Horsham, in September 1931, studying there till 1938. It was at this school that his considerable poetic talent and artistic ability were recognised. So was his cavalier attitude to authority and property, which nearly led to expulsion in 1935 over a purloined training rifle. In surprising contrast, he excelled as a member of the school's Officers Training Corps, particularly enjoying drill, although he was philosophically opposed to militarism.

University

After his bruising brush with authority in 1935, Douglas settled down to a less troubled and more productive period at school, during which he excelled both at studies and games, and at the end of which he won an open exhibition to Merton College, Oxford in 1938 to read History and English. The First World War-veteran and well-known poetEdmund Blunden was his tutor at Merton, and regarded his poetic talent highly. Blunden sent his poems to T. S. Eliot, the doyen of English poetry, who found Douglas's verses 'impressive'. Douglas became the editor of *Cherwell*, and one of the poets anthologised in the collection *Eight Oxford Poets* (1941), although by the time that volume appeared he was already in the army. He does not seem to have been acquainted with somewhat junior but contemporary Oxford poets such as Sidney Keyes, Drummond Allison, John Heath-Stubbs and Philip Larkin, who would make names for themselves.

At Oxford, Douglas entered a relationship with a sophisticated Chinese student named Yingcheng, or Betty Sze, the daughter of a diplomat. Her own sentiments towards him were less intense, and she refused to marry him. Yingcheng remained the unrequited love of Douglas's life and the source of his best romantic verse, despite his involvements with other women later, most notably Milena Guiterrez Penya.

Military service

Within days of the declaration of war he reported to an army recruiting centre with the intention of joining a cavalry regiment, but like many others keen to serve he had to wait, and it was not until July 1940 that he started his training. On 1 February 1941 he passed out from Sandhurst, the British Army officer training academy, and was posted to the Second Derbyshire Yeomanry at Ripon.

He was shipped to the Middle East in July 1941 and transferred to the Nottinghamshire (Sherwood Rangers) Yeomanry. Posted initially at Cairoand Palestine, he found himself stuck at Headquarters twenty miles behind El Alamein as a camouflage officer as the Second Battle of El Alamein began. At dawn on 24 October 1942, the Regiment advanced, and suffered numerous casualties from enemy anti-tank guns. Chafing at inactivity, Douglas took off against orders on 27 October, drove to the Regimental HQ in a truck, and reported to the C.O., Colonel E.O. Kellett, lying that he had been instructed to go to the front (luckily this escapade did not land him in serious trouble; in a reprise of 1935, Douglas got off with an apology). Desperately needing officer replacements, the Colonel posted him to A Squadron, and gave him the opportunity to take part as a fighting tanker in the Eighth Army's victorious sweep through North Africa vividly recounted in his memoir *Alamein to Zem Zem*, illustrated with his own drawings.

Death

Captain Douglas returned from North Africa to England in December 1943 and took part in the D-Day invasion of Normandy on 6 June 1944. He was killed by enemy mortar fire on 9 June, while his regiment was advancing from Bayeux. Captain Leslie Skinner (regimental chaplain) buried him by a hedge, close to where he had died on "forward slopes point 102". Shortly after the war his remains were reburied at Tilly-sur-Seulles War Cemetery (14 km south of Bayeux) in plot 1, row E, grave number 2.

BENJAMIN FONDANE

Benjamin Fondane or Benjamin Fundoianu (November 14, 1898 – October 2, 1944) was a Romanian and French poet, critic and existentialist philosopher, also noted for his work in film and theater. Known from his Romanian youth as a Symbolist poet and columnist, he alternated Neo-romantic and Expressionist themes with echoes from Tudor Arghezi, and dedicated several poetic cycles to the rural life of his native Moldavia. Fondane, who was of Jewish Romanian extraction and a nephew of Jewish intellectuals Elias and Moses Schwartzfeld, participated in both minority secular Jewish culture and mainstream Romanian culture. During and after World War I, he was active as a cultural critic, avant-gardepromoter and, with his brother-in-law Armand Pascal, manager of the theatrical troupe *Insula*.

Fondane began a second career in 1923, when he moved to Paris. Affiliated with Surrealism, but strongly opposed to its communistleanings, he moved on to become a figure in Jewish existentialism and a leading disciple of Lev Shestov. His critique of political dogma, rejection of rationalism, expectation of historical catastrophe and belief in the soteriological force of literature were outlined in his celebrated essays on Charles Baudelaire and Arthur Rimbaud, as well as in his final works of poetry. His literary and philosophical activities helped him build close relationships with other intellectuals: Shestov, Emil Cioran, David Gascoyne, Jacques Maritain, Victoria Ocampo, Ilarie Voronca etc. In parallel, Fondane also had a career in cinema: a film critic and a screenwriter forParamount Pictures, he later worked on *Rapt* with Dimitri Kirsanoff, and directed the since-lost film *Tararira* in Argentina.

A prisoner of war during the fall of France, Fondane was released and spent the occupation years in clandestinity. He was eventually captured and handed to Nazi German authorities, who deported him to Auschwitz-Birkenau. He was sent to the gas chamber during the last wave of the Holocaust. His work was largely rediscovered later in the 20th century, when it became the subject of scholarly research and public curiosity in both France and Romania. In the latter country, this revival of interest also sparked a controversy over copyright issues.

Biography

Early life

Fondane was born in Ia˘i, the cultural capital of Moldavia, on November 14, 1898, but, as he noted in a diary he kept at age 16, his birthday was officially recorded as November 15. Fondane was the only son of Isac Wechsler and his wife Adela (née Schwartzfeld), who also bore the sisters Lina (b. 1892) and

Rodica (b. 1905), both of whom had careers in acting. Wechsler was a Jewish man from Hertza region, his ancestors having been born on the *Fundoaia* estate (which the poet later used as the basis for his signature). Adela was from an intellectual family, of noted influence within the urban Jewish community: her father, poet B. Schwartzfeld, was the owner of a book collection, while her uncles Elias and Moses both had careers in humanities. Adela herself was well acquainted with the intellectual elite of Ia^i, Jewish as well as ethnic Romanian, and kept recollections of her encounters with authors linked with the *Junimea* society. Through Moses Schwartzfeld, Fondane was also related with socialist journalist Avram Steuerman-Rodion, one of the literary men who nurtured the boy's interest in literature.

The young Benjamin was an avid reader, primarily interested in the Moldavian classics of Romanian literature (Ion Neculce, Miron Costin, Dosoftei, Ion Creangã), Romanian traditionalists or Neo-romantics (Vasile Alecsandri, Ion Luca Caragiale, George Co^buc, Mihai Eminescu) and French Symbolists. In 1909, after graduating from School No. 1 (an annex of the Trei Ierarhi Monastery), he was admitted into the Alexandru cel Bun secondary school, where he did not excel as a student. A restless youth (he recalled having had his first love affair at age 12, with a girl six years his senior), Fondane twice failed to get his remove before the age of 14.

Benjamin divided his time between the city and his father's native region. The latter's rural landscape impressed him greatly, and, enduring in his memory, became the setting in several of his poems. The adolescent Fondane took extended trips throughout northern Moldavia, making his debut in folkloristics by writing down samples of the narrative and poetic tradition in various Romanian-inhabited localities. Among his childhood friends was the future Yiddish-language writer B. Iosif, with whom he spent his time in Ia^i's Podul Vechi neighbourhood. In this context, Fondane also met Yiddishist poet Jacob Gropper—an encounter which shaped Fondane's intellectual perspectives on Judaismand Jewish history. At the time, Fondane became known to his family and friends as *Mielu^on* (from *miel*, Romanian for "lamb", and probably in reference to his bushy hairdo), a name which he later used as a colloquial pseudonym.

Although Fondane later claimed to have started writing poetry at age eight, his earliest known contributions to the genre date from 1912, including both pieces of his own and translations from such authors as André Chénier, Joseph Freiherr von Eichendorff, Heinrich Heine and Henri de Régnier. The same year, some of these were published, under the pseudonym *I. G. Ofir*, in the local literary review *Floare Albastrã*, whose owner, A. L. Zissu, was later a noted novelist and Zionist political figure. Later research proposed that these, like some other efforts of the 1910s, were collective poetry samples, resulting from a collaboration between Fondane and Gropper (the former was probably translating the latter's poetic motifs into Romanian). In 1913, Fondane also tried his hand at editing a student journal, signing his editorial with the pen name*Van Doian*, but only produced several handwritten copies of a single issue.

Debut years

Fondane's actual debut dates back to 1914, during the time when he became a student at the National High School Ia^i and formally affiliated with the provincial branch of thenation-wide Symbolist movement. That year, samples of lyric poetry were also published in the magazines *Valuri* and *Revista Noastrã* (whose owner, poetess Constan^a Hodo^, even offered Fondane a job on the editorial board, probably unaware that she was corresponding with a high school student). Also in 1914, the Moldavian Symbolist venue*Absolutio*, edited by Isac Ludo, featured pieces he signed with the pen name *I. Ha^ir*. Among his National High School colleagues was Alexandru Al. Philippide, the future critic, who remained one of Fondane's best friends (and whose poetry Fondane proposed for publishing in *Revista Noastrã*). Late in 1914, Fondane also began his short collaboration with the Ia^i Symbolist tribune *Viea^a Nouã*. While several of his poems were published there, the review's founder Ovid Densusianu issued objections to their content, and, in their subsequent correspondence, each writer outlines his stylistic disagreements with the other.

During the first two years of World War I and Romania's neutrality, the young poet established new contacts within the literary environments of Ia^i and Bucharest. According to his brother-in-law and biographer Paul Daniel, "it is amazing how many pages of poetry, translations, prose, articles, chronicles have been written by Fundoianu in this interval." In 1915, four of his patriotic-themed poems were published on the front page of *Diminea^a* daily, which campaigned for Romanian intervention against the Central Powers (they were the first of several contributions Fondane signed with the pen name *Alex. Vilara*, later *Al. Vilara*). His parallel contribution to the Bârlad-based review*Revista Criticã* (originally, *Cronica Moldovei*) was more strenuous: Fondane declared himself indignant that the editorial staff would not send him the galley proofs, and received instead an irritated reply from manager Al. ^tefãnescu; he was eventually featured with poems in three separate issues of *Revista Criticã*. At around that time, he also wrote amemoir of his childhood, *Note dintr-un confesional* ("Notes from a Confessional").

Around 1915, Fondane was discovered by the journalistic tandem of Tudor Arghezi and Gala Galaction, both of whom were also modernist authors, left-wing militants and Symbolist promoters. The pieces Fondane sent to Arghezi and Galaction's *Cronica* paper were received with enthusiasm, a reaction which surprised and impressed the young author. Although his poems went unpublished, his Ia^i-themed article *A doua capitalã* ("The Second Capital"), signed*Al. Vilara*, was featured in an April 1916 issue. A follower of Arghezi, he was personally involved in raising awareness about Arghezi's unpublished verse, the *Agate negre* ("Black Diamonds") cycle.

Remaining close friends with Fondane, Galaction later made persistent efforts of introducing him to critic Garabet Ibrăileanu, with the purpose of having him published by thePoporanist *Via^a Românească* review, but Ibrăileanu refused to recognize Fondane as an affiliate. Fondane had more success in contacting *Flacăra* review and its publisherConstantin Banu: on July 23, 1916, it hosted his sonnet *Eglogă marină* ("Marine Eglogue"). Between 1915 and 1923, Fondane also had a steady contribution to Romanian-language Jewish periodicals (*Lumea Evree*, *Bar-Kochba*, *Hasmonaea*, *Hatikvah*), where he published translations from international representatives of Yiddish literature (Hayim Nahman Bialik, Semyon Frug, Abraham Reisen etc.) under the signatures *B. Wechsler*, *B. Fundoianu* and *F. Benjamin*. Fondane also completed work on a translation of the *Ahasverus* drama, by the Jewish author Herman Heijermans.

His collaboration with the Bucharest-based *Rampa* (at the time a daily newspaper) also began in 1915, with his debut as theatrical chronicler, and later with his Carpathian-themed series in the travel writing genre, *Pe drumuri de munte* ("On Mountain Roads"). With almost one signed or unsigned piece per issue over the following years, Fondane was one of the more prolific contributors to that newspaper, and frequently made use of either pseudonyms (*Diomed*, *Dio*, *Funfurpan*, *Const. Meletie*) or initials (*B. F.*, *B. Fd.*, *fd.*). These included his January 1916 positive review of *Plumb*, the first major work by Romania's celebrated Symbolist poet, George Bacovia.

In besieged Moldavia and relocation to Bucharest

In 1917, after Romania joined the Entente side and was invaded by the Central Powers, Fondane was in Ia^i, where the Romanian authorities had retreated. It was in this context that he met and befriended the doyen of Romanian Symbolism, poet Ion Minulescu. Minulescu and his wife, author Claudia Millian, had left their home in occupied Bucharest, and, by spring 1917, hosted Fondane at their provisional domicile in Ia^i. Millian later recalled that her husband had been much impressed by the Moldavian teenager, describing him as "a rare bird" and "a poet of talent". The same year, at age 52, Isac Wechsler fell ill with typhus and died in Ia^i's Sfântul Spiridon Hospital, leaving his family without financial support.

At around that time, Fondane began work on the poetry cycle *Priveli^ti* ("Sights" or "Panoramas", finished in 1923). In 1918, he became one of the contributors to the magazine *Chemarea*, published in Ia^i by the leftist journalist N. D. Cocea, with help from Symbolist writer Ion Vinea. In the political climate marked by the Peace of Bucharestand Romania's remilitarization, Fondane used Cocea's publication to protest against the arrest of Arghezi, who had been accused of collaborationism with the Central Powers. In this context, Fondane spoke of Arghezi as being "Romania's greatest contemporary poet" (a verdict which was later to be approved of by mainstream critics).According to one account, Fondane also worked briefly as a fact checker for *Arena*, a periodical managed by Vinea and N. Porsenna.

His time with *Chemarea* also resulted in the publication of his Biblical-themed short story *Tãgãduin^a lui Petru* ("Peter's Denial"). Issued by *Chemarea*'s publishing house in 41 bibliophile copies (20 of which remained in Fondane's possession), it opened with the tract *O lãmurire despre simbolism* ("An Explanation of Symbolism").

In 1919, upon the war's end, Benjamin Fondane settled in Bucharest, where he stayed until 1923. During this interval, he frequently changed domicile: after a stay at his sister Lina's home in Obor area, he moved on Lahovari Street (near Pia^a Romanã), then in Mo^ilor area, before relocating to Vãcãre^ti (a majority Jewish residential area, where he lived in two successive locations), and ultimately to a house a short distance away from Foi^orul de Foc. Between these changes of address, he established contacts with the Symbolist and avant-garde society of Bucharest: a personal friend of graphic artist Iosif Ross, he formed an informal avant-garde circle of his own, attended by writers F. Brunea-Fox, Ion Cãlugãru, Henri Gad, Sa^a Panã, Claude Sernet-Cosma and Ilarie Voronca, as well as by artist-director Armand Pascal (who, in 1920, married Lina Fundoianu). Panã would later note his dominant status within the group, describing him as the "stooping green-eyed youth from Ia^i, the standard-bearer of the iconoclasts and rebels of the new generation".

The group was occasionally joined by other friends, among them Millian and painter Nicolae Tonitza. In addition, Fondane and Cãlugãru frequented the artistic and literary club established by the controversial Alexandru Bogdan-Pite^ti, a cultural promoter and political militant whose influence spread over several Symbolist milieus. In a 1922 piece for *Rampa*, he remembered Bogdan-Pite^ti in ambivalent terms: "he could not stand moral elevation. [...] He was made of the greatest of joys, in the most purulent of bodies. How many generations of ancient boyars had come to pass, like unworthy dung, for this singular earth to be generated?"

Pressed on by his family and the prospects of financial security, Fondane contemplated becoming a lawyer. Having passed his baccalaureate examination in Bucharest, he was, according to his own account, a registered student at the University of Ia^i Law School, obtaining a graduation certificate but prevented from becoming a licentiate by the opposition of faculty member A. C. Cuza, the antisemitic political figure. According to a recollection of poet Adrian Maniu, Fondane again worked as a fact checker for some months after his arrival to the capital. His activity as a journalist also allowed him to interview Arnold Davidovich Margolin, statesman of the defunct Ukrainian People's Republic, with whom he discussed the fate of Ukrainian Jews before and after the Soviet Russian takeover.

Sburãtorul, Contimporanul, Insula

Over the following years, he restarted his career in the press, contributing to various nationally circulated newspapers: *Adevãrul*, *Adevãrul Literar ^i Artistic*, *Cuvântul Liber*,*Mântuirea*, etc. The main topics of his interest were literary reviews, essays reviewing the contribution of Romanian and French authors, various art chronicles, and opinion pieces on social or cultural issues. A special case was his collaboration with *Mântuirea*, a Zionist periodical founded by Zissu, where, between August and October 1919, he published his studies collection *Iudaism ^i elenism* ("Judaism and Hellenism"). These pieces, alternating with similar articles by Galaction, showed how the young man's views in cultural anthropology had been shaped by his relationship with Gropper (with whom he nevertheless severed all contacts by 1920).

Fondane also renewed his collaboration with *Rampa*. He and another contributor to the magazine, journalist Tudor Teodorescu-Brani^te, carried out a debate in the magazine's pages: Fondane's articles defended Romanian Symbolism against criticism from Teodorescu-Brani^te, and offered glimpse into his personal interpretation of Symbolist attitudes. One piece he wrote in 1919, titled *Noi, simboli^tii* ("Us Symbolists") stated his proud affiliation to the current (primarily defined by him as an artistic transposition of eternal idealism), and comprised the slogan: "We are too many not to be strong, and too few not to be intelligent." In May 1920, another of his *Rampa* contributions spoke out against Octavian Goga, Culture Minister of the Alexandru Averescu executive, who contemplated sacking George Bacovia from his office of clerk. The same year, *Lumea Evree* published his verse drama fragment *Monologul lui Baltazar* ("Belshazzar's Soliloquy").

Around the time of his relocation to Bucharest, Fondane first met the moderate modernist critic Eugen Lovinescu, and afterwards became both an affiliate of Lovinescu's circle and a contributor to his literary review *Sburãtorul*. Among his first contributions there was a retrospective coverage of the boxing match between Jack Dempsey andGeorges Carpentier, which comprised his reflections on the mythical power of sport and the clash of cultures. Although a *Sburãtorist*, he was still in contact with Galaction and the left-wing circles. In June 1921, Galaction paid homage to "the daring Benjamin" in an article for *Adevãrul Literar ^i Artistic*, calling attention to Fondane's "overwhelming originality."

A year later, Fondane was employed by Vinea's new venue, the prestigious modernist venue *Contimporanul*. Having debuted in its first issue with a comment on Romanian translation projects (*Ferestre spre Occident*, "Windows on the Occident"), he was later assigned the theatrical column. Fondane's work was again featured in *Flacăra*magazine (at the time under Minulescu's direction): the poem *Ce simplu* ("How Simple") and the essay *Istoria Ideii* ("The History of the Idea") were both published there in 1922. The same year, with assistance from fellow novelist Felix Aderca, Fondane grouped his earlier essays on French literature as *Imagini ^i căr^i din Fran^a* ("Images and Books from France"), published by Editura Socec company. The book included what was probably the first Romanian study of Marcel Proust's contribution as a novelist.The author announced that he was planning a similar volume, grouping essays about Romanian writers, both modernists (Minulescu, Bacovia, Arghezi, Maniu, Galaction) and classics (Alexandru Odobescu, Ion Creangã, Constantin Dobrogeanu-Gherea, Anton Pann), but this work was not published in his lifetime.

Also in 1922, Fondane and Pascal set up the theatrical troupe *Insula* ("The Island"), which stated its commitment to avant-garde theater. Probably named after Minulescu's earlier Symbolist magazine, the group was likely a local replica of Jean Copeau's nonconformist productions in France. Hosted by the Maison d'Art galleries in Bucharest, the company was joined by, among others, actresses Lina Fundoianu-Pascal and Victoria Mierlescu, and director Sandu Eliad. Other participants were writers (Cocea, Panã, Zissu, Scarlat Callimachi, Mãrgãrita Miller Verghy, Ion Pillat) and theatrical people (George Ciprian, Marietta Sadova, Soare Z. Soare, Dida Solomon, Alice Sturdza, Ionel ^ãranu).

Although it stated its goal of revolutionizing the Romanian repertoire (a goal published as an art manifesto in *Contimporanul*), *Insula* produced mostly conventional Symbolist andNeo-classical plays: its inaugural shows included *Legenda funigeilor* ("Gossamer Legend") by ^tefan Octavian Iosif and Dimitrie Anghel, one of Lord Dunsany's *Five Plays* and (in Fondane's own translation) Molière's *Le Médecin volant*. Probably aiming to enrich this programme with samples of Yiddish drama, Fondane began, but never finished, a translation of S. Ansky's *The Dybbuk*. The troupe ceased its activity in 1923, partly because of significant financial difficulties, and partly because of a rise in antisemitic activities, which put its Jewish performers at risk. For a while, *Insula* survived as a conference group, hosting modernist lectures on classical Romanian literature—with the participation of Symbolist and post-Symbolist authors such as Aderca, Arghezi, Millian, Pillat, Vinea, N. Davidescu, Perpessicius, and Fondane himself. He was at the time working on his own play, *Filoctet* ("Philoctetes", later finished as *Philoctète*).

Move to France

In 1923, Benjamin Fondane eventually left Romania for France, spurred on by the need to prove himself within a different cultural context. He was at the time interested in the success of Dada, an avant-garde movement launched abroad by the Romanian-born author Tristan Tzara, in collaboration with several others. Not dissuaded by the fact that his sister and brother-in-law (the Pascals) had returned impoverished from an extended stay in Paris, Fondane crossed Europe by train and partly by foot.

The writer (who adopted his Francized name shortly after leaving his native country) was eventually joined there by the Pascals. The three of them continued to lead a bohemian and at times precarious existence, discussed in Fondane's correspondence with Romanian novelist Liviu Rebreanu, and described by researcher Ana-Maria Tomescu as "humiliating poverty". The poet acquired some sources of income from his contacts in Romania: in exchange for his contribution to the circulation of Romanian literature in France, he received official funds from the Culture Ministry's directorate (at the time headed by Minulescu); in addition, he published unsigned articles in various newspapers, and even relied on handouts from Romanian actressElvira Popescu (who visited his home, as did avant-garde painter M. H. Maxy). He also translated into French Zissu's novel*Amintirile unui candelabru* ("The Recollections of a Chandelier"). For a while, the poet also joined his colleague Ilarie Voronca on the legal department of L'Abeille insurance company.

After a period of renting furnished rooms, Fondane accepted an offer from Jean, brother of the deceased literary theorist Remy de Gourmont, and, employed as a librarian-concierge, moved into the Gourmonts' museum property on Rue des Saints-Pères, some distance away from to the celebrated literary café *Les Deux Magots*. In the six years before Pascal's 1929 death, Fondane left Gourmont's house and, with his sister and brother-in-law, moved into a succession of houses (on Rue Domat, Rue Jacob, Rue Monge), before settling into a historical building once inhabited by author Bernardin de Saint-Pierre (Rue Rollin, 6). Complaining about eye trouble and exhaustion, and several times threatened with insolvency, Fondane often left Paris for the resort of Arcachon.

Claudia Millian, who was also spending time in Paris, described Fondane's new focus on studying Christian theology and Catholic thought, from Hildebert to Gourmont's own*Latin mystique* (it was also at this stage that the Romanian writer acquired and sent home part of Gourmont's bibliophile collection). He coupled these activities with an interest in grouping together the cultural segments of the Romanian diaspora: around 1924, he and Millian were founding members of the Society of Romanian Writers in Paris, presided upon by the aristocrat Elena Văcărescu. Meanwhile, Fondane acquired a profile on the local literary scene, and, in his personal notes, claimed to have had his works praised by novelist André Gide and philosopher Jules de Gaultier. They both were his idols: Gide's work had shaped his own contribution in the prose poem genre, while Gaultier did the same for his philosophical outlook. The self-exiled debutant was nevertheless still viewing his career with despair, describing it as languishing, and noting that there was a chance of him failing to earn a solid literary reputation.

Surrealist episode

The mid-1920s brought Benjamin Fondane's affiliation with Surrealism, the post-Dada avant-garde current centered in Paris. Fondane also rallied with Belgian Surrealist composers E. L. T. Mesens and André Souris (with whom he signed a manifesto on modernist music), and supported Surrealist poet-director Antonin Artaud in his efforts to set up a theater named after Alfred Jarry (which was not, however, an all-Surrealist venue). In this context, he tried to persuade the French Surrealist group to tour his native country and establish contacts with local affiliates.

By 1926, Fondane grew disenchanted with the communist alignment proposed by the main Surrealist faction and its mentor, André Breton. Writing at the time, he commented that the ideological drive could prove fatal: "Perhaps never again will [a poet] recover that absolute freedom that he had in the bourgeois republic." A few years later, the Romanian writer expressed his support for the anti-Breton dissidents of *Le Grand Jeu* magazine, and was a witness at the 1930 riot which opposed the two factions. His anti-communist discourse was again aired in 1932: commenting on indictment of Surrealist poet Louis Aragon for communist texts (read by the authorities as instigation to murder), Fondane stated that he did believe Aragon's case was covered by the freedom of speech. His ideas also brought him into conflict with Pierre Drieu La Rochelle, who was moving away from an avant-garde background and into the realm of far right ideas. By the early 1930s, Fondane was in contact with the mainstream modernist Jacques Rivière and his *Nouvelle Revue Française* circle.

In 1928, his own collaboration with the Surrealists took shape as the book *Trois scenarii: ciné-poèmes* ("Three Scenarios: Cine-poems"), published by *Documents internationaux de l'esprt nouveau* collection, with artwork by American photographer Man Ray and Romanian painter Alexandru Brătă^anu (one of his other contacts in the French Surrealist photographers' group was Eli Lotar, the illegitimate son of Arghezi and nephew of Zissu). The "cine-poems" were intentionally conceived as unfilmable screenplays, in what was his personal statement about artistic compromise between experimental film and the emerging worldwide film industry. The book notably comprised his verdict about cinema being "the only art that was never classical."

Philosophical debut

With time, Fondane became a contributor to newspapers or literary journals in France, Belgium, and Switzerland: a regular presence in *Cahiers du Sud* of Carcassonne, he had his work featured in the Surrealist press (*Discontinuité*,

Le Phare de Neuilly, Bifur), as well as in *Le Courrier des Poètes, Le Journal des Poètes*, Romain Rolland's *Europe*, Paul Valéry's *Commerce* etc. In addition, Fondane's research was hosted by specialized venues such as *Revue Philosophique, Schweizer Annalen* and Carlo Suarès' *Cahiers de l'Étoile*. After a long period of indecision, the Romanian poet became a dedicated follower of Lev Shestov, a Russian-born existentialist thinker whose ideas about the eternal opposition between faith and reason he expanded upon in later texts. According to intellectual historian Samuel Moyn, Fondane was, with Rachel Bespaloff, one of the "most significant and devoted of Shestov's followers". In 1929, as a frequenter of Shestov's circle, Fondane also met Argentinian female author Victoria Ocampo, who became his close friend (after 1931, he became a contributor to her modernist review, *Sur*). Fondane's essays were more frequently than before philosophical in nature:*Europe* published his tribute Shestov (January 1929) and his comments of Edmund Husserl's phenomenology, which included his own critique of rationalism (June 1930).

Invited (on Ocampo's initiative) by the *Amigos del Arte* society of Buenos Aires, Fondane left for Argentina and Uruguay in summer 1929. The object of his visit was promoting French cinema with a set of lectures in Buenos Aires, Montevideo and other cities (as he later stated in a *Rampa* interview with Sarina Cassvan-Pas, he introduced South Americans to the work of Germaine Dulac, Luis Buñuel and Henri Gad). In this context, Fondane met essayist Eduardo Mallea, who invited him to contribute in *La Nación*'s literary supplement. His other activities there included conferencing on Shestov at the University of Buenos Aires and publishing articles on several subjects (from Shestov's philosophy to the poems of Tzara), but the fees received in return were, in his own account, too small to cover the cost of decent living.

In October 1929, Fondane was back in Paris, where he focused on translating and popularizing some of Romanian literature's milestone texts, from Mihai Eminescu's *Sãrmanul Dionis* to the poetry of Ion Barbu, Minulescu, Arghezi and Bacovia. In the same context, the expatriate writer helped introduce Romanians to some of the new European tendencies, becoming, in the words of literary historian Paul Cernat, "the first important promoter of French Surrealism in Romanian culture."

Integral *and* unu

In the mid-1920s, Fondane and painter János Mattis-Teutsch joined the external editorial board of *Integral* magazine, an avant-garde tribune published in Bucharest by Ion Cãlugãru, F. Brunea-Fox and Voronca. He was assigned a permanent column, known as *Fenêtres sur l'Europe/Ferestre spre Europa* (French and Romanian for "Windows on Europe"). With Barbu Florian, Fondane became a leading film reviewer for the magazine, pursuing his agenda in favour of non-commercial and "pure" films (such as René Clair's *Entr'acte*), and praising

Charlie Chaplin for his lyricism, but later making some concessions to talkies and the regular Hollywood films. Exploring what he defined as "the great ballet of contemporary French poetry", Fondane also published individual notes on writers Aragon, Jean Cocteau, Joseph Delteil, Paul Éluard and Pierre Reverdy.In 1927, *Integral* also hosted one of Fondane's replies to the communist Surrealists in France, as *Le surréalisme et la révolution* ("Surrealism and Revolution").

He also came into contact with *unu*, the Surrealist venue of Bucharest, which was edited by several of his avant-garde friends at home. His contributions there included a text on Tzara's post-Dada works, which he analyzed as Valéry-like "pure poetry". In December 1928, *unu* published some of Fondane's messages home, as *Scrisori pierdute* ("Lost Letters"). Between 1931 and 1934, Fondane was in regular correspondence with the *unu* writers, in particular Stephan Roll, F. Brunea-Fox and Sa^a Panã, being informed about their conflict with Voronca (attacked as a betrayer of the avant-garde) and witnessing from afar the eventual implosion of Romanian Surrealism on the model of French groups. In such dialogues, Roll complains about right-wing political censorship in Romania, and speaks in some detail about his own conversion to Marxism.

With Fondane's approval and Minulescu's assistance, *Priveli^ti* also saw print in Romania during 1930. Published by Editura Cultura Na^ionalã, it sparked significant controversy with its non-conformist style, but also made the author the target of critics' interest. As a consequence, Fondane was also sending material to Isac Ludo's *Adam*review, most of it notes (some hostile) clarifying ambiguous biographical detail discussed in Aderca's chronicle to *Priveli^ti*. His profile within the local avant-garde was also acknowledged in Italy and Germany: the Milanese magazine *Fiera Letteraria* commented on his poetry, reprinting fragments originally featured in *Integral*; in its issue of August–September 1930, the Expressionist tribune *Der Sturm* published samples of his works, alongside those of nine other Romanian modernists, translated by Leopold Kosch.

As Paul Daniel notes, the polemics surrounding *Priveli^ti* only lasted for a year, and Fondane was largely forgotten by the Romanian public after this moment. However, the discovery of Fondane's avant-garde stance by traditionalist circles took the form of bemusement or indignation, which lasted into the next decades. The conservative criticConst. I. Emilian, whose 1931 study discussed modernism as a psychiatric condition, mentioned Fondane as one of the leading "extremists", and deplored his abandonment of traditionalist subjects. Some nine years later, the antisemitic far right newspaper *Sfarmã-Piatrã*, through the voice of Ovidiu Papadima, accused Fondane and "the Jews" of having purposefully maintained "the illusion of a literary movement" under Lovinescu's leadership. Nevertheless, before that date, Lovinescu himself had come to criticize his former pupil (a disagreement which echoed his larger conflict with the *unu* group). Also in the 1930s, Fondane's work received coverage in the articles of two other maverick modernists: Perpessicius, who viewed it with noted sympathy, and Lucian Boz, who found his new poems touched by "prolixity".

Rimbaud le voyou, Ulysse *and intellectual prominence*

Back in France, where he had become Shestov's assistant, Fondane was beginning work on other books: the essay on 19th-century poet Arthur Rimbaud—*Rimbaud le voyou* ("Rimbaud the Hoodlum")—and, despite an earlier pledge not to return to poetry, a new series of poems. His eponymously titled study-portrait of German philosopher Martin Heidegger was published by *Cahiers du Sud* in 1932. Despite his earlier rejection of commercial films, Fondane eventually became an employee ofParamount Pictures, probably spurred on by his need to finance a personal project (reputedly, he was accepted there with a second application, his first one having been rejected in 1929). He worked first as an assistant director, before turning to screenwriting. Preserving his interest in Romanian developments, he visited the Paris set of*Televiziune*, a Romanian cinema production for which he shared directorial credits. His growing interest in Voronca's own poetry led him to review it for Tudor Arghezi's Bucharest periodical, *Bilete de Papagal*, where he stated: "Mr. Ilarie Voronca is at the top of his form. I'm gladly placing my stakes on him."

In 1931, the poet married Geneviève Tissier, a trained jurist and lapsed Catholic. Their home on Rue Rollin subsequently became a venue for literary sessions, mostly grouping the *Cahiers du Sud* contributors. The aspiring author Paul Daniel, who became Rodica Wechsler's husband in 1935, attended such meetings with his wife, and recalls having met Gaultier, filmmaker Dimitri Kirsanoff, music critic Boris de Schlözer, poets Yanette Delétang-Tardif and Thérèse Aubray, as well as Shestov's daughter Natalie Baranoff. Fondane also enjoyed a warm friendship with Constantin Brâncuˆi, the Romanian-born modern sculptor, visiting Brâncuˆi's workshop on an almost daily basis and writing about his work in *Cahiers de l'Étoile*. He witnessed first-hand and described Brâncuˆi's primitivist techniques, likening his work to that of a "savage man".

Rimbaud le voyou was eventually published by Denoël and Steele company in 1933, the same year when Fondane published his poetry volume *Ulysse* ("Ulysses") with *Les Cahiers du Journal des Poètes*. The Rimbaud study, partly written as a reply to Roland de Renéville's monograph *Rimbaud le Voyant* ("Rimbaud the Seer"),consolidated Fondane's international reputation as a critic and literary historian. In the months after its publication, the book earned much praise from scholars and writers—fromJoë Bousquet, Jean Cocteau, Benedetto Croce and Louis-Ferdinand Céline, to Jean Cassou, Guillermo de Torre and Miguel de Unamuno. It also found admirers in the English poet David Gascoyne, who was afterwards in correspondence with Fondane, and the American novelist Henry Miller. *Ulysse* itself illustrated Fondane's interest in scholarly issues:

he sent one autographed copy to Raïssa Maritain, wife of Jacques Maritain (both of whom were Catholic thinkers). Shortly after this period, the author was surprised to read Voronca's own French-language volume *Ulysse dans la cité* ("Ulysses in the City"): although puzzled by the similarity of titles with his own collection, he described Voronca as a "great poet." Also then, in Romania, B. Iosif completed the Yiddish translation of Fondane's *Psalmul leprosului* ("The Leper's Psalm"). The text, left in his care by Fondane before his 1923 departure, was first published in *Di Woch*, a periodical set up in Romania by poet Yankev Shternberg (October 31, 1934).

Anti-fascist causes and filming of **Rapt**

The 1933 establishment of a Nazi regime in Germany brought Fondane into the camp of anti-fascism. In December 1934, his *Apelul studen ˆimii* ("The Call of Students") was circulated among the Romanian diaspora, and featured passionate calls for awareness: "Tomorrow, in concentration camps, it will be too late". The following year, he outlined his critique of all kinds of totalitarianism, *L'Écrivain devant la révolution* ("The Writer Facing the Revolution"), supposed to be delivered in front of the Paris-held International Congress of Writers for the Defence of Culture (organized by left-wing and communist intellectuals with support from the Soviet Union). According to historian Martin Stanton, Fondane's activity in film, like Jean-Paul Sartre's parallel beginnings as a novelist, was itself a political statement in support of the Popular Front: "[they were] hoping to introduce critical dimensions in the fields they felt the fascists had colonized." Fondane nevertheless ridiculed the communist version of pacifism as a "parade of big words", noting that it opposed mere slogans to concrete German re-armament. Writing for the film magazine *Les Cahiers Jaunes* in 1933, he expressed the ambition of creating "an absurd film about something absurd, to satisfy [one's] absurd taste for freedom".

Fondane left the Paramount studios the same year, disappointed with company policies and without having had any screen credit of his own (although, he claimed, there were over 100 Paramount scripts to which he had unsigned contributions). During 1935, he and Kirsanoff were in Switzerland, for the filming of *Rapt*, with a screenplay by Fondane (adapted from Charles Ferdinand Ramuz's *La séparation des races* novel). The result was a highly poetic production, and, despite Fondane's still passionate defence of silent film, the first talkie in Kirsanoff's career. The poet was enthusiastic about this collaboration, claiming that it had enjoyed a good reception from Spain toCanada, standing as a manifesto against the success of more "chatty" sound films. In particular, French critics and journalists hailed *Rapt* as a necessary break with the*comédie en vaudeville* tradition. In the end, however, the independent product could not compete with the Hollywood industry, which was at the time monopolizing theFrench market. In parallel with these events, Fondane followed Shestov's personal guidance and, by means of *Cahiers du Sud*, attacked philosopher Jean Wahl's secularreinterpretation of Søren Kierkegaard's Christian existentialism.

From **Tararira** *to World War II*

Despite selling many copies of his books and having *Rapt* played at the Panthéon Cinema, Benjamin Fondane was still facing major financial difficulties, accepting a 1936 offer to write and assist in the making of *Tararira*, an avant-garde musical product of the Argentine film industry. This was his second option: initially, he contemplated filming a version of Ricardo Güiraldes' *Don Segundo Sombra*, but met opposition from Güiraldes' widow. While en route to Argentina, he became friends with Georgette Gaucher, aBreton woman, with whom he was in correspondence for the rest of his life.

Under contract with the Falma-film company, Fondane was received with honours by the Romanian Argentine community, and, with the unusual cut of his preferred suit, is said to have even become a trendsetter in local fashion. For Ocampo and the *Sur* staff, literary historian Rosalie Sitman notes, his visit also meant an occasion to defy thexenophobic and antisemitic agenda of Argentine nationalist circles. Centered on the tango, Fondane's film enlisted contributions from some leading figures in several national film and music industries, having Miguel Machinandiarena as producer and John Alton as editor; in starred, among others, Orestes Caviglia, Miguel Gómez Bao andIris Marga. The manner in which *Tararira* approached its subject scandalized the Argentine public, and it was eventually rejected by its distributors (no copies survive, but writer Gloria Alcorta, who was present at a private screening, rated it a "masterpiece"). Fondane, who had earlier complained about the actors' resistance to his ideas, left Argentina before the film was actually finished. It was on his return trip that he met Jacques and Raïssa Maritain, with whom he and Geneviève became good friends.

With the money received in Buenos Aires, the writer contemplated returning on a visit to Romania, but he abandoned all such projects later in 1936, instead making his way to France. He followed up on his publishing activity in 1937, when his selected poems, *Titanic*, saw print. Encouraged by the reception given to *Rimbaud le voyou*, he published two more essays with Denoël and Steele: *La Conscience malheureuse* ("The Unhappy Consciousness", 1937) and *Faux traité d'esthétique* ("False Treatise ofAesthetics", 1938). In 1938, he was working on a collected edition of his *Ferestre spre Europa*, supposed to be published in Bucharest but never actually seeing print. At around that date, Fondane was also a presenter for the Romanian edition of 20th Century Fox's international newsreel, *Movietone News*.

In 1939, Fondane was naturalized French. This followed an independent initiative of the *Société des écrivains français* professional association, in recognition for his contribution to French letters. *Cahiers du Sud* collected the required 3,000 francs fee through a public subscription, enlisting particularly large contributions from music producer Renaud de Jouvenel (brother of Bertrand de Jouvenel) and philosopher-ethnologist Lucien Lévy-Bruhl. Only months after this event, with the outbreak of World War II, Fondane was drafted into the French Army. During most of the "Phoney War" interval, considered too old for active service, he was in the military reserve force, but in February 1940 was called under arms with the 216 Artillery Regiment. According to Lina, "he left [home] with unimaginable courage and faith." Stationed at the Sainte Assise Castle in Seine-Port, he edited and stenciled a humorous gazette, *L'Écho de la I C-ie* ("The 1st Company Echo"), where he also published his last-ever work of poetry, *Le poète en patrouille*("The Poet on Patrolling Duty").

First captivity and clandestine existence

Fondane was captured by the Germans in June 1940 (shortly before the fall of France), and was taken into a German camp as a prisoner of war. He managed to escape captivity, but was recaptured in short time. After falling ill with appendicitis, he was transported back to Paris, kept in custody at the Val-de-Grâce, and operated on.Fondane was eventually released, the German occupiers having decided that he was no longer fit for soldierly duty.

He was working on two poetry series, *Super Flumina Babylonis* (a reference to *Psalm 137*) and *L'Exode* ("The Exodus"), as well as on his last essay, focusing on 19th-century poet Charles Baudelaire, and titled *Baudelaire et l'expérience du gouffre* ("Baudelaire and the Experience of the Abyss"). In addition to these, his other French texts, incomplete or unpublished by 1944, include: the poetic drama pieces *Philoctète*, *Les Puits de Maule* ("Maule's Well", an adaptation of Nathaniel Hawthorne's *The House of the Seven Gables*) and *Le Féstin de Balthazar* ("Belshazzar's Feast"); a study about the life and work of Romanian-born philosopher Stéphane Lupasco; and the selection from his interviews with Shestov, *Sur les rives de l'Illisus* ("On the Banks of the Illisus"). His very last text is believed to be a philosophical essay, *Le Lundi existentiel* ("The Existential Monday"), on which Fondane was working in 1944. Little is known about *Provèrbes* ("Proverbs"), which, he announced in 1933, was supposed to be an independent collection of poems.

According to various accounts, Fondane made a point of not leaving Paris, despite the growing restrictions and violence. However, others note that, as a precaution against the antisemitic measures in the occupied north, he eventually made his way into the more permissive *zone libre*, and only made returns to Paris in order to collect his books. Throughout this interval, the poet refused to wear the yellow badge (mandatory for Jews), and, living in permanent risk, isolated himself from his wife, adopting an even more precarious lifestyle. He was still in contact with writers of various ethnic backgrounds, and active on the clandestine literary scene. In this context, Fondane stated his intellectual affiliation to the French Resistance: his former Surrealist colleague Paul Éluard published several of his poems in the pro-communist *Europe*, under the name of *Isaac Laquedem* (a nod to the Wandering Jew myth). Such pieces were later included, but left unsigned, in the anthology *L'Honneur des poètes* ("The Honour of Poets"), published by the Resistance activists as an anti-Nazi manifesto. Fondane also preserved his column in *Cahiers du Sud* for as long as it was possible, and had his contributions published in several other clandestine journals.

After 1941, Fondane became friends with another Romanian existentialist in France, the younger Emil Cioran. Their closeness signaled an important stage in the latter's career: Cioran was slowly moving away from his fascist sympathies and his antisemitic stance, and, although still connected to the revolutionary fascist Iron Guard, had reintroduce dcosmopolitanism to his own critique of Romanian society. In 1943, transcending ideological boundaries, Fondane also had dinner with Mircea Eliade, the Romanian novelist and philosopher, who, like their common friend Cioran, had an ambiguous connection with the far right. In 1942, his own Romanian citizenship rights, granted by theJewish emancipation of the early 1920s, were lost with the antisemitic legislation adopted by the Ion Antonescu regime, which also officially banned his entire work as "Jewish". At around that time, his old friends outside France made unsuccessful efforts to obtain him a safe conduct to neutral countries. Such initiatives were notably taken by Jacques Maritain from his new home in the United States and by Victoria Ocampo in Argentina.

Arrest, deportation and death

He was eventually arrested by collaborationist forces in spring 1944, after unknown civilians reported his Jewish origin. Held in custody by the Gestapo, he was assigned to the local network of Holocaust perpetrators: after internment in the Drancy transit camp, he was sent on one of the transports to the extermination camps inoccupied Poland, reaching Auschwitz-Birkenau. In the meantime, his family and friends remained largely unaware of his fate. After news of his arrest, several of his friends reportedly intervened to save him, including Cioran, Lupasco and writer Jean Paulhan. According to some accounts, such efforts may have also involved another one of Cioran's friends, essayist Eugène Ionesco (later known for his work in drama).

Accounts differ on what happened to his sister Lina. Paul Daniel believes that she decided to go looking for her brother, also went missing, and, in all probability, became a victim of another deportation. Other sources state that she was arrested at around the same time as, or even together with, her brother, and that they were both on the same transport to Auschwitz. According to other accounts, Fondane was in custody while his sister was not, and sent her a final letter from Drancy; Fondane, who had theoretical legal grounds for being spared deportation (a Christian wife), aware that Lina could not invoke them, sacrificed himself to be by her side. While in Drancy, he sent another letter, addressed to Geneviève, in which he asked for all his French poetry to be published in the future as *Le Mal des fantômes* ("The Ache of Phantoms"). Optimistically, Fondane referred to himself as "the traveler who isn't done traveling".

While Lina is believed to have been marked for death upon arrival (and immediately after sent to the gas chamber), her brother survived the camp conditions for a few more months. He befriended two Jewish doctors, Moscovici and Klein, with whom he spent his free moments engaged in passionate discussions about philosophy and literature. As was later attested by a survivor of the camp, the poet himself was among the 700 inmates selected for extermination on October 2, 1944, when the Birkenau subsection outsideBrzezinka was being evicted by SS guards. He was aware of impending death, and reportedly saw it as ironic that it came so near to an expected Allied victory. After a short interval in Block 10, where he is said to have awaited his death with dignity and courage, he was driven to the gas chamber and murdered. His body was cremated, along with those of the other victims.

Literary work and philosophical contribution

Symbolist and traditionalist beginnings

As a young writer, Benjamin Fondane moved several times between the extremes of Symbolism and Neo-romantic traditionalism. Literary historian Mircea Martin analyzed the very first of his as pastiches of several, sometimes contradictory, literary sources. These influences, he notes, come from local traditionalists, Romantics and Neo-romantics—Octavian Goga (the inspiration for Fondane's earliest pieces), Grigore Alexandrescu, Vasile Alecsandri, George Co^buc, ^tefan Octavian Iosif; from French Symbolists—Paul Verlaine; and from Romanian disciples of Symbolism—Dimitrie Anghel, George Bacovia, Alexandru Macedonski, Ion Minulescu. The young author had a special appreciation for the 19th century national poet, Mihai Eminescu. Familiar with Eminescu's entire poetic work, he was one of the young poets who tried to reconcile Eminescu's Neo-romantic, ruralizing, traditionalism with the urban phenomenon that was Symbolism. While Fondane continued to credit Minulescu's radical and jocular Symbolism as a main influence on his own poems, this encounter was overall less significant than his enthusiasm for Eminescu; in contrast, Bacovia's desolate and macabre poetry left enduring traces in Fondane's work, shaping his depiction of provincial environments and even transforming his worldview.

Fondane's early affiliation with Ovid Densusianu's version of Romania's Symbolist current was, according to literary historian Dumitru Micu, superficial. Micu notes that the young Fondane sent his verse to be published by magazines with incompatible agendas, suggesting that his collaboration with *Viea^a Nouã* was therefore incidental, but also that, around 1914, Fondane's own style was a "conventional Symbolism". Writing in 1915, the poet himself explained that his time with the magazine in question ought not be interpreted as anything other than conjectural. During his polemic with Tudor Teodorescu-Brani^te, he defined himself as an advocate of an "insolent" Symbolism, a category defined by and around Remy de Gourmont. This perspective was further clarified in *O lãmurire...*, which explained how *Tãgãduin^a lui Petru* was to be read: "A clear, although Symbolist, book. For it is, unmistakably, Symbolist. [...] Symbolism doesn't necessarily mean neo-logism, morbid, bizarre, decadent, confusing and badly written. But rather—if there is talent—original, commonsensical, depth, non-imitation, lack of standard, subconscious, new and sometimes healthy." From a regional point of view, the young Fondane is sometimes included with Bacovia in the Moldavian branch of Romanian Symbolism, or, more particularly, in the Jewish Moldavian subsection.

The various stylistic directions of Fondane's early poetry came together in *Priveli^ti*. Mircea Martin reads in it the poet's emancipation from both Symbolism and traditionalism, despite it being opened with a dedication to Minulescu, and against Eugen Lovinescu's belief that such pastorals were exclusively traditionalist. According to Martin, *Priveli^ti*parts from its Romantic predecessors by abandoning the "descriptive" and "sentimentalist" in pastoral conventions: "Everything seems designed on purpose to confound and defy the traditional mindset." Similarly, writer-critic Gheorghe Crãciun found the *Priveli^ti* texts contiguous with other early forms of Romanian modernism.

Nevertheless, much of the volume still adheres to lyricism and the conventional idyll format, primarily by identifying itself with the slow rhythms of country life. These traits were subsumed by literary historian George Cãlinescu into a special category, that of "traditionalist Symbolism", centered on "that which brings man closer to Creation's interior life". The same commentator suggested that the concept linked modernism and traditionalism through the common influence of Charles Baudelaire, whom Fondane himself credited as the "mystical power" behind *Priveli^ti*. The cycle also recalls Fondane's familiarity with another pastoral poet, Francis Jammes. Of special note is anode, *Lui Taliarh* ("At Thaliarchus"), described by Cãlinescu as the masterpiece of *Priveli^ti*. Directly inspired by Horace's *Odes I.9*, and seen by Martin as Fondane's will to integrate death into life (or "plenary living"), it equates existence with the seasonal cycle:

Ca mâne, toamna iarã se va mãri prin grâne,^i vinul toamnei poate nu-l vom mai bea. Ca mâne,poate s-o duce boii cu ochi de râu în ^tiri,sã tragã cu urechea la noile-ncol^iri.^i-atuncea, la bra^, umbre, nu vom mai ^ti de toate;poate-am sã uit nevasta ^i vinul acru; poate...Ei, poate la ospe^e nu vei mai fi monarh.E toamnã. Bea cotnarul din cupã, Taliarh. T o m o r r o w maybe, autumn will expand over the fields of grain,and autumn wine us two we may no longer drink. Tomorrow maybe,the river-eyed oxen will head for the amaranth,so they may eavesdrop on the new germination.And then, shadows arm in arm, we won't remember things;I might forget my wife and bitter wine; I might...Well, maybe you'll no longer be a monarch for the feasts.It's autumn. Drink your cup of *cotnar*, Taliarchus.

Arghezian modernism and Expressionist echoes

From its traditionalist core, *Priveli^ti* created a modernist structure of uncertainty and violent language. According to Mircea Martin, the two tendencies were so intertwined that one could find both expressed within the same poem. The very preference for vitalism and the energy of wilderness, various critics assess, is a modernist reaction to the drama of World War I, rather than a return to Romantic ideals. In this interval, Fondane had also discovered the poetic revolution promoted by Tudor Arghezi, who united traditionalist discourse with modernist themes, creating new poetic formats. Martin notes that Fondane, more than any other, tried to replicate Arghezi's abrupt prosody and "tooth and nail" approach to the literary language, but lacked his mentor's "verbal magic." The same critic suggests that the main effect of Arghezi's influence on Fondane was not in poetic form, but in determining the disciple to "discover himself", to seek his own independent voice. Paul Cernat also sees Fondane as indebted to Arghezi's mix of "cruelty" and "formal discipline". In contrast to such assessments, Călinescu saw Fondane not as an Arghezian pupil, but as a traditionalist "spiritually related" to Ion Pillat's own post-Symbolist avatar. This verdict was implicitly or explicitly rejected by other commentators: Martin argued that Pillat's omnipresent "calm joy", modulated with "impeccable taste", clashed with Fondane's "tension", "surprises" and "intelligence superior to [his] talent"; Cernat assessed that *Priveli^ti* was at "the antipode" of Pillat and Jammes, that its themes pointed to social alienation and a patriarchal universe gone "off its rocker".

Statements made by the young Fondane, in which he explains his indifference towards the landscape as it is, and his preference for the landscape as the poet himself creates it, have been a traditional source for critical commentary. As Martin notes, this attitude led the poet and travel writer to express an apathy, or even boredom, in regard to the wild landscape, to promote "withdrawal" rather than "adhesion", "solitude" rather than "communion". However, as a way of cultivating a cosmic level of poetry, Fondane's work veered into synesthesia and vitalism, being commended by critics for its tactile, aural or olfactory suggestions. In one such poem, cited by Călinescu as a sample of "exquisite freshness", the author imagines being turned into a ripe watermelon. These works also part with convention in matters of prosody (with a modern treatment ofalexandrines) and vocabulary (a stated preference for Slavic versus Romance terminologies). In addition, Martin, who declared himself puzzled at noting that Fondane would not publish some of his most accomplished poems of youth, made special note of their occasional disregard for Romanian grammar and other artistic licenses (left uncorrected by Paul Daniel on Fondane's explicit request). Some of the *Priveli^ti* poems look upon nature with ostentatious sarcasm, focusing on its grotesque elements, its rawness and its repetitiveness, as well as attacking the idyllic portrayal of peasants in traditionalist literature. Martin notes in particular one of the untitled pieces about Hertza region:

[...] ^i trec ^ãrani cu rapãn, ca ni^te boi; trec boicu pântecele pline de miros de trifoi^i idio^i de toamnã; ^i toamna e cumintepeste ^ãrani, ^i peste ovãz, ^i peste linte. [...] and mangy peasants pass, like oxen; oxen passwith bellies full of clover scentand autumn idiots; and autumn is cozyon the peasants, and on oats, and on lentils.

Literary historian Ovid Crohmãlniceanu was the first to suggest, in the 1960s, that the underlying traits of such imagery made the post-Symbolist Fondane an Expressionist poet, who had detected "the fundamental anarchy of the universe". The verdict was echoed and amended by those of other critics. Martin finds that it applies to many of Fondane's early poems, where "explosive" imagery is central, but opines that, generally toned down by melancholy, their message too blends into a new form of "crepuscular wisdom". Scholar Dan Grigorescu stresses that the Neo-romantic and Symbolist element is dominant throughout the *Priveli^ti* volume and, contrary to Crohmãlniceanu's thesis, argues that Fondane's projection of the self into the nature is not Expressionist, but rather a convention borrowed from Romanticism (except for "perhaps, [...] the exacerbated dilatation" in scenes in which terrified cattle are driven into town). In Grigorescu's interpretation, the volume has some similarities with the pastoral Expressionism of Romanian writers Lucian Blaga and Adrian Maniu, as well as with the wilderness paintings of Franz Marc, but is at "the opposite pole" from the "morbid hallucination" Expressionism of H. Bonciu and Max Blecher. He indicates that, overall, Fondane's contributions confuse critics by following "contradictory directions", a mix that "hardly finds any grounds for comparison within [Romanian] poetry." In contrast, Paul Cernat sees both Fondane's poetry and Ion Cãlugãru's prose as "Expressionist *écorchés*", and connects Fondane's "modern attitude" to his familiarity with the poems of Arthur Rimbaud.

Avant-garde critique of parochialism

The introduction of rhetorical violence within a traditional poetic setting announced Fondane's transition into the more radical wing of the modernist movement. During his*Priveli^ti* period, in his articles for *Contimporanul*, the poet stated that Symbolism was dead, and in subsequent articles drew a line between the original and non-original sides of Romanian Symbolism, becoming particularly critical of Macedonski. Defining his programatic approach as leading, through the avant-garde, into a Neoclassicalmodernism (or a "new Classicism"), Benjamin Fondane argued: "To be excessive: that is the only way of being innovative." His perspective, mixing revolt and messages about creating a new tradition, was relatively close to *Contimporanul*'s own artistic programme, and as such a variant of Constructivism. During his own transition from Symbolism, Fondane looked on the avant-garde itself with critical distance. Discussing it as the product of a tradition leading back to Stéphane Mallarmé, he reproachedCubism for displaying a limitation of range, and viewed Futurism as essentially destructive (but also useful for having created a virgin territory to support "constructive man"); likewise, he found Dada a solid, but limited, method of combating interwar period's "metaphysical despair".

The affiliation to the avant-garde came with a sharp critique of Romanian culture, accused by Fondane of promoting imitation and parochialism. During a period which ended with his 1923 departure, the young poet sparked polemic with a series of statements in which, reviewing the impact of local Francophilia, he equated Romania with a colony of France. This theory proposed a difference between Westernization and "parasitism": "If a foreign intellectual direction is always useful, an alien soul is always a danger." He did not cease to promote foreign culture at home, but stated a complex argument about the need to recognize differences in culture: his global conclusion about civilizations, which he viewed as equal but not identical, built on Gourmont's theory about an "intellectual constancy" throughout human history, as well as on philosopherHenri Bergson's critique of mechanism. In parallel, Fondane criticized the cultural setting of Greater Romania, noting that it was so Bucharest-focused that Transylvanianauthors only became widely known by attending the capital's Casa Cap^a restaurant. In his retrospective interpretation of Romanian literature, the avant-garde essayist stated that there were precious few authors who could be considered original, primarily citing Ion Creangã, the peasant writer, as a model of authenticity. While stating this point in his *Imagini ^i cãr^i din Fran^a*, Fondane cited in his favour a traditionalist culture critic, historian Nicolae Iorga.

However, during a virtual polemic with Poporanism (hosted by *Sburãtorul* in 1922), Fondane also questioned the originality and Thraco-Roman origin of Romanian folklore, as well as, through it, historical myths surrounding the Latin ethnogenesis: "Present-day Romania, of obscure origins, Thraco-Roman-Slavic-Barbarian, owes its existence and present-day European inclusion to a fecund error [...]: *it is the idea of our Latin origin* [Fondane's italics]." Likewise, the author put forth the thesis according to which traditionalists such as Mihail Sadoveanu and George Co^buc invoked literary themes present not just in Romania's archaic tradition, but also in Slavic folklore. Fondane went on to draw a comparison between the idea of Jewish chosenness and that of Romanian Latinity, concluding that they both resulted in positive national goals (in the case of Romania and its inhabitants, that of "becoming part of Europe"). Paul Cernat found his perspective "more reasonable" than that of his *Contimporanul* colleagues, who speculated about creating a modernity on folkloric roots.

Scholar Constantin Pricop interprets Fondane's overall perspective as that of a "constructive" critic, citing a fragment of *Imagini ˆi cãrˆi din Franˆa*: "Let us hope the time will come when we may bring our personal contribution into Europe. [...] Until such time, let's keep a check on the continuous assimilation of foreign culture [...]; let's therefore return tocultural criticism." Commenting at length on the probable motivations of Fondane's discourse, Cernat suggests that, like many of his avant-garde colleagues, Fondane experienced a "peripheral complex", merging Bovarysme and frustrated ambition. According to Cernat, the poet surpassed this moment after experiencing success in France, and his decision to have *Priveliˆti* printed at home was intended as a special tribute to Romania and its language. There is however a pronounced difference between Fondane's French and Romanian work, as discussed by critics and by Fondane himself. The elements of continuity are highlighted in Crãciun's account: "French literature and culture signified for Fundoianu a process of clarification and self-definition, but not a change of identity."

Jewish tradition and Biblical language

Several of Fondane's exegetes have discussed the links between his apparent traditionalism and the classical themes of either secular Jewish culture or Judaism, with a focus on his Hasidic roots. According to Swedish researcher Tom Sandqvist (who discusses the Jewish background of many Romanian avant-garde authors and artists), the Hasidic and Kabbalah connection is enhanced by both the pantheistic vision of *Tãgãduinˆa lui Petru* and the "Ein Sof-like emptiness" suggested in *Priveliˆti*. Paul Cernat too argued that the traditionalist elements in Fondane's work reflected Hasidism as it was experienced in Galicia or Bukovina, as well as the direct influence of Jacob Gropper. According to George Cãlinescu's analysis (originally stated in 1941), Fondane's origin within the rural minority of Romanian Jews (and not the urban Jewish mainstream) was of special psychological interest: "The poet is a Jew from Moldavia, where Jews have almost pastoral professions, but are nevertheless prevented by a tradition of market agglomerations from fully enjoying the sincerity of rustic life." The fond memory of Judaic practice is notably intertwined with the *Priveliˆti* pastorals:

Deodatã, dupã geamuri se aprindeau fãclii;o umbrã liniˆtitã intra în prãvãliiprin uˆile-ncuiate ˆi s-aˆeza la masã.Tãcerea de salinã încremenea în casãˆi-n sloiul nopˆii jgheabul ogrãzii adãpa.Bunicul între flãcãri de sfeˆnic se ruga:"Sã-mi cadã dreapta, limba sã se usuce-n minede te-oi lua vreodatã-n de^ert, Ierusalime!" At once, flames lit up behind windows;a quiet shadow crept into the shopsthrough the locked doors and took place at the table.The silence of a salt mine was tightened in the houseand an icy night flowed into the outside gutter.Grandfather was praying around candle flames:"May my right arm fall off, my tongue dry up in meif ever I take in vain thy name, Jerusalem!"

Fondane expanded on his interest in the Jewish heritage in his early prose and drama. The various pre-1923 articles, including his obituary pieces for Elias Schwartzfeld andAvram Steuerman-Rodion, speak at length about Jewish ethics (which Fondane described as unique and idealistic), assimilation and Jewish nationalism. They also offer his answer to antisemitism, including his case, relying on proof of Jewish exogamy, against all theories about a distinct Semitic race. In other such pieces, he comments at length on Gropper's Yiddishist literature and corrects opinions expressed on the same topic by their common friend Gala Galaction. As he explains in this context, Gropper quelled his adolescent identity crisis, helping him find a core Judaism, more "vital" to him than the political scope of Zionism. During these dialogues, Fondane recalled, he first discovered his interest in philosophy: he played the "Sophist", paradoxical and abstract, in front of the "sentimental" Gropper. This antithesis also inspired the core essay in*Iudaism ^i elenism*, where Fondane writes at length about the hostile dialogue between Jewish philosophy, in search of fundamental truths, and Greek thought, with its ultimate value of beauty.

Tãgãduin^a lui Petru, believed by Mircea Martin to be a sample of Fondane's debt to André Gide, is the first of his works to take inspiration from the Bible (in this case, looking beyond the Talmud). Also Biblical in subject, *Monologul lui Baltazar* has been interpreted by Crohmãlniceanu as a negative comment on nihilism and the *Übermensch*theory, notions embodied by the protagonist Belshazzar, legendary ruler of Babylon during the Jewish captivity. Fondane's progressive focus on Jewish Biblical sources mirrored the Christian interests of his mentor Arghezi. Like Arghezi, Fondane wrote a series of *Psalms*—although, according to Martin, his tone was "too cadenced and solemn for one to expect a confrontation or a touching confession". However, Martin notes, the Jewish author either adopted or anticipated (depending on the reliability of his manuscripts' dating) Arghezi's poetry of exhortation and curses, in which ugliness, baseness and destitution speak directly to divinity. These sentiments are found in Fondane's *Psalmul leprosului*, which the same critic identifies as "the series' masterpiece":

Cãci trupul meu se crapã de buboaie —^i din obraji,vinete coji au curs vânãt puroaie;[...]^i sufletul meu, broascã, de urâtorãcãie, o, Doamne, cãtre tine.For my body is breaking up in boils—and from my cheeks,indigo scabs have leaked indigo pus;[...]And my soul, a frog, in desperationcroaks, o my Lord, unto thee.

Surrealism, anti-communism and Jewish existentialism

Throughout and beyond his participation in the Surrealist milieus (an affiliation illustrated primarily by his filmmaker and popularizer activities, rather than by his literary creation), Benjamin Fondane remained an existentialist, primarily following Lev Shestov's views on the human condition. This came as a critique of the scientific method andrationalism as human explanations of the world, notably outlined in his own *Faux traité d'esthétique*. Probably developed independently from Shestovist thought, his overall objection towards abstract projects has been likened by essayist Gina Sebastian Alcalay to the later stances of André Glucksmann or Edgar Morin. These attitudes shaped his assessments of Surrealism.

In one of *Integral* chronicles, Fondane himself explained that the movement, described as superior to Dada's "joyous suicide", had created a "new continent" with its rediscovery of dreams. Poet and critic Armelle Chitrit notes that, in part, Fondane's later dissidence was also motivated on an existentialist level, since Surrealism "had stopped asking questions"; instead, she notes, Fondane "believed neither in reason nor in any system based on it. It is folly, he wrote, to perpetuate the attempt to make man and history cohabitable. One of [S]hestov's rare disciples, he sets only the powers of life against those of chaos." As Fondane wrote to Claude Sernet, *Rimbaud le voyou* was in part at attempt at preventing the other Surrealists from confiscating Rimbaud's mythical status. According to Romanian-born writer Lucian Raicu, its "somber" tone and allusive language are also early clues that Fondane had a nightmarish vision of the political and intellectual climate.

His Shestovist interpretation, opposing existence to ideas, was contested by intellectual figure Raymond Queneau: himself a former Surrealist, Queneau suggested that Fondane was relying on blind faith, having a distorted perspective on science, literature and the human intellect. Furthermore, he noted that, under the influence of Lucien Lévy-Bruhl, Fondane described reality exclusively in primitivist terms, as the realm of savagery and superstition.

Fondane's objection to the communist flirtations of the main Surrealist wing had roots in his earlier discourse: before leaving Romania, Fondane had criticized socialism as a modern myth, symptomatic of a generalized desecration, suggesting that Leninist and Labour Zionist projects were economically unsound.

Much admired by Emil Cioranfor his rejection of all modern ideology, the poet argued that a critical distance imposed itself between artists and social structures, and, although he too reacted against "bourgeois" culture, concluded that communism carried a greater risk for the independent mind. In particular, he objected to the Marxist theory on base and superstructure: although his planned address for the Writers' Congress spoke of Marxian economics as being justified by reality, it also argued that economic relationships could not be used to explain all historical developments. His critique of the Soviet Union as an equally "bourgeois" society also came with the argument that Futurism, not Surrealism, could transform into art the communist version of voluntarism.

Fondane found himself opposed to the general trend of intellectual partisanship, and took pride in defining himself as a politically independent skeptic. Around 1936, he reacted strongly against Julien Benda's rationalist political essays, with their overall critique of intellectual passions, describing them as revived and "excruciatingly boring" versions of positivism, but ignoring their primary, anti-totalitarian, agenda. However, *La Conscience malheureuse* (with essays on Shestov, Edmund Husserl, Friedrich Nietzsche and Søren Kierkegaard) was noted as Fondane's own contribution to the debate surrounding Popular Front activities and the rise of fascism: titled after a concept in Hegelian philosophy, which originally referred to the thinking process generating its own divisions, it referred to the possibility of thinkers to interact with the larger world, beyond subjectivity.

Rallying himself with the main trends of Jewish existentialism, the poet remained critical of other existentialist schools, such as those of Martin Heidegger and Jean-Paul Sartre, believing them to be overly reliant on dialectics, and therefore on rational thought; likewise, citing Kierkegaard as his reference point, Fondane criticized Jean Wahl for not discussing existential philosophy as an act of faith. His dislike for secular existentialism was also outlined in a text he authored shortly before his 1944 arrest, where he spoke of the Bible as being, "whether or not it wants to", the original reference for all existential philosophy. Geneviève Tissier-Fondane later recalled that her husband was "profoundly Jewish" to his death, but also that he would not abide by any formal regulation within the *Halakha* tradition. This approach also implied a measure of ecumenism:Jacques Maritain, who cultivated his relationship with Fondane across the religious and philosophical divides, described his friend as "a disciple of Shestov but one inhabited by the Gospel"; Fondane himself explained to Maritain that Shestov and himself were aiming for a new Judaic philosophy that would be equally indebted to the Christianity of Kierkegaard, Martin Luther and Tertullian. He was critical of Maritain's worldview, but remained a passionate reader of his work; in contrast, Geneviève attested that the Maritains' beliefs shaped her own, leasing her back into the Church.

Late poetry and drama

The spiritual crisis experienced in France was the probable reason why Fondane refused to write poems between 1923 and 1927. As he stated in various contexts, he mistrusted the innate ability of words to convey the tragedy of existence, describing poetry as the best tool for rendering a universal "wordless scream", an "ultimate reality", or an eternal expression of things ephemeral. In his essays, he suggested that the invention of art, like the invention of theory and rhetoric, had deprived poets of their existential function; beyond letting themselves be guided by their art, he argued, writers needed to confirm that the principles of life, negative as well as positive, exist. He saw poets as waging an unequal battle with both scientific perspectives and moralism, urging them to place their unique faith "in the mysterious virtue of poetry, in the existential virtue that poetry upholds". *Rimbaud le voyou* was in part a study of how, during his self-exile to Harar, Rimbaud had not merely abandoned poetry for the sake of adventure, but rather transformed his lifestyle into a poetry of incertitude and personal ambition. As Fondane explained in his *Baudelaire et l'expérience du gouffre*, a poet and thinker could also evidence the abyss he faced, and alleviate his own anxiety, through the use of irony: "Laugh in the face of tragedy, or disappear!"

According to Cernat, his articles for *Integral* show Fondane as an ally of the "anti-political" and lyrical side of Surrealism, a poet placing his trust in "the negative-soteriological, liberating function of poetry". The impact of existentialist philosophy was even traced to the "cine-poems" by Martin Stanton (who called the pieces "amazing"). In contrast to the Surrealists, Fondane did not believe in a need to circulate poems as universal messages, but rather saw them as the basis for a very personal relationship with the reader: "This is not a time for print. Poetry is seeking its friends, not an audience. [...] Poetry will be for the few—or it will not be at all." Chitrit, who parallels Fondane's definitions with the similar views of Romanian poet and Holocaust survivor Paul Celan, concludes: "This is probably the closest that we can come to seeing contemporary poetry." Fondane's other literary works also evidence the impact of his philosophical preoccupations. With *Le Féstin de Balthazar*, the writer modified his earlier *Monologul* by adopting Shestivist themes (introducing allegorical characters who discuss Aristotelianism, capitalism and revolution) and by introducing some elements from the burlesque. Originally conceived in 1918 and completed in 1933, *Philoctète* reworked Sophocles' play of the same title, interpreting it through the style of Gide's dramas.

Ulysse was an epic poem in free verse, the first such work in Fondane's career, and testing a format later adopted in *Titanic* and *L'Exode*. Although quite similar to Voronca's own work, which also used Homer's *Odyssey* as the pretext for a comment on social alienation, it included an additional allegory of Jewishness (according to critic Petre Răileanu, Voronca had stripped his own text of Jewish symbolism, in the hope of not entering a competition with Fondane). Fondane's 1933 text echoes his earlierintertextual Homeric references (present in poems he wrote back in 1914), but, to their adventurous escapism, it opposes the Ithaca metaphor—an ideal of stability in the assumption of one's destiny. Claude Sernet referred to *Ulysse* as "painful and sober, a cry of anxiety, of revolt and resignation, a fraternal and noble song to mankind".The poem is also Fondane's comment on the Wandering Jew story (the mythical figure is rescaled into an urban Ulysses), and, according to cultural historian Andrei Oi^teanu, reinterprets the Christian prejudice about Jews being eternal "witnesses" of Christ's Passion. Together, such motifs intimated the writer's own experiences, leading various commentators to conclude that he too was "the Jewish Ulysses". Italian academic Gisèle Vanhese, who connects this lyrical discourse with Fondane's "experience of the abyss" concept, notes that ocean waters are the vehicles of nomadism in *Ulysse*, while, in *Titanic*, the same environment serves as a metaphor of dying.

In Cioran's account, Benjamin Fondane lived his final years permanently aware "of a misfortune that was about to happen", and built a "complicity with the unavoidable". The same is noted by German Romanian poet and Cioran exegete Dieter Schlesak, who suggests: "Fondane was a man who wished to bear the absolute uncertainty of the outside; that which exists is an intermittent, not continuous, reality. But [true misfortune] is the boredom of faint unliving, [...] of things implied, these being the ones [Fondane] hated."Fondane's visions about history and the role of poetry were notably outlined in *L'Exode*, a portion of which is dedicated to the powerlessness of Jews in front of prejudice. According to Oi^teanu, this text, where the narrative voice speaks of sufferings and defects common in all humans, was probably inspired by the famous monologue in William Shakespeare's *The Merchant of Venice*. Another part, called "astonishingly prophetic" and "cynical apocalyptic" by Chitrit, reads:

Que l'on nous brûle ou que l'on nous clouteet que se soit chance ou déveine,que voulez-vous que ça nous foute?Il n'est de chanson que l'humaine. No matter if you burn or nail uswhether it be good luck or illit is to us of little consequence.There is no chant except the human song.

Similar themes were being explored by the *Super Flumina Babylonis* cycle, described by Sernet as "a terrible foreshadowing of events into which peoples and continents were about to sink, into which the author himself was to be dragged without the possibility of return." Writing about the entirety of Fondane's French poetry (*Le Mal des fantômes*), poet and language theorist Henri Meschonnic argued that the Romanian author was unique in depicting "the revolt and the flavour of life mixed into the sense of death".

Legacy

Family and estate

After her husband's death (of which she was for long ignorant) and the end of the war, Geneviève Tissier-Fondane, aided by the Maritains, moved into Kolbsheim Castle, tutoring the children of Antoinette and Alexander Grunelius. A devout Catholic, she eventually retreated from public life, becoming a nun in the Congregation of Notre-Dame de Sion (dedicated to Catholic missionary work among the Jews). Relocating to the Montagne Sainte-Geneviève, she died, after a long battle with cancer, in March 1954. Fondane was also survived by his mother Adela, who died in June 1953 at age 94, and sister Rodica (d. 1967).

The writer was the subject of several visual portrayals by noted artists, some of whom were his personal friends. During his collaboration with *Integral* and *unu*, Victor Braunerand Jules Perahim both drew his vignette portraits (the former as part of a series titled *film unu*). He is the subject of a 1930 sketch by Constantin Brâncu^i, a 1931 Surrealist painting by Brauner (who also painted one of Adela Schwartzfeld), and an artistic photograph by Man Ray. The 1934 edition of *Psalmul leprosului* featured Fondane's portrait in the hand of graphic artist Sigmund Maur (the original version of which was dated to 1921). A posthumous image of the poet in military attire was drawn by Romanian-born artist Eugen Drãgu^escu. Benjamin Fondane was also commemorated with a mention on the Panthéon plaque, among the *Morts pour la France*(reportedly, his name was added upon a request from Cioran). There is a similar landmark in Ia^i's Eternitatea cemetery, set up by the Writers' Union of Romania near his family grave.

The poet-philosopher left behind a large manuscript collection, a personal library and a set of works due for publishing. His book collection was split into individual documentary funds, some located in France and others in Romania. In February 1930, Benjamin Fondane explained that he did not consider revisiting his land of birth until such time as his earlier volumes would be printed, indicating that these included (in addition to *Priveli^ti*): *Ferestre spre Europa*, *Imagini ^i scriitori români* ("Images and Romanian Writers"),*Caietele unui inactual* ("The Notebooks of an Outdated Man"), *Probleme vesele* ("Merry Problems"), *Dialoguri* ("Dialogues") and an introduction to the work of art critic Walter Pater. Among Fondane's other Romanian works, unpublished at the time of his death, were the prose poem *Her^a* ("Hertza"), *Note dintr-un confesional* and many other prose fragments and poems, all preserved in Daniel's manuscript collection. According to Paul Daniel, part of the poet's book collection in Romania was left in the care of literary critic Lucian Boz, who sold it upon his departure for Australia. In France, the copyright to Fondane's work was passed on in the late 20th century to scholar Michel Carassou, who was personally involved in several publication projects.

Western echoes

In France, the caretaker of documentary enterprises regarding Fondane was for long Sernet (Voronca's brother-in-law), who released part of *Super Flumina Babylonis* and other previously unknown texts (published in various issues of *Cahiers du Sud*and other journals), while supervising a new edition of *L'Honneur des poètes*, where Fondane was properly credited. In 1945, philosopher Jean Grenier edited the first-ever version of *Le Lundi existentiel*. A Fondane reader (comprising *L'Exode*) was being planned around 1946, and supposed to be published by Les Éditions de Minuit, with contributions from poets Jean Lescure and Paul Éluard. *Baudelaire et l'expérience du gouffre* was eventually published by Éditions Seghers in 1947, under the supervision of Jean Cassou (second edition 1972; third edition 1973). Sernet was also the author of the poem *À Benjamain Fondane, déporté* ("To Benjamin Fondane, Upon His Deportation"), reportedly dated June 3, 1944.Recollections of Fondane's activity and his friendship with Victoria Ocampo are also found in Ocampo's series *Testimonios*("Testimonies").

With support from Culture Minister André Malraux, Sernet also published a 1965 bound version of *L'Exode* and *Super Flumina...*, reconstructed from the fragmentary manuscripts. Also on Sernet's initiative, Le Chant du Monde record label and comedienne Ève Griliquez released an LP album of public recitations from his work. Other collections of his written work were published in later years, including his *Écrits pour le cinéma* ("Writings for the Cinema", 1984), *Le Féstin de Balthazar* (1985), *Le Lundi existentiel* (1989), and*Le Mal des fantômes* (1996). His interviews with Shestov, left by the poet in Ocampo's care, were collected in 1982, as *Rencontres avec Léon Chestov*("Meetings with Lev Shestov"). Fondane's notes on Dada, as well as other documents, saw print in 1996, as *Le voyageur n'a pas fini de voyager* ("The Traveler Isn't Done Traveling"). The following year, Fondane scholar Monique Jutrin discovered and published his manuscript speech for the 1935 Congress, *L'Écrivain devant la révolution*.Another previously unknown text, the screenplay sketch *Une journée d'ivresse* ("A Day of Drunkenness"), was included by editors Carassou and Petre Rãileanu in a critical edition of 1999.

In the Western world (including the Romanian diaspora), there were a few authors whose work was influenced directly by Fondane's, among them Voronca and David Gascoyne. Gascoyne, the author of "I.M. Benjamin Fondane" poem and recollection pieces on their friendship, spoke of the Romanian as a mentor, with a "decisive and lasting influence" on his own writings. France is home to a Benjamin Fondane Studies Society, which organizes an annual workshop in Peyresq. Since 1994, it publishes the academic review *Cahiers Benjamin Fondane*, which has recovered and published much of Fondane's correspondence and political texts. In 2006, following a Fondane Society request, a square on Paris' Rue Rollin was renamed in honour of the Romanian-born writer. Three years later, on the 65th commemoration of Fondane's killing, the Mémorial de la Shoah museum hosted a special exhibit dedicated his life and literary work. In Israel, a fragment from his *L'Exode* is engraved in English and Hebrew versions on the entrance of Yad Vashem memorial.

By the late 1970s, Fondane's Romanian work was attracting researchers and authors of monographs from various other countries, in particular the United States (John Kenneth Hyde, Eric Freedman etc.) and Communist Czechoslovakia (Libuše Valentová). In West Germany, Fondane's poetic and philosophical contributions were in focus by 1986, when exiled poet Dieter Schlesak published translated samples in *Akzente* journal. Preceded by Gascoyne's French-to-English translation attempts from Fondane,American film editor Julian Semilian's contribution as a translator from Romanian is credited with having played an important part in introducing the Anglosphere to the writings of Fondane and various other Romanian modernists. The first-ever volume of Hebrew translations from Fondane's verse saw print in 2003, with support from Tel Aviv University. Other international echoes include the publication of Odile Serre's Romanian-to-French translations from his early poems.

Recognition of Fondane's overall contribution was however rare, as noted in 1989 by Martin Stanton: "[Fondane is] surely the most underestimated intellectual of the 1930s".Writing some nine years later, Chitrit also argued: "His works [...] are as important as they are unknown." Cioran, who in 1986 dedicated a portion of his *Exercises in Admiration* collection to his deceased friend, mentioned that *Baudelaire et l'expérience du gouffre*, made memorable by its study of boredom as a literary subject, had since found numerous readers. Cioran kept a fond memory of his friend, and recalled not being able to pass on Rue Rollin without experiencing "terrible pain". Awareness of Fondane's philosophy was nevertheless judged unsatisfactory by scholar Moshe Idel. Speaking in 2007, he suggested that Fondane the philosopher remained less familiar toJewish studies academics in Israel than his various counterparts in Germanic Europe.

Argentinian director Edgardo Cozarinsky, who was inspired in his youth by Fondane's introduction of avant-garde films (preserved in the Argentine Film Archives), staged and narrated a dramatized version of his biography, performed at the Villa Ocampo. Fondane scholar Olivier Salazar-Ferrer also authored a theatrical adaptation of *L'Exode*(premiered by France's *Théâtre de La Mouvance* company in 2008).

Romanian echoes

In his native country, Benjamin Fondane was present in the memoirs of several authors. One special case is Arghezi, who, despite his disciple's admiration, left a sarcastic and intentionally demoralizing portrayal of Fondane in his 1930 volume *Poarta Neagrã*. A year after the poet's death at Auschwitz, Arghezi returned with a sympathetic obituary, printed in *Revista Funda^iilor Regale*. Fondane was also the subject of a Surrealist poem in prose, or "short-circuit", by Stephan Roll, where he was referred to as "a Don Juan of the brain's lineage from God". A very hostile depiction of Fondane and other Jewish writers, noted for its antisemitic undertones, was present in the 1942 memoirs of writer Victor Eftimiu. A reflection of the late 1940s communization of Romania, Sa^a Panã's recollection piece *De la B. Fundoianu la Benjamin Fondane* ("From B.

Fundoianu to Benjamin Fondane"), published by *Orizont* review, reinterpreted some of the poet's activities, and avant-garde history in general, from a partisan Marxist vantage point. Later memoirs mentioning the writer include a piece by Adrian Maniu in the Cluj-based magazine *Steaua* (December 1963) and a new tribute by Panã in *Luceafãrul*(October 1964). Panã's recollections were later turned into a larger narrative, the 1973 autobiographical novel *Nãscut în 02* ("Born in '02"). Fondane also features prominently in Claudia Millian's *Cartea mea de aduceri-aminte* ("My Book of Recollections"), published the same year as Panã's volume. Also in 1973, the former Surrealist campaigner Geo Bogza dedicated Fondane an eponymous prose poem, centered on an existential contradiction: "To be born in Moldavia, in sweet, gentle Moldavia... and to end up in the furnaces at Auschwitz." Among the younger Romanian poets, who debuted during communism, Nichita Stãnescu was influenced by *Priveli ^ti* in some of his own earliest works, as was Andrei Codrescu.

Posthumous Romanian editions of Fondane's works included the selection *Poezii* ("Poems"), edited by the former Surrealist author Virgil Teodorescu (Editura pentru Literaturã, 1965), and Daniel's new version of *Priveli ^ti* (Cartea Româneascã, 1974), followed in 1978 by the Martin and Daniel selection, and in 1980 by Teodorescu and Martin's*Imagini ^i cãr ^i* ("Images and Books", grouping Fondane's French literary studies, as translated by Sorin Mãrculescu). Translated by Romulus Vulpescu, *Le poète en patrouille* was featured in *Manuscriptum* review (1974). During communism, various Romanian scholars who dedicated significant portions of their work to Fondane studies; in addition to Martin, Ovid Crohmãlniceanu and Dumitru Micu, they include: Paul Cornea, Nicolae Manolescu, Dan Mãnucã, Marin Mincu, Dan Petrescu, Mihail Petroveanu andIon Pop. In the 1980s, modern classical composer Doru Popovici completed the cantata *In memoriam Beniamin Fundoianu* (lyrics by Victor Bârlãdeanu).

Writing in 1978, Martin noted that the focus of such recoveries was on Fondane's poetry, while Fondane the thinker and "informed commentator", "one of the most evolved critical voices in 1920s Romanian culture", remained unfamiliar to Romanians. The limits on Fondane's posthumous circulation were partly dictated by the policies ofCommunist Romania. In 1975, the censorship apparatus (who followed national communist ideas about restricting references to Judaism) removed references to Fondane's ethnic and religious background from a reprint of Arghezi's 1945 text. In 1980, a version of his *Mântuirea* series, *Iudaism ^i elenism*, was purged from *Imagini ^i cãr ^i*, on orders from the same institution. Martin's 1984 monograph, *Introducere în opera lui B. Fundoianu* ("An Introduction to B. Fundoianu's Work"), was saluted as "penetrating" by his colleague Gheorghe Crãciun. The same study is primarily noted by Paul Cernat as a "problem-oriented" text about the "complexes" of Romanian culture, and therefore an implicit reaction against the national communism promoted under Nicolae Ceau^escu. The hidden parts of Benjamin Fondane's contribution became accessible only after the anti-communist uprising of 1989. In 1999, the Jewish community publishers, Editura Hasefer, issued *Iudaism ^i elenism* (with scholars Leon Volovici and Remus Zăstroiu as editors). The same year, the Federation of Jewish Communities of Romaniapublished an anthology of his texts, *Strigăt întru eternitate* ("A Shout unto Eternity"), and Editura Echinox a concordance dictionary of his poetry (one of several such projects initiated by linguist Marian Papahagi). In 2004, Mircea Martin and Ion Pop also collected Fondane's political essays as *Scriitorul în fa^a revolu^iei* (titled after the Romanian version of *L'Écrivain devant la révolution*). Writing in 2001, Crăciun assessed that the poet was still "non-integrated" into his native Romanian culture, which mostly perceived him as estranged, and his work in the vernacular as traditionalist.

Eight years later, comparatist Irina Georgescu assessed that interest in the more unknown aspects of Fondane's work had been rekindled by public conferences and new monographs (among which she cites the contributions of scholars Mariana Boca, Nedeea Burcă and Ana-Maria Tomescu). *Le Féstin de Balthazar* was performed in its Romanian version (*Ospă^ul lui Baltazar*), directed by Alexandru Dabija for the Nottara Theater company. The 65th commemoration of Fondane's death was marked locally with several events, including the premiere of Andreea Tănăsescu's *Exil în pământul uitării* ("Exile to the Land of Oblivion"), a contemporary ballet and performance art show loosely inspired by his poetry. In 2006, the Romanian Cultural Institute set up the Benjamin Fondane International Award for Francophone literature in countries outside France. Fondane's literary posterity was also touched by an extended controversy, notably involving Mircea Martin and philosopher Mihai ^ora. The scandal was ignited after October 2007, when ^ora and poet Luiza Palanciuc set up the *Restitutio Benjamin Fondane* translation programme, with support from Editura Limes and *Observator Cultural*magazine. Martin contested this initiative, arguing that he had earlier publicized his intent of editing a Romanian-language Fondane reader, and claiming legal precedence on copyrights. A parallel conflict ensued between Editura Limes and *Observator Cultural*, after which the *Restitutio* programme split into separate projects.

RANDALL JARRELL

Randall Jarrell (May 6, 1914 – October 14, 1965) was an American poet, literary critic, children's author, essayist, novelist, and the 11th Consultant in Poetry to the Library of Congress, a position that now bears the title Poet Laureate.

Life

Jarrell was a native of Nashville, Tennessee. He attended Hume-Fogg High

School where he "practiced tennis, starred in some school plays, and began his career as a critic with satirical essays in a school magazine." He received his B.A. from Vanderbilt University in 1935. While at Vanderbilt, he edited the student humor magazine *The Masquerader*, was captain of the tennis team, made Phi Beta Kappa and graduated *magna cum laude*. He studied there under Robert Penn Warren, who first published Jarrell's criticism; Allen Tate, who first published Jarrell's poetry; and John Crowe Ransom, who gave Jarrell his first teaching job as a Freshman Composition instructor at Kenyon College in Gambier, Ohio. Although all of these Vanderbilt teachers were heavily involved with the conservative Southern Agrarian movement, Jarrell did not become an Agrarian himself. According to Stephen Burt, "Jarrell—a devotee of Marx and Auden— embraced his teachers' literary stances while rejecting their politics." He also completed his Masters degree in English at Vanderbilt in 1937, beginning his thesis on A. E. Housman (which he completed in 1939).

When Ransom left Vanderbilt for Kenyon College in Ohio that same year, a number of his loyal students, including Jarrell, followed him to Kenyon. Jarrell taught English at Kenyon for two years, coached tennis, and served as the resident faculty member in an undergraduate dormitory that housed future writers Robie Macauley, Peter Taylor, and poet Robert Lowell. Lowell and Jarrell remained good friends and peers until Jarrell's death. According to Lowell biographer Paul Mariani, "Jarrell was the first person of [Lowell's] own generation [whom he] genuinely held in awe" due to Jarrell's brilliance and confidence even at the age of 23.

Jarrell went on to teach at the University of Texas at Austin from 1939 to 1942, where he began to publish criticism and where he met his first wife, Mackie Langham. In 1942 he left the university to join the United States Army Air Forces. According to his obituary, he "[started] as a flying cadet, [then] he later became a celestial navigation tower operator, a job title he considered the most poetic in the Air Force." His early poetry would focus on the subject of his war-time experiences in the Air Force.

The Jarrell obituary goes on to state that "after being discharged from the service he joined the faculty of Sarah Lawrence College in Bronxville, N.Y., for a year. During his time in New York, he also served as the temporary book review editor for *The Nation* magazine." However, Jarrell was uncomfortable living in the city and "claimed to hate New York's crowds, high cost of living, status-conscious sociability, and lack of greenery." He didn't end up staying in the city for long. Instead, he left for the Woman's College of the University of North Carolina where, as an associate professor of English, he taught modern poetry and "imaginative writing."

Jarrell divorced his first wife and married Mary von Schrader, a young woman whom he met at a summer writer's conference in Colorado, in 1952. They first lived together while Jarrell was teaching for a term at the University of Illinois at Champaign-Urbana. Then the couple settled back in Greensboro with Mary's daughters from her previous marriage. The couple also moved temporarily to Washington D.C. in 1956 when Jarrell served as the consultant in poetry at the Library of Congress (a position that later became titled "Poet Laureate") for two years, returning to Greensboro and the University of North Carolina after his term ended.

Towards the end of his life, in 1963, Stephen Burt notes, "Randall's behaviour began to change. Approaching his fiftieth birthday, he seems to have worried deeply about his advancing age... After President Kennedy was shot, Randall spent days in front of the television weeping. Sad to the point of inertia, Randall sought help from a Cincinnatipsychiatrist, who prescribed [the antidepressant drug] Elavil." The drug made him manic and in 1965, he was hospitalized and taken off Elavil. At this point, he was no longer manic, but he became depressed again. Burt also states, "In April *The New York Times* published a viciously condescending review of [Jarrell's most recent book of poems] *The Lost World*. Soon afterwards, Jarrell slashed a wrist and returned to the hospital." After leaving the hospital, he stayed at home that summer under his wife's care and returned to teaching at the University of North Carolina that fall.

Then, near dusk on October 14, 1965, while walking along U.S. highway 15-501 near Chapel Hill, N.C., where he had gone seeking medical treatment, Jarrell was struck by a car and killed. In trying to determine the cause of death, "[Jarrell's wife] Mary, the police, the coroner, and ultimately the state of North Carolina judged his death accidental, a verdict made credible by his apparent improvements in health...and the odd, sidelong manner of the collision; medical professionals judged the injuries consistent with an accident and not with suicide." Nevertheless, because Jarrell had recently been treated for mental illness and a previous suicide attempt, some of the people closest to him weren't entirely convinced that his death was accidental and suspected that he might have committed suicide. In a letter to Elizabeth Bishop about a week after Jarrell's death,Robert Lowell wrote, "There's a small chance [that Jarrell's death] was an accident... [but] I think it was suicide, and so does everyone else, who knew him well." Jarrell's death being a suicide has since become accepted practically as fact, even by people who were not personally close to him. The idea has been perpetuated by some well known writers. A. Alvarez, in his book *The Savage God*, lists Jarrell as a twentieth-century writer who killed himself, and James Atlas refers to Jarrell's "suicide" multiple times in his biography of Delmore Schwartz. The idea of Jarrell's death being a suicide was always denied by his wife.

On February 28, 1966, a memorial service was held in Jarrell's honour at Yale University, and some of the best-known poets in the country attended and spoke at the event, including Robert Lowell, Richard Wilbur, John

Berryman, Stanley Kunitz, and Robert Penn Warren. Reporting on the memorial service, *The New York Times* quoted Lowell who said that Jarrell was "'the most heartbreaking poet of our time'... [and] had written 'the best poetry in English about the Second World War.'" These memorial tributes formed the basis for the book *Randall Jarrell 1914-1965* which Farrar, Straus and Giroux published the following year.

In 2004, the Metropolitan Nashville Historical Commission approved placement of a historical marker in his honour, to be placed at his alma mater, Hume-Fogg High School. Some of the awards that he received during his lifetime included a Guggenheim Fellowship for 1947-48, a grant from the National Institute of Arts and Letters in 1951, and theNational Book Award for Poetry in 1961.

Writing

Poetry

In terms of the subject matter of Jarrell's work, the scholar Stephen Burt observed, "Randall Jarrell's best-known poems are poems about the Second World War, poems about bookish children and childhood, and poems, such as 'Next Day,' in the voices of aging women." Burt also succinctly summarizes the essence of Jarrell's poetic style as follows:

Jarrell's stylistic particularities have been hard for critics to hear and describe, both because the poems call readers' attention instead to their characters and because Jarrell's particular powers emerge so often from mimesis of speech. Jarrell's style responds to the alienations it delineates by incorporating or troping speech and conversation, linking emotional events within one person's psyche to speech acts that might take place between persons...Jarrell's style pivots on his sense of loneliness and on the intersubjectivity he sought as a response.

Jarrell's first collection of poetry, *Blood for a Stranger*, which was heavily influenced by W.H. Auden, was published in 1942 – the same year he enlisted in the United States Army Air Corps. His second and third books, *Little Friend, Little Friend* (1945) and *Losses* (1948), drew heavily on his Army experiences. The short lyric "The Death of the Ball Turret Gunner" is Jarrell's most famous war poem and one that is frequently anthologized.

His reputation as a poet was not firmly established until 1960 when his National Book Award-winning collection *The Woman at the Washington Zoo* was published. Starting with this book, Jarrell broke free of Auden's influence and the influence of the New Critics and developed a style that mixed Modernist and Romantic influences, incorporating the aesthetics of William Wordsworth in order to create more sympathetic character sketches and dramatic monologues. The scholar Stephen Burt notes, "Jarrell took from Wordsworth the idea that poems had to be 'convincing as speech' before they were anything else." His final volume, *The Lost World*, published in 1965, continued in the same style and cemented Jarrell's reputation as a poet; many critics consider it to be his best work. Stephen Burt states that "in the 'Lost World' poems and throughout Jarrell's oeuvre...he took care to define and defend the self [and]...his lonely personae seek intersubjective confirmation and...his alienated characters resist the so-called social world." Burt identifies the chief influences on Jarrell's poetry to be "Proust, Wordsworth, Rilke, Freud, and the poets and thinkers of Jarrell's era [particularly his close friend,Hannah Arendt]."

Criticism

From the start of his writing career, Jarrell earned a solid reputation as an influential poetry critic. Encouraged by Edmund Wilson, who published Jarrell's criticism in *The New Republic*, Jarrell developed his style of critique which was often witty and sometimes fiercely critical. However, as he got older, his criticism began to change, showing a more positive emphasis. His appreciations of Robert Lowell, Elizabeth Bishop, and William Carlos Williams helped to establish or resuscitate their reputations as significant American poets, and his poet/friends often returned the favour, as when Lowell wrote a review of Jarrell's book of poems, *The Seven League Crutches* in 1951. Lowell wrote that Jarrell was "the most talented poet under forty, and one whose wit, pathos, and grace remind us more of Pope or Matthew Arnold than of any of his contemporaries." In the same review, Lowell calls Jarrell's first book of poems, *Blood for A Stranger*, "a tour-de-force in the manner of Auden." And in another book review for Jarrell's *Selected Poems*, a few years later, fellow-poet Karl Shapiro compared Jarrell to "the great modern Rainer Maria Rilke" and stated that the book "should certainly influence our poetry for the better. It should become a point of reference, not only for younger poets, but for all readers of twentieth-century poetry."

Jarrell is also noted for his essays on Robert Frost — whose poetry was a large influence on Jarrell's own — Walt Whitman, Marianne Moore, Wallace Stevens, and others, which were mostly collected in *Poetry and the Age* (1953). Many scholars consider him the most astute poetry critic of his generation, and in 1979, the poet and scholar Peter Levi went so far as to advise younger writers, "Take more notice of Randall Jarrell than you do of any academic critic."

In an introduction to a selection of Jarrell's essays, the poet Brad Leithauser wrote the following assessment of Jarrell as a critic:

[Jarrell's] multiple and eclectic virtues —originality, erudition, wit, probity, and an irresistible passion —combined to make him the best American poet-critic sinceEliot. Or one could call him, after granting Eliot the English citizenship he so actively embraced, the best poet-critic we have ever had. Whichever side of the Atlantic one chooses to place Eliot, Jarrell was his superior in at least one significant respect. He captured a world that any contemporary poet will recognize as "the poetry scene"; his *Poetry and the Age* might even now be retitled *Poetry and Our Age*.

Fiction, Translations, and Children's Books

In addition to poetry and criticism, Jarrell also published a satiric novel, *Pictures from an Institution*, in 1954 (a National Book Award for Fiction finalist) — drawing upon his teaching experiences at Sarah Lawrence College, which served as the model for the fictional Benton College. He also wrote several children's books, among which *The Bat-Poet*(1964) and *The Animal Family* (1965) are considered prominent (and feature illustrations by Maurice Sendak). Jarrell translated poems by Rainer Maria Rilke and others, a play by Anton Chekhov, and several Grimm fairy tales.

SIDNEY KEYES

Sidney Arthur Kilworth Keyes (27 May 1922 – 29 April 1943, Tunisia) was an English poet of World War II.

Life

Early years

Keyes was born May 27, 1922. He boarded at Tonbridge School (Hillside, 1935-1940) during his secondary education, after which he attended the Queen's College, Oxford.While at college, Keyes wrote the only two books of his lifetime, *The Cruel Solstice* and *The Iron Laurel*. During his time in Oxford, Keyes fell in love with the young German artist Milein Cosman, but his love was not returned.

Military service

Keyes left Oxford and joined the army in April 1942, entering active service that same year. He was sent with his regiment to fight in the Tunisia Campaign of World War II.Prior to his service, Keyes had already written more than half of the 110 poems that would later be gathered in *The Collected Poems of Sidney Keyes*. During combat, he was reported to have continued writing poetry. However, these works have not survived.

Death

Keyes fought and died in action on 29 April 1943, shortly before his 21st birthday. It has also been stated that he died at the hands of the enemy, following his capture.

ALUN LEWIS

Alun Lewis (1 July 1915 – 5 March 1944) was a Welsh poet. He is one of the best-known English-language poets of the Second World War

Life and work

Alun Lewis was born on 1 July 1915 at Cwmaman, near Aberdare in Cynon Valley in the South Wales Coalfield. His father was a school teacher; and he had a younger sister, Mair. By the time he attended Cowbridge Grammar School, he was already interested in writing. He went on to study at Aberystwyth University and the University of Manchester. Although he was born in South Wales, he wrote in English only.

Lewis was unsuccessful as a journalist, and instead earned his living as a supply teacher. He met the poet Lynette Roberts (whose poem "Llanybri" is an invitation to him to visit her home), but she was married to another poet, Keidrych Rhys. In 1939 Lewis met Gweno Ellis, a teacher, whom he married before the year was out.

After the outbreak of the Second World War Lewis joined the British army, although he inclined to pacifism. In 1941 he collaborated with artists John Petts and Brenda Chamberlain on the "Caseg broadsheets". His first published book was the collection poetry *Raider's Dawn and other poems* (1942) (in which he makes a reference to Saints Peter and Paul), which was followed up by volume of short stories, *The Last Inspection* (1942) In 1942 he was sent to India with the South Wales Borderers.

Lewis died on 5 March 1944 in Burma, in the course of the campaign against the Japanese. He was found shot in the head, after shaving and washing, near the officers' latrines, with his revolver in his hand, and died from the wound six hours later. Despite a suggestion of suicide, an army court of enquiry concluded that he had tripped and that the shooting was an accident.

His second book of poems, *Ha!Ha! among the trumpets. Poems in transit*, was published in 1945, and his *Letters from India* in 1946. Several collections of his poems, letters and stories have been published subsequently.

One of his stories

All Day it has Rained

All day it has rained, and we on the edge of the moors
Have sprawled in our bell-tents, moody and dull as boors,
Groundsheets and blankets spread on the muddy ground
And from the first grey wakening we have found
No refuge from the skirmishing fine rain
And the wind that made the canvas heave and flap
And the taut wet guy-ropes ravel out and snap,
All day the rain has glided, wave and mist and dream,
Drenching the gorse and heather, a gossamer stream
Too light to stir the acorns that suddenly
Snatched from their cups by the wild south-westerly

Pattered against the tent and our upturned dreaming faces.
And we stretched out, unbuttoning our braces,
Smoking a Woodbine, darning dirty socks,
Reading the Sunday papers – I saw a fox
And mentioned it in the note I scribbled home;
And we talked of girls and dropping bombs on Rome,
And thought of the quiet dead and the loud celebrities
Exhorting us to slaughter, and the herded refugees;
– Yet thought softly, morosely of them, and as indifferently
As of ourselves or those whom we
For years have loved, and will again .
Tomorrow maybe love; but now it is the rain
Possesses us entirely, the twilight and the rain.
And I can remember nothing dearer or more to my heart
Than the children I watched in the woods on Saturday
Shaking down burning chestnuts for the schoolyard's merry play
Or the shaggy patient dog who followed me
By Sheet and Steep and up the wooded scree
To the Shoulder o' Mutton where Edward Thomas brooded long
On death and beauty – till a bullet stopped his song.

BORIS PASTERNAK

Boris Leonidovich Pasternak (10 February [O.S. 29 January] 1890 – 30 May 1960) was a Russian poet, novelist, and literary translator. In his native Russia, Pasternak's first book of poems, *My Sister, Life* (1917), is one of the most influential collections ever published in the Russian language. Pasternak's translations of stage plays by Johann Wolfgang von Goethe, Friedrich Schiller, Pedro Calderón de la Barca, and William Shakespeare remain very popular with Russian audiences.

Outside Russia, Pasternak is best known as the author of *Doctor Zhivago* (1958), a novel which takes place between the Russian Revolution of 1905 and the Second World War. Given its independent-minded stance on the socialist state, *Doctor Zhivago* was rejected for publication in the USSR. At the instigation of Giangiacomo Feltrinelli, *Doctor Zhivago* was smuggled to Milan and published in 1957. Pasternak was awarded the Nobel Prize for Literature in 1958, an event which both humiliated and enraged theCommunist Party of the Soviet Union. It forced him to refuse to accept the prize. His descendants accepted it in his name in 1988.

Early life

Pasternak was born in Moscow on 10 February, (Gregorian), 1890 (Julian 29 January) into a wealthy assimilated Russian Jewishfamily. His father was the Post-Impressionist painter, Leonid Pasternak, professor at the Moscow School of Painting, Sculpture, and Architecture. His mother was Rosa Kaufman, a concert pianist and the daughter of Odessa industrialist Isadore Kaufman and his wife. Pasternak had a younger brother Alex and sister Josephine.

In a 1959 letter to Jacqueline de Proyart, Pasternak recalled,

I was baptized as a child by my nanny, but because of the restrictions imposed on Jews, particularly in the case of a family which was exempt from them and enjoyed a certain reputation in view of my father's standing as an artist, there was something a little complicated about this, and it was always felt to be half-secret and intimate, a source of rare and exceptional inspiration rather than being calmly taken for granted. I believe that this is at the root of my distinctiveness. Most intensely of all my mind was occupied by Christianity in the years 1910–12, when the main foundations of this distinctiveness – my way of seeing things, the world, life – were taking shape...

Shortly after his birth, Pasternak's parents had joined the Tolstoyan Movement. Novelist Leo Tolstoy was a close family friend, as Pasternak recalled, "my father illustrated his books, went to see him, revered him, and...the whole house was imbued with his spirit."

In a 1956 essay, Pasternak recalled his father's feverish work creating illustrations for Tolstoy's novel *Resurrection*. The novel was serialized in the journal *Niva* by the publisher Fyodor Marx, based in St Petersburg. The sketches were drawn from observations in such places as courtrooms, prisons and on trains, in a spirit of realism. To ensure that the sketches met the journal deadline, train conductors were enlisted to personally collect the illustrations. Pasternak wrote,

My childish imagination was struck by the sight of a train conductor in his formal railway uniform, standing waiting at the door of the kitchen as if he were standing on a railway platform at the door of a compartment that was just about to leave the station. Joiner's glue was boiling on the stove. The illustrations were hurriedly wiped dry, fixed, glued on pieces of cardboard, rolled up, tied up. The parcels, once ready, were sealed with sealing wax and handed to the conductor.

According to Max Hayward, "In November 1910, when Tolstoy fled from his home and died in the stationmaster's house at Astapovo, Leonid Pasternak was informed by telegram and he went there immediately, taking his son Boris with him, and made a drawing of Tolstoy on his deathbed."

Regular visitors to the Pasternak's home also included Sergei Rachmaninoff, Alexander Scriabin, Lev Shestov, Rainer Maria Rilke. Pasternak aspired first to be a musician.Inspired by Scriabin, Pasternak briefly was a student at the Moscow Conservatory. In 1910 he abruptly left for the German University of Marburg, where he studied under Neo-Kantian philosophers Hermann Cohen and Nicolai Hartmann.

Career

Early career

Pasternak fell in love with Ida Wissotzkaya, a girl from a notable Moscow family of tea merchants, whose company Wissotzky Tea was the largest tea company in the world. Pasternak had tutored her in the final class of high school. He helped her prepare for finals. They met in Marburg during the summer of 1912 when Boris' father, Leonid Pasternak, painted her portrait.

Although Professor Cohen encouraged him to remain in Germany and to pursue a Philosophy doctorate, Pasternak decided against it. He returned to Moscow upon the outbreak of World War I. His first book of poems was published later that year. In the aftermath, Pasternak proposed marriage to Ida. However, the Wissotzky family was disturbed by Pasternak's poor prospects and persuaded Ida to refuse him. She turned him down and he told of his love and rejection in the poem "Marburg" (1917).

Another failed love affair in 1917 inspired the poems in his first book, *My Sister, Life*. His early verse cleverly dissimulates his preoccupation with Immanuel Kant's philosophy. Its fabric includes striking alliterations, wild rhythmic combinations, day-to-day vocabulary, and hidden allusions to his favourite poets such as Rilke, Lermontov, Pushkin and German-language Romantic poets.

During World War I, Pasternak taught and worked at a chemical factory in Vsevolodovo-Vilve near Perm, which undoubtedly provided him with material for *Dr. Zhivago* many years later. Unlike the rest of his family and many of his closest friends, Pasternak chose not to leave Russia after the October Revolution of 1917. According to Max Hayward,

'Pasternak remained in Moscow throughout the Civil War (1918–1920), making no attempt to escape abroad or to the White-occupied south, as a number of other Russian writers did at the time. No doubt, like Yuri Zhivago, he was momentarily impressed by the "splendid surgery" of the Bolshevik seizure of power in October 1917, but – again to judge by the evidence of the novel, and despite a personal admiration for Vladimir Lenin, whom he saw at the 9th Congress of Soviets in 1921 – he soon began to harbour profound doubts about the claims and credentials of the regime, not to mention its style of rule. The terrible shortages of food and fuel, and the depredations of the Red Terror, made life very precarious in those years, particularly for the "bourgeois" intelligentsia. In a letter written to Pasternak from abroad in the twenties, Marina Tsvetayeva reminded him of how she had run into him in the street in 1919 as he was on the way to sell some valuable books from his library in order to buy bread. He continued to write original work and to translate, but after about the middle of 1918 it became almost impossible to publish. The only way to make one's work known was to declaim it in the several "literary" cafes which then sprang up, or – anticipating samizdat – to circulate it in manuscript. It was in this way that *My Sister, Life* first became available to a wider audience.

When it finally was published in 1921, Pasternak's *My Sister, Life* revolutionised Russian poetry. It made Pasternak the model for younger poets, and decisively changed the poetry of Osip Mandelshtam, Marina Tsvetayeva and others.

Following *My Sister, Life*, Pasternak produced some hermetic pieces of uneven quality, including his masterpiece, the lyric cycle *Rupture*(1921). Both Pro-Soviet writers and their White emigre equivalents applauded Pasternak's poetry as pure, unbridled inspiration.

In the late 1920s, he also participated in the much celebrated tripartite correspondence with Rilke and Tsvetayeva. As the 1920s wore on, however, Pasternak increasingly felt that his colourful style was at odds with a less educated readership. He attempted to make his poetry more comprehensible by reworking his earlier pieces and starting two lengthy poems on the Russian Revolution of 1905. He also turned to prose and wrote several autobiographical stories, notably "The Childhood of Luvers" and "Safe Conduct".

In 1922 Pasternak married Evgeniya Lurye, a student at the Art Institute. The following year they had a son, Evgenii.

Evidence of Pasternak's support of still-revolutionary members of the leadership of the Communist Party as late as 1926 is indicated by his worshipful poem "In Memory of Reissner" presumably written upon the shockingly premature death from typhus of legendary Bolshevik leader Larisa Reisner at age 30 in February of that year.

By 1927, Pasternak's close friends Vladimir Mayakovsky and Nikolai Aseyev were advocating the complete subordination of the Arts to the needs of the Communist Party of the Soviet Union. In a letter to his sister Josephine, Pasternak wrote of his intentions to, "break off relations," with both of them. Although he expressed that it would be deeply painful, Pasternak explained that it could not be prevented. He explained,

They don't in any way measure up to their exalted calling. In fact, they've fallen short of it but – difficult as it is for me to understand – a modern sophist might say that these last years have actually demanded a reduction in conscience and feeling in the name of greater intelligibility. Yet now the very spirit of the times demands great, courageous purity. And these men are ruled by trivial routine. Subjectively, they're sincere and conscientious. But I find it increasingly difficult to take into account the personal aspect of their convictions. I'm not out on my own – people treat me well. But all that only holds good up to a point. It seems to me that I've reached that point.

By 1932, Pasternak had strikingly reshaped his style to make it more understandable to the general public and printed the new collection of poems, aptly titled *The Second Birth*. Although its Caucasian pieces were as brilliant as the earlier efforts, the book alienated the core of Pasternak's refined audience abroad, which was largely composed of anti-communist emigres.

In 1932 Pasternak fell in love with Zinaida Neigauz, the wife of the composer Genrikh Neigauz. They both got divorces and married two years later.

He continued to change his poetry, simplifying his style and language through the years, as expressed in his next book, *Early Trains* (1943).

Stalin Epigram

After Joseph Stalin was acclaimed as leader of the CPSU in 1929, Pasternak became further disillusioned with the Party's tightening censorship of literature. Still unwilling to conform, Pasternak remained a close friend of Anna Akhmatova and Osip Mandelstam. Mandelstam recited his searing indictment of Stalin, the "Stalin Epigram," to Pasternak soon after its composition in late April 1934. After listening, Pasternak told Mandelstam,

"I didn't hear this, you didn't recite it to me, because, you know, very strange and terrible things are happening now: they've begun to pick people up. I'm afraid the walls have ears and perhaps even these benches on the boulevard here may be able to listen and tell tales. So let's make out that I heard nothing."

On the night of 14 May 1934, Mandelstam was arrested at his home based on a warrant signed by NKVD boss Genrikh Yagoda. Devastated, Pasternak went immediately to the offices of *Izvestia* and begged Nikolai Bukharin to intercede on Mandelstam's behalf.

According to Olga Ivinskaya, later Pasternak's lover, Pasternak was deeply upset by Mandelstam's arrest. He was concerned for his friend but he also worried that he might be blamed for betraying Mandelstam to the secret police. Ivinskaya writes that Pasternak "raced frantically all over town, telling everybody that he was not to blame and denying responsibility for Mandelstam's disappearance, which for some reason he thought might be laid at his door.

Soon after his meeting with Bukharin, the telephone rang in Pasternak's Moscow apartment. A voice from The Kremlin said, "Comrade Stalin wishes to speak with you."According to Ivinskaya, Pasternak was struck dumb. "He was totally unprepared for such a conversation. But then he heard *his* voice, the voice of Stalin, coming over the line. The Leader addressed him in a rather bluff uncouth fashion, using the familiar *thou* form: 'Tell me, what are they saying in your literary circles about the arrest of Mandelstam?'" Flustered, Pasternak denied that there was any discussion or that there were any literary circles left in Soviet Russia. Stalin went on to ask him for his own opinion of Mandelstam. In an "eager fumbling manner" Pasternak explained that he and Mandelstam each had a completely different philosophy about poetry. Ivinskaya writes that he "went on for quite a time in this vein. Stalin gave him no encouragement whatsoever, not interjecting, or uttering a sound of any kind. At last B[oris] L[eonidovich] came to a halt. Stalin then said, in a mocking tone of voice: "I see, you just aren't able to stick up for a comrade," and put down the receiver.

Years later, Pasternak recalled that he was horrified at how the conversation had ended. He repeatedly telephoned the Kremlin's number, begging to be reconnected to Stalin. Instead, Pasternak was told, "Comrade Stalin is busy." Pasternak became frantic, pacing around his apartment repeating over and over that he must write to Stalin to explain what he had meant and to also say that injustices were being committed in the name of the Leader. Pasternak later did write and send just such a letter.

According to Ivinskaya,

If ever the conversation turned to Mandelstam, [Boris Leonidovich] would always hark back to the same thing: that he was not to blame for his misfortunes, and that if he had not written to Bukharin and in general made a great fuss about his arrest, then perhaps Mandelstam would not even have had the respite, brief as it was, which was granted to him – with the result that the *Voronezh Notebooks* might never have been written. It was clear, however, that [Boris Leonidovich] himself felt he had not come as well as he should out of his unexpected conversation with the Leader. He had done something not quite right...

Great Purge

According to Pasternak, during the 1937 show trial of General Iona Yakir and Marshal Mikhail Tukhachevsky, the Union of Soviet Writers requested all members to add their names to a statement supporting the death penalty for the defendants. They demanded Pasternak's signature as well, but he refused to give it. Vladimir Stavski, the chairman of the Union, was terrified that he would be punished for Pasternak's dissent. The leadership of the Union travelled to Pasternak's dacha at Peredelkino and severely threatened the writer, who refused to sign the statement and returned to his dacha. Hearing this, Zinaida Pasternak, who was pregnant, was terribly upset, accusing him of risking the destruction of their family. Pasternak went to bed. He and Zinaida expected to be arrested that evening. They later learned that an NKVD agent was hiding in the bushes outside their window and wrote down every word they said to each other.

Soon after, Pasternak appealed directly to Stalin. He wrote about his family's strong Tolstoyan convictions, which he still held dear. He declared that his own life was at the Leader's disposal. He said, that he could not stand as a self-appointed judge of life and death. Pasternak was certain that he would be instantly arrested, but he was not.Stalin is said to have crossed Pasternak's name off an execution list during the Great Purge. According to Pasternak,

Stalin declared, "Do not touch this cloud dweller" (or, in another version, "Leave that holy fool alone!")

Although Pasternak was never arrested by the Soviet secret police, his close friend Titsian Tabidze fell victim to the Great Purge. In an autobiographical essay published in the 1950s, Pasternak described the execution of Tabidze and the suicides of Marina Tsvetaeva and Paolo Iashvili as the greatest heartbreaks of his entire life.

According to Stalin's biographer, Simon Sebag Montefiore, Stalin was well aware that Mandelstam, Pasternak, and Bulgakov were geniuses, but ordered their writings suppressed. As Bulgakov and Pasternak never attacked him openly, they were never arrested. Ivinskaya wrote, "I believe that between Stalin and Pasternak there was an incredible, silent duel."

World War II

Pasternak was elated by the outbreak of war between Nazi Germany and the Soviet Union. When the Luftwaffe began bombing Moscow, Pasternak immediately began to serve as a fire warden on the roof of the writer's building on Lavrushinski Street. According to Ivinskaya, he repeatedly helped to dispose of German bombs which fell on it.

In 1943, Pasternak was finally granted permission to visit the soldiers at the front. He bore up well, considering the hardships of the journey (he had a weak leg from an old injury), and he wanted to go to the most dangerous places. He read his poetry and talked extensively with the active and injured troops.

With the end of the war in 1945, the Soviet people expected to see the end of the devastation of Nazism, and hoped for the end of Stalin's Purges. But, sealed trains began carrying large numbers of prisoners to the Soviet Gulags. Some were Nazi collaborators who had fought under General Andrey Vlasov, but most were ordinary Soviet officers and men. Pasternak watched as ex-POWs were directly transferred from Nazi Germany to Soviet concentration camps. White emigres who had returned due to pledges ofamnesty were also sent directly to the Gulag, as were Jews from the Anti-Fascist Committee and other organizations. Many thousands of innocent people were incarcerated in connection with the Leningrad Affair and the so-called Doctor's Plot, while whole ethnic groups were deported to Siberia. Pasternak later said, "If, in a bad dream, we had seen all the horrors in store for us after the war, we should not have been sorry to see Stalin fall, together with Hitler. Then, an end to the war in favour of our allies, civilized countries with democratic traditions, would have meant a hundred times less suffering for our people than that which Stalin again inflicted on it after his victory."

Olga Ivinskaya

In October 1946, the married Pasternak met Olga Ivinskaya, a single mother employed by *Novy Mir*. Deeply moved by her resemblance to his first love Ida Vysotskaya, Pasternak gave Ivinskaya several volumes of his poetry and literary translations. Although Pasternak never left his wife Zinaida, he started an extramarital relationship with Ivinskaya that would last for the remainder of Pasternak's life. Ivinskaya later recalled, "He phoned almost every day and, instinctively fearing to meet or talk with him, yet dying of happiness, I would stammer out that I was "busy today." But almost every afternoon, towards the end of working hours, he came in person to the office and often walked with me through the streets, boulevards, and squares all the way home to Potapov Street. 'Shall I make you a present of this square?' he would ask."

She gave him the phone number of her neighbour Olga Volkova who resided below. In the evenings, Pasternak would phone and Volkova would signal by Olga banging on the water pipe which connected their apartments.

When they first met, Pasternak was translating the verse of the Hungarian national poet, Sándor Petõfi. Pasternak gave his lover a book of Petõfi with the inscription, "Petõfi served as a code in May and June 1947, and my close translations of his lyrics are an expression, adapted to the requirements of the text, of my feelings and thoughts for you and about you. In memory of it all, B.P., 13 May 1948."

Pasternak later noted on a photograph of himself, "Petõfi is magnificent with his descriptive lyrics and picture of nature, but you are better still. I worked on him a good deal in 1947 and 1948, when I first came to know you. Thank you for your help. I was translating both of you." Ivinskaya would later describe the Petõfi translations as, "a first declaration of love."

According to Ivinskaya, Zinaida Pasternak was infuriated by her husband's infidelity. Once, when his younger son Leonid fell seriously ill, Zinaida extracted a promise from her husband, as they stood by the boy's sickbed, that he would end his affair with Ivinskaya. Pasternak asked Luisa Popova, a mutual friend, to tell Ivinskaya about his promise. Popova told him that he must do it himself. Soon after, Ivinskaya happened to be ill at Popova's apartment, when suddenly Zinaida Pasternak arrived and confronted her.

Ivinskaya later recalled,

But I became so ill through loss of blood that she and Luisa had to get me to the hospital, and I not longer remember exactly what passed between me and this heavily built, strong-minded woman, who kept repeating how she didn't give a damn for our love and that, although she no longer loved [Boris Leonidovich] herself, she would not allow her family to be broken up. After my return from the hospital, Boris came to visit me, as though nothing had happened, and touchingly made his peace with my mother, telling her how much he loved me. By now she was pretty well used to these funny ways of his.

In 1948, Pasternak advised Ivinskaya to resign her job at *Novy Mir*, which was becoming extremely difficult due to their relationship. In the aftermath,

Pasternak began to instruct her in translating poetry. In time, they began to refer to her apartment on Potapov Street as, "Our Shop."

On the evening of 6 October 1949, Ivinskaya was arrested at her apartment by the KGB. Ivinskaya relates in her memoirs that, when the agents burst into her apartment, she was at her typewriter working on translations of the Korean poet Won Tu-Son. Her apartment was ransacked and all items connected with Pasternak were piled up in her presence. Ivinskaya was taken to the Lubyanka Prison and repeatedly interrogated, where she refused to say anything incriminating about Pasternak. At the time, she was pregnant with Pasternak's child and had a miscarriage early in her ten-year sentence in the GULAG.

Upon learning of his mistress' arrest, Pasternak telephoned Liuisa Popova and asked her to come at once to Gogol Boulevard. She found him sitting on a bench near the Palace of Soviets Metro Station. Weeping, Pasternak told her, "Everything is finished now. They've taken her away from me and I'll never see her again. It's like death, even worse."

According to Ivinskaya, "After this, in conversation with people he scarcely knew, he always referred to Stalin as a 'murderer.' Talking with people in the offices of literary periodicals, he often asked: 'When will there be an end to this freedom for lackeys who happily walk over corpses to further their own interests?' He spent a good deal of time with Akhmatova—who in those years was given a very wide berth by most of the people who knew her. He worked intensively on the second part of *Doctor Zhivago*."

In a 1958 letter to a friend in West Germany, Pasternak wrote, "She was put in jail on my account, as the person considered by the secret police to be closest to me, and they hoped that by means of a gruelling interrogation and threats they could extract enough evidence from her to put me on trial. I owe my life, and the fact that they did not touch me in those years, to her heroism and endurance."

Translating Goethe

Pasternak's translation of the first part of *Faust* led him to be attacked in the August 1950 edition of *Novy Mir*. The critic accused Pasternak of distorting Goethe's "progressive" meanings to support "the reactionary theory of 'pure art'", as well as introducing aesthetic and individualist values. In a subsequent letter to the daughter of Marina Tsvetaeva, Pasternak explained that the attack was motivated by the fact that the supernatural elements of the play, which *Novy Mir* considered, "irrational," had been translated as Goethe had written them. Pasternak further declared that, despite the attacks on his translation, his contract for the second part had not been revoked.

Khrushchev thaw

When Stalin died of a stroke on 5 March 1953, Olga Ivinskaya was still imprisoned in the Gulag, and Pasternak was in Moscow. Across the nation, there were waves of panic, confusion, and public displays of grief. Pasternak wrote, "Men who are not free... always idealize their bondage."

After her release, Pasternak's relationship with Ivinskaya picked up where it had left off. Soon after he confided in her, "For so long we were ruled over by a madman and a murderer, and now by a fool and a pig. The madman had his occasional flights of fancy, he had an intuitive feeling for certain things, despite his wild obscurantism. Now we are ruled over by mediocrities." During this period, Pasternak delighted in reading a clandestine copy of George Orwell's *Animal Farm* in English. In conversation with Ivinskaya, Pasternak explained that the pig dictator Napoleon, in the novel, "vividly reminded " him of Soviet Premier Nikita Khrushchev.

Doctor Zhivago

Although it contains passages written in the 1910s and 1920s, *Doctor Zhivago* was not completed until 1956. Pasternak submitted the novel to "Íîâûé Ìèð" (*Novy Mir*), which refused publication due to its rejection of socialist realism. The author, like his protagonist Yuri Zhivago, showed more concern for the welfare of individual characters than for the "progress" of society. Censors also regarded some passages as anti-Soviet, especially the novel's criticisms of Stalinism, Collectivisation, the Great Purge, and the Gulag.

In March 1956, the Italian Communist Party dispatched a young journalist, Sergio d'Angelo, to work in the Soviet Union... His membership of the Communist Party and his job as a journalist allowed d'Angelo to plunge immediately into the cultural life of the Soviet capital. Besides his official appointment, he also had a private commission from a Milan publisher – the communistGiangiacomo Feltrinelli – to find new works of Soviet literature that would be of interest to the Western reader.

Upon learning of *Doctor Zhivago*'s existence, d'Angelo travelled immediately to Peredelkino and offered to submit Pasternak's novel to Feltrinelli's company for publication. At first Pasternak was stunned. Then he brought the manuscript from his study and told d'Angelo with a laugh, "You are hereby invited to watch me face the firing squad."

According to Lazar Fleishman, Pasternak was aware that he was taking a huge risk. No Soviet author had attempted to deal with Western publishers since the 1920s, when such behaviour led the Soviet State to declare war on Boris Pilnyak and Evgeny Zamyatin. Pasternak, however, believed that Feltrinelli's Communist affiliation would not only guarantee publication, but might even force the Soviet State to publish the novel in Russia.

In a rare moment of agreement, both Olga Ivinskaya and Zinaida Pasternak were horrified by the submission of *Doctor Zhivago* to a Western publishing house. Pasternak, however, refused to change his mind and informed an emissary from Feltrinelli that he was prepared to undergo any sacrifice in order to see *Doctor Zhivago* published.

In 1957, Feltrinelli announced that the novel would be published by his company. Despite repeated demands from visiting Soviet emissaries, Feltrinelli refused to cancel or delay publication. According to Ivinskaya, "He did not believe that we would ever publish the manuscript here and felt he had no right to withhold a masterpiece from the world – this would be an even greater crime." The Soviet government forced Pasternak to cable the publisher to withdraw the manuscript, but he sent separate, secret letters advising Feltrinelli to ignore the telegrams.

Helped considerably by the Soviet campaign against the novel (as well as by the U.S. Central Intelligence Agency's secret purchase of hundreds of copies of the book as it came off the presses around the world - see "Nobel Prize" section below), *Doctor Zhivago* became an instant sensation throughout the non-Communist world upon its release in November 1957. In the State of Israel, however, Pasternak's novel was sharply criticized for its assimilationist views towards the Jewish people. When informed of this, Pasternak responded, "No matter. I am above race..." According to Lazar Fleishman, Pasternak had written the disputed passages prior to Israeli independence. At the time, Pasternak had also been regularly attending Russian Orthodox Divine Liturgy. Therefore, he believed that Soviet Jews converting to Christianity was preferable to assimilating into atheism and Stalinism.

The first English translation of *Doctor Zhivago* was hastily produced by Max Hayward and Manya Harari in order to coincide with overwhelming public demand. It was released in August 1958, and remained the only edition available for more than fifty years. Between 1958 and 1959, the English language edition spent 26 weeks at the top of *The New York Times'* bestseller list.

Ivinskaya's daughter Irina circulated typed copies of the novel in Samizdat. Although no Soviet critics had read the banned novel, *Doctor Zhivago* was pilloried in the State-owned press. Similar attacks led to a humorous Russian saying, "I haven't read Pasternak, but I condemn him".

During the aftermath of the Second World War, Pasternak had composed a series of poems on Gospel themes. According to Ivinskaya, Pasternak had regarded Stalin as a, "giant of the pre-Christian era." Therefore, Pasternak's Christian-themed poems were, "a form of protest."

On 9 September 1958, the *Literary Gazette* critic Viktor Pertsov retaliated by denouncing, "the decadent religious poetry of Pasternak, which reeks of mothballs from theSymbolist suitcase of 1908–10 manufacture." Furthermore, the author received much hate mail from Communists both at home and abroad. According to Ivinskaya, Pasternak continued to receive such letters for the remainder of his life. In a letter written to his sister Josephine, however, Pasternak recalled the words of his friend Ekaterina Krashennikova upon reading *Doctor Zhivago*. She had said, "Don't forget yourself to the point of believing that it was you who wrote this work. It was the Russian people and their sufferings who created it. Thank God for having expressed it through your pen."

Nobel Prize

According to Yevgeni Borisovich Pasternak, "Rumors that Pasternak was to receive the Nobel Prize started right after the end of World War II. According to the former Nobel Committee head Lars Gyllensten, his nomination was discussed every year from 1946 to 1950, then again in 1957 (it was finally awarded in 1958). Pasternak guessed at this from the growing waves of criticism in USSR. Sometimes he had to justify his European fame: 'According to the Union of Soviet Writers, some literature circles of the West see unusual importance in my work, not matching its modesty and low productivity...'"

According to journalist Ivan Tolstoi, the British MI6 and the American CIA lent a hand to ensure that *Doctor Zhivago* was submitted to theNobel Committee in the original Russian. According to Tolstoi, this was done so that Pasternak could win the Nobel prize and harm the international credibility of the Soviet Union. He repeats and elaborates upon Feltrinelli's claims that the CIA operatives had photographed a manuscript of the novel and secretly printed a small number of books in the Russian language. More recently, Anna Sergeyeva-Klyatis wrote that the first Russian edition of *Doctor Zhivago*, which was a pirated version with numerous typographical errors and omissions, was actually initiated by the Central Association of Postwar Émigrées, in response to a growing demand among Russian émigrés.

The issue of whether or not the CIA had a hand in creating the international controversy that led to Pasternak's winning the Nobel Prize was definitively settled on 11 April 2014 when the U.S. Central Intelligence Agency released "nearly 100 declassified documents"confirming that it had, in fact, undertaken a massive propaganda campaign to influence the Nobel Prize committee to consider *Zhivago* for the award, starting as early as 12 December 1957: "*Dr. Zhivago* should be published in a maximum number of foreign editions, for maximum free world discussion and acclaim and consideration for such honour as the Nobel prize" [sic] In order to turn Pasternak's novel into an international bestseller worthy of consideration for the Nobel Prize, the CIA purchased thousands of copies of the novel as they came off the presses throughout Europe. When in the summer of 1958 the Dutch publishing house of Mouton brought out an edition of *Zhivago*, the CIA secretly arranged to "obtain first thousand copies of the book off the press and of these send 500 copies to the Brussels Fair" (*i.e.* the World's Fair held that summer in Brussels, Belgium). In its announcement of the declassification of the *Zhivago* documents the CIA states that it also published "thousands" of copies of *Zhivago* and gave them out to

Soviet tourists on holiday in Western Europe and had them smuggled into the Soviet Union: "After working secretly to publish the Russian-language edition in the Netherlands, the CIA moved quickly to ensure that copies of Doctor Zhivago were available for distribution to Soviet visitors at the 1958 Brussels World's Fair. By the end of the Fair, 355 copies of Doctor Zhivago had been surreptitiously handed out, and eventually thousands more were distributed throughout the Communist bloc. [...] Subsequently, the CIA funded the publication of a miniature, lightweight paperback edition of Doctor Zhivago that could be easily mailed or concealed in a jacket pocket. Distribution of the miniature version began in April 1959."

Meanwhile, Pasternak wrote to Renate Schweitzer and his sister, Lydia Pasternak Slater. In both letters, the author expressed hope that he would be passed over by the Nobel Committee in favour of Alberto Moravia. Pasternak wrote that he was wracked with torments and anxieties at the thought of placing his loved ones in danger.

On 23 October 1958, Boris Pasternak was announced as the winner of the Nobel Prize. The citation credited Pasternak's contribution to Russian lyric poetry and for his role in, "continuing the great Russian epic tradition." On 25 October, Pasternak sent a telegram to the Swedish Academy: "Infinitely grateful, touched, proud, surprised, overwhelmed." That same day, the Literary Institute in Moscow demanded that all its students sign a petition denouncing Pasternak and his novel. They were further ordered to join a "spontaneous" demonstration demanding Pasternak's exile from the Soviet Union. On 26 October, the *Literary Gazette* ran an article by David Zaslavski entitled,*Reactionary Propaganda Uproar over a Literary Weed.*

According to Solomon Volkov,

The anti-Pasternak campaign was organized in the worst Stalin tradition: denunciations in *Pravda* and other newspapers; publications of angry letters from, "ordinary Soviet workers," who had not read the book; hastily convened meetings of Pasternak's friends and colleagues, at which fine poets like Vladimir Soloukin,Leonid Martynov, and Boris Slutsky were forced to censure an author they respected. Slutsky, who in his brutal prose-like poems had created an image for himself as a courageous soldier and truth-lover, was so tormented by his anti-Pasternak speech that he later went insane.

On October 29, 1958, at the plenum of the Central Committee of the Young Communist League, dedicated to the Komsomol's fortieth anniversary, its head, Vladimir Semichastny, attacked Pasternak before an audience of 14,000 people, including Khrushchev and other Party leaders. Semishastny first called Pasternak, "a mangy sheep," who pleased the enemies of the Soviet Union with, "his slanderous so-called work." Then Semichastny (who became head of the KGB in 1961) added that, "this man went and spat in the face of the people." And he concluded with, "If you compare Pasternak to a pig, a pig would not do what he did," because a pig, "never shits where it eats." Khrushchev applauded demonstratively. News of that speech drove Pasternak to the brink of suicide. It has recently come to light that the real author of Semichastny's insults was Khrushchev, who had called the Komsomol leader the night before and dictated his lines about the mangy sheep and the pig, which Semichastny described as a, "typically Khrushchevian, deliberately crude, unceremoniously scolding."

Furthermore, Pasternak was informed that, if he traveled to Stockholm to collect his Nobel Medal, he would be refused re-entry to the Soviet Union. As a result, Pasternak sent a second telegram to the Nobel Committee: "In view of the meaning given the award by the society in which I live, I must renounce this undeserved distinction which has been conferred on me. Please do not take my voluntary renunciation amiss." The Swedish Academy announced: "This refusal, of course, in no way alters the validity of the award. There remains only for the Academy, however, to announce with regret that the presentation of the Prize cannot take place."

According to Yevgenii Pasternak, "I couldn't recognize my father when I saw him that evening. Pale, lifeless face, tired painful eyes, and only speaking about the same thing: 'Now it all doesn't matter, I declined the Prize.'"

Deportation plans

Despite his decision to decline the award, the Soviet Union of Writers continued to demonise Pasternak in the State-owned press. Furthermore, he was threatened at the very least with formal exile to the West. In response, Pasternak wrote directly to Soviet Premier Nikita Khrushchev,

I am addressing you personally, the C.C. of the C.P.S.S., and the Soviet Government. From Comrade Semichastny's speech I learn that the government, 'would not put any obstacles in the way of my departure from the U.S.S.R.' For me this is impossible.

I am tied to Russia by birth, by my life and work. I cannot conceive of my destiny separate from Russia, or outside it. Whatever my mistakes or failings, I could not imagine that I should find myself at the center of such a political campaign as has been worked up round my name in the West. Once I was aware of this, I informed the Swedish Academy of my voluntary renunciation of the Nobel Prize. Departure beyond the borders of my country would for me be tantamount to death and I therefore request you not to take this extreme measure with me. With my hand on my heart, I can say that I have done something for Soviet literature, and may still be of use to it.

In *The Oak and the Calf*, Alexander Solzhenitsyn sharply criticized Pasternak, both for declining the Nobel Prize and for sending such a letter to Khrushchev. In her own memoirs, Olga Ivinskaya blames herself for pressuring her lover into making both decisions.

According to Yevgenii Pasternak, "She accused herself bitterly for persuading Pasternak to decline the Prize. After all that had happened, open shadowing, friends turning away, Pasternak's suicidal condition at the time, one can... understand her: the memory of Stalin's camps was too fresh, [and] she tried to protect him."

On 31 October 1958, the Union of Soviet Writers held a trial behind closed doors. According to the meeting minutes, Pasternak was denounced as an internal White emigre and a Fascist fifth columnist. Afterwards, the attendees announced that Pasternak had been expelled from the Union. They further signed a petition to the Politburo, demanding that Pasternak be stripped of his Soviet citizenship and exiled to, "his Capitalist paradise." According to Yevgenii Pasternak, however, author Konstantin Paustovsky refused to attend the meeting. Yevgeny Yevtushenko did attend, but walked out in disgust.

According to Yevgenii Pasternak, his father would have been exiled had it not been for Indian Prime Minister Jawaharlal Nehru, who telephoned Khrushchev and threatened to find a Committee for Pasternak's protection.

It is possible that the 1958 Nobel Prize prevented Pasternak's imprisonment due to the Soviet State's fear of international protests. Yevgenii Pasternak believes, however, that the resulting persecution fatally weakened his father's health.

Meanwhile, Bill Mauldin produced a political cartoon which won the 1959 Pulitzer Prize for Editorial Cartooning. The cartoon depicts Pasternak and another GULAG inmate, splitting trees in the snow. The caption reads, "I won the Nobel Prize for literature. What was your crime?"

Last years

Pasternak's post-*Zhivago* poetry probes the universal questions of love, immortality, and reconciliation with God. Boris Pasternak wrote his last complete book, *When the Weather Clears*, in 1959.

According to Ivinskaya, Pasternak continued to stick to his daily writing schedule even during the controversy over *Doctor Zhivago*. He also continued translating the writings of Juliusz S³owacki and Pedro Calderón de la Barca. In his work on Calderon, Pasternak received the discreet support of Nikolai Mikhailovich Liubimov, a senior figure in the Party's literary apparatus. Ivinskaya describes Liubimov as, "a shrewd and enlightened person who understood very well that all the mudslinging and commotion over the novel would be forgotten, but that there would always be a Pasternak." In a letter to his sisters in Oxford, England, Pasternak claimed to have finished translating one of Calderon's plays in less than a week.

During the summer of 1959, Pasternak began writing *The Blind Beauty*, a trilogy of stage plays set before and after Alexander II's abolition of serfdom in Russia. In an interview with Olga Carlisle from *The Paris Review*, Pasternak enthusiastically described the play's plot and characters. He informed Olga Carlisle that, at the end of *The Blind Beauty*, he wished to depict "the birth of an enlightened and affluent middle class, open to occidental influences, progressive, intelligent, artistic". However, Pasternak fell ill with terminal lung cancer before he could complete the first play of the trilogy.

Death

Boris Pasternak died of lung cancer in his dacha in Peredelkino on the evening of 30 May 1960. He first summoned his sons, and in their presence said, "Who will suffer most because of my death? Who will suffer most? Only Oliusha will, and I haven't had time to do anything for her. The worst thing is that she will suffer." Pasternak's last words were, "I can't hear very well. And there's a mist in front of my eyes. But it will go away, won't it? Don't forget to open the window tomorrow."

Shortly before his death, a priest of the Russian Orthodox Church had given Pasternak the last rites. Later, in the strictest secrecy, aRussian Orthodox funeral liturgy, or Panikhida, was offered in the family's dacha.

Funeral demonstration

Despite only a small notice appearing in the *Literary Gazette*, handwritten notices carrying the date and time of the funeral were posted throughout the Moscow subway system. As a result, thousands of admirers braved Militia and KGB surveillance to attend Pasternak's funeral in Peredelkino.

Before Pasternak's civil funeral, Olga Ivinskaya had a conversation with Konstantin Paustovsky. According to Ivinskaya,

"He began to say what an authentic event the funeral was—an expression of what people really felt, and so characteristic of the Russia which stoned its prophets and did its poets to death as a matter of longstanding tradition. At such a moment, he continued indignantly, one was bound to recall the funeral of Pushkin and the Tsar's courtiers – their miserable hypocrisy and false pride. 'Just think how rich they are, how many Pasternaks they have—as many as there were Pushkins in the Russia of Tsar Nicholas... Not much has changed. But what can one expect? They are afraid...'"

Then, in the presence of a large number of foreign journalists, the body of Pasternak was removed to the cemetery. According to Ivinskaya,

The graveside service now began. It was hard for me in my state to make out what was going on. Later, I was told that Paustovski had wanted to give the funeral address, but it was in fact Professor Asmus who spoke. Wearing a light coloured suit and a bright tie, he was dressed more for some gala occasion than for a funeral. "A writer has died," he began, "who, together with Pushkin, Dostoevsky, and Tolstoy, forms part of the glory of Russian literature. Even if we cannot agree with him in everything; we all none the less owe him a debt of gratitude for setting an example of unswerving honesty, for his incorruptible conscience, and for his heroic view of his duty as a writer." Needless to say, he mentioned [Boris Leonidovich]'s, "mistakes and failings," but hastened to add that, "they do not, however, prevent us from recognizing the fact that he was a great poet." "He was a very modest man," Asmus said in conclusion, "and he did not like people to talk about him too much, so with this I shall bring my address to a close."

To the horror of the assembled Party officials, however, someone with, "a young and deeply anguished voice," began reciting Pasternak's banned poem *Hamlet*.

The murmurs ebb; onto the stage I enter.I am trying, standing at the door,To discover in the distant echoesWhat the coming years may hold in store.The nocturnal darkness with a thousandBinoculars is focused onto me.Take away this cup, O Abba, Father,Everything is possible to Thee.I am fond of this Thy stubborn project,And to play my part I am content.But another drama is in progress,And, this once, O let me be exempt.But the plan of action is determined,And the end irrevocably sealed.I am alone; all round me drowns in falsehood:Life is not a walk across a field.

According to Ivinskaya,

At this point, the persons stage-managing the proceedings decided the ceremony must be brought to an end as quickly as possible, and somebody began to carry the lid towards the coffin. For the last time, I bent down to kiss Boria on the forehead, now completely cold... But now something unusual began to happen in the cemetery. Someone was about to put the lid on the coffin, and another person in gray trousers... said in an agitated voice: "That's enough, we don't need any more speeches! Close the coffin!" But people would not be silenced so easily. Someone in a coloured, open-necked shirt who looked like a worker started to speak: "Sleep peacefully, dear Boris Leonidovich! We do not know all your works, but we swear to you at this hour: the day will come when we shall know them all. We do not believe anything bad about your book. And what can we say about all you others, all you brother writers who have brought such disgrace upon yourselves that no words can describe it. Rest in peace, Boris Leonidovich!" The man in gray trousers seized hold of other people who tried to come forward and pushed them back into the crowd: "The meeting is over, there will be no more speeches!" A foreigner expressed his indigation in broken Russian: "You can only say the meeting is over when no more people wish to speak!"

The final speaker at the graveside service said,

God marks the path of the elect with thorns, and Pasternak was picked out and marked by God. He believed in eternity and he will belong to it... We excommunicated Tolstoy, we disowned Dostoevsky, and now we disown Pasternak. Everything that brings us glory we try to banish to the West... But we cannot allow this. We love Pasternak and we revere him as a poet... Glory to Pasternak!

As the spectators cheered, the bells of Peredelkino's Church of the Transfiguration began to toll. Written prayers for the dead were then placed upon Pasternak's forehead and the coffin was closed and buried. Pasternak's gravesite would go on to become a major shrine for members of the Soviet dissident movement.

Legacy

After Pasternak's death, Olga Ivinskaya was arrested for the second time, with her daughter, Irina Emelyanova. Both were accused of being Pasternak's link with Western publishers and of dealing in hard currency for *Doctor Zhivago*. All of Pasternak's letters to Ivinskaya, as well as many other manuscripts and documents, were seized by the KGB. The KGB quietly released them, Irina after one year, in 1962, and Olga in 1964. By this time, Ivinskaya had served four years of an eight-year sentence, in retaliation for her role in *Doctor Zhivago*s publication. In 1978, her memoirs were smuggled abroad and published in Paris. An English translation by Max Haywardwas published the same year under the title *A Captive of Time: My Years with Pasternak*.

Ivinskaya was rehabilitated only in 1988. After the dissolution of the Soviet Union, Ivinskaya sued for the return of the letters and documents seized by the KGB in 1961. The Russian Supreme Court ultimately ruled against her, stating that, "there was no proof of ownership," and that the, "papers should remain in the state archive". Olga Ivinskaya died of cancer on 8 September 1995. A reporter on NTV compared her role to that of other famous muses for Russian poets: "As Pushkin would not be complete without Anna Kern, and Yesenin would be nothing without Isadora, so Pasternak would not be Pasternak without Olga Ivinskaya, who was his inspiration for *Doctor Zhivago*.".

Meanwhile, Boris Pasternak continued to be pilloried by the Soviet State until Mikhail Gorbachev proclaimed Perestroika during the 1980s.

In 1988, after decades of circulating in Samizdat, *Doctor Zhivago* was serialized in the literary journal *Novy Mir*.

In December 1989, Yevgenii Borisovich Pasternak was permitted to travel to Stockholm in order to collect his father's Nobel Medal. At the ceremony, acclaimed cellist and Soviet dissident Mstislav Rostropovich performed a Bach serenade in honour of his deceased countryman.

A 2009 book by Ivan Tolstoi reasserts claims that British and American intelligence officers were involved in ensuring Pasternak's Nobel victory however another Russian researcher disagrees. When Yevgeny Borisovich Pasternak was questioned about this, he responded that his father was completely unaware of the actions of Western intelligence services. Yevgeny further declared that the Nobel Prize caused his father nothing but severe grief and harassment at the hands of the Soviet State. The Pasternak family papers are stored at the Hoover Institution Archives, Stanford University. They contain correspondence, drafts of *Doctor Zhivago* and other writings, photographs, and other material, of Boris Pasternak and other family members.

Cultural influence

A minor planet (3508 Pasternak) discovered by Soviet astronomer Lyudmila Georgievna Karachkina in 1980 is named after him.

Russian-American singer and songwriter Regina Spektor recites a verse from "Black Spring", a 1912 poem by Pasternak in her song "Apres Moi" from her album *Begin to Hope*.

In 1990, the book "Twenty Thousand Faces of Pasternak" was published in USA. It was published to the 100th Anniversary of the birth of Boris Pasternak by Ilya Rudiak. The book includes the selected photographs of Boris Pasternak by the famous photographer, Moses Nappelbaum (1869-1958), and several poems by Pasternak from his novel "Doctor Zhivago". The book design, cover and illustrations to the poems from "Doctor Zhivago" by Natalia G. Toreeva. The English translations to the text by Erick Esrach. In October 2010, Random House released Richard Pevear and Larissa Volokhonsky's translation of *Doctor Zhivago*. In 1997, the "Washington Museum of Russian Poetry and Music" was founded in the USA by Dr. Uli Zislin, the songwriter and singer. The museum includes the work of five famous Russian poets of the Silver Age (1920th), which includes the poets such as Boris Pasternak, Marina Tsvetaeva, Anna Akhmatova, Nikolay Gumilev, and Osip Mandelstam.

Adaptations

The first screen adaptation of *Doctor Zhivago*, adapted by Robert Bolt and directed by David Lean, appeared in 1965. The film, which toured in the roadshow tradition, starredOmar Sharif, Geraldine Chaplin, and Julie Christie. Concentrating on the love triangle aspects of the novel, the film became a worldwide blockbuster, but was unavailable in Russia until Perestroika.

In 2002, the novel was adapted as a television miniseries. Directed by Giacomo Campiotti, the serial starred Hans Matheson, Alexandra Maria Lara, Keira Knightley, and Sam Neill.

The Russian TV version of 2006, directed by Alexander Proshkin and starring Oleg Menshikov as Zhivago, is considered more faithful to Pasternak's novel than David Lean's 1965 film.

Work

Poetry

Thoughts on poetry: According to Ivinskaya,

In Pasternak the 'all-powerful god of detail' always, it seems, revolted against the idea of turning out verse for its own sake or to convey vague personal moods. If 'eternal' themes were to be dealt with yet again, then only by a poet in the true sense of the word – otherwise he should not have the strength of character to touch them at all. Poetry so tightly packed (till it crunched like ice) or distilled into a solution where 'grains of true prose germinated,' a poetry in which realistic detail cast a genuine spell – only such poetry was acceptable to Pasternak; but not poetry for which indulgence was required, or for which allowances had to be made – that is, the kind of ephemeral poetry which is particularly common in an age of literary conformism. [Boris Leonidovich] could weep over the 'purple-gray circle' which glowed above Blok's tormented muse and he never failed to be moved by the terseness of Pushkin's sprightly lines, but rhymed slogans about the production of tin cans in the so-called 'poetry' of Surkov and his like, as well as the outpourings about love in the work of those young poets who only echo each other and the classics – all this left him cold at best and for the most part made him indignant."

For this reason, Pasternak regularly avoided literary cafes where young poets regularly invited them to read their verse. According to Ivinskaya, "It was this sort of thing that moved him to say: 'Who started the idea that I love poetry? I can't stand poetry.'"

Also according to Ivinskaya, "'The way they could write!' he once exclaimed – by 'they' he meant the Russian classics. And immediately afterwards, reading or, rather, glancing through some verse in the *Literary Gazette*: 'Just look how tremendously well they've learned to rhyme! But there's actually nothing there – it would be better to say it in a news bulletin. What has poetry got to do with this?' By 'they' in this case, he meant the poets writing today."

Translation

Reluctant to conform to Socialist Realism, Pasternak turned to translation in order to provide for his family. He soon produced acclaimed translations of Sándor Petõfi, Johann Wolfgang von Goethe, Rainer Maria Rilke, Paul Verlaine, Taras Shevchenko, and Nikoloz Baratashvili. Osip Mandelstam, however, privately warned him, "Your collected works will consist of twelve volumes of translations, and only one of your own work."

In a 1942 letter, Pasternak declared, "I am completely opposed to contemporary ideas about translation. The work of Lozinski, Radlova, Marshak, and Chukovski is alien to me, and seems artificial, soulless, and lacking in depth. I share the nineteenth century view of translation as a literary exercise demanding insight of a higher kind than that provided by a merely philological approach."

According to Ivinskaya, Pasternak believed in not being too literal in his translations, which he felt could confuse the meaning of the text. He instead advocated observing each poem from afar to plumb its true depths. Pasternak's translations of William Shakespeare (*Romeo and Juliet*, *Antony and Cleopatra*, *Othello*, *King Henry IV* (Parts I and II), *Hamlet*, *Macbeth*, *King Lear*) remain deeply popular with Russian audiences because of their colloquial, modernised dialogues. Paternak's critics, however, accused him of "pasternakizing" Shakespeare. In a 1956 essay, Pasternak wrote, "Translating Shakespeare is a task which takes time and effort. Once it is undertaken, it is best to divide it into sections long enough for the work to not get stale and to complete one section each day. In thus daily progressing through the text, the translator finds himself reliving the circumstances of the author. Day by day, he reproduces his actions and he is drawn into some of his secrets, not in theory, but practically, by experience."

According to Ivinskaya,

Whenever [Boris Leonidovich] was provided with literal versions of things which echoed his own thoughts or feelings, it made all the difference and he worked feverishly, turning them into masterpieces. I remember his translating Paul Verlaine in a burst of enthusiasm like this – *Art poétique (Verlaine)* was after all an expression of his own beliefs about poetry.

While they were both collaborating on translating Rabindranath Tagore from Bengali into Russian, Pasternak advised Ivinskaya, "1) Bring out the theme of the poem, its subject matter, as clearly as possible; 2) tighten up the fluid, non-European form by rhyming internally, not at the end of the lines; 3) use loose, irregular meters, mostly ternary ones. You may allow yourself to use assonances." Later, while she was collaborating with him on a translation of Vítìzslav Nezval, Pasternak told Ivinskaya,

"Use the literal translation only for the *meaning*, but do not borrow words as they stand from it: they are absurd and not always comprehensible. Don't translate everything, only what you can manage, and by this means try to make the translation more precise than the original – an absolute necessity in the case of such a confused, slipshod piece of work."

According to Olga Ivinskaya, however, translation was not a genuine vocation for Pasternak. She later recalled, One day someone brought him a copy of a British newspaper in which there was a double feature under the title, "Pasternak Keeps a Courageous Silence." It said that if Shakespeare had written in Russian he would have written in the same way he was translated by Pasternak... What a pity, the article continued, that Pasternak published nothing but translations, writing his own work for himself and a small circle of intimate friends. "What do they mean by saying that my silence is courageous?" [Boris Leonidovich] commented sadly after reading all this. "I am silent because I am not printed."

Music

Boris Pasternak was also a composer, and had a promising musical career as a musician ahead of him, had he chosen to pursue it. He came from a musical family: his mother was a concert pianist and a student of Anton Rubinstein and Theodor Leschetizky, and Pasternak's early impressions were of hearing piano trios in the home. The family had adacha – country house – close to one occupied by Alexander Scriabin; Sergei Rachmaninoff, Rainer Maria Rilke and Leo Tolstoy were all visitors to the family home. His father Leonid was a painter who produced one of the most important portraits of Scriabin, and Pasternak wrote many years later of witnessing with great excitement the creation of Scriabin's Symphony No. 3, "The Divine Poem", in 1903.

Pasternak began to compose at the age of 13. The high achievements of his mother discouraged him from becoming a pianist, but – inspired by Scriabin – he entered theMoscow Conservatory, but left abruptly in 1910 at the age of twenty, to study philosophy in Marburg University. Four years later he returned to Moscow, having finally decided on a career in literature, publishing his first book of poems, influenced by Alexander Blok and the Russian Futurists, the same year.

Pasternak's early compositions show the clear influence of Scriabin. His single-movement Piano Sonata of 1909 shows a more mature and individual voice. Nominally in B minor, it moves freely from key to key with frequent changes of key-signature and a chromatic dissonant style that defies easy analysis. Although composed during his time at the Conservatory, the Sonata was composed at Raiki, some 27 miles north-east of Moscow, where Leonid Pasternak had his painting studio and taught his students. (NB. This is not the site of the Pasternak family dacha, now open to the public, in the writers' colony at Peredelkino, which is about 16 miles south-west of the capital.)

HENRY REED (POET)

Henry Reed (22 February 1914 – 8 December 1986) was a British poet, translator, radio dramatist and journalist.

Background

Reed was born in Birmingham and educated at King Edward VI School, Aston, followed by the University of Birmingham. At university he associated with W. H. Auden, Louis MacNeice and Walter Allen. He went on to study for an MA and then worked as a teacher and journalist. He was called up to the Army in 1941, spending most of the war as a Japanese translator. Although he had studied French and Italian at university and taught himself Greek at school, Reed did not take to Japanese, perhaps because he had learned an almost entirely military vocabulary.

Walter Allen, in his autobiography *As I Walked down New Grub Street,* quoted Reed as saying "He intended...to devote every day for the rest of his life to forgetting another word of Japanese."

After the war he worked for the BBC as a radio broadcaster, translator and playwright, where his most memorable set of productions was the *Hilda Tablet* series in the 1950s, produced by Douglas Cleverdon. The series started with *A Very Great Man Indeed*, which purported to be a documentary about the research for a biography of a dead poet and novelist called Richard Shewin. This drew in part on Reed's own experience of researching a biography of the novelist Thomas Hardy. However, the 'twelve-tone composeress' Hilda Tablet, a friend of Richard Shewin, became the most interesting character in the play; and in the next play, she persuades the biographer to change the subject of the biography to her - telling him "not more than twelve volumes". Dame Hilda, as she later became, was based partly on Ethel Smyth and partly on Elisabeth Lutyens (who was not pleased, and considered legal action).

Reed's most famous poem is "Lessons of the War", a witty parody of British army basic training during World War II, which suffered from a lack of equipment at that time. Originally published in *New Statesman and Nation* (August 1942), the series was later published in *A Map of Verona* in 1946, and was his only collection to be published within his lifetime. Another anthologised poem is "Chard Whitlow", a satire of T. S. Eliot's *Burnt Norton*. Eliot himself was amused by "Chard Whitlow"'s mournful imitations of his poetic style ("As we get older we do not get any younger...").

Unfortunately for Reed he was forever being confused with the much better known Sir Herbert Read; the two men were unrelated. Reed responded to this confusion by naming his 'alter ego' biographer in the *Hilda Tablet* plays "Herbert Reeve" and then by having everyone else get the name slightly wrong.

The Papers of Henry Reed are kept safe at the University of Birmingham Special Collections.

KARL SHAPIRO

Karl Jay Shapiro (November 10, 1913 – May 14, 2000) was an American poet. He was appointed the fifth Poet Laureate Consultant in Poetry to the Library of Congress in 1946.

Biography

Karl Shapiro was born in Baltimore, Maryland and graduated from the Baltimore City College high school. He attended theUniversity of Virginia before World War II, and immortalized it in a scathing poem called "University," which noted that "to hate the Negro and avoid the Jew is the curriculum." He did not return after his military service.

Karl Shapiro, a stylish writer with a commendable regard for his craft, wrote poetry in the Pacific Theater while he served there during World War II. His collection *V-Letter and Other Poems*, written while Shapiro was stationed in New Guinea, was awarded thePulitzer Prize for Poetry in 1945, while Shapiro was still in the military. Shapiro was American Poet Laureate in 1946 and 1947. (At the time this title was Consultant in Poetry to the Library of Congress which was changed by Congress in 1985 to Poet Laureate Consultant in Poetry to the Library of Congress.)

Poems from his earlier books display a mastery of formal verse with a modern sensibility that viewed such topics as automobiles, house flies, and drug stores as worthy of attention. In 1963, the poet/critic Randall Jarrell praised Shapiro's work:

Karl Shapiro's poems are fresh and young and rash and live; their hard clear outlines, their flat bold colours create a world like that of a knowing and skillful neo-primitive painting, without any of the confusion or profundity of atmosphere, of aerial perspective, but with notable visual and satiric force. The poet early perfected a style, derived from Auden but decidedly individual, which he has not developed in later life but has temporarily replaced with the clear Rilke-like rhetoric of his Adam and Eve poems, the frankly Whitmanesque convolutions of his latest work. His best poem—poems like "The Leg," "Waitress," "Scyros," "Going to School," "Cadillac"—have a real precision, a memorable exactness of realization, yet they plainly come out of life's raw hubbub, out of the disgraceful foundations, the exciting and disgraceful surfaces of existence.

In his later work, he experimented with more open forms, beginning with *The Bourgeois Poet* (1964) and continuing with *White-Haired Lover* (1968). The influences of Walt Whitman, D. H. Lawrence, W. H. Auden and William Carlos Williams were evident in his work.

Shapiro's interest in formal verse and prosody led to his writing multiple books on the subject including the long poem *Essay on Rime* (1945), *A Bibliography of Modern Prosody*(1948), and *A Prosody Handbook* (with Robert Beum, 1965; reissued 2006).

His *Selected Poems* appeared in 1968. Shapiro also published one novel, *Edsel* (1971) and a three-part autobiography simply titled, "Poet" (1988–1990).

Shapiro edited the prestigious magazine, *Poetry* for several years, and he was a professor of English at the University of Nebraska, Lincoln, where he edited *Prairie Schooner*, and at the University of California, Davis, from which he retired in the mid-1980s.

His other works include *Person, Place and Thing* (1942), (with Ernst Lert) the libretto to Hugo Weisgall's opera *The Tenor* (1950), *To Abolish Children* (1968), and *The Old Horsefly* (1993). Shapiro received the 1969 Bollingen Prize for Poetry, sharing the award that year with John Berryman.

He died in New York City, aged 86, on May 14, 2000.

More recent editions of his work include *The Wild Card: Selected Poems Early and Late* (1998) and *Selected Poems* (2003). Shapiro's last work, *Coda: Last Poems,* (2008) was recently published in a volume organized posthumously by editor Robert Phillips. The poems, divided into three sections according to love poems to his last wife, poems concerning roses, and other various poems, were discovered in the drawers of Shapiro's desk by his wife two years after his death.

LEONID VYSHESLAVSKY

Leonid Vysheslavsky (Ukrainian: Ëåîí³ä Ìèêîëàéîâè÷ Âèøåñëàâñüêèé; born March 18, 1914, Nikolayev, died December 26, 2002, Kyiv) was a Soviet and Ukrainian poet, literary critic and translator. He wrote in the Russian and Ukrainian languages and published more than 60 books of poems, prose and translations. Vysheslavsky's works were published in the Ukrainian, Polish,German, French and other languages. He had supporters and friends in many countries.

Biography and creation

Leonid Vysheslavsky was born in Nikolayev 18 March 1914. His father Nikolai Vysheslavsky (1888–1979) was engineer, his mother Cleopatra Platonova (1892–1939) was the daughter of a priest. He spent his childhood in the family's maternal grandfather, a priest Harlampy Platonov, in a family with great cultural and spiritual traditions. His wife Agnessa Baltaga (1905–1991) was literary critic. Their daughter — Irina Vysheslavska — is artist, their grandson — Glib Vysheslavsky — is artist and art critic.

In his youth he was interested in futurist poets, especially Vladimir Mayakovsky, (many years later, he wrote about him literary studies). First poems he published in 1931 inKharkiv and in Moscow. He graduated from Taras Shevchenko University of Kyiv in 1938, philological department. Since 1948 until 2002 Vysheslavsky was the editor of the magazine *Raduga* (means: rainbow), (renamed in 1963 from "Soviet Ukraine").

One of the main themes in the Vysheslavsky's poetry is a flight into space, as a human contact with the Universe. After Yuri Gagarin's flight Vysheslavsky wrote several poetry books. The First Astronaut liked his poems very much and ever wrote himself introduction to one of them. Vysheslavsky had active creative life and communication with prominent contemporaries: priest Alexander Men, poets David Burliuk, Boris Pasternak, Mikola Zerov, Pavlo Tychina, Ivan Druch and other.

FRANZ WERFEL

Franz Viktor Werfel (10 September 1890 – 26 August 1945) was an Austrian-Bohemian novelist, playwright, and poet whose career spanned World War I, the Interwar period, and World War II. He is primarily known as the author of *The Forty Days of Musa Dagh* (1933, English tr. 1934, 2012), a novel based on events that took place during the Armenian Genocide of 1915, and

The Song of Bernadette (1941), a novel about the life and visions of the French Catholic saint Bernadette Soubirous, which was made into a Hollywood film of the same name.

Biography

Born in Prague (then part of the Austro-Hungarian Empire), Werfel was the first of three children of a wealthy Jewish manufacturer of gloves and leather goods, Rudolf Werfel. His mother, Albine Kussi, was the daughter of a mill owner. His two sisters were Hanna(born 1896) and Marianne Amalie (born 1899). As a child, Werfel was raised by his Czech Catholic governess, Barbara Šimunková, who often took him to mass in Prague's main cathedral. Like the children of other progressive German-speaking Jews in Prague, Werfel was educated at a Catholic school run by the Piarists, a teaching order that allowed for a rabbi to instruct Jewish students for their Bar Mitzvahs. This, along with his governess's influence, gave Werfel an early interest (and expertise) inCatholicism, which soon branched out to other faiths, including Theosophy and Islam, such that reading his fiction, as well as his nonfiction, can be an exercise in comparative religion.

Werfel began writing at an early age and, by 1911, had published his first book of poems, *Der Weltfreund*, which can be translated as "the friend to the world" as well as philanthropist, humanitarian, and the like. By this time, Werfel had befriended other German Jewish writers who frequented Prague's Café Arco, chief among them Max Brod and Franz Kafka, and his poetry was praised by such critics as Karl Kraus, who published Werfel's early poems in Kraus's journal, *Die Fackel* (The Spark). In 1912, Werfel moved to Leipzig, where he became an editor for Kurt Wolff's new publishing firm, where Werfel championed and edited Georg Trakl's first book of poetry. While he lived in Germany, Werfel's milieu grew to include Else Lasker-Schüler, Martin Buber, Rainer Maria Rilke, among other German-language writers, poets, and intellectuals in the first decades of the twentieth century.

With the outbreak of World War I, Werfel served in the Austro-Hungarian Army on the Russian front as a telephone operator. His duties both exposed him to the vicissitudes oftotal war as well as provided him with enough of a haven to continue writing Expressionist poems, ambitious plays, and letters voluminously. His strange mix of humanism,confessionalism, autobiography, as well as mythology and religiosity developed further during this time. His poems and plays ranged from scenes of ancient Egypt (notably themonotheism of Akhenaton) to occult allusions (Werfel had participated in séances with his friends Brod and Kafka) and incorporate a parable from the Bahá'í Faith in the poem "Jesus and the Carrion Path." His bias for Christian subjects, as well as his antipathy for Zionism, eventually alienated many of his Jewish friends and readers, including early champions such as Karl Kraus. Others, however, stood by him, including, Martin Buber, who published a sequence of poems from Werfel's wartime manuscript, *Der Gerichtstag*(Judgement Day, published in 1919) in his monthly journal, *Der Jude* (*The Jew*). and wrote of Werfel in his prefatory remark:

Since I was first moved by his poems, I have opened (knowing well, I should say, it's a problem) the gates of my invisible garden [*i.e.*, an imaginarium] to him, and now he can do nothing for all eternity that would bring me to banish him from it. Compare, if you will, a real person to an anecdotal one, a late book to an earlier, the one you see to you yourself; but I am not putting a value on a poet, only recognizing that he is one—and the way he is one.

In the summer of 1917, Werfel left the frontline for the Military Press Bureau in Vienna, where he joined other notable Austrian writers serving as propagandists, among themRobert Musil, Rilke, Hugo von Hofmannsthal, and Franz Blei. Through the latter, Werfel met and fell in love with Alma Mahler, widow of Gustav Mahler, the former lover of the painter Oskar Kokoschka, and the wife of the architect Walter Gropius, then serving in the Imperial German Army on the Western Front. Alma, who was also a composer, had already set one of Werfel's poems to music, reciprocated despite Werfel being much younger, shorter, and having Jewish features that she, being both anti-Semitic and attracted to Jewish men, found initially distasteful. Their love affair culminated in the premature birth of a son, Martin, in August 1918. Martin, who was given the surname of Gropius, died in May of the following year. Despite attempts to save his marriage to Alma, with whom he had a young daughter, Manon, Gropius reluctantly agreed to a divorce in 1920. Ironically, Alma refused to marry Werfel for the next nine years. However, Alma, more so than with her first two husbands and lovers, lent herself to the development of Werfel's career and influenced it in such a way that he became an accomplished playwright and novelist as well as poet. They married on 6 July 1929.

In April 1924, "Verdi - Roman der Oper" (Novel of the Opera) was published by Zsolnay Verlag, establishing Werfel's reputation as a novelist. In 1926, Werfel was awarded the Grillparzer Prize by the Austrian Academy of Sciences, and in Berlin, Max Reinhardt performed his play "Juarez and Maximilian". By the end of the decade, Werfel had become one of the most important and established writers in German and Austrian literature and had already merited one full-length critical biography.

A journey in 1930 to the Middle East and encountering starving refugees inspired his novel *The Forty Days of Musa Dagh* which drew world attention to the Armenian Genocideat the hands of the Ottoman government. Werfel lectured on this subject across Germany. The Nazi newspaper *Das Schwarze Corps* denounced him as a propagandist of "alleged Turkish horrors perpetrated against the Armenians." The same newspaper, suggesting a link between the

Armenian and the later Jewish genocide, condemned "America's Armenian Jews for promoting in the U.S.A. the sale of Werfel's book."

Werfel was forced to leave the Prussian Academy of the Arts in 1933. His books were burned by the Nazis. Werfel left Austria after the Anschluss in 1938 and went to France, where they lived in a fishing village near Marseille. Visitors to their home at this time included Bertolt Brecht and Thomas Mann. After the German invasion and occupation of France during World War II, and the deportation of French Jews to the Nazi concentration camps, Werfel had to flee again. With the assistance of Varian Fry and the Emergency Rescue Committee in Marseille, he and his wife narrowly escaped the Nazi regime, finding shelter for five weeks in the pilgrimage town of Lourdes. He also received much help and kindness from the Catholic orders that staffed the shrine. He vowed to write about the experience and, safe in America, he published *The Song of Bernadette* in 1941.

Fry organized a secret crossing over the Pyrenees on foot. They went to Madrid and then Lisbon where they boarded a ship for New York, arriving 13 October 1940. Werfel and his family settled in Los Angeles, where they met other German and Austrian emigrants, such as Mann, Reinhardt, and Erich Wolfgang Korngold. In southern California, Werfel wrote his final play, *Jacobowsky and the Colonel* (*Jacobowsky und der Oberst*) which was made into the 1958 film *Me and the Colonel* starring Danny Kaye; Giselher Klebe'sopera *Jacobowsky und der Oberst* (1965) is also based on this play. Before his death, he completed the first draft of his last novel *Star of the Unborn* (*Stern der Ungeborenen*), which was published posthumously in 1946.

Franz Werfel died in Los Angeles in 1945 and was interred there in the Rosedale Cemetery. However, his body was returned in 1975 to Vienna for reburial in theZentralfriedhof.

8

World War II as Seen through Children's Literature

My rationale for choosing this subject is found in the aim of the course itself. World War II, although enduring only four years for Americans, has played a sizable part in the history of American Children's Literature, both in itself and in its preparation and wake. There have been many books written about the war that pertain to the people who were children at the time of siege and about their coping and survival. I myself was a child during the war years and remember quite keenly that at the time my reading habits were being formed and becoming fixed.

I thought that there was very little literature then about the war and that most, if not all of it, had been written immediately after and beyond the war itself. However, Jean Wood Garrison's survey shows that over 300 books with war-related themes were published for children during World Wars I and II in England and over 400 in the United States. She categorizes her plots as follows: (a) home front, (b) home front in other countries, (c) evacuation, (d) flying, (e) sea action, (f) spies, (g) land fighting, (h) animals, (i) sabotage, (j) girls in action, (k) training and (l) miscellaneous or undetermined. Garrison found that there is no significant difference in the English and American books. She found very few books of quality and only a few that are now still in print. (Garrison, 1981)

I remember being an avid reader, consuming as it were multitudes of books in all of my spare time, that included my favourite fairy tale author/editor, Andrew Lang. I also remember reading some "romantic novels" during my literacy development, that I preferred to "tuck away" in my fancy as I grew older. This is not to say that I was ashamed of having read so many of them, but rather to hold them in a safe place in my imagination to be able to escape to from time to time. Needless to say, I, as a child during the war, was not bothered, in my quest for literacy, about the crimes and atrocities and the ultimate futility of the waste of human lives. It was not until this fellowship programme at Yale that I was made to recall that scurrilous period in my "reading trek."

My choice of topics led me to find out what other authors (different from my early authors) felt about the war through children's literature. My unit, through many studies, reviews and surveys, will show the pervasive influence of World War II on children's literature. Because I was a child during this event, I felt legitimately led to this rationale for my unit.

Marcia Shutze and Dr. Jean Greenlaw (1975) examine twenty-two books in their survey of the trends in juvenile books set during the war. The books they survey were written after the war itself into the 1970s. The authors say that books with World War II settings have increased in number since the late 1950s, beginning then and increasing throughout the 1960s into the 1970s before waning. Jane Yolen, who wrote *The Devil's Arithmetic*, points out that mass media has brought societal conflicts within everyone's immediate sight, including children. The print media has a larger readership today than ever before because more people, including children, are able to read. A change in attitude from the "Peter Pan Principle" has brought more realism to children's literature. Some of the books that I will use could be considered realistic fiction as well as historical fiction. Shutze's and Greenlaw's books are broken down into two subgroups: (1) those published in the late fifties and early sixties, and (2) those published since 1965. Authors in the first subgroup portray war poignantly and realistically, by pointing out war's horrors and tragedies.

Some significant titles in this group are: Meindert DeJong's *The House of Sixty Fathers* (1956), John Tunis' *Silence over Dunkerque (1962),* Hilda Van Stockum's *The Winged Watchman* (1962), James Forman's *The Skies of Crete* (1963), and Margaretha Shemin's *The Little Riders* (1963) and *I Never Saw Another Butterfly* (1964).

The second subgroup, those published since 1965, make the strongest war statements and do not always end on a happy note. Some titles are: John Tunis' *His Enemy, His Friend* (1967), Betty Jean Lifton's*Return to Hiroshima* (1970), and James Forman's *Ceremony of Innocence* (1970).

Betty Jean Lifton's *Return to Hiroshima* (1970) is a nonfiction book showing the effects of the atomic bomb dropped on the city on August 6, 1945. The book contains pictures, so that there is no way to escape the reality of war.

James Forman's *Ceremony of Innocence* (1970) is a work of fiction but based on factual events. Two close friends and all of Munich University's students, during the time of the war, wrote and published*White Rose* leaflets denouncing Hitler and Nazism.

Some books that do not show the horrors and cruelties of war, by not ending in death and destruction, are: Esther Hautzig's *The Endless Steppe: Growing Up in Siberia* (1973), Judith Kerr's *When Hitler Stole Pink Rabbit* (1972), Elliott Arnold's *A Kind of Secret Weapon* (1969). Here, Peter Andersen and his mother escape from the Gestapo in Denmark and begin a new life in Sweden. Erik Haugaard's *The Little Fishes* realistically portrays a picture of a war victim's life. Shutze and Greenlaw survey other books that show examples of war's maturing effect on all different types of children. James Forman's six novels are cited: *The Skies of Crete*, *Ring the Judas Bell* (1965),*Horses of Anger* (1967), *The Traitors* (1968), *My Enemy, My Brother* (1969), and *Ceremony of Innocence.*

In *Ring the Judas Bell,* Shutze and Greenlaw tell us that in postwar Greece, Nicholos and Angela, after having lost their mother to Nazi execution and being kidnapped by Andarte, the Communist guerrillas, escape from prison and lead several other youths home.

In *Horses of Anger*, fifteen-year-old Hans is helping to man an anti-aircraft tower near Munich and wondering how long it will be before he himself will be killed.

In *The Traitors*, Paul engages in subversive work against the Reich in order to save his town from destruction by the Nazis. Sixteen-year-old Daniel survives a Jewish concentration camp at the end of World War II when the story begins, so for him, childhood has already ended. Two more nationally acclaimed, award-winning books reflecting the maturing effect are Bette Greene's *Summer of My German Soldier*(1973), and Johanna Reiss' *The Upstairs Room* (1972). The latter chronicles the life of Annie, a Jewish child of six, from 1938-1945, war's end. The problems of the terror of hiding are much more vivid when seen through the eyes of a child.

In summarizing their review, Shutze and Greenlaw state that children today have available to them an excellent collection of quality books with World War II settings, which make sensitive statements about the harsh realities of War and what it does to people.

I also consulted Joan Stadium Nist's review, "Perspective on World War II" (1981). She reviews six books on World War II for two pages each, stating in her rationale that even though each of the books shares a common theme in the historic events, each author presents his/her own country and each condemns war.

She uses Alki Zei's *Petros' War.* She explains that even though this book portrays the war in Greece (a minor theater), Zei shows that no suffering or courage is minor.

In Robert Westall's *The Machine Gunners*, Nist writes that Westall realistically portrays the relationship between an enemy airman and a group of working-class youngsters. She also credits him with going beyond the conflicts of the war into the ageless conflicts between generations. "The Germans cease to be the only enemies. All the adults were a kind of enemy now." (p. 95).

Yevgeny Ryss's *Search Behind the Lines* tells of two young people in Russia, which suffered the highest casualties of any nation during the war, who hide and survive in Robinson-Crusoe-like fashion from the enemy for three years. Nist describes Ryss as a war correspondent who wrote several children's works including "Search," which became a prize-winning film in 1946, in Russia but which was not translated until 1974. Hans Peter Richter's *Friedrich*, Nist describes as autobiographical. She writes that German authors are haunted by the memory of the war because of the "degradations perpetrated by the Nazi regime." The book has an unnamed, first-person narrator and emphasizes the theme of pervasive helplessness and horror. Richter's historical chronology parallels the Third Reich and the Holocaust.

Bette Greene's *Summer of My German Soldier* is a book that I intend to use in my curriculum. Nist assesses it as "the story of a young girl seeking close relationships during her struggle to maturity." Greene adds Anti-Semitism to the mix. Patty is a Jew, who comes to be called "Jew Nazi" (p. 160) when she befriends the German prisoner, Anton. Yet the book does not reflect military action.

Bel Ria, by Sheila Burnford, is a book that shows more scenes of the war's devastation and destruction than do the others in Nist's discussion. Bel Ria is a dog which several characters in the book credit for their survival. Burnford shows that throughout the book, he has been an "innocent... caught up in man's lethal affairs" (p. 198), sharing the suffering in the desecration of war."

Nist feels that World War II gains deeper dimension and scope when children are able to read stories from their own background as well as those written for children of another country, especially those reflecting that nation's perspective on the conflict.

David L. James (1977) offers a review of recent books on World War II in his survey. He bemoans the fact that so many writers are reluctant to "probe the troublesome, psychological and spiritual questions that war should provoke." Of the fourteen books that he reviews, he chooses two for detailed discussion: Robert Westall's *The Machine Gunners,* and Nina Bowden's *Carrie's War*.

Robert Westall says of *The Machine Gunners* that he is preoccupied with the way the violence is kept in check. A group of children salvage a working machine-gun from a crashed Heinkel. With the help of a surviving German airman, whom they are holding hostage, they get it working and use it against a Polish corps which they mistake for German invaders. The battle ruins many adult reputations and the airman is seriously wounded.

James does not feel that Westall has sufficiently shown how people keep their violence in check. He feels that we are being asked to salute physical courage in the book. At the end the two fathers admire their sons' courage.

In Nina Bowden's *Carrie's War*, James feels that the author makes a serious comment on violence without really trying. Carrie Willow, the character, is developing an awareness of other people's mystery and misery. He cites two scenes in the book, the hay making scene in which Frederick Evans taunts Mr. Johnny and is in turn attacked with a pitchfork, and Carrie's farewell to Mr. Evans who tells her his unhappy love story. The other books are discussed briefly. In Jill Paton Walsh's *The Dolphin Crossing*, two boys eager to serve the nation defy their parents and assist in Dunkirk's epic evacuation. John Aston, who initially protects Pat Riley from prejudice and insults, has a brother who is a conscientious objector. This further complicates the plot.

Hester Burton's *In Spite of All Terror* also deals with the retreat from Dunkirk. Jill Paton Walsh's *Fireweed* again deals with two children who escape their parents to accomplish daring deeds. James applauds Walsh's historical recreation, at the children's level, of the London Blitz.

Susan Cooper's *Dawn of Fear* develops the idea of a local squabble between rival groups going on beneath the German bombing of London.

Willi Fahrmann's *The Year of the Wolves* tells of the end of the war in rural East Prussia. James thinks that it is admirable the way this German novel owns up to its nation's complicity in the extermination of the Jews. "None of us raised our voice in protest. We're glad we're not going there (to the... "camps"). Our silence is our sin."

Yuri Suhl's book, *Uncle Mischa's Partisans,* confirms prejudice. The wife of a German officer hypocritically defends her Jew-hating husband, who, as a German officer, has spent his life plundering Jewish homes.

Noel Streatfield's *When the Siren Wailed* tells a story of bombing and evacuation, but is steeped in class stereotypes and snobbery. Pygmalion-like.

Sylvia Sherry's *Dark River, Dark Mountain* takes place in wartime Britain. An aura of mystery and confusion is created when crews are used to change signposts and remove milestones to confound the potential invader. This is a revealing study in national and personal paranoia.

Penelope Lively's *Going Back* is a story told retrospectively about a brother and sister who substitute the place, Medleycott, for their remote father. Both children run away to a Commanding Officer, whom the father has dismissed earlier. The book ends with Edward, the boy, dying in the Korean War.

Peggy Woodford's *Backwater War* book set in the Channel Islands has as its theme the moral issue of collaboration or resistance. There are many instances of heroism. Morgenstein is partly English and hates the leader but feels he must fight for his country anyway. He finds himself with men whose attitudes and opinions are so anti-human that he shudders.

Nathaniel Benchley's *Bright Candle* tells about the Danish resistance. The author did a lot of research and uses long historical explanations of the Maginot Line etc. The Danish underground movement is sabotaging Nazi-sponsored industry. There is a lot of action and little sympathy for the enemy.

In Mara Kay's *Storm Warning,* an English girl smuggles a Jewish family out of Nazi Germany. She finds that her friend Eleonore is really a Nazi agent who betrays her own Jewish mother. The last episode is the final car journey taking concealed Jews to freedom in Switzerland. Kay's method of conveying the political background by long lectures on the economic position of Germany and her attitude towards Jews is subtly done.

Betsy Hearne (1980) gives an overview of United States children's literature. She feels that since the United States was neither an occupied country nor a battleground during World War II, the flavour of the fiction published here is different. There are almost twice as many non-fiction books describing military, political and social events as there are fiction books about individual experiences.

She mentions that *Petros' War*, *Fly Away Home*, *The Diary of Anne Frank*, and others have been absorbed into United States Literature. Other sources of first-hand experience on the war front come from refugees who escaped to America and have written of their ordeals. Authentic stories of personally known situations are: *The Survivor,* which chronicles the deaths of all but one Dutch Jewish family, and *On the Other Side of the Gate,* which tells of Jewish resistance to persecution in Poland. Hearne says that these are not necessarily autobiographical, but carefully researched war-time situations.

There are also stories of the non-immigrant Americans' experience of World War II; soldiers at the battle front and those who waited and worked on the home front. *Alan and Naomi*, and *The Summer of My German Soldier* focus on the victims of the war, but none so poignantly as Uchida's *Journey to Topaz* which tells of the United States government's mistreatment of Japanese Americans in internment camps. Most of the home front stories feature the war as a backdrop. Such books as *Make Me a Hero*, *Autumn Street*, and *Hut School and the War Time Home-Front Heroes* reveal in varied degrees the involvement and understanding of American youth at that time.

Hearne says that few children's books have glorified the war but there seem to be three kinds of juvenile literature written about World War II. The first is written by people who have experienced some phase of it, but are not skilled in writing about it. The second is written by people who have no first-hand experience about the war but know how to write a story. The third is written by a person with first-hand experience and knowledge of how to craft a story. The last kind brings the war waged half-way around the world painfully close to home. Hearne also says that it is extremely important that children experience the human cost of war through literature. Each classroom history assignment should include not just names and events but the reality of separation, death, and the destruction that disfigures the true face of war. "Students drawn by tanks, airplanes and battle strategies can realize through some of these books, the difference between toy history and personal tragedy." Hearne feels that that understanding is crucial to those who hold future peace in their hands.

In 1979 and 1980, the journal *Bookbird* published a series of brief essays under the general title "World War II Reflected in Children's Books" (Kaminski, et al., 1979 and 1980): Kaminski (1979) writes that there is a considerable amount of literature for young people informing them about World War II. She has included books that by their narrative have influenced the reader; books that give the impression that when the Germans had to flee, the misery then began. Her selection of books came about because she felt moved to include them, not only because they met her standards but also because they should still be available.

Lucia Binder (1979) says that reading materials for Austrian children have always been influenced by the German book market. In 1938 when Austria was incorporated into the Third Reich, a change came about. Two characteristic books of the time aimed at winning over young people for Hitler are *Hitler Boy* and *Quex and Austrian Girl*. Binder says that not even first graders were spared from propaganda. Binder tells of her own experience of having won a photo book as a prize and visiting Hitler in Bavaria and giving him a kiss. She remembers being the envy of the entire class.

The first Austrian book of the war was set in Japan *The Day of the Bomb*. Then a number of books from other countries came to Austria. She says the first book about the war set in Austria did not appear until 1965 (*The Net of Shadows* by Kathe Recheis). It dealt with the dissolution of the Austrian concentration camp for Jews. Binder feels that Austrian books have made the contribution of "arousing reader interest and making them knowledgeable" about the war.

Sheila Ray (1979) looks at British books that were written forty years after the beginning of the war and are still available today and also books that were written from 1939-1945. She lists several books already mentioned: Streatfield's *The Children of Primrose Lane* (1941); (1967-1973) Walsh's *The Dolphin Crossing* (1967); *Burton's In Spite of Terror* (1968); and Turner's *Dunkirk Summer* (1973). Ray says that much of her understanding of the real war issues came from the "Chalet" books (*Chalet School in Exile*, and *The Chalet School Goes to It*). She writes of the objectivity of Westall's *The Machine Gunners* (1975) and Nina Bowden's *Carrie's War* (1973). She feels that British writers of the 1960s and 1970s have set their stories during World War II because (1) they can vividly recall what it was like to be a child during that period, (2) "it" provides a useful catalyst for an interesting story and (3) they want to show today's children the realities of war, both its issues and its horrors.

Genevieve Humbert (1980) attempts an analysis of the abundant war material for young French people. She discusses in detail a few books and lists their goals in a three-fold category: (1) they aim to acquaint the youth of today with a part of the national history so that they can better understand the present-day situation (2) these books describe the war's atrocities without overly dramatizing them (3) they can teach the reader what the German Philosopher Ernst Bloch called the "Prinzip Hoffnung," hope.

Yoshiko Kogochi (1980) breaks his books down into these categories: A) Early works (4 books), produced fifteen years after the war: *Harp of Burma*,

Twenty-Four Eyes, *Yuri and the Little People*, and*Captain Bamboo-Grass-Boat* which gives a picture of a group of boys who had to tackle life on their own at that time; B) The Atomic Bomb and the Air Raids (11 books); C) Evacuation of Children and Other Themes (6 books). *Journey to Topaz*, one of these six books, tells the story of Yuki, a Japanese-American citizen of California who is sent to a concentration camp when war breaks out between the United States and Japan. (p. 13).

Mary Jean Laubenfels' 1975 dissertation was "A Study of the Theme of War in Selected Literature for Junior High Readers (1940-1975)." The main purpose of her study was to examine juvenile books on the theme of war. "If war is to be rejected as an unthinkable reaction to group conflicts, then it is vital that the present generation of school children be informed as to the vast tragedy and suffering it has caused." She finds that early adolescence, grades seven to nine, is optimum for studying social concepts such as war and peace and contemporary literature on the theme of war. Her dissertation is six chapters long.

This Fellowship programme has enhanced my curriculum immensely. I will now be able to introduce much more literature to my students. Those who are non-readers and those who are super-readers will all benefit from the prose, stories, novels, and films. I have done a lot of research and have found many authors, both American and foreign, who use World War II as a background for their books. The research will help me to teach subjects across the curriculum. My unit, however, will focus primarily on the American books which I have included in my bibliography.

Since I teach Reading/Language Arts, Mathematics, Science, and Social Studies every day, I will have the opportunity to use many books. My students will be able to critique such books. They will be able to orate. They will learn the essence of story-writing; the how and the why stories are written. They will also learn about author's styles. They will be introduced to some classic literature within the genre.

I cannot think of a better subject to use in order to teach my students. I have often told them that from kindergarten to third grade "they learn to read and from fourth grade on, they read to learn." There is no more effective or more appropriate tool to use in order to bring them into the realm of beautiful literature. It could be an easy and delightful task to use Historical Fiction, and the many cultures that Multicultural/International literature offer, especially, to teach Social Studies. Traditional Literature (including the Classics), Modern Fantasy, Realistic Fiction and Non-Fiction also offer a plethora of learning opportunities and enjoyment. Even Music and Art could be intertwined with Children's Literature. I have studied Children's Literature before and will welcome the chance to develop and use this curriculum unit in my classroom.

I intend to use all of the books in my bibliography, eventually. Some are stories of actual war experiences and some are well written fabrications. I have chosen four books to critique here, fully, and to use simultaneously with the videos that I have been able to secure. Two of the books take place in Europe, one totally in the United States and one in the Dutch West Indies. *Stepping on the Cracks* by Mary Downing Hahn takes place in the United States. Lois Lowry's *Number the Stars*, and Jane Yolen's *The Devil's Arithmetic* take place in Europe, and Theodore Taylor's *The Cay* takes place in the Dutch West Indies. These are all stories that are happening because of and during the war. Some of my objectives will be to provide students not only with bibliography, videos, maps, and tapes, but also with study guides with easy-to-follow lessons on mediation skills and realistic cases that they can mediate; creative problem solving activities; and reproducible pages with activities to accompany the selections on peace. The value of my unit will be seen in the achievement of my objectives.

Students will study some of the reasons for the war, its outcomes and the fallout. They will write book reports, reenact battles, and talk of legislative controls and the governments involved. They will research the way that things might have been changed or had different results. Some of the fun ideas will be learning of and discovering the fashions, foods, temperaments, and economics of the time.

The study of World War II can be used, as I said, across the curriculum. In doing so, students will have the opportunity to study technology. My research has provided ample material for them to do so. There are more than enough resources. Even if used broadly, it will probably take years to completely finish the unit. My critiques follow.

Stepping on the Cracks (1991), is an autobiographical, historical novel by Mary Downing Hahn. In 20 chapters, Hahn relates what she remembers about the war time when she is only a child, in first-person narration. The book opens with Margaret Baker and her best friend trying to fend off a bully, Gordy Smith. Gordy is constantly taunting them. He seems not to care that they are girls. It is during the war time and both heroines have a brother in the service. Even though American children have not been directly exposed to war, Hahn parallels the "war" with Gordy with the real event, happening at that time.

The girls are constantly thinking of ways to outdo Gordy and ways in which to make him keep his distance. Gordy's story starts to unfold when they follow him into the woods one day and find that he is visiting Stuart, his older brother who is supposedly in the army. Hahn portrays him as a conscientious objector, who runs away from the armed services because of his belief. He is hiding in the woods, apparently afraid to return home to a tyrannical father. They discover too, that Gordy probably behaves the way that he does because of the father. The father is always drinking and abusive to the mother, children and pet.

Gordy, fiercely loyal to his brother, is helping to hide him and has been visiting him as often as he can. The situation probably would have gone on for a much longer period of time if Stuart had not become ill. The girls begin to feel a little pity for Gordy after seeing how poorly his father treats him. They try to help with Stuart, but as he seems to be getting worse, they decide to tell an adult and get some real help. Stuart goes to Barbara's for a while, and there he mends. Her parents do not know that he is AWOL. Barbara decides not to tell them. Elizabeth's father is a policeman and the girls want him to know how Mr. Smith is so that he can arrest him. Mrs. Baker tells her daughter Margaret, our story teller, that only Mrs. Smith can have Mr. Smith arrested. She does when Stuart returns home and is almost beaten to death by his father.

The story ends happily, with Barbara and Stuart getting married and Mr. Smith being arrested. Despite all of the nuances, when Hahn weaves in bits and pieces of the war, the girls call Stuart a "deserter." Mrs. Baker cannot believe that Margaret would help a deserter, while her brother is fighting for our country and ultimately gives his life for it. Hahn keeps the war at a distance in her story. That is the way she sees it, as a child. She has a way of weaving in domestic problems; Gordy's bullying others, Mrs. Smith being a battered wife, poor whites in a middle-class neighbourhood. The war seems to be the thread tying the book together. The death of the heroine's brother is as close as the harshness of the war ever comes. The town is still concerned with its domestic problems; the children at school, etc. The interweaving of the war into the lives of the townspeople is subtly done. In this way, the almost perfect balance of this fictional town is never upset. The war is seen through the eyes of a child, (our narrator).

In the Newbery Award winning book, *Number the Stars* (1989), Lois Lowry tells of a family in occupied Denmark who help their Jewish friends escape to Sweden and safety. Annemarie Johansen and Ellen Rosen are best friends during the Nazi occupation of Denmark. The Germans are "relocating" Jews and the war is brought home to the children in the book when Jews start disappearing. When Ellen's mother and father disappear, she is told that they have gone away for a while and she has to stay with the Johansen's. As it turns out, each member of the Johansen family plays a part in the Danish Resistance movement which helps the Rosens escape to Sweden and safety. Annemarie's family hide Ellen "in plain sight" as one of their children, when the Nazis come to check for Jews. It is not revealed until the end of the book that the older Johansen sister has also been a member of the Resistance.

Annemarie and her mother go to visit Annemarie's uncle. Suddenly, people gather as if at a wake, for an aunt which Annemarie has never heard of. Mother has made a basket of lunch for her fisherman brother, who is sailing Jews to freedom. It is very exciting and informative to find out that hidden in the lunch basket are hankies, doused with a chemical that dulls the senses of the German police dogs, so that they can not sniff out the Jews hidden in the fishing fleet waiting to sail to freedom.

The family is right in the middle of the war. We see it through the eyes of the children. It is Annemarie who goes through the forest at night, risking being caught and found out by the Nazis. Her mother has sprained her ankle on the trip back from her brother's fishing boat. When almost at the clearing leading to the boat where her uncle awaits, Annemarie is stopped by three Germans and her basket searched. The fact that she does not know that she is carrying contraband is probably significant in her success. The Germans who stop her have dogs. They take each item out of her basket and either offer it or actually feed it to the dogs. When they come to the hankies, which Annemarie's mother has wrapped in a napkin, they make a joke about the uncle throwing them back into the basket. She leaves the discarded items with the dogs or on the ground and runs on to give her uncle the basket, just in time before he sets sail. There are enough drug-soaked hankies for all the other fishing boats.

Lowry treats the war in her book in a very dignified fashion. There are no atrocities seen. As Shutze and Greenlaw (1975) say, the further away we move from the war, the less it is written about. However, Lowry's coverage is realistic. I think that "Number" fits into Shutze and Greenlaw's subgroup number two.

The Cay by Theodore Taylor is a nineteen-chapter book of fiction that deals with the war in the Dutch West Indies. The book won the Jane Addams Children's Book Award when it was published in 1969. It can be considered realistic fiction of Shutze and Greenlaw's subgroup number two. The story takes place in February, 1942. It starts on the island of Curacao, the largest of the Dutch islands just off the coast of Venezuela, where Phillip, our narrator lives. Phillip is an eleven-year-old boy, whose father works in a refinery for lake oil tankers.

When the big British Tanker, S.S. Empire Tern, is torpedoed, Phillip's mother, Grace, decides to take him home to the United States (Norfolk, VA). They leave the patriotic father behind and sail for home on the S.S.Hato, a small Dutch freighter. Two days after leaving Panama, they are torpedoed. Something happens to the life boats and Phillip and Grace find themselves in the water.

They are near each other but Phillip loses consciousness when a heavy piece of debris hits him on the head. When he awakens, he finds himself on a raft with only one other person, a huge Negro, named Timothy, and a cat. Timothy tells him, in his West Indian accent, that he thinks that Phillip's mother is probably safe on a raft like theirs. After a couple of days, Phillip goes blind, having had a delayed reaction to the bump on the head when the ship had sunk. Timothy takes care of him and Stew Cat until they sight land and drift into the cay, a small island with no inhabitants. Here Phillip, Timothy and Stew Cat survive for several weeks. Timothy teaches Phillip how to take care of himself.

They build a shelter and lay white rocks out on the beach so that they might be rescued. They store berries and fish. Timothy has taught Phillip how to fish and to keep time by dropping a pebble in a can, daily. A couple of times airplanes fly over the cay but do not see their "H E L P" sign. They go on with their daily routines until a furious hurricane kills Timothy and slashes away most of their home. Phillip manages to survive (after having been saved by Timothy), clumsily, until he and Stew Cat are rescued. He has survived, even though blind, from April until late August. The war, after the torpedoing of the ship, seemingly has no connection to them, although it is probably the reason that they are not picked up sooner. This is realistic fiction at its best, but with the war being seen through the eyes of an eleven-year-old and old Timothy. At the end of the war, Phillip's father, not being needed anymore at the Royal Dutch Shell Company, takes the family (mother and son) away from Curacao. Phillip has three operations on his eyes and although he has to wear glasses, he is grateful for having regained his sight. He vows to revisit the cays to try to find the lonely little cay where Timothy is buried.

This is truly a poignant story, which happens because of World War II. Once the war events are set in the Dutch West Indies, we are no longer concerned about it except for an occasional reference to it by Phillip's parents and friends. He has grown up on the island while trying to stay alive. I agree with Shutze and Greenlaw when they say that the war has a maturing effect on children who live through it. This is a realistic experience that Phillip has to go through away from his family. While they have their own problems, we are not told that they are survivors until the very end of the book.

This is a delightful book to read. I think that fifth grade students will have a lot to identify with even though most of them have not had to live through a war. Phillip also brings a lot of cultural "baggage" with him. Society has already taught him to look, even at his tender age, disdainfully on Timothy, whom he immediately assigns to the same class of people that he has seen hanging around the docks at home. His scorn is short-lived, however, when he realizes that he has to depend on this person for his very survival. He, slowly at first, tries to scoff at Timothy and "puts him down" with every phrase and thought. But Taylor weaves these two lives together so tightly, that Phillip begins to depend on Timothy as he has his own father. As we read, we feel, vicariously, that these two are becoming closer and closer. The war is only a distant background. I recommend this book as a brilliantly-written piece of historical as well as realistic fiction. It certainly will be one of my curriculum items next year.

The Devil's Arithmetic, a novel by Jane Yolen, was published in 1988 by Viking Kestrel. As a piece of realistic and historical fiction, it falls into the Shutze, Greenlaw subgroup number two. The book depicts the Holocaust, time travel and fantasy. Hannah, a twelve-year-old Jew, resents all of the ceremony attached to the traditional Passover feast and celebration. At one of the holiday gatherings when she is selected to symbolically open the door for the prophet Elijah's entrance, she finds herself transported back in time to another place. She is in Nazi-occupied Poland, known by another name (Chaya) and very uncomfortable. While she is attending the wedding of a member of her new "time" family, Germans herd the entire wedding party, guests and others into box cars, which have no windows or any other kind of ventilation, and take them to concentration camps.

There, unspeakable horrors and atrocities are done to them. The war is an everyday experience for this young girl. They are branded. The stronger ones of the group try to support the frailer ones. They are starved and brutalized. The children are allowed to survive by one German officer, if they agree to run into the rotted, sloppy garbage dump and hide in the muck, while Jews are being chosen for extermination. The situation of course, reminds me of the biblical Jews in Egypt, who are also scathed and mistreated. Pharaoh, having been given every message and chance to mend his ways, refuses them all, while still chastising the Jews. They are tattooed, for life, not only physically, but mentally as well. The scars never heal.

Hannah and her family do not realize at first, what is happening. It gradually comes to them when they are let out of the box cars, and herded together behind barbed-wire fences and given one piece of clothing apiece with no shoes, that they have been abducted and placed in "camps." They are all cold and hungry. Yolen exemplifies that spirit which the war seems to develop in them, that helps them to survive. Her little village of people are prime examples of the victims of the Holocaust. After several months, Chaya (Hannah) finally escapes from the camp and the "time warp" to return to contemporary time and home, now a person full of respect for the traditions of her race. Even though there are many heart-rending events in the book and the war is recounted on practically every page, it is an interesting study in courage. I think that this will be an excellent book to have my fifth grade class read and study. It should lead to some very active research on World War II.

Yolen, who gave her children English names as well as Hebrew ones, wants them always to remember the Holocaust. She feels that she comes from a typical "blended" American family, which means that they are a product of dis-memorification, which they prize so highly, but she states that some things should not be forgotten. The Holocaust is one of them.

The book list in my bibliography is long and I will have enough material for more than one curriculum, but doing a thorough job will not only stretch out the curriculum, but also have a more lasting effect.

There are several videos and films, described below, that I will use in my unit. The fifteen *Crucial Turning points of World War II* are highlighted in detail in three Reader's Digest films; five on land, five by sea and five by air. *The*

Diary of Anne Frank, and *Schindler's List* are movies starring famous actors. *Sink the Bismarck*, and *Survivors of the Holocaust* are documentaries that I found and am sure will be of great value.

LAND: FIVE CRUCIAL TURNING POINTS IN THE WAR

1. Hitler was trying to take the Kremlin and the Volga at the same time. Russia had learned not to defend exposed places. Hitler's determination to take both at once gave Russia time to regroup. When Hitler was ready, so was Russia. The Russian winter set in and the Germans were put on the defensive for the rest of the war.
2. If the Guadalcanal airstrip was successfully taken by the Japanese, Australia would be vulnerable to attack by Japan. The allies chased the Japanese away and took over the airstrip. The Japanese, however, came back to fight at Iron Bottom Sound. While allies unloaded their supplies, the Japanese had time to regroup. Luckily, the marines had an early warning system by Australian and native coast watchers, so they were able, if only barely, to get away. Henderson Field was the crucial prize. Six thousand Japanese were again turned back by the allies.

   Admiral Bull Halsey was appointed to crush Japanese naval support. November 12-15, 1942 was the fiercest battle. Halsey crushed the Japanese navy and won the island of Guadalcanal. Five thousand Japanese tried again in their last ditch effort to regain the island but were annihilated by American airmen.

   Had we not taken Guadalcanal, the Japanese could have extended their domination of the Pacific to Australia and the United States might never have been able to push them back.
3. In North Africa, Erwin Rommel, the Desert Fox, was appointed to seal off the Mediterranean from the allies. Morocco, Libya, Algeria, and Tunisia were Hitler's. The British had Egypt and nearby Gibraltar. General Dwight D. Eisenhower led our invasion, called "Operation Torch." It was successful. British General Bernard Law Montgomery (Monty to his men) was appointed by Winston Churchill. The success of the invasion gained us needed experience and opened the back door to Hitler's Europe. Rommel's illness gave Montgomery a good chance to win El Alamein. This was the pivot point of the North African war campaign.

   Rommel asked Hitler for fresh troops, but Hitler's distraction with Russia made him deny Rommel. This was a mistake and a third turning point of the war. As German officers surrendered, America prepared to enter the war. "Operation Torch" was America's North African theatre (Algiers, French Morocco near Casablanca and Iran).

The American army approached from the north and the British army from the south. If successful, they could squeeze the German army out of North Africa. We lost, however, and the Germans broke through Kasserine, but their troops and supplies were depleted. They withdrew. Now Germany had a two-front war to fight.

4. General Eisenhower led "Operation Overlord," which culminated on June 6, 1944, D-Day! The British had its Armada. America was creating, each month, one hundred forty ships, two thousand five hundred tanks, fifteen thousand jeeps, and eight thousand airplanes. With all of this, the success lay in keeping the Germans guessing. General George Patton's "Operation Fortitude" was the hoax that led the Germans to believe that the invasion would take place at Pas de Calais, the narrowest part of the Channel. Patton kept himself visible. Dummy tanks and trucks were placed throughout England to complete the deception. The invasion took place on the five beaches of Normandy; Gold, Juno, Sword, Omaha, and Utah. Hitler, convinced that the invasion would be at Calais, delayed his decision to move for seven hours. This was a pivotal point in the war.
5. Iwo Jima was General Douglas MacArthur's and Admiral Chester Nimitz's war theatre. Mount Suribachi was strategic to Tokyo.The Japanese army, led by General Tatabishi Kuribayashi, entrenched itself inside the mountain. After only four days of battle, Old Glory was raised. The Japanese were prepared to fight to the death, but flame throwers were used. More than five thousand marines were lost in thirty-six days of battle, but of twenty-two thousand Japanese, only one thousand survived. Kuribayashi's body was never found.

SEA: FIVE CRUCIAL TURNING POINTS IN THE WAR

1. England's fleet had to have one million tons of supplies by ship each month.

   German U-Boats plagued the fleet. During the Battle of the Atlantic, Merchant Marines brought fifty-five million tons of their yearly supplies to Britain. The Graf Spee hunted allied ships and was successful until it was attacked off the coast of Uruguay by four small British ships. Captain Hans Leinsdorf scuttled the ship and killed himself.

   Admiral Karl Dernitz asked for extra U-Boats. Hitler refused, so Dernitz used what he had. Forty-one British supply ships were sunk by German mines and U-Boats. Hitler was building ships in France. British supplies were cut off, so they started sailing in convoy to avoid detection. U-Boats then hunted the seas in wolf-packs. Churchill asked Roosevelt for help. The Lend-lease act was born. Through the

Atlantic Charter, Great Britain and America protected the Atlantic together. Two hundred forty-nine of the three hundred U-Boats that Dernitz had originally asked for were made. America was turning out three ships a day. Fifteen hundred in all were made. American ships were being made faster than the Germans could sink them. Ninety-two ships were sunk off the coasts of Boston, New York City, Washington D.C., and Miami. Twenty-five ships were sunk off the coast of Florida because residents fearing that their tourist trade would be hurt, refused to turn off their lights. The war had actually been brought to our shores. This is a little-known fact.

Finally, in 1942, "Enigma," the German code, was broken. Sonar enabled us to pinpoint German U-Boats. Airships destroyed U-Boats with two depth charges called "Hedgehogs" and "Squibbs." Some German captains surrendered their U-Boats rather than risk capture. The German Kriegsmarine had been beaten.

2. The Battle of the Coral Sea introduced "Carrier" warfare. Moresby Port had to be captured by the Japanese if the United States was to be stopped from using Australia as an ally. United States' intelligence broke the Japanese code. This was a turning point in the war. The Lexington and Yorktown carriers were used. The Japanese used dive bombers, fighters and torpedo planes. In the battle, the Lexington was sunk, but the Yorktown was saved. After that the Japanese called off the attack. No battleship salvoes were fired.

3 The film shows our and the Japanese Imperial Navy's power at Midway. Admirals Nimitz, Spruance and Fletcher were used on their carriers, Hornet, Enterprise and Yorktown. Because the United States had broken the Japanese code, Americans were ready for the attack. The Japanese, however, mistakenly launched a second attack. This mistake was a turning point in the war. American carriers sank three Japanese carriers. The Yorktown was unfortunate this time and sank. The last Japanese carrier, Hiryu, was sunk, but Admiral Izaroku Yamamoto's defeat was hidden from the Japanese people. At Midway the Americans avenged Pearl Harbour.

4. General MacArthur and Admiral Nimitz fought in the Philippines at Leyte Gulf. If the Japanese lost the Philippines, they would also lose their oil supply in the Dutch East Indies. They used decoys, but America launched its battle on Leyte in October. Our aircraft shot down one third of the inexperienced Japanese pilots. The Princetown was sunk, but so was a Japanese battleship. Japanese Admiral Kurita called off the attack and fled, fearing that he was headed for a trap. MacArthur had, as he had promised, come back.

5 The Japanese Kamikazes fought in the battle of Okinawa. Under

General Mitsuru Ushijima, they engaged the United States carriers Intrepid, Franklin, and Wasp. General Buckner was asked to call off the attack to save our threatened supplies. Japanese General Isamu Cho, assistant to Ushijima, as a last ditch effort, asked Ushijima to counter attack to regain lost ground. This mistake was a turning point of the war. Japanese aircraft ran out. Cho's attack had left the battleships unprotected and exposed to our artillery fire. Okinawa was the last battle. Ushijima committed harakiri.

Air: Five crucial turning points in the war

1. The German Luftwaffe air force fought the Battle of Britain. The RAF was in top condition. General Hermann Goering had the fast Messerschmitts. The British Hawker Hurricane and the Spitfire were slower than the Messerschmitts. British radar, however, could locate the Germans before they could attack. The British won the first battle. The RAF destroyed the German air force two to one. An accidental bombing of London on August 24, 1940, was a pivotal point in the war. The RAF in turn bombed Berlin. Churchill was goading Hitler into attacking London so that the RAF could have time to regroup. The Blitz was a success. The RAF had refreshed, repaired and regrouped. Well-rested RAF Spitfire pilots engaged Messerschmitts over London and won. The invasion was canceled because the Germans could not launch an attack before the Channel became impassable by winter.
2. The point of Lieutenant Colonel James Doolittle's Raid was to use a carrier to launch bombers. It was thought that the carrier runway would be too short. He and Admiral Mark Mitcher, commander of the Hornet, used the Hornet and Yorktown to get near Japan. However, surprise was destroyed so the bombers were launched five hundred miles earlier than planned. Sixteen bombers led the attack. They landed in China. This was one turning point of the war.
3. The battle for the sky over Europe was fought by the United States B-17's, the Flying Fortress and Germany's speedy Focke-Wulf. Production of the P-47 Thunderbolt and the P-51 Mustang was stepped up. These gave the allied bombers protection and shot down more than four hundred German fighter planes. Allied control of the air led to control on the ground.
4. Carrier war waged. "The Great Marianas Turkey Shoot" was the name given to the battle that American airmen won near Japan. The B-29's could carry more payloads, but an airstrip was needed near Japan. Admiral Mark Mitcher had an armada of fifteen aircraft carriers. They landed at Saipan. Japanese Admiral Jisaburu Ozawa said, "The

fate of the empire rests with us." Inexperienced Japanese pilots were put in the air. The Mitsubishi Zero was outdated. United States pilots commanded the sky with the Hellcat fighter planes. Dozens of Japanese planes were downed in minutes. Admiral Ozawa launched his third and fourth wave of planes into the meat grinder, believing that the first and second waves had gone on to refuel. That mistake was the pivotal point of the battle. Two Japanese carriers were also sunk. Only twenty United States airplanes were shot down. Eighty more ran out of fuel and were ditched. The capture of the Marianas was a turning point.

5. Roosevelt died three weeks before the collapse of Nazi Germany, with the Atomic Bomb secret. Now Iwo Jima, Okinawa and the Marianas could be used to launch B-29s to crush Japanese industry and morale. The allied invasion was launched. Japan knew that she could not win the war but she would not give up. Children were used as human bombs and women were given sharpened bamboo sticks to ward off allies. At Oak Ridge, under Brigadier General Leslie Grove, Americans were working on "The Manhattan Project," creating the bomb. The bomb, called "Fat Man," was detonated in New Mexico for practice. The Japanese rejected the "Potsdam Agreement."

Colonel Paul Tibbets, in the "Enola Gay," dropped "little boy" on Hiroshima. Japan still did not surrender. The second target was Kokura, but since it was obscured by clouds, Nagasaki was chosen. Japan surrendered on August 15, 1945. On September 8, 1945, General MacArthur presided over the surrender.

The Diary of Anne Frank is a movie that was produced by George Stevens in 1959. It was an academy award winning film in black and white, in two parts that ran for 170 minutes. A thirteen-year-old girl chronicles the lives of two Jewish families hiding from the Nazis in a cramped, tiny attic in Amsterdam. She and seven others struggle to survive for two years with Hitler's sirens in the streets below as a constant reminder that his army is always waiting. Anne's inquisitive mind and unceasing belief in the future transcend their tragic confinement. The film is a profound presentation of the human spirit. It has been a moving and uplifting movie for generations. It is one that I will be able to adapt easily to my unit.

Schindler's List is a Steven Spielberg movie also in two parts. It is a more recent presentation of the Holocaust that took place during World War II. It is a black and white film with some colour segments. It runs for three hours and seventeen minutes. It was made in 1993 and presents the indelible, true story of the enigmatic Oskar Schindler. Schindler is a member of the Nazi Party, a womanizer and war profiteer who manages to save more than eleven hundred Jews during the Holocaust. It is the triumph of one man who made a difference and the drama of those who survived one of the darkest periods in human history because of what he did.

Sink the Bismarck is a documentary that I viewed recently on television. The Bismarck was a huge German Battleship that plagued the Atlantic, sinking as many British ships as it could. So successful was this "seemingly" unsinkable craft in its devastation on the high seas that the battle cry became, "Sink the Bismarck!" The ship ruled the Atlantic in early 1941. When it was sunk in May, only one hundred fifteen crewmen out of more than two thousand survived. Thinking that they were going to be attacked again, the British ship that was taking on the prisoners left over eight hundred in the ocean to drown while they sailed to safety. The British captain, Hood, finally felt avenged when the Bismarck went down. The sinking was the beginning of the end of "battleship war." Air battle power took over and aircraft carriers became the demons of the sea.

Survivors of the Holocaust is an historic documentary which chronicles the events of Shoah (Holocaust) as witnessed by those who survived. The programme weaves together archival footage and an original music score with survivors' personal testimonies and photographs, chronicling life in prewar Europe, the devastating impact of Nazism, the liberation of the concentration camps, and life fifty years later. As survivors relive their stories on camera, many for the first time, those who watch can not come away without being deeply affected.

It was the profound impact of the survivors' stories that prompted Steven Spielberg to establish "Survivors of the Shoah Visual History Foundation," a non-profit effort to videotape tens of thousands of these precious accounts and make them available for education around the world.

The video contains an additional segment, hosted by Ben Kingsley, which takes the viewer behind the scenes at "Survivors." Footage of Spielberg is included discussing and describing this ambitious project. This is a very fitting document for my unit.

9

American Poetry, 1945-1990: The Anti-Tradition

AMERICAN POETRY, 1945-1990: THE ANTI-TRADITION

Traditional forms and ideas no longer seemed to provide meaning to many American poets in the second half of the 20th century. Events after World War II produced for many writers a sense of history as discontinuous: Each act, emotion, and moment was seen as unique. Style and form now seemed provisional, makeshift, reflexive of the process of composition and the writer's self-awareness. Familiar categories of expression were suspect; originality was becoming a new tradition.

The break from tradition gathered momentum during the 1957 obscenity trial of Allen Ginsberg's poem *Howl*. When the San Francisco customs office seized the book, its publisher, Lawrence Ferlinghetti's City Lights, brought a lawsuit. During that notorious court case, famous critics defended *Howl*'s passionate social criticism on the basis of the poem's redeeming literary merit. *Howl*'s triumph over the censors helped propel the rebellious Beat poets – especially Ginsberg and his friends Jack Kerouac and William Burroughs – to fame.

It is not hard to find historical causes for this dissociated sensibility in the United States. World War II itself, the rise of anonymity and consumerism in a mass urban society, the protest movements of the 1960s, the decade-long Vietnam conflict, the Cold War, environmental threats – the catalog of shocks to American culture is long and varied. The change that most transformed American society, however, was the rise of the mass media and mass culture. First radio, then movies, and later an all-powerful, ubiquitous television presence changed American life at its roots. From a private, literate, elite culture based on the book and reading, the United States became a media culture attuned to the voice on the radio, the music of compact discs and cassettes, film, and the images on the television screen. American poetry was directly influenced by the mass media and electronic technology. Films, videotapes, and tape recordings of poetry readings and interviews with poets became available, and new inexpensive photographic methods of printing encouraged young poets to self-publish and young editors to begin literary magazines – of which there were more than 2,000 by 1990.

At the same time, Americans became uncomfortably aware that technology, so useful as a tool, could be used to manipulate the culture. To Americans seeking alternatives, poetry seemed more relevant than before: It offered people a way to express subjective life and articulate the impact of technology and mass society on the individual.

A host of styles, some regional, some associated with famous schools or poets, vied for attention; post-World War II American poetry was decentralized, richly varied, and difficult to summarize. For the sake of discussion, however, it can be arranged along a spectrum, producing three overlapping camps – the traditional on one end, the idiosyncratic in the middle, and the experimental on the other end. Traditional poets have maintained or revitalized poetic traditions. Idiosyncratic poets have used both traditional and innovative techniques in creating unique voices. Experimental poets have courted new cultural styles.

TRADITIONALISM

Traditional writers include acknowledged masters of established forms and diction who wrote with a readily recognizable craft, often using rhyme or a set metrical pattern. Often they were from the U.S. eastern seaboard or the southern part of the country, and taught in colleges and universities. Richard Eberhart and Richard Wilbur; the older Fugitive poets John Crowe Ransom, Allen Tate, and Robert Penn Warren; such accomplished younger poets as John Hollander and Richard Howard; and the early Robert Lowell are examples. In the years after World War II, they became established and were frequently anthologized.

The refinement, respect for nature, and profoundly conservative values of the Fugitives. These qualities grace much poetry oriented to traditional modes. Traditionalist poets were generally precise, realistic, and witty; many, like Richard Wilbur (1921-), were influenced by British metaphysical poets brought to favour by T.S. Eliot. Wilbur's most famous poem, "A World Without Objects Is a Sensible Emptiness" (1950), takes its title from Thomas Traherne, a 17th century English metaphysical poet. Its vivid opening illustrates the clarity some poets found within rhyme and formal regularity:

The tall camels of the spirit
Steer for their deserts, passing the last
groves loud
With the sawmill shrill of the locust,to the
whole honey of the arid
Sun. They are slow, proud...

Traditional poets, unlike many experimentalists who distrusted "too poetic" diction, welcomed resounding poetic lines. Robert Penn Warren (1905-1989) ended one poem with the words: "To love so well the world that we may believe, in the end, in God." Allen Tate (1899-1979) ended a poem: "Sentinel of the grave who counts us all!" Traditional poets also at times used a somewhat rhetorical diction of obsolete or odd words, using many adjectives (for example, "sepulchral owl") and inversions, in which the natural, spoken word order of English is altered unnaturally. Sometimes the effect is noble, as in the line by Warren; other times, the poetry seems stilted and out of touch with real emotions, as in Tate's line: "Fatuously touched the hems of the hierophants."

Occasionally, as in Hollander, Howard, and James Merrill (1926-1995), self-conscious diction combines with wit, puns, and literary allusions. Merrill, who was innovative in his urban themes, unrhymed lines, personal subjects, and light conversational tone, shares a witty habit with the traditionalists in "The Broken Heart" (1966), writing about a marriage as if it were a cocktail:

Always that same old story —
Father Time and Mother Earth,
A marriage on the rocks.

Obvious fluency and verbal pyrotechnics by some poets, including Merrill and John Ashbery, made them successful in traditional terms, although they redefined poetry in radically innovative ways. Stylistic gracefulness made some poets seem more traditional than they were, as in the case of Randall Jarrell (1914-1965) and A.R. Ammons (1926-2001). Ammons created intense dialogues between humanity and nature; Jarrell stepped into the trapped consciousness of the dispossessed – women, children, doomed soldiers, as in "The Death of the Ball Turret Gunner" (1945):

From my mother's sleep I fell into the State,
And I hunched in its belly till my wet fur froze.
Six miles from earth, loosed from its dream
of life,
I woke to black flak and the nightmare
fighters.
When I died they washed me out of the turret
with a hose.

Although many traditional poets used rhyme, not all rhymed poetry was traditional in subject or tone. Poet Gwendolyn Brooks (1917-2000) wrote of the difficulties of living – let alone writing – in urban slums. Her "Kitchenette Building" (1945) asks how

could a dream send up through
onion fumes
Its white and violet, fight with
fried potatoes

And yesterday's garbage ripening
in the hall...

Many poets, including Brooks, Adrienne Rich, Richard Wilbur, Robert Lowell, and Robert Penn Warren, began writing traditionally, using rhyme and meters, but abandoned these in the 1960s under the pressure of public events and a gradual trend towards open forms.

Robert Lowell (1917-1977)

The most influential poet of the period, Robert Lowell, began traditionally but was influenced by experimental currents. Because his life and work spanned the period between the older modernist masters like T.S. Eliot and the recent antitraditional writers, his career places the later experimentalism in a larger context.

Lowell fits the mold of the academic writer: white, male, Protestant by birth, well educated, and linked with the political and social establishment. He was a descendant of the respected Boston Brahmin family that included the famous 19th-century poet James Russell Lowell and a 20th-century president of Harvard University.

Robert Lowell found an identity outside his elite background, however. He left Harvard to attend Kenyon College in Ohio, where he rejected his Puritan ancestry and converted to Catholicism. Jailed for a year as a conscientious objector in World War II, he later publicly protested the Vietnam conflict.

Lowell's early books, *Land of Unlikeness* (1944) and *Lord Weary's Castle* (1946), which won a Pulitzer Prize, revealed great control of traditional forms and styles, strong feeling, and an intensely personal yet historical vision. The violence and specificity of the early work is overpowering in poems like "Children of Light" (1946), a harsh condemnation of the Puritans who killed Indians and whose descendants burned surplus grain instead of shipping it to hungry people. Lowell writes: "Our fathers wrung their bread from stocks and stones/ And fenced their gardens with the Redman's bones."

Lowell's next book, *The Mills of the Kavanaughs* (1951), contains moving dramatic monologues in which members of his family reveal their tenderness and failings. As always, his style mixes the human with the majestic. Often he uses traditional rhyme, but his colloquialism disguises it until it seems like background melody. It was experimental poetry, however, that gave Lowell his breakthrough into a creative individual idiom.

On a reading tour in the mid-1950s, Lowell heard some of the new experimental poetry for the first time. Allen Ginsberg's *Howl* and Gary Snyder's *Myths and Texts*, still unpublished, were being read and chanted, sometimes to jazz accompaniment, in coffee houses in North Beach, a section of San Francisco. Lowell felt that next to these, his own accomplished poems were too stilted, rhetorical, and encased in convention; when reading them aloud, he made spontaneous revisions towards a more colloquial diction. "My own poems seemed like prehistoric monsters dragged down into a bog and death by their ponderous armor," he wrote later. "I was reciting what I no longer felt."

At this point Lowell, like many poets after him, accepted the challenge of learning from the rival tradition in America – the school of William Carlos Williams. "It's as if no poet except Williams had really seen America or heard its language," Lowell wrote in 1962. Henceforth, Lowell changed his writing drastically, using the "quick changes of tone, atmosphere, and speed" that Lowell most appreciated in Williams.

Lowell dropped many of his obscure allusions; his rhymes became integral to the experience within the poem instead of superimposed on it. The stanzaic structure, too, collapsed; new improvisational forms arose. In *Life Studies* (1959), he initiated confessional poetry, a new mode in which he bared his most tormenting personal problems with great honesty and intensity. In essence, he not only discovered his individuality but celebrated it in its most difficult and private manifestations. He transformed himself into a contemporary, at home with the self, the fragmentary, and the form as process.

Lowell's transformation, a watershed for poetry after the war, opened the way for many younger writers. In *For the Union Dead* (1964), *Notebook 1967-68* (1969), and later books, he continued his autobiographical explorations and technical innovations, drawing upon his experience of psychoanalysis. Lowell's confessional poetry has been particularly influential. Works by John Berryman, Anne Sexton, and Sylvia Plath (the last two his students), to mention only a few, are impossible to imagine without Lowell.

Idiosyncratic Poets

Poets who developed unique styles drawing on tradition but extending it into new realms with a distinctively contemporary flavour, in addition to Plath and Sexton, include John Berryman, Theodore Roethke, Richard Hugo, Philip Levine, James Dickey, Elizabeth Bishop, and Adrienne Rich.

Sylvia Plath (1932-1963)

Sylvia Plath lived an outwardly exemplary life, attending Smith College on scholarship, graduating first in her class, and winning a Fulbright grant to Cambridge University in England. There she met her charismatic husband-to-be, poet Ted Hughes, with whom she had two children and settled in a country house in England.

Beneath the fairy-tale success festered unresolved psychological problems evoked in her highly readable novel *The Bell Jar* (1963). Some of these problems were personal, while others arose from her sense of repressive attitudes towards women in the 1950s. Among these were the beliefs – shared by many women themselves – that women should not show anger or ambitiously pursue a career, and instead find fulfillment in tending their husbands and children. Professionally successful women like Plath felt that they lived a contradiction.

Plath's storybook life crumbled when she and Hughes separated and she cared for the young children in a London apartment during a winter of extreme cold. Ill, isolated, and in despair, Plath worked against the clock to produce a series of stunning poems before she committed suicide by gassing herself in her kitchen. These poems were collected in the volume *Ariel* (1965), two years after her death. Robert Lowell, who wrote the introduction, noted her poetry's rapid development from the time she and Anne Sexton had attended his poetry classes in 1958.

Plath's early poetry is well crafted and traditional, but her late poems exhibit a desperate bravura and proto-feminist cry of anguish. In "The Applicant" (1966), Plath exposes the emptiness in the current role of wife (who is reduced to an inanimate "it"):

A living doll, everywhere you look.
It can sew, it can cook.
It can talk, talk, talk.
It works, there is nothing wrong with it.
You have a hole, it's a poultice.
You have an eye, it's an image.
My boy, it's your last resort.
Will you marry it, marry it, marry it.

Plath dares to use a nursery rhyme language, a brutal directness. She has a knack for using bold images from popular culture. Of a baby she writes, "Love set you going like a fat gold watch." In "Daddy," she imagines her father as the Dracula of cinema: "There's a stake in your fat black heart/ And the villagers never liked you."

Anne Sexton (1928-1974)

Like Sylvia Plath, Anne Sexton was a passionate woman who attempted to be wife, mother, and poet on the eve of the women's movement in the United States. Like Plath, she suffered from mental illness and ultimately committed suicide.

Sexton's confessional poetry is more autobiographical than Plath's and lacks the craftedness Plath's earlier poems exhibit. Sexton's poems appeal powerfully to the emotions, however. They thrust taboo subjects into close focus. Often they daringly introduce female topics such as childbearing, the female body, or marriage seen from a woman's point of view. In poems like "Her Kind" (1960), Sexton identifies with a witch burned at the stake:

I have ridden in your cart, driver,
waved my nude arms at villages going by,
learning the last bright routes, survivor

where your flames still bite my thigh
and my ribs crack where your wheels wind.
A woman like that is not ashamed to die.
I have been her kind.

The titles of her works indicate their concern with madness and death. They include *To Bedlam and Part Way Back* (1960), *Live or Die* (1966), and the posthumous book *The Awful Rowing Towards God* (1975).

John Berryman (1914-1972)

John Berryman's life paralleled Robert Lowell's in some respects. Born in Oklahoma, Berryman was educated in the Northeast – at prep school and at Columbia University, and later was a fellow at Princeton University. Specializing in traditional forms and meters, he was inspired by early American history and wrote self-critical, confessional poems in his *Dream Songs* (1969) that feature a grotesque autobiographical character named Henry and reflections on his own teaching routine, chronic alcoholism, and ambition.

Like his contemporary, Theodore Roethke, Berryman developed a supple, playful, but profound style enlivened by phrases from folklore, children's rhymes, clichìœŠ"ØÈŠ"- and slang. Berryman writes, of Henry, "He stared at ruin. Ruin stared straight back." Elsewhere, he wittily writes, "Oho alas alas/ When will indifference come, I moan and rave."

Theodore Roethke (1908-1963)

The son of a greenhouse owner, Theodore Roethke evolved a special language evoking the "greenhouse world" of tiny insects and unseen roots: "Worm, be with me./ This is my hard time." His love poems in *Words for the Wind* (1958) celebrate beauty and desire with innocent passion. One poem begins: "I knew a woman, lovely in her bones,/ When small birds sighed, she would sigh back at them." Sometimes his poems seem like nature's shorthand or ancient riddles: "Who stunned the dirt into noise?/ Ask the mole, he knows."

Richard Hugo (1923-1982)

Richard Hugo, a native of Seattle, Washington, studied under Theodore Roethke. He grew up poor in dismal urban environments and excelled at communicating the hopes, fears, and frustrations of working people against the backdrop of the northwestern United States. Hugo wrote nostalgic, confessional poems in bold iambics about shabby, forgotten small towns in his part of the United States; he wrote of shame, failure, and rare moments of acceptance through human relationships. He focused the reader's attention on minute, seemingly inconsequential details in order to make more significant points. "What Thou Lovest Well, Remains American" (1975) ends with a person carrying memories of his old hometown as if they were food:

in case you're stranded in some
odd empty town
and need hungry lovers for
friends, and need feel
you are welcome in the street
club they have formed.

Philip Levine (1928-)

Philip Levine, born in Detroit, Michigan, deals directly with the economic sufferings of workers through keen observation, rage, and painful irony. Like Hugo, his background is urban and poor. He has been the voice for the lonely individual caught up in industrial America. Much of his poetry is somber and reflects an anarchic tendency amid the realization that systems of government will endure.

In one poem, Levine likens himself to a fox who survives in a dangerous world of hunters through his courage and cunning. In terms of his rhythmic pattern, he has traveled a path from traditional meters in his early works to a freer, more open line in his later poetry as he expresses his lonely protest against the evils of the contemporary world.

James Dickey (1923-1997)

James Dickey, a novelist and essayist as well as poet, was a native of Georgia. At Vanderbilt University he studied under Agrarian poet and critic Donald Davidson, who encouraged Dickey's sensitivity to his southern heritage. Like Randall Jarrell, Dickey flew in World War II and wrote of the agony of war.

As a novelist and poet, Dickey was often concerned with strenuous effort, "outdoing, desperately/ Outdoing what is required." He yearned for revitalizing contact with the world – a contact he sought in nature (animals, the wild), sexuality, and physical exertion. Dickey's novel *Deliverance* (1970), set in a southern wilderness river canyon, explores the struggle for survival and the dark side of male bonding. When filmed with the poet himself playing a southern sheriff, the novel and film increased his renown. While *Selected Poems* (1998) includes later work, Dickey's reputation rests largely on his early collection *Poems 1957-1967* (1967).

Elizabeth Bishop (1911-1979) and Adrienne Rich (1929-)

Among women poets of the idiosyncratic group, Elizabeth Bishop and Adrienne Rich have garnered the most respect in recent years. Bishop's crystalline intelligence and interest in remote landscapes and metaphors of travel appeal to readers for their exactitude and subtlety. Like her mentor Marianne Moore, Bishop wrote highly crafted poems in a descriptive style that contains hidden philosophical depths. The description of the ice-cold North Atlantic in "At the Fishhouses" (1955) could apply to Bishop's own poetry: "It is like what we imagine knowledge to be:/ dark, salt, clear, moving, utterly free."

With Moore, Bishop may be placed in a "cool" female poetic tradition harking back to Emily Dickinson, in comparison with the "hot" poems of Plath, Sexton, and Adrienne Rich. Though Rich began by writing poems in traditional form and meter, her works, particularly those written after she became an ardent feminist in the 1980s, embody strong emotions.

Rich's special genius is the metaphor, as in her extraordinary work "Diving Into the Wreck" (1973), evoking a woman's search for identity in terms of diving down to a wrecked ship. Rich's poem "The Roofwalker" (1961), dedicated to poet Denise Levertov, imagines poetry writing, for women, as a dangerous craft. Like men building a roof, she feels "exposed, larger than life,/ and due to break my neck."

EXPERIMENTAL POETRY

The force behind Robert Lowell's mature achievement and much of contemporary poetry lies in the experimentation begun in the 1950s by a number of poets. They may be divided into five loose schools, identified by Donald Allen in The New American Poetry, 1945-1960 (1960), the first anthology to present the work of poets who were previously neglected by the critical and academic communities.

Inspired by jazz and abstract expressionist painting, most of the experimental writers are a generation younger than Lowell. They have tended to be bohemian, counterculture intellectuals who disassociated themselves from universities and outspokenly criticized "bourgeois" American society. Their poetry is daring, original, and sometimes shocking. In its search for new values, it claims affinity with the archaic world of myth, legend, and traditional societies such as those of the American Indian. The forms are looser, more spontaneous, organic; they arise from the subject matter and the feeling of the poet as the poem is written, and from the natural pauses of the spoken language. As Allen Ginsberg noted in "Improvised Poetics," "first thought best thought."

THE BLACK MOUNTAIN SCHOOL

The Black Mountain School centered around Black Mountain College, an experimental liberal arts college in Asheville, North Carolina, where poets Charles Olson, Robert Duncan, and Robert Creeley taught in the early 1950s. Ed Dorn, Joel Oppenheimer, and Jonathan Williams studied there, and Paul Blackburn, Larry Eigner, and Denise Levertov published work in the school's magazines *Origin*and *Black Mountain Review*. The Black Mountain School is linked with Charles Olson's theory of "projective verse," which insisted on an open form based on the spontaneity of the breath pause in speech and the typewriter line in writing. Robert Creeley (1926-2005), who writes with a terse, minimalist style, was one of the major Black Mountain poets. In "The Warning" (1955), Creeley imagines the violent, loving imagination:

For love – I would
split open your head and put
a candle in
behind the eyes.
Love is dead in us
if we forget
the virtues of an amulet
and quick surprise

THE SAN FRANCISCO SCHOOL

The work of the San Francisco School owes much to Eastern philosophy and religion, as well as to Japanese and Chinese poetry. This is not surprising because the influence of the Orient has always been strong in the U.S. West. The land around San Francisco – the Sierra Nevada Mountains and the jagged seacoast – is lovely and majestic, and poets from that area tend to have a deep feeling for nature. Many of their poems are set in the mountains or take place on backpacking trips. The poetry looks to nature instead of literary tradition as a source of inspiration.

San Francisco poets include Jack Spicer, Lawrence Ferlinghetti, Robert Duncan, Phil Whalen, Lew Welch, Gary Snyder, Kenneth Rexroth, Joanne Kyger, and Diane diPrima. Many of these poets identify with working people. Their poetry is often simple, accessible, and optimistic.

At its best, as seen in the work of Gary Snyder (1930-), San Francisco poetry evokes the delicate balance of the individual and the cosmos. In Snyder's "Above Pate Valley" (1955), the poet describes working on a trail crew in the mountains and finding obsidian arrowhead flakes from vanished Indian tribes:

On a hill snowed all but summer,
A land of fat summer deer,
They came to camp. On their
Own trails. I followed my own
Trail here. Picked up the
cold-drill,
Pick, singlejack, and sack
Of dynamite.
Ten thousand years.

BEAT POETS

The San Franciso School blends into the next grouping – the Beat poets, who emerged in the 1950s. The term beat variously suggests musical downbeats, as in jazz; angelical beatitude or blessedness; and "beat up" – tired or hurt. The Beats (beatniks) were inspired by jazz, Eastern religion, and the wandering life. These were all depicted in the famous novel by Jack Kerouac *On the Road*, a sensation when it was published in 1957. An account of a 1947 cross-country car trip, the novel was written in three hectic weeks on a single roll of paper in what Kerouac called "spontaneous bop prose." The wild, improvisational style, hipster-mystic characters, and rejection of authority and convention fired the imaginations of young readers and helped usher in the freewheeling counterculture of the 1960s.

Most of the important Beats migrated to San Francisco from America's East Coast, gaining their initial national recognition in California. The charismatic Allen Ginsberg (1926-1997) became the group's chief spokesperson. The son of a poet father and an eccentric mother committed to Communism, Ginsberg attended Columbia University, where he became fast friends with fellow students Kerouac (1922-1969) and William Burroughs (1914-1997), whose violent, nightmarish novels about the underworld of heroin addiction include *The Naked Lunch* (1959). These three were the nucleus of the Beat movement.

Other figures included publisher Lawrence Ferlinghetti (1919-), whose bookstore, City Lights, established in San Francisco's North Beach in 1951, became a gathering place. One of the best educated of the mid-20th century poets (he received a doctorate from the Sorbonne), Ferlinghetti's thoughtful, humorous, political poetry included *A Coney Island of the Mind* (1958); *Endless Life* (1981) is the title of his selected poems.

Gregory Corso (1930-2001), a petty criminal whose talent was nurtured by the Beats, is remembered for volumes of humorous poems, such as the often-anthologized "Marriage." A gifted poet, translator, and original critic, as seen in his insightful *American Poetry in the Twentieth Century* (1971), Kenneth Rexroth (1905-1982) played the role of elder statesman to the anti-tradition. A labour organizer from Indiana, he saw the Beats as a West Coast alternative to the East Coast literary establishment. He encouraged the Beats with his example and influence.

Beat poetry is oral, repetitive, and immensely effective in readings, largely because it developed out of poetry readings in underground clubs. Some might correctly see it as a great-grandparent of the rap music that became prevalent in the 1990s. Beat poetry was the most anti-establishment form of literature in the United States, but beneath its shocking words lies a love of country. The poetry is a cry of pain and rage at what the poets see as the loss of America's innocence and the tragic waste of its human and material resources.

Poems like Allen Ginsberg's *Howl* (1956) revolutionized traditional poetry.

I saw the best minds of my
generation destroyed by

madness, starving hysterical
naked,
dragging themselves through the
negro streets at dawn
looking for an angry fix,
angelheaded hipsters burning
for the ancient heavenly
connection to the starry
dynamo in the
machinery of night...

THE NEW YORK SCHOOL

Unlike the Beat and San Francisco poets, the poets of the New York School were not interested in overtly moral questions, and, in general, they steered clear of political issues. They had the best formal educations of any group.

The major figures of the New York School – John Ashbery, Frank O'Hara, and Kenneth Koch – met while they were undergraduates at Harvard University. They are quintessentially urban, cool, non-religious, witty with a poignant, pastel sophistication. Their poems are fast moving, full of urban detail, incongruity, and an almost palpable sense of suspended belief.

New York City is the fine arts center of America and the birthplace of abstract expressionism, a major inspiration of this poetry. Most of the poets worked as art reviewers or museum curators, or collaborated with painters. Perhaps because of their feeling for abstract art, which distrusts figurative shapes and obvious meanings, their work is often difficult to comprehend, as in the later work of John Ashbery (1927-), perhaps the most critically esteemed poet of the late 20th century.

Ashbery's fluid poems record thoughts and emotions as they wash over the mind too swiftly for direct articulation. His profound, long poem, *Self-Portrait in a Convex Mirror* (1975), which won three major prizes, glides from thought to thought, often reflecting back on itself:

A ship
Flying unknown colours has
entered the harbour.
You are allowing extraneous
matters
To break up your day...

SURREALISM AND EXISTENTIALISM

In his anthology defining the new schools, Donald Allen includes a fifth group he cannot define because it has no clear geographical underpinning. This vague group includes recent movements and experiments. Chief among these are surrealism, which expresses the unconscious through vivid dreamlike imagery, and much poetry by women and ethnic minorities that has flourished in recent years. Though superficially distinct, surrealists, feminists, and minorities appear to share a sense of alienation from mainstream literature.

Although T.S. Eliot, Wallace Stevens, and Ezra Pound had introduced symbolist techniques into American poetry in the 1920s, surrealism, the major force in European poetry and thought in Europe during and after World War II, did not take root in the United States. Not until the 1960s did surrealism (along with existentialism) become domesticated in America under the stress of the Vietnam conflict.

During the 1960s, many American writers – W.S. Merwin, Robert Bly, Charles Simic, Charles Wright, and Mark Strand, among others – turned to French and especially Spanish surrealism for its pure emotion, its archetypal images, and its models of anti-rational, existential unrest.

Surrealists like Merwin tend to be epigrammatic, as in lines such as: "The gods are what has failed to become of us/ If you find you no longer believe enlarge the temple."

Bly's political surrealism criticized values that he felt played a part in the Vietnam War in poems like "The Teeth Mother Naked at Last."

It's because we have new
packaging for smoked
oysters
that bomb holes appear in the
rice paddies.

The more pervasive surrealist influence has been quieter and more contemplative, like the poem Charles Wright describes in "The New Poem" (1973):

It will not attend our sorrow.
It will not console our children.
It will not be able to help us.

Mark Strand's surrealism, like Merwin's, is often bleak; it speaks of an extreme deprivation. Now that traditions, values, and beliefs have failed him, the poet has nothing but his own cavelike soul:

I have a key
so I open the door and walk in.
It is dark and I walk in.
It is darker and I walk in.

WOMEN POETS AND FEMINISM

Literature in the United States, as in most other countries, was long evaluated on standards that often overlooked women's contributions. Yet there are many women poets of distinction in American writing. Not all are feminists, nor do their subjects invariably voice women's concerns. Also, regional, political, and racial differences have shaped their work. Among distinguished women poets are Amy Clampitt, Rita Dove, Louise Glorie Graham, Carolyn Kizer, Maxine Kumin, Denise Levertov, Audre Lorde, Gjertrud Schnackenberg, May Swenson, and Mona Van Duyn.

Before the 1960s, most women poets had adhered to an androgynous ideal, believing that gender made no difference in artistic excellence. This gender-blind position was, in effect, an early form of feminism that allowed women to argue for equal rights. By the late 1960s, American women – many active in the civil rights struggle and protests against the Vietnam conflict, or influenced by the counterculture – had begun to recognize their own marginalization. Betty Friedan's outspoken *The Feminine Mystique* (1963), published in the year Sylvia Plath committed suicide, decried women's low status. Another landmark book, Kate Millett's *Sexual Politics* (1969), made a case that male writings revealed a pervasive misogyny, or contempt for women.

In the 1970s, a second wave of feminist criticism emerged following the founding of the National Organization for Women (NOW) in 1966. Elaine Showalter's *A Literature of Their Own* (1977) identified a major tradition of British and American women authors. Sandra Gilbert and Susan Gubar's *The Madwoman in the Attic* (1979) traced misogyny in English classics, exploring its impact on works by women, such as Charlotte Bront*Jane Eyre*. In that novel, a wife is driven mad by her husband's ill treatment and is imprisoned in the attic; Gilbert and Gubar compare women's muffled voices in literature to this suppressed female figure.

Feminist critics of the second wave challenged the accepted canon of great works on the basis that aesthetic standards were not timeless and universal but rather arbitrary, culture bound, and patriarchal. Feminism became in the 1970s a driving force for equal rights, not only in literature but in the larger culture as well. Gilbert and Gubar's *The Norton Anthology of Literature by Women*(1985) facilitated the study of women's literature, and a women's tradition came into focus.

Other influential woman poets before Sylvia Plath and Anne Sexton include Amy Lowell (1874-1925), whose works have great sensuous beauty. She edited influential Imagist anthologies and introduced modern French poetry and Chinese poetry in translation to the English-speaking literary world. Her work celebrated love, longing, and the spiritual aspect of human and natural beauty. H.D. (1886-1961), a friend of Ezra Pound and William Carlos Williams who had been psychoanalyzed by Sigmund Freud, wrote crystalline poems inspired by nature and by the Greek classics and experimental drama. Her mystical poetry celebrates goddesses. The contributions of Lowell and H.D., and those of other women poets of the early 20th century such as Edna St. Vincent Millay, are only now being fully acknowledged.

MULTIETHNIC POETS

The second half of the 20th century witnessed a renaissance in multiethnic literature that has continued into the 21st century. In the 1960s, following the lead of African Americans, ethnic writers in the United States began to command public attention. The 1970s saw the founding of ethnic studies programmes in universities.

In the 1980s, a number of academic journals, professional organizations, and literary magazines focusing on ethnic groups were initiated. Conferences devoted to the study of specific ethnic literatures had begun, and the canon of "classics" had been expanded to include ethnic writers in anthologies and course lists. Important issues included race and ethnicity, spiritual life, familial and gender roles, and language.

Minority poetry shares the variety and occasionally the anger of women's writing. It has flowered in works by Latino and Chicano Americans such as Gary Soto, Alberto Rios, and Lorna Dee Cervantes; in Native Americans such as Leslie Marmon Silko, Simon Ortiz, and Louise Erdrich; in African-American writers such as Amiri Baraka (LeRoi Jones), Michael S. Harper, Rita Dove, Maya Angelou, and Nikki Giovanni; and in Asian-American poets such as Cathy Song, Lawson Inada, and Janice Mirikitani.

Chicano/Latino Poetry

Spanish-influenced poetry encompasses works by many diverse groups. Among these are Mexican Americans, known since the 1950s as Chicanos, who have lived for many generations in the southwestern U.S. states annexed from Mexico in the Mexican-American War ending in 1848.

Among Spanish Caribbean populations, Cuban Americans and Puerto Ricans maintain vital and distinctive literary traditions. For example, the Cuban-American genius for comedy sets it apart from the elegiac lyricism of Chicano writers such as Rudolfo Anaya. New immigrants from Mexico, Central and South America, and Spain constantly replenish and enlarge this literary realm.

Chicano, or Mexican-American, poetry has a rich oral tradition in the *corrido*, or ballad, form. Seminal works stress traditional strengths of the Mexican community and the discrimination it has sometimes met with among whites. Sometimes the poets blend Spanish and English words in a poetic fusion, as in the poetry of Alurista and Gloria Anzald, heir poetry is much influenced by oral tradition and is very powerful when read aloud.

Some poets have written largely in Spanish, in a tradition going back to the earliest epic written in the present-day United States – Gaspar Pérez de Villagrá's *Historia de la Nueva México*, commemorating the 1598 battle between invading Spaniards and the Pueblo Indians at Acoma, New Mexico.

A central text in Chicano poetry, *I Am Joaquin* by Rodolfo Gonzales (1928-2005) evokes acculturation: the speaker is "Lost in a world of confusion/Caught up in a whirl of gringo society/Confused by the rules..." Many Chicano writers have found sustenance in their ancient Mexican roots. Thinking of the grandeur of Mexico, Lorna Dee Cervantes (1954-) writes that "an epic corrido" chants through her veins, while Luis Omar Salinas (1937-) feels himself to be "an Aztec angel."

Much Chicano poetry is highly personal, dealing with feelings and family or members of the community. Gary Soto (1952-) writes out of the ancient tradition of honoring departed ancestors, but these words, written in 1981, describe the multicultural situation of Americans today:

A candle is lit for the dead
Two worlds ahead of us all

In the 1980s, Chicano poetry achieved a new prominence, and works by Cervantes, Soto, and Alberto Rios were widely anthologized.

NATIVE-AMERICAN POETRY

Native Americans have written fine poetry, most likely because a tradition of shamanistic song plays a vital role in their cultural heritage. Their work has excelled in vivid, living evocations of the natural world, which become almost mystical at times. Indian poets have also voiced a tragic sense of irrevocable loss of their rich heritage.

Simon Ortiz (1941-), an Acoma Pueblo, bases many of his hard-hitting poems on history, exploring the contradictions of being an indigenous American in the United States today. His poetry challenges Anglo readers because it often reminds them of the injustice and violence at one time done to Native Americans. His poems envision racial harmony based on a deepened understanding.

In "Star Quilt," Roberta Hill Whiteman (1947-), a member of the Oneida tribe, imagines a multicultural future like a "star quilt, sewn from dawn light," while Leslie Marmon Silko (1948-), who is part Laguna Pueblo, uses colloquial language and traditional stories to fashion haunting, lyrical poems. In "In Cold Storm Light" (1981), Silko achieves a haiku-like resonance:

out of the thick ice sky
running swiftly
pounding
swirling above the treetops
The snow elk come,
Moving, moving
white song
storm wind in the branches.

Louise Erdrich (1954-), like Silko also a novelist, creates powerful dramatic monologues that work like compressed dramas. They unsparingly depict families coping with alcoholism, unemployment, and poverty on the Chippewa reservation. In Erdrich's "Family Reunion" (1984), a drunken, abusive uncle returns from years in the city. As he suffers from a heart disease, the abused niece, who is the speaker, remembers how this uncle had killed a large turtle years before by stuffing it with a firecracker. The end of the poem links Uncle Ray with the turtle he has victimized:

Somehow we find our way back,
Uncle Ray
sings an old song to the body
that pulls him
towards home. The gray fins that
his hands have become
screw their bones in the
dashboard. His face
has the odd, calm patience of a
child who has always
let bad wounds alone, or a
creature that has lived
for a long time underwater.
And the angels come
lowering their slings and litters.

AFRICAN-AMERICAN POETRY

Black Americans have produced many poems of great beauty with a considerable range of themes and tones. African-American literature is the most developed ethnic writing in America and is extremely diverse. Amiri Baraka (1934-), the best-known African-American poet of the 1960s and 1970s, has also written plays and taken an active role in politics. The writings of Maya Angelou (1928-) encompass various literary forms, including poetry, drama, and her well-known memoir, *I Know Why the Caged Bird Sings* (1969).

Rita Dove (1952-) was named poet laureate of the United States for 1993-1995. Dove, a writer of fiction and drama as well, won the 1987 Pulitzer Prize for *Thomas and Beulah* (1986), in which she celebrates her grandparents through a series of lyric poems. She has said that she wrote the work to reveal the rich inner lives of poor people.

Michael S. Harper (1938-) has similarly written poems revealing the complex lives of African Americans faced with discrimination and violence. His dense, allusive poems often deal with crowded, dramatic scenes of war or urban life. They make use of surgical images in an attempt to heal. His "Clan Meeting: Births and Nations: A Blood Song" (1971), which likens cooking to surgery ("splicing the meats with fluids"), begins "we reconstruct lives in the intensive/ care unit, pieced together in a buffet." The poem ends by splicing together images of the hospital, racism in the early American film *Birth of a Nation*, the Ku Klux Klan, film editing, and x-ray technology:

We reload our brains as the
cameras,
the film overexposed
in the x-ray light,
locked with our double door
light meters: race and sex
spooled and rung in a hobby;
we take our bundle and go
home.

History, jazz, and popular culture have inspired many African Americans, from Harper (a college professor) to West Coast publisher and poet Ishmael Reed (1938-), known for spearheading multicultural writing through the Before Columbus Foundation and a series of magazines such as *Yardbird*, *Quilt*, and *Konch*.

Many African-American poets, such as Audre Lorde (1934-1992), have found nourishment in Afrocentrism, which sees Africa as a center of civilization since ancient times. In sensuous poems such as "The Women of Dan Dance With Swords in Their Hands To Mark the Time When They Were Warriors" (1978), she speaks as a woman warrior of ancient Dahomey, "arming whatever I touch" and "consuming" only "What is already dead."

ASIAN-AMERICAN POETRY

Like poetry by Chicano and Latino writers, Asian-American poetry is exceedingly varied. Americans of Japanese, Chinese, and Filipino descent may often have lived in the United States for eight generations, while Americans of Korean, Thai, and Vietnamese heritage are likely to be fairly recent immigrants. Each group has grown out of a distinctive linguistic, historical, and cultural tradition.

Developments in Asian-American literature have included an emphasis on the Pacific Rim and women's writing. Asian Americans generally have resisted the common stereotypes as the "exotic" or "good" minority. Aestheticians have compared Asian and Western literary traditions – for example, comparing the concepts of *Tao and Logos*.

Asian-American poets have drawn on many sources, from Chinese opera to Zen Buddhism, and Asian literary traditions, particularly Zen, have inspired numerous non-Asian poets, as can be seen in the 1991 anthology Beneath *a Single Moon: Buddhism in Contemporary American Poetry*. Asian-American poets span a spectrum, from the iconoclastic posture taken by Frank Chin (1940-), co-editor of *Aiiieeeee*! (an early anthology of Asian-American literature), to the generous use of tradition by writers such as Maxine Hong Kingston (1940-).

Janice Mirikitani (1942-), a sansei (third-generation Japanese American), evokes Japanese-American history and has edited several anthologies, such as *Third World Women* (1973); *Time To Greez! Incantations From the Third World*(1975); and *Ayumi: A Japanese American Anthology* (1980).

The lyrical *Picture Bride* (1983) of Chinese-American Cathy Song (1955-) also dramatizes history through the lives of her family. Many Asian-American poets explore cultural diversity. In Song's "The Vegetable Air" (1988), a shabby town with cows in the plaza, a Chinese restaurant, and a Coca-Cola sign hung askew becomes an emblem of rootless multicultural contemporary life made bearable by art, in this case an opera on cassette:

then the familiar aria,
rising like the moon,
lifts you out of yourself,
transporting you to another country
where, for a moment, you travel light.

THE LANGUAGE SCHOOL, EXPERIMENTATION, AND NEW FORMALISM

At the end of the 20th century, directions in American poetry included the Language Poets loosely associated with *Temblor* magazine and Douglas Messerli, editor of *"Language" Poetries: An Anthology* (1987). Among them: Bruce Andrews, Lyn Hejinian, Bob Perelman, and Barrett Watten, author of *Total Syntax* (1985), a collection of essays. These poets stretch language to reveal its potential for ambiguity, fragmentation, and self-assertion within chaos. Ironic and postmodern, they reject "meta-narratives" – ideologies, dogmas, conventions – and doubt the existence of transcendent reality. Michael Palmer writes:

This is Paradise, a mildewed book
Left too long in the house

Bob Perelman's "Chronic Meanings" (1993) begins:

The single fact is matter.
Five words can say only.
Black sky at night, reasonably.
I am, the irrational residue...

Viewing art and literary criticism as inherently ideological, they oppose modernism's closed forms, hierarchies, ideas of epiphany and transcendence, categories of genre and canonical texts or accepted literary works. Instead they propose open forms and multicultural texts. They appropriate images from popular culture and the media, and refashion them. Like performance poetry, language poems often resist interpretation and invite participation.

Performance-oriented poetry – sets of chance operations such as those of composer John Cage, jazz improvisation, mixed media work, and European surrealism – have influenced many U.S. poets. Well-known figures include Laurie Anderson (1947-), author of the international hit *United States* (1984), which uses film, video, acoustics and music, choreography, and space-age technology. Sound poetry, emphasizing the voice and instruments, has been practiced by poets David Antin (who extemporizes his performances) and New Yorkers George Quasha (publisher of Station Hill Press), the late Armand Schwerner, and Jackson Mac Low. Mac Low has also written visual or concrete poetry, which makes a visual statement using placement and typography.

Ethnic performance poetry entered the mainstream with rap music, while across the United States over the last decade, poetry slams – open poetry reading contests that are held in alternative art galleries and literary bookstores – have become inexpensive, high-spirited, participatory entertainments.

At the opposite end of the theoretical spectrum are the self-styled New Formalists, who champion a return to form, rhyme, and meter. All groups are responding to the same problem – a perceived middle-brow complacency with the status quo, a careful and overly polished sound, often the product of poetry workshops, and an overemphasis on the personal lyric as opposed to the public gesture.

The Formal School is associated with Story Line Press; Dana Gioia, the poet who became chairman of the National Endowment for the Arts in 2003; Philip Dacey and David Jauss, poets and editors of *Strong Measures: Contemporary American Poetry in Traditional Forms* (1986); Brad Leithauser; and Gjertrud Schnackenberg. Robert Richman's *The Direction of Poetry: An Anthology of Rhymed and Metered Verse Written in the English Language Since 1975* is a 1988 anthology. Though these poets have been accused of retreating to 19th-century themes, they often draw on contemporary stances and images, along with musical languages and traditional, closed forms.

10

Poets of the Civil War II

POEMS AND SONGS OF THE AMERICAN CIVIL WAR

"The poems and songs of the Civil War era are gripping and powerful. From the secession of South Carolina and the opening battle at Fort Sumter to Lee's surrender at Appomattox and Lincoln's assassination, this wealth of literature records a remarkable period in American history from an urgent, contemporary perspective.

Moved by the currents of the divergent principles and needs that tore the nation in half, northern and southern authors alike express their horror at the bloodshed and sacrificed lives. in these patriotic and sentimental works, they tell tales of heroes and daring deeds, find solace in memory, and commemorate their dead. Finally, after the bitter end of the war, they assume the burdens of the peace and begin to reconstruct the nation. in the voices of these poets-speaking, writing, singing-lies the full spectrum of the history and emotions of the Civil War."

—Lois Hill

There are many sites on the Internet that have poems and songs of the Civil War, but in order to find all the ones I like I have had to go to several different ones. So I decided to put the ones I like up in hopes there may be some of you folks out there that might enjoy them also.

POEMS

A Message Written by Elizabeth Stuart Phelps Ward. A dandy! This one will give you something to think about.

Brother Jonathan's Lament For Sister Caroline Written by Oliver Wendell Holmes. It's about the Secession of South Carolina. 'Course you would never know it by the title.

Civil War Written by Charles Dawson Shanly and is about one of the great tragedies of a Civil War. Now there's an oxymoron if I've ever heard one. Since when is any war civil. Come Up From The Fields, Father Written by Walt Whitman. Got to be a terrible feeling to receive news such as this about your child. Little Giffen What courage for one so young. Stonewall Jackson's WayWritten by John Williamson Palmer. Dang good poem, but Bobby Horton put it to music and I kinda like that too. However, I think I will leave it in the poem category.

O Captain! My Captain! Written by Walt Whitman. Shades of my High School days! Still a dang good poem about ole Abe.

The Blue and the Gray A dandy one by Francis Miles Finch. It don't matter which side you were one, dead is dead.

SONGS

Battle Hymn of the Republic Written by Julia Ward Howe. This one never fails to stir my emotions no matter how many times I hear it.

Bonnie Blue Flag No Civil War Poems and Song site would be complete without this one. My personal favourite.

Dixie Now what kind of webmaster would I be if I didn't put this beauty on my web site!

Lorena If this one don't pull your heart strings nothing will. Caused many a good soldier from both sides to desert during the late Rebellion.

O' I'm a Good Old Rebel This one sure expressed the feelings of many a Reb after the war. You reenactors can't sing this one around your campfires. 'Cause if ya do, you gonna be "wrong as snow in July," it's post war!

Yellow Rose of Texas Great marching song. At least the Rebs thought so.

SOUTHERN ART AND POETRY FROM THE CIVIL WAR

The American Civil War, also known as The War Between the States, was fought during the 1860s, a time when romantic art and poetry flourished. Poetry was prominently featured in newspapers and periodicals. War was an ever-present topic that stirred deep emotions among writers and artists, especially in the South. Southerners believed the war was not only about political ideologies and slavery but also involved defence of a pastoral and genteel way of life. Because the war was primarily fought on Southern soil, many Southern poets and artists were both observers and participants in the conflict. Their works speak poignantly of bravery and loyalty, hardship and heartache, loss and despair.

PATRIOTISM

At the war's outset, Southern poets sought to rouse enthusiasm to the Confederate cause. Henry Timrod's "Ethnogenesis" reminded Southerners of the "noble land" they were fighting for and G.W. Hopkins "Hurrah for the South" was a patriotic cheer. In "The Southern Cross," E.K. Blunt reminds Southern men "On our side ... the God of battles fights!" Conrad Wise Chapman, the only Confederate artist who painted while actively serving, produced proud renderings of the Confederate submarine H.S. Hunley and the strong defences of Charleston Harbour. B.D. Julio paid homage to generals Robert E. Lee and Thomas J. "Stonewall" Jackson in "The Heroes of Chancellorsville."

SOLDIER LIFE

Confederate soldiers' musings were shared through poetry of both established and anonymous writers. In "Christmas," poet Henry Timrod wonders how he can celebrate the holiday while recalling the horrors at the Battle of Shiloh. In "Dreaming in the Trenches," poet William Gordon McCabe imagines a woman back home and swears his loyalty to her. The unknown author of "Countersign" wonders if he will be ready if and when "the angelic sentries call." Detailed scenes of Confederate soldier life were sketched by illustrator Frank Viztelly. His "Night Amusements in the Confederate Camp" shows a lighter side of soldier life. A leisurely view of a soldier camp is portrayed in "The 59th Virginia Infantry — Wise's Brigade" by Conrad Wise Chapman.

WOMEN

Confederate women also used poetry to express their views of the Civil War. In "Song of the Southern Woman," poet Julia Midred Harriss tells Abraham Lincoln he will be contending with "Joans of Arc" if he threatens Southern households.

Alethea S. Burroughs wonders what consolation there is at the war's conclusion in her poem "They Cry Peace, Peace When There is No Peace." In art, Confederate women were portrayed as loyal and caring. "The Burial of Latane" by William D. Washington was inspired by the true story of two Southern women who conducted the funeral and burial of a cavalry soldier on their plantation. Women's volunteer service is illustrated in the painting "In the Hospital, 1861" by Confederate soldier William Ludwell Sheppard.

DEATH AND DESTRUCTION

Southern poets and artists had no shortage of material to draw from when illustrating the horror of war. The poem "Only One Killed" by Julia L. Keyes describes a battle where only one man was lost, but this one man was a son, husband and father-to-be.

The tremendous loss of life that marked battlefields across the South is described in the poem "Virginia's Dead" by Cornelia J.M. Jordan. The art of photography produced vivid images of the war's death toll and destruction in the South. Photographer Alexander Gardner's "Photographic Sketchbook of the War" shows in unflinching detail the Confederate dead at Antietam and documents the destruction Union General William Tecumseh Sherman left in his wake as he made his infamous march to the sea.

CIVIL WAR POETS IN THE SOUTH

Among the many reasons that have been suggested for the lack of literature in the ante-bellum South—the absorption in politics, the pre-eminence of the spoken word as compared with the written, the absence of centres of thought and life—must be considered the failure of the people as a whole to appreciate the literary efforts of their writers, and, what is more important, the failure of writers of talent to devote themselves to literature as a profession. The popular orator, William L.Yancey, expressed the views of many when he said in a grandiose way: 'Our poetry is our lives; our fiction will come when truth has ceased to satisfy us; as for our history, we have made about all that has glorified the United States.' A. B. Meek, author of The land of the South, in the preface to a volume of his poems (1857) said: 'The author is not a poet by profession or ambition; he has written only at long intervals or at the instigation of trivial or transient causes. The present volume is composed of occasional effusions through many years of my life.' Some years later Margaret J. Preston wrote to Hayne:

Poetry has been only my pastime, not the occupation or mission of my life, which has been too busy a one with the duties of wifehood, motherhood, mistress, hostess, neighbour, and friend.... I think I can truly say that I have never neglected the concoction of a pudding for the sake of a poem, or a sauce for a sonnet. Art is a jealous mistress and I have served her with my left hand only.

Of a great many Southern poets, then, it may be said that they were 'amateurs quick to feel the poetic instinct and the influence of other poets, content with an occasional poem or a single volume, and thenceforth prone to lead a life of culture rather than of creative activity.'

The result was that the South, in 1860, had found no adequate expression of her life, no interpretation of her ideals, not even a description of her natural scenery. What writing there was, with few exceptions, was not of the soil nor of the people.Poe, Edward Coate Pinkney (1802-28), author of the exquisite love-compliment *A Health*, and Richard Henry Wilde (1789-1847), who wrote the fragrant Stanzasbeginning 'My life is like the summer rose,' might have written anywhere. One poem of the War of 1812, one or two of the Mexican War, and some half dozen other lyrics constituted, despite the appearance of not a few volumes of well-meant verse, the poetic output of the South before the Civil War.

The Civil War aroused intense emotions that found expression in a large body of lyric poetry, written by some men who were professedly poets and by more who were but occasionally such. It is difficult for one of the present generation to realize the unity and the fervour of the Southern people at the beginning of the war. Most intelligent Southerners would now agree with President Wilson that the principles for which the South fought 'meant standstill in the midst of change; it was conservative, not creative; it was against drift and destiny; it protected an impossible institution and a belated order of society; it withstood a creative and an imperial idea, the idea of a united people and a single law of freedom.' But it was given to few men, if any, on either side to understand the issues thus clearly defined. In fact, as soon as Fort Sumter was attacked and Maryland was invaded there was no longer a question of political issues—it was rather, to Southerners, a struggle of human passions, of liberty against despotism, and of the invasion of the sacred rights of home and commonwealth. As Sidney Lanier, himself then a young man just graduating at a Georgia college, said:

An afflatus of war was breathed upon us. Like a great wind it drew on, and blew upon men, women, and children. Its sound mingled with the serenity of the church organ, and arose with the earnest words of preachers praying for guidance in the matter. It thundered splendidly in the impassioned appeals of orators to the people, it whistled through the streets, it stole into the firesides, it clinked glasses in bar-rooms, it lifted the gray hairs of our wise men in conventions, it thrilled through the lectures in college halls, it rustled the thumbed book leaves of the schoolrooms, it arrayed the sanctity of a righteous cause in the brilliant trappings of military display, it offered tests to all allegiances and loyalties,—of church, of state; of private loves, public devotions; of personal consanguinities, of social ties.

Of this solidarity of Southern opinion and feeling no better evidence could be given than the fact that practically all those who wrote poetry during the Civil War were either participants in the actual struggle or were intimately connected with those who were. Theodore O'Hara, who had been in active service during the Mexican War and had written The Bivouac of the dead in honour of those who died in that war, was colonel of an Alabama regiment and later a staff officer in the Confederate Army. Henry Rootes Jackson, who had also fought in the Mexican War and had written My wife and child and The red old Hills of Georgia, served under Hood in the battles around Atlanta, commanded a brigade in the Army of Tennessee, and was captured in the battle of Nashville.

Their poems of the Mexican War were frequently quoted, and in fact were printed in nearly all the Southern anthologies of the Civil War. James Barron Hope, who had been Virginia's official poet at theJamestown celebration and the unveiling of the Washington monument inRichmond (1858), was quartermaster and captain in the Army of Virginia, and came out of the struggle broken in fortune and in health. Albert Pike, born inMassachusetts and author of Hymns to the gods (1839), was ConfederateCommissioner to the Indians and afterwards a brigadier-general. Margaret JunkinPreston, born in Philadelphia, revealed in Beechenbrook—a poetical transcript of her experiences and impressions of the war—what the war meant to a woman who was the wife of one of the most distinguished colonels of Lee's army, the sister-in-law of Stonewall Jackson, and the friend of Lee. John R. Thompson, successor toPoe as the editor of The Southern literary Messenger, became assistant secretary to the Commonwealth of Virginia and was later sent to England in the hope that his poems and articles might help to win English sympathy for the Confederacy.

Of the younger poets Paul Hamilton Hayne, Henry Timrod, and James Ryder Randallvolunteered for service but were prevented by delicate constitutions from remaining in the army, though as staff officers, correspondents, or poets they followed the events of the war with the keenest interest. Henry Lynden Flash was on the staff of General Joseph Wheeler and was thus prepared by his experience to write his tributes to Zollicoffer, Polk, and Jackson. Dr. Francis O. Ticknor was in charge of the hospital work at Columbus, Georgia, and ministered to the needs of soldiers, among them the brave Tennessean whom he made immortal in Little Giffen. Abram J. (Father) Ryan could never have written The conquered Bannerand The sword of Robert Lee if he had not visualized as a chaplain the heroism and tragedy of the long struggle.

William Gordon McCabe, who went from the University of Virginia as one of the Southern Guards, was a poet of the trenches, giving expression in his Dreaming in the trenches and Christmas night of '62 to the quieter and gentler aspects of a soldier's life. Sidney Lanier and John B. Tabb,after living the romantic life of soldiers, sealed a memorable friendship by a common suffering in the prison at Point Lookout.

The feeling of the South as represented by all these poets first expressed itself in music. Southern soldiers were quick to seize upon Dixie, the words of which had been written by Dan D. Emmett for Bryant's minstrels in 1859. Except for the refrain and a few haunting phrases, the words were totally inadequate, but the music proved to be the chief inspiration of Southern armies throughout the long conflict.

Sung for the first time by Mrs. John Wood in New Orleans late in 1860, it was taken up by the Louisiana regiments and was soon heard by the campfires and hearthstones of the South. From New Orleans, too, came The Bonnie blue flag, an old Hibernian melody, with words written by an Irish comedian, Harry McCarthy, a volunteer soldier in the Confederate Army from Arkansas. The enthusiasm aroused by its first rendition at the Varieties Theatre in 1861 is well described by a later writer. The theatre was filled with soldiers from Texas, Arkansas, andLouisiana on their way to the front. McCarthy appeared on the stage accompanied by his sister waving a Confederate flag. 'Before the first verse was ended the audience was quivering with excitement. After he sang the second stanza the audience joined in the chorus and sang it over and over again amid the most intensive excitement. It was wafted to the streets and in twenty-four hours it was all over the Southern Army.' For the crude words of both these melodies were soon substituted various versions more dignified and intellectually more worthy of theSouthern cause. Of all these, the most striking version of Dixie was written by Albert Pike, and the most stirring words for The Bonnie blue flag by Mrs. Annie Chambers Ketchum. But not even these versions took the place in the army, or have since taken the place in the affections of the Southern people, held by the first forms.

If New Orleans may lay claim to the first popular melodies, it was natural that fromCharleston should come the first notable expression in verse of the South's feeling with regard to the war. Aside from the fact that this city was the meeting place of the convention which proclaimed the secession of South Carolina, aside from the fact, too, that the first incident of the war was connected with Fort Sumter,Charleston, at the outbreak of the war, was the one Southern city that might have been considered a literary centre. Here for many years Simms, as the editor of many magazines and as a prolific romancer, had made his brave fight for literary independence, and here he had gathered about him in his later years a group of young men, two of whom especially were to respond as poets to the call of the new nation. He himself was now an old man, moving among his friends 'like a Titan maimed.' As the struggle tightened about Charleston in the later years of the war, he wrote some fiery appeals against the besieging foe, but there is in his verse excitement rather than inspiration, heat rather than light.

Of the group of friends and younger men who gathered about Simms, the most promising was Paul Hamilton Hayne (1830-86). The descendant of several generations of Carolina gentlemen and gentlewomen, he had deliberately turned away from the attractive profession of law and politics and had definitely chosen literature as his profession. In his first published poem he had announced his dedication to the poet's life in words that are in striking contrast to the views of the Southern people in general, and even of Southern poets, who had looked on the writing of poetry as a pastime and not a passion.

Before the war he had editedRussell's magazine (1857-60) and had published three volumes of poetry—poems characterized by a certain imitativeness and yet a genuine love of nature and a feeling for idyllic life. When the war came he volunteered, only to find that his delicate health would not allow him to share the hardships of a campaign.

From the first, however, he hailed his native state as his mother, who, like a priestess 'blessed with wondrous vision of the things to come,' would not wait till the sister nations would join her in the conflict. While he wrote constantly of many incidents of the war in other places, Charleston was the centre of his tenderest affections; perhaps his greatest poem of those years was The battle of Charleston Harbour. In certain reminiscences that he wrote after the war, as well as in the poems written during the war, one realizes what a charm this city, with its distinct flavour and atmosphere, had for him. If to Henry James and Owen Wister Charleston is today 'the most appealing, the most lovely, the most wistful town in America,' how much more so was it to a sensitive soul who from infancy had known its legends and its history, and whose most tragic thought in his later life was that he was an-exile from the City by the Sea.

Henry Timrod (1829-67), the friend of Simms and Hayne, had also definitely dedicated himself to the work of a poet, having already published a volume of poems in Boston (1860) and many individual poems in Russell's magazine and The Southern literary Messenger. A poet by natural temperament, he was a critical student of the classics and of the best English poetry. A poet hitherto of nature and of love, he was now to show himself the greatest Southern poet of the Civil War. Even before the Southern Confederacy was formed he wrote The Cotton boll, which struck a new note in that it was almost the first Southern poem of local colour. The single boll of cotton which he holds in his hand as he reclines beneath an immemorial pine suggests the great plantation near Charleston from which it came, and then all the cotton fields of the South, from gray Atlantic dawns to the evening star; and not only cotton fields, but the rivers and mountains and forests of this land, which blesses the world with its mighty commerce, joining 'with a delicate web remotest strands.' In offices of peace and love his country's mission lies; but now the enemy is coming-war is inevitable. In words of passionate indignation and patriotism he exclaims:

Oh, help us, Lord! to roll the crimson flood
Back on its course, and, while our banners wing
Northward, strike with us! till the Goth shall cling
To his own blasted altar—stones, and crave
Mercy; and we shall grant it, and dictate
The lenient future of his fate
There, where some rotting ships and crumbling quays
Shall one day mark the Port which ruled the Western seas.

The closing lines—partly ridiculous and partly pathetic in the light of today—are typical of the absolute confidence of the South.

When the Confederate Congress met in Montgomery in February, 1861, Timrodhailed the birth of the new nation in his stateliest ode, Ethnogenesis. All nature's blessings are with the South and take part with her against the North, mad and blinded in its rage. The strength of pine and palm, the firmness and calm of the hills, the snow of Southern summers (cotton), the abundance of the harvests, the heart of woman, the chivalry of men are arrayed against materialism and fanaticism. To doubt the end were want of trust in God. The poem closes with a passage that still remains the most felicitous expression of the Southerntemperament. Although the poet's vision of a separate nation was an illusion, there will never be a time when these words should not be quoted in any characterization of the natural warmth and cordiality of the Southern people:

The hour perchance is not yet wholly ripe
When all shall own it, but the type
Whereby we shall be known in every land
Is that vast gulf which lips our Southern strand
And through the cold, untempered ocean pours
Its genial streams, that far off Arctic shores
May sometimes catch upon the softened breeze
Strange tropic warmth and hints of summer seas.

With the outbreak of hostilities in April, Timrod wrote his passionate lyric *A Cry to Arms*, and later, Carolina. But none of Timrod's poems had the lyric quality that fits them for popular music. The union of music and poetry in a splendid impassioned utterance came from James Ryder Randall (1839-1909). Seldom in history have the man, the moment, and the word met in such happy conjunction as in the composition of My Maryland. Randall, a native of Baltimore—just from college in Maryland, and, as he said, full of poetry and romance —was teaching English literature in Poydras College at Pointe Coupee, Louisiana, when he read in the New Orleans Delta an account of the attack on the Massachusetts troops as they passed through Baltimore:

This account [he said in later years] excited me greatly; I had long been absent from my native city, and the startling event there inflamed my mind. That night I could not sleep, for my nerves were all unstrung, and I could not dismiss what I had read in the paper from my mind. About midnight I arose, lit a candle, and went to my desk. Some powerful spirit appeared to possess me, and almost involuntarily I proceeded to write the song of My Maryland. I remember that the idea appeared to first take shape as music in the brain—some wild air that I cannot now recall. The whole poem was dashed off rapidly when once begun. It was not composed in cold blood, but under what may be called a conflagration of the senses, if not an inspiration of the intellect.

He read the poem the next morning to his students, and at their suggestion sent it to the New Orleans Delta, from which it was copied in nearly every Southern journal. The finding of an appropriate melody for the words was the achievement of the Cary sisters of Baltimore. A glee club, which was in the habit of singing at their home, sang the words to the tune Lauriger Horatius, well known as a college tune that had come from a modification of the German Tannenbaum, O Tannenbaum. A few weeks later, shortly after the battle of Manassas, the two sisters and their brother went through the Southern lines. One night while visiting the headquarters of General Beauregard they were serenaded by a regiment of soldiers from New Orleans, who in turn asked for a song. One of the sisters sangMy Maryland; the refrain was speedily caught up and tossed back from hundreds of rebel throats, who shouted, 'We will break her chains; she shall be free!' Soon the words which had been read far and wide were being sung in every part of the South—had become indeed a great national song, the Marseillaise of the Confederacy.

The words—too familiar to be quoted—suggest every aspect of the great struggle from the Southern standpoint. They summarize in passionate, concentrated lines the points of view that are scattered here and there throughout all the anthologies of Southern poetry. The feeling of an exiled son at the invasion of his home, the crushing of liberty under the despot's heel, the peerless chivalry of Maryland's former heroes of history and tradition, his love for the state as a mother, the appeal for a sister state's aid to Virginia, and, on the other hand, the fierce indignation at the 'vandal,' the 'despot,' the 'Northern scum'—all these are suggestive of the passion of a people giving themselves entirely to the great struggle.

The popular melodies, the odes of Timrod, and the lyric cry of Randall—all of them the best illustrations of their various types—were prophetic of an outburst of poetry in all parts of the South. Such papers as the Charleston Mercury, the RichmondExaminer, the Louisville Courier, the New Orleans Delta, and such magazines asThe Southern literary Messenger, The Southern field and Fireside, and The Southern illustrated news published constantly poems written by men and women in all sections. As there were no general means of communication, many poems were attributed to various authors and many were published anonymously. On account of the lack of publishing houses practically no volumes of poetry were published during the war. The problem, therefore, of making anthologies of these poems was a difficult one—much more difficult than was the case in the North, where so many poets already famous were writing constantly during the war, and where there were so many means of communication and of publication. Southern readers had to be satisfied with scrapbooks in which were treasured many of the poems that in this way became the common property of a good many people.

Of distinctly different quality from the poems already referred to, and all other 'literary' poems, are certain crude vernacular verses. With some of the characteristics of popular ballads, they had much currency in the camps. A writer in the Southern Bivouac (July, 1885) recalls and characterizes some of these as follows:

As the long contest dragged on, and war, losing much of its earlier illusions, became a stern, bitter, and exceedingly monotonous reality, these 'high-toned' lyrics were tacitly voted rather too romantic and poetical for the actual field, and were remitted to the parlor and the piano stool. The soldiers chanted in quite other fashion on the march or seated at the campfire. In these crude rhymes, some of them improvised for the moment, there was less of flourish but more of meaning, not so much bravado but a good deal more point. They were sappy with the homely satire of the camps, which stings friend and foe alike. Innumerable verses were composed and sung to popular refrains. The Army of Virginia and the Army of Tennessee had each its history rudely chronicled as fast as made in this rough minstrelsy. Every corps and command contributed some commemorative stanza. The current events of campaigns were told in improvised verse as rapidly as they occurred and were thereafter skillfully recited by the rhapsodist who professed to know the whole fragmentary epic.

Forms of such rhymed narratives may be seen in typical stanzas:

Marse Robert said, 'My soldiers,
You've nothing now to fear,
For Longstreet's on the right of them,
And Jackson's in the rear.'
The Fourteenth Louisiana,
They charged 'em with a yell;
They bagged them buck-tailed rangers
And sent 'em off to hell.
O Morgan crossed the river,
And I went across with him;
I was captured in Ohio
Because I could not swim.

No matter where this song was sung, or by whom, or which of its multitude of stanzas happened to be selected by the minstrel, the following verse always closed it:

But now my song is ended,
And I haven't got much time,
I'm going to run the blockade
To see that girl of mine.

Some of these poems are found in Rebel Rhymes and rhapsodies (1864) edited byFrank Moore as a companion volume to two other volumes of war poetry of theNorth. In his preface to this first anthology of Southern war poetry Moore says:

It has been the purpose of the editor to present as full a selection of the songs and ballads of the Southern people as will illustrate the spirit which actuates them in their rebellion against the government and laws of the United States. Most of these pieces have been published in the magazines and periodicals of the South, while many are copies of ballad-sheets and songs circulated in the Rebel armies, and which have come into the possession of the forces of the Union in their various moves and advances during the present conflict.

We find in the volume many humorous poems of the kind just described. The more serious include two poems each by Randall and Ticknor, one each by Hayne, Hope, Flash, Meek, Pike, Simms, and J. R. Thompson, Timrod's *A*

Cry to Arms andPalmer's Stonewall Jackson's way, the last two published, however, anonymously. There are also many parodies of famous songs such as Annie Laurie, Gideon's band, Bannockburn, Columbia, Wait for the wagon, The star Spangled Banner, etc.

It was probably this collection that formed the basis of the selections from Southern poetry published as an appendix to Richard Grant White's Poetry, lyrical, narrative, and satirical of the Civil War (1866). In his preface White says:

I have read all that I could discover of the war poetry, written by the confederated enemies of my government, and have preserved here all that, in a most catholic spirit, I deemed of any intrinsic merit or incidental interest. It was my original purpose to embody them with the substance of the volume, giving each piece its place in the order of time; but finding so little of this poetry which possesses any kind of interest, instead of scattering it sparsely through the collection. The secessionists fought much better than they wrote; and it is worthy of remark that the best poem on that side, 'The Conquered Banner' was published in a New York newspaper, The Freeman's journal.

Omitting the humorous poems published by Moore, White has only the ten or twelve of a more serious and important nature, and these, in the main, not the ones that might be considered the most important by the leading Southern poets. The selections are a good illustration either of the difficulty of getting hold of Southern poems or of a provincial point of view that happily no longer exists.

Inadequate as these anthologies were, they were much better than the volume entitled War lyrics and Songs of the South, published in London in 1866, and edited by 'a faithful few Southern women' who had thrown 'hastily together this book of poems,' in the hope that

its sale to the charitable might secure a fund for the relief of the crippled and invalid men who fought as soldiers in the war in the South; the impoverished women and children, widows and orphans, as well as those who from sorrow, need, sickness, and other adversity have lost their health and their *minds*.

In this volume The Virginians of the Valley, by Ticknor, and Stonewall Jackson's way and The conquered Banner, both published anonymously, are the only poems of any value. An illustration of the carelessness of the editors is that Henry R.Jackson's My wife and child is attributed to General J. T. [T. J., or Stonewall]Jackson. More than half of the volume is given up to Songs of the Southland and other poems by 'Kentucky.'

In the following year Miss Emily V. Mason of Virginia edited The Southern poems of the Civil War. She had from the beginning of the war conceived the design of 'collecting and preserving the various war poems which (born of the excited state of the public mind) then inundated our public newspapers.' With her collection, supplemented by those of her friends, she made an edition of

247 poems, not only as a memorial to the lost cause, but 'to aid the education of the daughters of our desolate land' and especially to fit a certain number to be teachers. The volume proved popular, for by 1869 a third and enlarged edition was published, consisting of 288 poems. The first edition is notable for the large number of women writers selected from, 71 in all, the only noteworthy one being Mrs. Preston. There are thirteen poems on Stonewall Jackson, only two poems by Timrod, an indiscriminate list by Randall, and many anonymous poems. In the third edition we have eight by Timrod, four by Father Ryan, and good, though not the best, selections by Lucas, McCabe, Flash, and others.

The improvement in this edition may doubtless be attributed to William GilmoreSimms's War poetry of the South (1866). It was a noble task undertaken by this 'weary old Titan' of Southern letters to preserve the writings of the younger poets, many of whom had been inspired by his friendship or by his lifelong devotion to Southern letters. The spirit in which he made the book is indicated in the following words from the preface:

Though sectional in its character, and indicative of a temper and a feeling which were in conflict with nationality, yet, now that the States of the Union have been resolved into one nation, this collection is essentially as much the property of the whole as are the captured cannon which were employed against it during the progress of the late war. It belongs to the national literature, and will hereafter be regarded as constituting a proper part of it, just as legitimately to be recognized by the nation as are the rival ballads of the cavaliers and roundheads by the English in the great civil conflict of their country.

Not much can be said for the critical standards which allowed Simms to publish so much unworthy poetry, none more so than the seven poems from his own pen. His desire to give a place to representative poets of all states, and especially to his personal friends, is in part responsible. Furthermore, the book was thrown hastily together without any arrangement of the material with regard to authorship or chronology. When all has been said, however, we find in this volume the first anthology of practically all the important poems produced by the South during the war—seven each by Randall, J. R. Thompson, and Simms himself, six by Hayne, three by Ticknor, three by Flash, and, above all, eleven by Timrod. It is this recognition of Timrod's greatness as a poet, this first setting him forth as the poet of the South who expressed in adequate verse every aspect of the struggle, that increases the value of the book and our appreciation of Simms's critical judgement.

In 1869 appeared The Southern Amaranth, characterized by its editor, Miss Sallie A. Brock, as 'a carefully selected collection of poems growing out of and in reference to the late war.' In the preface of March, 1868, she expresses a wish to render to her Southern sisters 'some assistance in gathering up the remains of theConfederate dead.' Her regret is that 'a vast number of beautiful and worthy productions are compelled for want of space to be crowded out of this volume.' In florid style she exclaims: The Muse of the Southland is one of tireless wing, and though her theme is lofty and glorious as the golden sunset splendor upon the purple sky of evening, her song is often as sad as the weary echoes of the winter wind through her matchless forests—the mournful wailings of broken hearts.

The most striking new features of the volume are Timrod's Ode on the Confederatedead (written in 1867) and Dr. Ticknor's Little Giffen of Tennessee, which, though probably written in 1863, was not published until October, 1867, in The land we love. The latter poem is not given, however, as it appears in the revised form of later years, the last stanza being especially faulty.

All these anthologies had appeared with but little introductory material or notes regarding the lives of the writers or the circumstances under which the poems were written. They were all practically a conglomeration of poems with little to aid the student of literary history. In 1869 James Wood Davidson's Living writers of the South was published in New York, with salient facts as to the biographies and bibliographies of some 241 writers—166 men and 75 women. Of these he puts down 112 as having written 'verse' and eight as having written 'poetry.' He adds:

Some of these specimens are poor enough, in all conscience,— some inartistic of course; and some, it may be, frivolous,— but each in its way and all together have their use in the general design. Some of the writers have talents and character, with corresponding results, which enable them to stand in the front rank of American authorship. Some have limited ability. And some have none.

These words are typical of the judgement and sense that run through the volume. There are, for instance, critical estimates, biographical sketches, and bibliographies of Simms, Hayne, Mrs. Preston, Flash, and Randall, and surprisingly short ones ofTicknor and Lucas. It required courage on the author's part to characterize the poems of the veteran Simms as 'prosaic, commonplace, and Tupperesque.' After citing some sixty-five titles of his books of all kinds he remarks: 'He has not written an epic; why, I have no idea, but we may be infinitely grateful that he has not.'

In his criticism of Flash, for whom he shows much enthusiasm, Davidson puts his finger upon the cardinal defects of many of the Southern poets. Flash, he says, 'has never written anything which was not finished at a single sitting, and has never been more than two hours writing anything he has ever published.' He wrote his poem on Polk when his foreman told him that he lacked six or seven inches for the makeup of The daily Confederate. 'You have written about Zollicoffer and Jackson, you might as well write about Polk, who was killed the other day.' Flash quickly responded to the suggestion, and in five minutes the poem was in the hands of the composer, and in twenty minutes was being printed. Paying full tribute to Flash's good qualities, the author warns him that without work there is not the remotest chance for an enduring reputation, and at the same time makes the same suggestion to others who may have acquired 'a reverence for inspiration so called, and a contempt for the art of versification.'

Apart from his critical judgement Davidson shows the ability of a careful editor in weighing evidence as to the authorship of All quiet along the Potomac—a poem that all Southerners had claimed as the work of Lamar Fontaine. Davidson publishesFontaine's letter claiming positively the authorship, but side by side with it is one from Joel Chandler Harris, who was at that time, according to the editor, planning an edition of Southern poems, and who after much deliberation expresses the opinion that Mrs. Beers is the author of the poem. He quotes also a letter to the same effect from the editor of Harper's magazine. While he himself does not express an opinion, it is not difficult for the reader to be convinced by the reasoning submitted by Joel Chandler Harris. The mention of Harris suggests that in this volume he himself appears as the author of several poems which are as unlike his later writings as anything could well be. Davidson has the credit too of publishing for the first time in this volume McCabe's Dreaming in the trenches and Christmas night of '62, and certain recent poems of Maurice Thompson and Sidney Lanier. He also has much to say of poems that do not relate to the war.

In 1882 Francis F. Browne of Chicago carried out the purpose that Richard GrantWhite had expressed by publishing Bugle echoes—a collection of poems of the Civil War, Northern and Southern. Drawing upon the anthologies that have been discussed and upon separate editions of Southern poets, such as Hayne's edition ofTimrod (1873), of Ticknor (1879), of Hayne (1882), he finds a much larger number of Southern poems that fit into his plan of suggesting the story of the Civil War by poems written at the time. Thus for the first time a systematic arrangement was made of this material. The result is altogether striking.

The Southern poems, while slightly fewer in number (the proportion is 60 to 85), measure up well with those of the North. Side by side in this volume appear Bryant's Our country's call andTimrod's *A Cry to Arms*, Whitman's Beat, beat drums and Randall's My Maryland,Pike's Dixie and The battle hymn of the republic, Holmes's Voyage of the good shipUnion and Ticknor's Virginians of the Valley, Lowell's Commemoration ode andTimrod's Ode to the Confederate dead, and at the very end Finch's The blue *and the Gray* and Lanier's The Tournament—both of them prophetic of a new national era. Not only was Browne's idea happy and well executed; his introduction and notes are invaluable. He established the fact that the author of StonewallJackson's way was Dr. J. W. Palmer. He printed in connection with the poems valuable letters as to the circumstances under which were written My Marylandand The conquered Banner. The volume as a whole was so marked by a careful critical judgement and good taste as to distinguish it from the hastily prepared anthologies by Southerners.

Two books of similar nature are Eggleston's American War ballads and Burton E.Stevenson's Poems of American history, in both of which the poems are published in chronological order, and in Stevenson's book with the historical setting which interprets many of the individual poems. In later years selections from Southern writers by Miss Manly and Miss Clarke and Professors Trent, Kent, and Fulton, and biographical sketches by Baskervill and Link, have brought the best poems and poets within the reach of a larger circle of students and readers. The Library of Southern literature is a valuable mine of selections and biographical material.

When one tries to make a general estimate of this war poetry as a whole, there are three standpoints from which it may be considered. Judged from the standpoint of absolute criticism, it affords another illustration of the contention that war produces a quantity of mediocre poetry but little of enduring worth. Four or five poems at best have stood the winnowing process of time and judicial criticism.Randall's My Maryland, Ticknor's Little Giffen of Tennessee, and Timrod's Ode on the Confederate dead in Magnolia Cemetery might well be included in any anthology of lyric poetry, ancient or modern. If we consider the poems from the standpoint of either literary or social history, a larger number must be considered significant. They rightly find their place in such a collection as Stedman's American Anthology as affording material for the comprehensive survey of American poetry; or in the books of Stevenson and Browne, where the various stages of the Civil Warare suggested in poems rather than in army orders, political tracts, or newspaper comment. When President Lincoln said at the end of the war that the Northern army had captured Dixie he might have extended his remarks to other poems that have become a part of our national heritage.

Still another interest attaches to it. Much of it is an adequate, if not felicitous and final, expression of the ideas and emotions of Southerners at a time when they felt as one people. The emotional fervour that swept over the South was somehow the inspiration of a literature different from that of any other era in its history. Southern literature before the war had been marked by its absorption in politics, or its divorce from real life, or its amateurishness and sentimentalism. A people that had been all too inclined to underrate poetry and to discourage literary production found their deepest emotions expressed in martial strains, or in meditative lyrics. Written for local newspapers, preserved in scrap-books, collected in volumes like those of Simms and Miss Mason, sifted by the later editors and collectors, they preserve heroes and incidents, landscapes and sentiments that will always endear them to the Southern people.

If we consider the poems from this last point of view, they serve to suggest the principal events of the war in rapid review. The gauntlet was thrown down in the poems hitherto cited and also in Tucker's The Southern Cross, Miles's God save theSouth, Randall's Battle Cry of the South, Mrs. Warfield's Chant of Defiance,Thompson's Coercion, and Hope's Oath of freedom. Among the group of Virginiapoets who wrote of the early battles on Virginia soil, John R. Thompson (1822-73) and Mrs. Preston (1820-97) stand out as the most conspicuous. Of distinctly higher quality than the crude rhymes already referred to were Thompson's humorous poems on some of the early Southern victories. His On to Richmond, modelled onSouthey's March to Moscow, is an exceedingly clever poem. His mastery of double and triple rhymes, his unfailing sense of the value of words, and his happy use of the refrain ('the pleasant excursion to Richmond') make this poem one of the marked achievements of the period. Scarcely less successful in their brilliant satire are his Farewell to Pope, England's Neutrality, and The Devil's delight.

The humour of these poems soon gave way, however, to the more heroic and tragic aspects of the war. Thompson himself wrote dirges for Ashby and Latane, both of them the finest types of Virginia gentlemen. Mrs. Preston wrote a still more beautiful tribute to Ashby, in which she expresses one of the favourite ideas of theSouth—that the struggle was between the cavaliers and men of low breeding. The tragic aspects of Virginia and the heroism of her people were visualized also by a Georgia poet, Francis O. Ticknor (1822-74), whose wife was one of the distinguished Nelsons of the Old Dominion. His Our left is the most vivid account of the second battle of Manassas. Virginia is the best tribute we have to the commonwealth that bore the brunt of the struggle. The more popular Virginians of the Valley suggests the most romantic story of early years and adds that the same spirit pervades their descendants:

We thought they slept! the men who kept
The names of noble sires,
And slumbered, while the darkness crept
Around their vigil fires!
But aye! the golden horse-shoe Knights
Their Old Dominion keep,
Whose foes have found enchanted ground,
But not a Knight asleep.

One phase of the struggle ends with Lee's whole army crossing the Potomac intoMaryland—an event celebrated by Hayne in his Beyond the Potomac. Then the fighting changed to the West, and we have Thompson's poem on Joseph E.Johnston in which he exhorts the West to emulate Virginia in its struggle for freedom. Requier's Clouds in the West is followed by Flash's tribute to Zollicoffer,Ticknor's poem on Albert Sidney Johnston, Hayne's The Swamp Fox—a spirited characterization of Morgan, who seems to the poet a reincarnation of the South Carolina Revolutionary patriot Marion. Connected also with the battles of the Westwere Ticknor's Loyal and Little Giffen of

Tennessee—the latter based on a story of real life and a striking illustration of the heroism with which the sons of the masses threw themselves into the Southern struggle. This poem, so dramatic in its quality, so concise in its expression, so vital in its phrasing, is destined to outlive all the tributes to the great leaders of the Confederacy. Mrs. Preston's Only a private andMrs. Townsend's The Georgia Volunteer and the anonymous Barefooted boysare poems of the same general tenor, but they lack the freshness and the vigour ofTicknor's poem.

With the publication of Hayne's poems on Vicksburg and the battle of New Orleans, the scene shifts again to Virginia, and especially to the dramatic death ofStonewall Jackson after some of the fiercest battles of the war. This event more than any other pierced the heart of the South and called forth scores of poems from all sections. One of the early collectors claimed to have found forty-eight of these; at least four or five rise to a high level of expression. No other poem gives anything like so adequate an expression of Jackson—his personal appearance, his religious faith, his impressive commands, his almost magical control of his men—asStonewall Jackson's way by John Williamson Palmer (1825-1906). Excellent also are Margaret J. Preston's Stonewall Jackson's grave and Under the shade of the trees, Flash's Death of Stonewall Jackson, Randall's The Lone Sentry, and the anonymous The brigade must not know, Sir.

In 1863 Charleston was attacked by the Northern fleet and her group of devoted poets gathered about her in suspense. Timrod described the dawn of the eventful day as the city in the broad sunlight of heroic deeds waited for the foe. The hostile smoke of the enemy's fleet 'creeps like a harmless mist above the brine.' He knows not what will happen—the triumph or the tomb. With his Carmen Triumphale he sings the rapturous joy of the victory. Paul Hamilton Hayne sang a nobler song of victory, giving the details of the battle, ending in the triumphant victory of Sumter's volleyed lightning, and closing with an apostrophe to his native city:

O glorious Empress of the main, from out thy storied spires
Thou well mayst peal thy bells of joy and light thy festal fires,—
Since Heaven this day hath striven for thee, hath nerved thy dauntless sons,
And thou in clear-eyed faith hast seen God's angels near the guns.

This victory was short-lived, however, for on 27 August, by a land attack, Fort Sumter was reduced to a shapeless mass of ruin, though the city itself stood unshaken. As the fate of the city became more and more uncertain, WilliamGilmore Simms, now in his old age, did all in his power to rouse the Spirit of the inhabitants. In a series of poems, *Do Ye Quail? The Angel of the Church*, andOur city by the sea, he presents in passionate words the claims of the historic city upon its inhabitants. Especially vivid is his plea for St. Michael's church, whose spire for full a hundred years had been a people's point of light, and the sweet, clear music of whose bells, made liquid-soft in Southern air, had been a benediction in the life of the city. But the words of her poets could not avail the doomed city when, in 1865,Sherman's army marched north from Savannah. Timrod, now a citizen ofColumbia, wrote his greatest lyric, Carolina, which comes nearest to My Marylandof all the poems of the war in its indignation and power.

He reproaches the idle hands and craven calm of the inhabitants, but calls upon the descendants ofRutledge, Laurens, and Marion to rouse themselves against the despot who treads their sacred sands. The answer to this appeal was the burning of Columbia. Hayneand John Dickson Bruns still had hope that Charleston might escape the doom. AsTimrod from Charleston had given to the world the first expression of the new nation's hope, so his friend and fellow townsman, Dr. Bruns, was to utter the last appeal for Charleston in his The foe at the Gates. There is nothing more tragic in the Civil War than the fall of Charleston—the proud, passionate, and romantic city that had issued her challenge to the South to join her in the conflict with the North. In her last despairing cry the poet calls upon her children to ring round her and catch one last glance from her imploring eye:

From all her fanes let solemn bells be tolled;
Heap with kind hands her costly funeral pyre,
And thus, with paean sung and anthem rolled,
Give her unspotted to the God of Fire.

The fall of Charleston was the beginning of the end. Various poems on Lee, notablyTicknor's Lee, Thompson's Lee to the Rear, and the anonymous Silent March, suggest the last battles in Virginia. The dominant note of the later poetry is that of melancholy, now and then tempered by a sort of pathetic longing for peace.Eggleston tells us that the most popular poem on both sides came to be C. C.Sawyer's *When This Cruel War Is Over.* The sentiment of the poem is echoed in poems on peace by George Herbert Sass, Ticknor, Bruns, and Timrod. Very different from the concluding lines of the Cotton boll is Timrod's pathetic yearning for peace, in the poem entitled Christmas:

Peace in the quiet dales,
Made rankly fertile by the blood of men,
Peace in the woodland, and the lonely glen,
Peace, in the peopled vales!
Peace on the whirring marts,
Peace where the scholar thinks, the hunter roams,
Peace, God of Peace! peace, peace, in all our homes,
And peace in all our hearts!

When peace came, the defeat of the South, its unconquerable loyalty to the lost cause, and its sad resignation at the inevitable found expression in Mrs. Preston'sAcceptation, Requier's Ashes of glory, Flash's The Confederate flag, and, above all,Father Ryan's The sword of Robert Lee and The conquered

Banner. Not until the end of the war did the last-named poet suddenly flash forth as the most popular of all Southern poets. The conquered Banner was written under somewhat the same circumstance as My Maryland—written in less than an hour as he brooded over the thought of the dead soldiers and the lost cause. He wrote other poems, chiefly religious, but none that has ever stirred the hearts of the people like these two written in the shadow of defeat.

Somewhat different in tone and spirit is The land where we were dreaming, byDaniel B. Lucas. Written and first printed in Montreal, whither the author had fled at the end of the war, it is a striking expression of a Southerner's awakening from the illusions which had so long dominated the thought of the people. There is the same loyalty to the leaders and the principles of the South, but a glimpse of reality that augured a readjustment for the future.

Two years after the war, Timrod, suffering from tuberculosis and the direst poverty, wrote his greatest poem, the Ode *Sung on the Occasion of Decorating the Graves of the Confederate Dead at Magnolia Cemetery,Charleston, S. C.*, 1867. The poem is a fit ending to any consideration of Southern War Poetry, for it is the last word to be said of those who died and of those who would honour their memory.

I

Sleep sweetly in your humble graves,
Sleep, martyrs of a fallen cause;
Though yet no marble column craves
The pilgrim here to pause.

II

In seeds of laurel in the earth
The blossom of your fame is blown,
And somewhere, waiting for its birth,
The shaft is in the stone!

III

Meanwhile, behalf the tardy years
Which keep in trust your storied tombs,
Behold! your sisters bring their tears
And these memorial blooms.

IV

Small tributes! but your shades will smile
More proudly on these wreaths to-day,
Than when some cannon-moulded pile
Shall overlook this bay.

V

Stoop, angels, hither from the skies!
There is no holier spot of ground
Than where defeated valor lies,
By mourning beauty crowned!

The question inevitably arises as to how these poets developed after the Civil War. One would naturally suppose that many of the younger ones especially would grow in power and influence. But all the causes generally assigned for the lack of poetry in the ante-bellum South prevailed in the new era; and thereto were added poverty, widespread disaster, and an overwhelming confusion in the public mind.Lanier tersely expressed the chief limitation under which the writer laboured when he wrote to Bayard Taylor: 'Perhaps you know that with us of the younger generation of the South since the war, pretty much the whole of life has been merely not dying.'

Simms wrote to Hayne just before his death in 1870: 'I am rapidly passing from a stage where you young men are to succeed me,' and inscribed for his tombstone the poignant words: 'Here lies one who, after a reasonably long life, distinguished chiefly by unceasing labours, has left all his better works undone.' Meek, O'Hara, John R. Thompson, and Henry Timrod were all dead by 1875. Randall spent many years in the drudgery of a newspaper office, never recapturing the first fine careless rapture of his great song. Ticknor andBruns followed with devotion the life of a doctor, while McCabe became one of the best-known schoolmasters of Virginia—a position which seemed to deaden his poetic inspiration, though he remained an inimitable raconteur, and the friend of some of the most gifted poets of England and America. Mrs. Preston continued to write as late as 1887, when she published Colonial ballads, but she added nothing to her fame. Flash became a merchant and lived for many years in the Far West.

Paul Hamilton Hayne alone made progress after the war. With magnificent courage and faith, after the destruction of his city and his home, he moved to a small cabin of his own building in the pine barrens near Augusta, Georgia. Here on a writing desk made out of a carpenter's work-bench he wrote poems for the remainder of his life. To Mrs. Preston he wrote: 'No, no! By my brain—my literary craft—I will win my bread and water; by my poems I will live or I will starve.' In 1872 he brought out a volume of Legends and lyrics; in 1875 The Mountain of the lovers and other poems; and in 1882, a complete edition of his poems. Two or three of his best poems were written in his last years, notably *A Little While I Fain Would Linger Yet*, and In Harbour. While Hayne did not strike a deeply original note, he cultivated faithfully the talents with which he was endowed. His best poems are characterized by delicacy of feeling, conscientious workmanship, and a certain assimilation of the best qualities of other poets. His magnanimous spirit after the war, as revealed in his tributes to Whittier and Longfellow, his revelation of the picturesqueness of the Southern landscapes and especially of the pine forests ofGeorgia, are the substantial features of his poetry. As a connecting link betweenSimms and Lanier he has a permanent place in the literary history of the South.

11

20th Century Literature

Two world wars, an intervening economic depression of great severity, and the austerity of life in Britain following the second of these wars help to explain the quality and direction of English literature in the 20th century. The traditional values of Western civilization, which the Victorians had only begun to question, came to be questioned seriously by a number of new writers, who saw society breaking down around them. Traditional literary forms were often discarded, and new ones succeeded one another with bewildering rapidity, as writers sought fresher ways of expressing what they took to be new kinds of experience, or experience seen in new ways.

POST-WORLD WAR I FICTION

Among novelists and short-story writers, Aldous Huxley best expressed the sense of disillusionment and hopelessness in the period after World War I (1914-1918) in his Point Counter Point (1928). This novel is composed in such a way that the events of the plot form a contrapuntal pattern that is a departure from the straightforward storytelling technique of the realistic novel.

Before Huxley, and indeed before the war, the sensitively written novels of E. M. Forster (A Room with a View, 1908; Howards End, 1910) had exposed the hollowness and deadness of both abstract intellectuality and upper-class social life. Forster had called for a return to a simple, intuitive reliance on the senses and for a satisfaction of the needs of one's physical being. His most famous novel, A Passage to India (1924), combines these themes with an examination of the social distance separating the English ruling classes from the native inhabitants of India and shows the impossibility of continued British rule there.

D. H. Lawrence similarly related his sense of the need for a return from the complexities, over-intellectualism, and cold materialism of modern life to the primitive; unconscious springs of vitality of the race. His numerous novels and short stories, among which some of the best known are Sons and Lovers (1913), Women in Love (1921), The Plumed Serpent (1926), and Lady Chatterley's Lover (1928), are for the most part more clearly experimental than Forster's. The obvious symbolism of Lawrence's plots and the forceful, straightforward preaching of his message broke the bonds of realism and replaced them with the direct projection of the author's own dynamically creative spirit. His distinguished but uneven poetry similarly deserted the fixed forms of the past to achieve a freer, more natural, and more direct expression of the perceptions of the writer.

Even more experimental and unorthodox than Lawrence's novels were those of the Irish writer James Joyce. In his novel Ulysses (1922) he focused on the events of a single day and related them to one another in thematic patterns based on Greek mythology. In Finnegans Wake (1939) Joyce went beyond this to create a whole new vocabulary of puns and portmanteau (merged) words from the elements of many languages and to devise a simple domestic narrative from the interwoven parts of many myths and traditions. In some of these experiments his novels were paralleled by those of Virginia Woolf, whose Mrs. Dalloway (1925) and To the Lighthouse (1927) skillfully imitated, by the so-called stream-of-consciousness technique, the complex of immediate, evanescent life experienced from moment to moment. Dame Ivy Compton-Burnett appeals to a small but discerning readership with her idiosyncratic dissections of family relationships, told almost entirely in sparse dialogue; her novels include Brothers and Sisters (1929), Men and Wives (1931), and Two Worlds and Their Ways (1949).

Among young novelists, Evelyn Waugh, like Aldous Huxley, satirized the foibles of society in the 1920s in Decline and Fall (1928). His later novels, similarly satirical and extravagant, showed a deepening moral tone, as in The Loved One (1948) and Brideshead Revisited (1945). Graham Greene, like Waugh a convert to Roman Catholicism, investigated in his more serious novels the problem of evil in human life (The Heart of the Matter, 1948; A Burnt-Out Case, 1961; The Comedians, 1966). Much of the reputation of George Orwell rests on two works of fiction, one an allegory (Animal Farm, 1945), the other a mordant satire (Nineteen Eighty-Four, 1949)—both directed against the dangers of totalitarianism. The same anguished concern about the fate of society is at the heart of his nonfiction, especially in such vivid reporting as The Road to Wigan Pier (1937), an account of life in the coal-mining regions of northern England during the Great Depression, and in Homage to Catalonia (1938), about the Spanish Civil War.

FICTION AFTER WORLD WAR II

No clearly definable trends have appeared in English fiction since the time of the post-World War II School of writers, the so-called angry young men of the 1950s and 1960s. This group, which included the novelists Kingsley Amis, John Wain, and John Braine, attacked outmoded social values left over from the prewar world. Interest in the 1970s focused on writers as disparate in their concerns and styles as V. S. Pritchett and Doris Lessing. Pritchett, considered a master of the short story (Selected Stories, 1978), is also noted as a literary critic of remarkable erudition. His easy but elegant, supple style illuminates both forms of writing. Lessing has moved from the early short stories collected as African Stories (1965) to novels increasingly experimental in form and concerned with the role of women in contemporary society. Notable among these is The Golden Notebook (1962), about a woman writer coming to grips with life through her art.

Anthony Powell, a friend and Oxford classmate of Evelyn Waugh, has also written wittily about the higher echelons of English society, but with more affection and on a broader canvas. His 12-volume series of novels, grouped under the title A Dance to the Music of Time (1951-1975), is a highly readable account of the intertwined lives and careers of people in the arts and politics from before World War II (1939-1945) to many years afterwards. His four-volume autobiography, To Keep the Ball Rolling (1977-1983), complements the fictionalized details that form the basis of his novels. Iris Murdoch, a teacher of philosophy as well as a writer, is esteemed for slyly comic analyses of contemporary lives in her many novels beginning with Under the Net (1954) and continuing with A Severed Head (1961), The Black Prince (1973), Nuns and Soldiers (1980), and The Good Apprentice (1986). Her effects are made by the contrast between her eccentric characters and the underlying seriousness of her ideas.

Other distinctive talents include Anthony Burgess, novelist and man of letters, most popular for his mordant novel of teenage violence, A Clockwork Orange (1962), which was made into a successful motion picture in 1971; and John Le Carré (pseudonym of David Cornwell), who has won popularity for ingeniously complex espionage tales, loosely based on his own experience in the British foreign service. His novels include The Spy Who Came in from the Cold (1963), Tinker, Tailor, Soldier, Spy (1974), A Perfect Spy (1986), The Russia House (1989), and The Night Manager (1993). William Golding displays a wide inventive range in fiction that explores human evil: the allegorical Lord of the Flies (1954); The Inheritors (1955), about Neanderthal life; The Spire (1964); and The Paper Men (1984), about an English novelist's cruel behaviour to an American scholar. Golding won the Nobel Prize for literature in 1983.

MODERN POETRY

Two of the most remarkable poets of the modern period combined tradition and experiment in their work. The Irish writer William Butler Yeats was the more traditional. In his romantic poetry, written before the turn of the century, he exploited ancient Irish traditions and then gradually developed a powerfully honest, profound, and rich poetic idiom, at its maturity in The Tower (1928) and The Winding Stair (1933). The younger poet, T. S. Eliot, born in the United

States, achieved more immediate acclaim with The Waste Land (1922), the most famous poem of the early part of the century. Through a mass of symbolic associations with legendary and historical events, Eliot expresses his despair over the sterility of modern life. His movement towards religious faith displayed itself in Four Quartets (1943). His surprising combination of colloquial and literary diction, his fusing of antithetical moods, and his startling, complex metaphorical juxtapositions relate him, among English poets, to John Donne. Eliot's style was intimately influenced by his study of such French poets as Jules Laforgue and Saint-John Perse. Eliot's essays, promulgating a style of poetry in which sound and sense are associated, were probably the most influential work in literary criticism in the first half of the century.

Both Yeats and Eliot exercised enormous influence on modern poets. A third influence was that of Gerard Manley Hopkins, a Victorian poet whose work was not introduced to the world until 1918. The conflict between his Roman Catholicism and his sense of the beauty of this world, and his complicated experiments in metrics and vocabulary have attracted much attention.

Of the many poets stimulated to indignant verse by World War I, Siegfried Sassoon, Wilfred Owen, and Robert Graves rank among the most lastingly important. Graves's ability to produce pure and classically perfect poetry kept his reputation strong long after World War II. His historical novels, such as I, Claudius and Claudius the God (both 1934), also helped to maintain his popularity. The verse of Dame Edith Sitwell, who communicated her disdain of commonplace propriety as much by the aristocratic individualism of her personal attitudes as by her poetry, was first published during World War I; her experimentalism had little directly to do, however, with social problems. Extravagantly imaginative metaphors after the manner of the metaphysical poets, and conscious distortion of sense impressions, somewhat as in modern painting, were among her poetic devices. After World War II she wrote more compassionate and moving poetry, as in The Canticle of the Sun (1949) and The Outcasts (1962).

The succeeding generation of poets, identified in the popular consciousness with the depression and social upheaval of the 1930s, made use at first of so much private or esoteric symbolism as to render the poetry barely intelligible to any but a small coterie of readers. The best known of these—W. H. Auden, Stephen Spender, and C. Day Lewis—filled their earlier poetry with political and ideological discussion and with expressions of horror at bourgeois society and nascent totalitarianism. After such verse plays as The Ascent of F-6, written in 1936 in collaboration with Christopher Isherwood, Auden's poetry became more reflective in The Double Man (1941) and, later, City Without Walls (1969). So, too, Day Lewis moved from The Magnetic Mountain (1935) to a more personal lyricism in World Above All (1943). His Poetic Image (1947) was a prose exposition of the modern poetic ideal. The position of poet laureate, held by Day Lewis from 1968 to 1972, subsequently passed to Sir John Betjeman, popular for his nostalgic humor.

Experimentalism continued in the exuberantly metaphorical poetry of the Welsh writer Dylan Thomas, whose almost mystical love of life and understanding of death were expressed in some of the most beautiful verse of the middle of the century. After Thomas's death in 1953, a new generation of British poets emerged, some influenced by him and some reacting against his influence. Among the leading younger poets were D. J. Enright, Philip Larkin, John Wain, Thom Gunn, and Ted Hughes. In 1984, after Betjeman's death, Hughes, whose poetry focuses on the savagery of life, became poet laureate.

MODERN DRAMA

Aside from the later plays of George Bernard Shaw, the most important drama produced in English in the first quarter of the 20th century came from another Irish writer, Sean O'Casey, who continued the movement known as the Irish Renaissance. Other playwrights of the period were James Matthew Barrie, John Galsworthy, Somerset Maugham, and Sir Noel Coward. Beginning in the 1950s the so-called angry young men became a new, salient force in English drama. The dramatists John Osborne, Arnold Wesker, Shelagh Delaney, and John Arden focused their attention on the working classes, portraying the drabness, mediocrity, and injustice in the lives of these people. Although Harold Pinter and the Irish writer Brendan Behan also wrote plays set in a working-class environment, they stand apart from the angry young men. In such works as The Birthday Party (1957) Pinter seems to offer reasonable interpretations of his characters' behaviour, only to withdraw the interpretations or set them slightly askew in an effort to keep the audience intent on every least hint in the action on stage. Outside the literary mainstream was the Irish-born novelist-dramatist Samuel Beckett, recipient in 1969 of the Nobel Prize for literature. Long a resident in France, he wrote his laconic, ambiguously symbolic works in French and translated them himself into English (Waiting for Godot, play, 1952; How It Is, novel, 1964).

Both English and American audiences have enthusiastically received the plays of Joe Orton and Tom Stoppard. Orton's Entertaining Mr. Sloane (1964), Loot (1967), and What the Butler Saw (1969) are farces dealing with the perverseness of modern morality; dazzling verbal ingenuity distinguishes Stoppard's Rosencrantz and Guildenstern Are Dead (1966), Travesties (1974), and The Real Thing (1984).

THE 20TH CENTURY

FROM 1900 TO 1945

THE EDWARDIANS

The 20th century opened with great hope but also with some apprehension, for the new century marked the final approach to a new millennium. For many, humankind was entering upon an unprecedented era. H.G. Wells's utopian studies, the aptly titled *Anticipations of the Reaction of Mechanical and Scientific Progress upon Human Life and Thought* (1901) and *A Modern Utopia* (1905), both captured and qualified this optimistic mood and gave expression to a common conviction that science and technology would transform the world in the century ahead. To achieve such transformation, outmoded institutions and ideals had to be replaced by ones more suited to the growth and liberation of the human spirit. The death of Queen Victoria in 1901 and the accession of Edward VII seemed to confirm that a franker, less inhibited era had begun.

Many writers of the Edwardian period, drawing widely upon the realistic and naturalistic conventions of the 19th century (upon Ibsen in drama and Balzac, Turgenev, Flaubert, Zola, Eliot, and Dickens in fiction) and in tune with the anti-Aestheticism unleashed by the trial of the archetypal Aesthete, Oscar Wilde, saw their task in the new century to be an unashamedly didactic one. In a series of wittily iconoclastic plays, of which *Man and Superman* (performed 1905, published 1903) and *Major Barbara* (performed 1905, published 1907) are the most substantial, George Bernard Shaw turned the Edwardian theatre into an arena for debate upon the principal concerns of the day: the question of political organization, the morality of armaments and war, the function of class and of the professions, the validity of the family and of marriage, and the issue of female emancipation. Nor was he alone in this, even if he was alone in the brilliance of his comedy.

John Galsworthy made use of the theatre in *Strife* (1909) to explore the conflict between capital and labour, and in *Justice* (1910) he lent his support to reform of the penal system, while Harley Granville-Barker, whose revolutionary approach to stage direction did much to change theatrical production in the period, dissected in *The Voysey Inheritance* (performed 1905, published 1909) and *Waste* (performed 1907, published 1909) the hypocrisies and deceit of upper-class and professional life.

Many Edwardian novelists were similarly eager to explore the shortcomings of English social life. Wells—in *Love and Mr. Lewisham* (1900); *Kipps* (1905); *Ann Veronica* (1909), his pro-suffragist novel; and *The History of Mr. Polly* (1910)—captured the frustrations of lower- and middle-class existence, even though he relieved his accounts with many comic touches. In *Anna of the Five Towns* (1902), Arnold Bennett detailed the constrictions of provincial life among the self-made business classes in the area of England known as the Potteries; in *The Man of Property* (1906), the first volume of *The Forsyte Saga*, Galsworthy described the destructive possessiveness of the professional bourgeoisie; and, in *Where Angels Fear to Tread* (1905) and *The Longest Journey* (1907), E.M. Forster portrayed with irony the insensitivity, self-repression, and philistinism of the English middle classes.

These novelists, however, wrote more memorably when they allowed themselves a larger perspective. In *The Old Wives' Tale* (1908), Bennett showed the destructive effects of time on the lives of individuals and communities and evoked a quality of pathos that he never matched in his other fiction; in *Tono-Bungay* (1909), Wells showed the ominous consequences of the uncontrolled developments taking place within a British society still dependent upon the institutions of a long-defunct landed aristocracy; and in *Howards End* (1910), Forster showed how little the rootless and self-important world of contemporary commerce cared for the more rooted world of culture, although he acknowledged that commerce was a necessary evil. Nevertheless, even as they perceived the difficulties of the present, most Edwardian novelists, like their counterparts in the theatre, held firmly to the belief not only that constructive change was possible but also that this change could in some measure be advanced by their writing.

Other writers, including Thomas Hardy and Rudyard Kipling, who had established their reputations during the previous century, and Hilaire Belloc, G.K. Chesterton, and Edward Thomas, who established their reputations in the first decade of the new century, were less confident about the future and sought to revive the traditional forms—the ballad, the narrative poem, the satire, the fantasy, the topographical poem, and the essay—that in their view preserved traditional sentiments and perceptions. The revival of traditional forms in the late 19th and early 20th century was not a unique event. There were many such revivals during the 20th century, and the traditional poetry of A.E. Housman (whose book *A Shropshire Lad*, originally published in 1896, enjoyed huge popular success during World War I), Walter de la Mare, John Masefield, Robert Graves, and Edmund Blunden represents an important and often neglected strand of English literature in the first half of the century.

The most significant writing of the period, traditionalist or modern, was inspired by neither hope nor apprehension but by bleaker feelings that the new century would witness the collapse of a whole civilization. The new century had begun with Great Britain involved in the South African War (the Boer War; 1899–1902), and it seemed to some that the British Empire was as doomed to destruction, both from within and from without, as had been the Roman Empire. In his poems on the South African War, Hardy (whose achievement as a poet in the 20th century rivaled his achievement as a novelist in the 19th) questioned simply and sardonically the human cost of empire building and established a tone and style that many British poets were to use in the course of the century, while Kipling, who had done much to engender pride in empire, began to speak in his verse and short stories of the burden of empire and the tribulations it would bring.

No one captured the sense of an imperial civilization in decline more fully or subtly than the expatriate American novelist Henry James. In *The Portrait of a Lady* (1881), he had briefly anatomized the fatal loss of energy of the English ruling class and, in *The Princess Casamassima*(1886), had described more directly the various instabilities that threatened its paternalistic rule. He did so with regret: the patrician American admired in the English upper class its sense of moral obligation to the community. By the turn of the century, however, he had noted a disturbing change. In *The Spoils of Poynton* (1897) and *What Maisie Knew* (1897), members of the upper class no longer seem troubled by the means adopted to achieve their morally dubious ends. Great Britain had become indistinguishable from the other nations of the Old World, in which an ugly rapacity had never been far from the surface. James's dismay at this condition gave to his subtle and compressed late fiction, *The Wings of the Dove* (1902), *The Ambassadors*(1903), and *The Golden Bowl* (1904), much of its gravity and air of disenchantment.

James's awareness of crisis affected the very form and style of his writing, for he was no longer assured that the world about which he wrote was either coherent in itself or unambiguously intelligible to its inhabitants. His fiction still presented characters within an identifiable social world, but he found his characters and their world increasingly elusive and enigmatic and his own grasp upon them, as he made clear in *The Sacred Fount* (1901), the questionable consequence of artistic will.

Another expatriate novelist, Joseph Conrad (pseudonym of Józef Teodor Konrad Korzeniowski, born in the Ukraine of Polish parents), shared James's sense of crisis but attributed it less to the decline of a specific civilization than to human failings. Man was a solitary, romantic creature of will who at any cost imposed his meaning upon the world because he could not endure a world that did not reflect his central place within it. In *Almayer's Folly* (1895) and *Lord Jim* (1900), he had seemed to sympathize with this predicament; but in "Heart of Darkness" (1902), *Nostromo*(1904), *The Secret Agent* (1907), and *Under Western Eyes* (1911), he detailed such imposition, and the psychological pathologies he increasingly associated with it, without sympathy. He did so as a philosophical novelist whose concern with the mocking limits of human knowledge affected not only the content of his fiction but also its very structure. His writing itself is marked by gaps in the narrative, by narrators who do not fully grasp the significance of the events they are retelling, and by characters who are unable to make themselves understood. James and Conrad used many of the conventions of 19th-century realism but transformed them to express what are considered to be peculiarly 20th-century preoccupations and anxieties.

Bibliography

Abraham Mathew: *The Making of English Literature*, Cyber Tech Publication, Delhi, 2011.

Aruna Sharma: *Women Writers in English Literature*, Ancient Publishing House, Delhi, 2011.

B.K. Jha: *The Long Journey of English Literature*, ALP Books, Delhi, 2011.

B.P. Sinha: *Studies and Essays in English Literature*, Book Enclave, Delhi, 2002.

Basavaraj Naikar: *Indian English Literature: Vol. VIII*, Atlantic Publication, Delhi, 2011.

Bhupal Singh: *Victorian English Literature : An Analytico-Critical Study*, Swastik Publication, Delhi, 2009.

Daniel Reed and Tim Horton: *Roots and Influences of English Literature*, Dominant Publication, Delhi, 2010.

Daniel Reed and Tim Horton: *Theatrical Traditions of Europe and Drama in English Literature*, Dominant Publication, Delhi, 2010.

George Sampson: *The Concise Cambridge History of English Literature*, Cambridge University Press, New York, 2000.

H A Taine: *Taine's Encyclopaedia of English Literature With Thirty Two Portraits (4 Vols-Set)*, Shubhi Publications, Delhi, 2003.

Kundan Bhardwaj: *Studies in English Literature*, Sonali Publications, Delhi, 2012.

L. D'Souza: *Studies in Contemporary English Literature*, Cyber Tech Publication, Delhi, 2011.

Malcolm Godden and Michael Lapidge: *The Cambridge Companion to Old English Literature*, Cambridge University Press, New York, 2003.

Mallikarjun Patil: *Karnataka Companion to Indian English Literature*, Sarup Book Publication, Delhi, 2011.

Mallikarjun Patil: *Studies In Indian English Literature*, Sarup & Sons, Delhi, 2010.

Mallikarjun Patil: *Trends and Techniques in Modern English Literature*, Authorspress, Delhi, 2011.

Malti Agarwal: *Women in Postcolonial Indian English Literature : Redefining the Self*, Atlantic Publication, Delhi, 2011.

Margaret Drabble: *The Oxford Companion to English Literature*, Oxford University Press, Delhi, 2008.

Naval Kishore Singh: *The Great Indian Novelists on English Literature*, Manglam Publication, Delhi, 2008.

Naval Kishore Singh: *The Great Indian Women Novelists in English Literature*, Manglam Publication, Delhi, 2009.

P. Varghese and Anita Jacob: *Landmarks of English Literature*, Alfa Publications, Delhi, 2012.

Partha Kumar Mukhopadhyay: *The Multicoloured Glass : Critical Essays on English Literature and Indian Writing in English*, Sarup & Sons, Delhi, 2006.

Pramod Kumar Singh and Sanju Kumari: *Indian English Literature: Issues and Trends*, Yking Books, Delhi, 2010.

Rashmi Kapoor: *The Masters of English Literature*, Pearl Books, Delhi, 2012.

Robert J. Fletcher: *The Concise History of English Literature : A Critical Assessment of Literature in English from Anglo-Saxon Period to Modern Times*, Dominant Publication, Delhi, 2011.

T. Sai Chandra Mouli and G.A. Ghanshyam: *Vignettes of Indian English Literature*, Authorspress, Delhi, 2010.

Tory Young: *Studying English Literature: A Practical Guide*, Cambridge University Press, New York, 2003.

Vipin Tomar: *The Twentieth Century English Literature : A Survey of Poetry Drama Fiction and Criticism*, Swastik Publication, Delhi, 2011.

Wallace: *The Cambridge History of Medieval English Literature*, Cambridge University Press, New York, 2003.

Index